THREE JEWISH PHILOSOPHERS

THREE JEWISH PHILOSOPHERS

Philo: Selections, edited by Hans Lewy

Saadya Gaon: Book of Doctrines and Beliefs,
edited by Alexander Altmann

Jehuda Halevi: Kuzari,
edited by Isaak Heinemann

A TEMPLE BOOK

ATHENEUM, NEW YORK, 1981

Published by Atheneum
Reprinted by arrangement with
The Jewish Publication Society of America
All rights reserved
Library of Congress catalog card number 60-9081
ISBN: *0-689-70126-8*
Manufactured in the United States of America by
The Murray Printing Company
Forge Village, Massachusetts
Published in Canada by McClelland and Stewart Ltd.
First Atheneum Printing August 1969
Second Printing January 1972
Third Printing March 1973
Fourth Printing July 1974
Fifth Printing March 1976
Sixth Printing March 1977
Seventh Printing April 1979
Eighth Printing March 1981

CONTENTS

Philo: Selections

Saadya Gaon: Book of Doctrines and Beliefs

Jehuda Halevi: Kuzari

HANS LEWY *was born in Berlin in 1901 and died in Jerusalem in 1945. Educated at the University of Berlin and the Hochschule für Wissenschaft des Judentums, he acquired mastery both of classic Hebrew thought and Greek and Hellenistic philosophy. He made Philo his particular specialty, although he concentrated as well on the view of Judaism reflected in the work of such classic writers as Tacitus, Cicero, and particularly Josephus. The last twelve years of his life were spent in the Department of Classics at the Hebrew University in Jerusalem.*

ALEXANDER ALTMANN *was born in Hungary in 1906. He was rabbi and lecturer in the Berlin Rabbinical Seminary until 1938, when he was appointed chief rabbi of Manchester, England. He founded the Institute of Jewish Studies, Manchester, which he later transferred to London. He is presently Professor of Jewish Philosophy at Brandeis University. He has published extensively in the fields of medieval Jewish philosophy and mysticism as well as modern Jewish thought. Among his works are:* ISAAC ISRAELI *(with S. M. Stern) and several volumes in the Brandeis Studies and Texts Series which he co-authored and edited.*

ISAAK HEINEMANN *was born in Germany in 1876 and died in Israel in 1957. From 1919 he lectured at the Breslau Rabbinical Seminary and from 1920 he served as editor of the* MONATSCHRIFT FÜR GESCHICHTE UND WISSENSCHAFT DES JUDENTUMS. *Having settled in Palestine in 1939, he continued to pursue his studies of Jewish philosophy in the classical and medieval world.*

PHILO: SELECTIONS

Edited by Hans Lewy

INTRODUCTION

IF the extent of the influence exercised by an author formed a true measure of his eminence, Philo would probably rank with the greatest not only of Jewish, but also of Greek thinkers. He was a pioneer in a number of important fields of human thought. He was not only the first theologian, i.e. the first who tried to bring into harmony the teachings of a supernatural revelation and the conclusions of speculative thought, but also the first psychologist of faith, the first mystic among professors of monotheism, and—last but not least—the first systematizer of Biblical allegory. The contributions which he made to these and other branches of inquiry give to his writing an importance of the first degree for the history of religious thought.

Yet notable as was his achievement, we can hardly credit him with any great depth or originality of thought. He owes his dominant position less to his own personal qualities than to the circumstances of the time in which he wrote. He lived in an age which had become ripe for a synthesis of Jewish creed and Greek thought. Judaism had for long been slowly, but steadily, developing the universalistic tendencies of its great prophets, the rational trend of its moral legislation and the consciousness of individual piety; while Hellenism had similarly been developing the idea of a cosmopolitan community united by the bond of Greek education and a rigid canon of rules for ethical conduct, along with a strong bent towards the theological side of philosophical speculation. These two spiritual movements met in Alexandria, at once the chief home of the Jewish Dispersion and the chief centre of Hellenistic culture; and their conjunction provided the material, to a writer conscious of this convergence, for a new presentment of religious and philosophical problems. It was the merit of Philo that he seized this opportunity.

Posterity has been duly grateful to him for this. While it has neglected to keep the works of greater thinkers of his era, it has preserved more than three-quarters of the vast expanse of his writings (about 2,500 pages). Oddly enough the transmittors were not the genuine sons of his nation, to the glorification of whose Law the whole labour of his literary life was devoted, but the abrogators of Mosaic Legislation, the theological scholars of the Christian Church. The spread of the rival creed, to which the literary productions of the Jewish hellenizing movement appealed so strongly, led the spiritual leaders of the Synagogue to cut away this entire branch from the stock of Jewish tradition. In rabbinic literature there is (except for some faded echoes in the writings of remote sectarians) no mention either of Philo's name or of his work, and even the Jewish philosophers of the Middle Ages who revived his ideas in a new setting, had no notion of the existence of their forerunner. Only in the sixteenth century did a Jewish scholar of broader education, who breathed the humanistic air of Italy and was in touch with the theological literature of the Church, Azarya dei Rossi, rediscover, as it were, Philo; and since then Jewish learning has—somewhat reluctantly and not nearly so readily as modern research on Christian theology or Greek philosophy—received the writings of this forgotten son into the domain of its own interests.

Of the outward life of Philo as little is known as befits a devotee of religious contemplation. He was born about 25 B.C. as the son of one of the noblest and wealthiest members of the Jewish community in Alexandria, brought up in the faith of his fathers and instructed according to the best standards of Greek education. His brother Alexander rose, by virtue of his economic and diplomatic talents, to be a high official of the Roman administration in Egypt, the confidant of Agrippa (the grandson of Herod and later King of Judaea) and even a friend of the Emperor Claudius. But Philo despised the honours of a worldly career and devoted himself to the study of Greek wisdom. Some elaborations of philosophical problems, which are probably works of his early years, bear witness of his extensive acquaintance with the subjects of higher Greek education and his thorough knowledge of the principal teachings of classic and of contemporary philosophy (especially of the Stoic, Platonic and Pythagorean schools, but they are totally devoid of any originality of thought. A third feature of these tracts (and one which remained a characteristic of his entire literary production) is the elaborate and flowery style. Rhetoric, the disease of Hellenistic literature, has left its deep impress also on this scorner of verbose vanity.

There was apparently in Philo's development a phase in which he was content with the modest role of an author of moral treatises presenting the ideas then current in the philosophical schools in a popular form and elegant style. Fortunately, however, he managed to emerge from this barren track and found a worthier scope for his talents in the great work of interpreting the Pentateuch. This occupation filled the main part of his life. It was as an expositor of Scripture that he won his fame, and in that activity he was at his best. In his exegetical writings he presents himself as a man fully sensible of the claims of social intercourse, and well acquainted with the refinements of civilization, but also as one passionately attached to meditation and the search for wisdom. He was by temper a philosopher who derived his ideas of human nature more from abstract thought than from experience. Hence his portraits of ethical types lack the delicate shadows of true life; they give vague phrases instead of pictures, and personified qualities instead of human beings. He felt really at home, as he himself avows, only when his mind rose from the 'images' of this changeful world to the realms of the Absolute.

From his tranquil meditations on the inner meaning of the Divine Laws Philo was rudely torn by disturbances in the outside world. The peaceful era of the government of Augustus and Tiberius came to an end. The new Emperor Caligula, instigated by his Egyptian friends, conceived a grudge against the Jews, who alone firmly resisted his megalomaniac plan of self-deification. The Alexandrinian populace, quick to perceive the imperial ill-humour and annoyed by the efforts of its Jewish neighbours to enlarge their special privileges into full citizenship, found in some trifling accident the long-sought opportunity for anti-Jewish riots, and a veritable civil war ensued (A.D. 38). When, shortly afterwards, Caligula ordered his own effigy to be set up in the temple of Jerusalem, an upheaval of all Jewry within the boundaries of the Roman empire seemed to be inevitable. On this critical moment (still before the news of the last fateful decree of the Emperor had been received) the Jews of Alexandria decided to send an embassy of notables to Rome (A.D. 40) and appointed as its head Philo—a proof of the reputation which he had won in his community and of the hopes which were based on the relations of his family with Roman notables. The story of this unsuccessful mission is related, with a vividness hardly surpassed in the historical writings of the period, in his *Legacy to Gaius*. As we might expect this work exhibits clearly the moral dignity of its author; what surprises us is its realistic tone. It shows that Philo was not only ready to stand firm by the beliefs of his fathers in the hour of stress, but also that he had the wit to elude the snares of court-intrigue and the courage to face without flinching the imperial madman. Philo published this account (together with a story of the fate of the Roman prefect in Egypt, Flaccus, who was convicted of supporting the rioters in Alexandria) after Caligula was murdered (A.D. 41). Claudius had then ascended the throne and peace had been restored both in Alexandria and in Palestine. The dramatic turn of events appeared to him the work of Providence; this theological idea runs through the account and gives life and vigour to it. Its author was, as he says, already an old man when circumstances 'dragged him down into the vast sea of political cares'. Not long after the storm abated he retired from public life and resumed his exegetical work, to which he had added considerably by the time of his death (before A.D. 50).

These are almost all the facts known about the life of Philo. He was certainly a great teacher; but it is by no means easy to present his teaching in systematic shape. One reason is that in form his main work is an exegesis of the Bible and not a working out of first principles. Consequently his philosophical concepts lie scattered throughout his writings, and the reader has to piece together cognate ideas which he has disjoined. Another reason is the variety of his interests, which is reflected in a kaleidoscopic transition from one theme to another. Often Philo opens his exegetical expositions with a literal explanation after the pattern of the rabbinic Midrash jumps from this to a philosophical or moral disquisition (it is in the latter that he is especially prone to rhetorical flourishes), and concludes with some remark of a highly spiritual nature. The student is left wondering whether this author was a 'reformed' Rabbi who dressed up the simple teachings of his fathers in the fashionable garb of the Greek theory, or a moralizing preacher with a professional weakness for sonorous effects, or perhaps a mystic with a distressing penchant for the dry formulas of philosophical dogmatism. That under all these guises Philo spoke with the voice of his age may be granted; yet it would be unfair not to see in him something more than a mere sounding-board for the current and diverse theories of his time and surroundings. Through all his desultory ramblings the attentive hearer, who has grown accustomed to his sudden changes of theme and has learnt to tolerate his interludes of dull verbosity will discern the voice of the human soul which has commenced the eternal dialogue with her inward God, *sola cum solo*.

Two seemingly contradictory concepts of the deity dominate Philo's thought: the one of a Supreme Being, self-sufficient, removed from mankind and incomprehensible in its nature; and the other, of a personal God, close to human life at every turn. It has been aptly said that in Philo's God-idea the First Cause of the metaphysicians has been blended with the Lord of the Bible. The same, however, might be said of every man of intellect in whom the emotional side is stronger than the intellectual. Philo's idea of divine perfection was such as to compel him to equip the Godhead both with the absolute abstractness which strict logic required, and with the moral qualities which Jewish piety indicated. The two aspects of perfection were united in the concept of the Divine Logos, the Word and Wisdom of the Supreme Being, who also is represented as being simultaneously abstract and personal. He is, on the one side, the sum of the divine thoughts (the ideas) and the force of the deity, on the other side God's first-born son (after Proverbs viii, 22), who executes the volition of his father (hence the prominence of this idea in Christian dogma), and his deputy in the character of head of the angels. This many-faced entity is the connecting link between the Inaccessible creation; it embodies God's presence in the world. In its secret primordial existence, in its primary manifestation as a creative and a ruling power, in its subsequent unfolding in the potencies of stern judgement and man-loving mercy, in its establishment in the material world as law of nature and its codification in the legislation of Moses, this Logos forms one of the most sublime subjects of Philo's theosophy. The rich variations which he plays on this particular theme are the expression of a peculiar form of religious consciousness, equally remote from anthropomorphic concreteness and philosophical abstraction. The 'inner eye' beholds a higher world of symbolic reality in which Philo calls that type of man who beholds this vision by the name of 'Israel, the Seer of God', according to what he supposes to be the Hebrew etymology of the name, and in so doing creates a new type of Jewish piety. The descriptions of the religious experiences of this God-seeker constitute one of the main features of Philo's discourses. This search is, according to his view, identical with the exposition of Scripture, because the Bible, rightly understood, i.e. read with the eye of Spirit, is nothing else but the account of the soul's striving for God. The clue to this higher understanding is allegory.

In his explanations of the Biblical text Philo looks for a twofold meaning: the literal and the symbolic (or allegorical). The first represents, as he says, the 'body', the second the 'soul' of the divine revelations. If the first seems to him unworthy of divine thought, he recognizes only the allegorical meaning. His literal explanations, generally confined to moral or legal expositions, are too often of a rather common place nature. Their ornate and well-rounded sentences extolling virtue and denouncing vice do not rise above the level of pulpit oratory, and the rhetorical flights by which many incidents of the Bible are 'embellished' destroy the verve and incisiveness of the original. They show that their author had no ear either for the simple beauty or for the natural wisdom of the Biblical tales. Quite another impression, however, is conveyed by the allegorical explanations: here the ingenuity and imagination of the expositor are displayed in full—and frequently remarkable—strength.

In modern times allegorizing has become a hopelessly discredited method of exegesis. It is not convincing, and it easily becomes ridiculous through the contrast between the plain and the symbolic sense of the same passage. Philo's use of this method creates between him and readers of our times a barrier which will probably prevent the majority of them from studying any one of his exegetical treatises from end to end (hence, by the way, the main justification for a Selection). Against this instinctive prejudice, a reminder of the changeableness in fashions of thought will be, probably, of small avail. Yet a just appreciation of the incontestable services rendered by the allegorizing method to the progress of human thought should help to reconcile, if not the taste, at least the reason, to its use. As is well known, allegory has often performed the important task of freeing the intellect from the heavy bonds of dogmatic oppression. Under the safe cover afforded by a respectful interpretation of a sacred text (the questioning of which was neither possible nor even desired) new ideas were allowed to creep in. The history of Biblical exegesis itself gives the most celebrated examples; Philo's allegorism is only one manifestation of this process. He himself, it is true (like many of his kind) was never aware of the incompatibility of his method with the original intention of the Biblical author; the fact remains that his expositions reflect a religious attitude quite different from that inculcated by Scripture. If one learns to appreciate his allegories as the embodiment of a new-found consciousness of belief, he may perhaps find in them sufficient interest to overcome the tedium caused by the frigid toying with exegetical fancies.

With such new consciousness Philo approached the explanation of the Biblical narratives. They are no longer accounts of the historical development of the Chosen People, but images of moral and metaphysical truths. The events related are to be understood as signs of spiritual happenings independent of time and space; their scene is man's soul and their content his everlasting struggle for salvation. Thus allegory becomes the instrument for the expression of a strictly personal form of religious experience. Philo uses the method of symbolic interpretation according to a more or less consistent system. Each personality recorded in Scripture is regarded (mostly by reference to the Hebrew significance of his name) as the type of a special moral quality or the embodiment of a certain way of life. Thus, for instance, Abraham represents the man who arrives at the true apprehension of God through instruction, Isaac through inspiration, and Jacob through ascetic exercise. In the characters of the patriarchs the drama of the human soul in its relation to God is performed. Whole sets of Biblical tales are transformed, in the same way, into symbolic descriptions of religious progress. Two of the most conspicuous examples are the story of the inner development of Abraham from a believer in astral (Chaldaean) world rulership to a venerator of the supercelestial deity, and that of the migration of the Israelites from the land of Egypt, figuring the emancipation of the individual from bodily passion. Each of these allegories reveals a different aspect of the struggle towards spiritual self-realization, and the whole Torah is transformed into a mystic philosophy.

Philo did not invent allegory nor was he the first to use it for eliciting a purified sense from the homely scenes of Scripture. This method had been introduced by Pre-Platonic philosophers and was fully developed by the Stoics, who employed it in order to reconcile the grossness of Greek mythological theology, hallowed by long tradition and glorified by poetic treatment, with the principles of their philosophy. Through them Alexandrine Jews became acquainted with this procedure. A considerable period before Philo there arose a special school of Jewish expositors who used allegory to defend Biblical imagery against the mockery of rationalists and to bring Jewish religion into line with the thought of the Greek world. These Jewish allegorists were the teachers of Philo. He refers to them sometimes expressly, and quotes them still more often without acknowledgement. To them he owed also his vocabulary of Hebrew etymologies which forms the basis of his typology. While, however, these Jewish predecessors applied allegory rather haphazardly, Philo constructed with its help a comprehensive system containing what he considered to be the major tenets of religious philosophy. The apologetic tendency was relegated to the background (although it did not disappear) and gave room to the mystical vision of a great spiritual world.

We have dealt first with the allegorical writings of Philo, because they are, in the general view, his most interesting products. They constitute, however, only one (although the main) section of his literary work. For Philo the commentator had a twofold aim: to show his co-religionists the identity of their holy tradition with Hellenic wisdom, and to prove to the Greeks the conformity of all that was best in their philosophy with the teachings of the Bible. Accordingly, he embarked upon two comprehensive enterprises which he pursued at one and the same time. For the educated members of his own religious community he composed an allegoric commentary on Genesis consisting of a long series of special treatises of which twenty-one covering Genesis, ii–xx, are preserved. In this work the Biblical text is expounded continuously and in great detail, with numerous illustrations from parallel passages; the frequent digressions with which it is swollen deprive it of all trace of literary form. It is further disfigured by wearisome repetitions of the same topic and it suffers from a complete absence of philosophical observations or reflections. Besides this *opus magnum* Philo composed for the same audience a shorter commentary on Genesis and Exodus in the form of 'Questions and Answers' providing a running verse by verse exegesis of the literal and symbolical sense. He borrowed this method of explanation from Hellenistic scholars who used it for commentaries on Homer and other Greek classics. This second work is preserved only in part, and that part (except for a few Greek fragments) only in an Armenian translation.

From these two classes of compositions are to be distinguished the writings addressed to the Gentiles. These consist of a large number of monographs which aim at exhibiting the essence of Judaism from the historical, legislative, moral and philosophical points of view. This vast work, in which allegory is only seldom employed, was divided, as it seems, into three major parts. It began with a treatise on the creation of the world (Gen. i–ii) and passed to a description of the lives of Abraham, Isaac and Jacob (only the first is preserved) and of Joseph. In the accounts of the three great Patriarchs it was maintained that they observed the laws of Moses while still unwritten and therefore had themselves to be regarded as 'living laws'. There followed a lengthy biography of Moses, who is pictured as the ideal king, law-giver, priest, prophet and sage. The third part of this work consisted of a series of separate books: *On the Decalogue* and *On the Special Laws*, which contained a systematic review of Mosaic legislation; *On the Virtues*, the purpose of which was to show the conformity of the Jewish Law with Greek ethics; and, lastly, a treatise *On Rewards and Punishments* dealing mainly with the blessings and punishments mentioned in two particular chapters in Leviticus and Deuteronomy. To the group of writings intended for Gentile readers belong also some other tracts, among which the treatise *On the Contemplative Life* deserve special mention. This gives a description of the life of the Therapeutæ, a group of Jewish monks living near the desert of Egypt. We have also a fragment of an Apology for the Jews giving a similar account of the sect of Essenes living in Palestine. We may pass over here Philo's purely philosophical treatises, which are not more than exercises, as also his historical works.

Although the esoteric and exoteric writings of Philo differ widely in their subject matter and literary character, they are in harmony in their main views and complete each other in many respects. Their common object, to bring about a full synthesis of Greek thought and Jewish tradition, explains many peculiarities of Philo's way of thinking. Philo ascribes all the doctrines which he had, in reality, derived from Greek sources, to the Old Testament. Scripture is, formally, the sole authority which he acknowledges. Yet, as he could, through a symbolic explanation, disengage himself from this obligation at any moment he wished, he was, as a matter of fact, dependent only on Greek philosophy. This, however, was never represented by a single system of axioms, but comprised a great variety of rival systems. Therefore Philo was, on this side also, at liberty to accept or to decline according to his own judgement. In practice, therefore, the two principles on which he based his entire work proved to be rather flexible. We arrive in this way at the paradoxical result (not at all uncommon in the history of theology) that this seemingly strict dogmatist was in reality less bound to principles than many 'unprejudiced' thinkers of his time and after, who were caught up in a network of school-tradition without being fully aware of the fact. This actual liberty places Philo among those thinkers who establish standards of valuation according to their own ideas. To determine these standards is the ultimate goal of a critical analysis of Philo's mentality. Before, however, we try to fix them more closely we have to examine how and to what extent he made use of his right of selection.

It lies in the nature of the subject itself that Philo's personal faith should be less conspicuous in his exoteric writings. As he wished there to demonstrate that the most valuable conclusions of Greek thought are contained in the Mosaic Law, he had to handle his material in such a way that an educated Greek should easily recognize the doctrines familiar to him in the new surroundings. He was therefore reduced to a more or less mechanical reproduction of Greek teachings brought loosely into connection with kindred Jewish precepts. The result of this procedure was a vast collection of metaphysical, ethical, social and political rules and claims mostly taken from Stoic, Pythagorean and Platonic sources, with frequent reference to the civil and moral law of his Greek environment. Every Jewish conception which had no (real or seeming) counterpart in Greek morals had to remain in the background, as it would not be properly understood and so might endanger the validity of his main thesis. This limitation deprived Philo in advance of the possibility of considering the deeper implications of a Greek-Jewish synthesis. Instead of an organic combination of the two elements we are presented with a large set of correlations. While the general humanitarian spirit which pervades these exoteric writings bears witness to the high moral character of their author, they show a certain lack of concreteness which places them on a par with the flavourless declamations of some modern humanitarians. 'The sound is forced, the notes are few.' It may, however, be worth while to dwell for a moment on the actual tendency of this group of writings.

Since the days when the prophet had declared it the mission of Israel to be a light to enlighten the nations, Judaism had devoted itself to proclaiming the superiority of its creed by word and writing. When in the Hellenistic epoch it came in touch with the culture of the Greeks, it soon became aware of the affinity between the theism of their enlightened representatives and its own monotheistic creed, of the similarities between hellenistic (especially Stoic) morality and Mosaic Law, and of the parallel between philosophic interpretation of cultic ceremonies as symbols of philosophical truths and its own attitude to ritual tradition. In this spiritual atmosphere, in which the differences, real as they were, faded into insignificance, the vision of a universal Judaism embracing the sum of human wisdom arose. This idea was fostered in the circles of hellenistic Jews and ran through many and various stages, until it received its fullest expression in the exoteric writings of Philo. Its hold was strengthened by the enormous success of proselytism. The proud words of Philo about the constant spread of Jewish rites among the Gentiles show that he believed firmly in the realization of his dream of Judaism as the religion of a whole world united by the belief in the one only God, whose command was justice and humanity. In this way, the 'particularistic' concept of the Chosen People is merged in the universalistic idea of enlightenment: philosophy becomes the content of the message of salvation, and *vice versa*. This is, however, only one side of the Philonic version of the Jewish legacy. As the history of the Chosen People represents, in his opinion, a consistent advance towards the accomplishment of this ideal, it becomes the guarantor of its ultimate fulfilment for the benefit of humanity as a whole. This view of Jewish history is the national component in Philo's outlook. His racial feelings, stirred by the persecutions of his time, burst out with full passion in his writings on contemporary events and breathe the spirit of Biblical confidence in the God of Israel who has chosen His people in order to teach the nations the ways of Providence. We do not understand Philo's exoteric writings rightly if we do not take into account both sides, the universal and the national, of his missionary enthusiasm, which deserves the admiration even of those who are inclined to hold that his intellectual capacities were not adequate to the attainment of his lofty purpose.

The restrictions which prevented Philo from giving expression to his personal faith in his works intended for Gentiles affected in a much lesser degree the writings in which he addressed himself to his own community. For one thing, the task which he set himself in them—to show the philosophical meaning of the Biblical narratives—did not as a rule require to take note of Greek manners and precepts of life. For the inward sense of the Bible is not concerned with the external affairs of daily life, but with the moral progress of the God-seeking soul. Thus Greek philosophy becomes the language of spiritual piety and changes, often insensibly, its original meaning through being brought into connection with religious ideas. Philo frequently employs the philosophical mode of speech while meaning by it something quite different from what was meant by its originators. Often, it is true, he aims at nothing higher than embellishing a narrative with familiar reflections borrowed from Greek thought, but not rarely, when his own religious consciousness has been roused, he knows how to elicit from the arid technicalities of his Greek source profound hints of higher stages of piety unknown to the Greek theologians of his time. Sometimes he treats these lofty topics as a secret to be imparted only to a minority of spiritually gifted men, and adopts in these cases, after the pattern of Plato and the later Platonists, the technical terms of the pagan mysteries; yet this is scarcely more than one of his many literary mannerisms.

We may now proceed to examine more closely those leading ideas of Philo which may be regarded as inner directives of his religious speculation. Philo's basic concept on which his whole view of life rests is the contrast between Spirit and Matter. Man is placed by nature midway between the remote deity, the essence and fountain of pure intellect, and the material substance, the domain of sinful passions. He is linked with the world of Intellect by the higher portion of his soul, reason, and with the physical world by the lower portion of his soul and by his body. The first tries to elevate man towards her heavenly origin, the second drags him down into earthly desires. Man's task is to abandon his lower existence and to rise to God. The way of perfection is Wisdom. The souls of those who have walked in this way during their life-time will return afterwards to heaven; they have gained immortality.

This duality of human nature imposes on man the duty of regarding with complete detachment the material side of life. Not that Philo recommends flight from the world; in theory at any rate, he looks upon the practical life as the prerequisite for the contemplative life. He emphasizes the social duties devolving on man (and he himself fulfilled them, when called upon by his brethren to defend their cause) but the abandonment of sensual perception which he demands for the purpose of concentrating the mind on the thought of God comes very close in practice to complete seclusion. He shows a deep sympathy for the solitary lives of the Therapeutæ and Essenes, who devoted themselves wholly to the service of God. It goes without saying that he rejects luxury. After the model of Cynic asceticism, he prescribes a simple diet sufficient only to satisfy the barest needs of the body.

The renunciation of the physical pleasures of life is the preliminary condition for a spiritual activity of which the ultimate aim is an intuition of God. The path leading to this goal is philosophy. It is both long and arduous. At first one has to pass through the 'encyclic studies' (the scientific education of the day), which explain separately the various component parts of the universe and form the gateway to the higher knowledge of philosophy. This higher knowledge provides the key for the right apprehension of the universe as a whole, its law and creator, and paves the way for a true self-knowledge. Yet, like the Socratic quest, though with a deeper insight, this philosophic self-examination brings man back to the recognition of his own nothingness, as also of God's omnipotence. Thus philosophy itself declares its abdication in the face of the inconceivable greatness of God. Scepticism becomes, as often, the stepping-stone to mystic exaltation. For, as Philo says, he who wishes to know God, has to abandon himself, or, conversely, only he who despairs of himself is able to know the Infinite. Wisdom renounces its claim to independence and consents to serve as a guide to higher knowledge in which the rational mind submits itself to the divine Will.

Philo's meditations on the process by which God is apprehended form one of the most fascinating chapters of his theology. The human mind is able to know only God's existence, not His nature, and even this neither by sensible perception nor even by logical reasoning, but by intuition. For the Godhead, as the absolute and perfect being, is limited by no attribute and can be reached by mystical illumination only. In order to prepare itself for this final illumination the human mind must free itself of all earthly desire and ascend not only beyond the pale of the sensible world, but also above the highest sphere of the ideas which fringe the Absolute Being. When it has come near the Presence of God, bright beams of a spiritual light issuing from His hidden dwelling-place and representing His virtues irradiate the soul, fill her with its ineffable beauty, produce a 'fine frenzy', a sort of 'sober intoxication, and dazzle her mental eye so that it cannot discern the Face of the Inconceivable. The mystical consummation is, thus, a state of highest strain, emotion, delight and ignorance. Philo spares no effort to bring home to his readers the full beauty of this beatific vision. His descriptions of it are inspired with a glowing enthusiasm, and are perhaps, apart from certain passages of Plotinus, finished and impressive accounts of mystical experience preserved in ancient Greek literature. One of the symbols used by him as an illustration of this kind of vision is the cloud which covered Mount Sinai wrapping God from sight, and into which Moses ascended in order to speak with the Attainable; this symbol recurs in the writings of medieval mystics as the Cloud of Unknowing, 'dark with excessive bright' (Milton, P.L. iii, 380). Elsewhere, Philo discards the spatial precepts which he took mostly from ancient cosmology and describes ecstasy, on the analogy of prophetic inspiration, as the entrance of the Divine Spirit into the mortal, in whose mind reason makes room for the highest presence. Using the imagery of light, as in most of his similes, Philo says that the Divinity comes as a beam which we cannot apprehend until the light of our mind is extinguished; for when the divine light shines, the human light sets, and when the divine light sets the human light rises. All these descriptions constitute variations on the same central idea: that the apprehension of God comes to the mind spontaneously and cannot be forced. The individual's share is limited to the preparation for the reception of the divine ray, the actual apparition of which is an act of Grace. Thus, at the end of the long, hard journey from bodily purification to philosophizing contemplation stands the genuine Jewish idea of Revelation.

Such, in brief outline, is the structure of Philo's thought and we may now inquire into the sources of his religious outlook. These coincide only in part with the sources of his actual knowledge. Philo received a double education: as a Jew and as a Greek philosopher. The extent of his Jewish learning was very small. He was, of course, acquainted with Scripture, but was really well versed only in the Pentateuch. Even this he did not know in Hebrew (which he understood, if at all, very imperfectly), but in the Greek translation of the Seventy which was regarded by him as inspired as by all Hellenistic Jews. Of Rabbinical interpretation of Law (Halakah) and Bible narrative (Haggadah) he had very dim notions; he owed both his exegetical training and his actual knowledge in matters Jewish to that school of Alexandrine commentators whose methods were perfected by himself. These matters had developed a peculiar form of Midrash into which many speculative ideas of Jewish Hellenism (among them the concept of Wisdom as a personified hypostasis, presenting God's pre-ordained world-plan), had found their way, but of Haggadic teaching only a few scraps. We must remember that in Philo's environment there did not exist anything like an authorized, canonized tradition of religious learning. Judaism has never been freer from dogmatical restrictions than it was in his time. Everyone who believed in the revelation of the Torah and followed its precepts was allowed to cherish his own views on the 'spirit' of the revealed letter and its religious content. Only by bearing this in mind can we account for the formation of the countless sects and types of piety which characterize this epoch of Jewish history. It is true that in Philo's time the so-called Oral Teaching on which Talmudic law was ultimately based began to take definite shape; this development, however, occurred in Palestine and exercised, at that time, no sensible influence upon the hellenized Dispersion. As Rabbinical opinion was no criterion for orthodoxy, Philo considered himself with full right a devout Jew; he was a strict observer of the religious rites and defended them against the freethinkers among his own people.

Philo's Greek scholarship was incomparably wider than his Jewish. It equalled that of a Greek of the highest standard of erudition. The abounding use he made of this store of knowledge has made him an important source for research in the history of Hellenistic philosophy. Owing to the loss of original sources, he is one of the main authorities for this branch of study.

If we were to form our estimate of Philo only from the doctrines which he has borrowed from others, we should be tempted to label him a Hellenistic philosopher with a special interest in religion. Such a judgement would, however, be essentially mistaken. For even were we to assume that every philosophical tenet held by Philo had its counterpart in contemporary Greek speculation (an assumption which would be quite arbitrary, since this literature is largely lost), the fact remains that the formation of a system like his would not have been possible for a mind working on purely Greek lines. The way in which he correlates theocentric and anthropocentric thought, his complete indifference to speculative research and his consistent transmutation of statements of fact into religious beliefs are the fruits not of philosophy, but of religious meditation. His attitude to Greek speculation generally betrays the same mentality. He regards Greek philosophical literature as a treasure-house containing a vast stock of solutions from which he is at liberty to pick out those which he considers most suitable. This process of selection was, it is true, in vogue among many Greek philosophers of his time, who were led to it by their scepticism as to the absolute validity of any single system. Philo, however, derived his criteria for selection from experiences which lay beyond the realm of logical reasoning. He was guided, as we have seen, by a vivid consciousness of the duality of human existence—its entanglement in sin by the bodily passions and its longing for salvation through the mind, the divine portion of mankind. This ethical dualism transposed itself for him into an analogous conception of the world as a whole; Spirit and Matter, the two rival elements in human being, became the opposing powers of the Universe, while the Deity, the purest embodiment of the better principle, withdrew to inaccessible heights. The gulf between man and God widened, and the path to salvation became more steep. Matter became preponderant, the sense of human weakness became keener and confidence in the mind's self-sufficiency faded away. Yet this increase of sensitiveness produced its own corrective; for that spark of divine life which is man's soul developed the capacity of leaving the domain of terrestrial evil and rising to the sublime height of the divine realm. This ascent ceases, however, to be within the range of the mind's own powers and becomes dependent upon an inspiration granted by Divine Grace to those who, by ascetic life, have overcome the material bonds and purified themselves for the reception of the supra celestial light. The union with God's radiance eradicates the dross or mortality and sanctifies the soul for an eternal beatitude.

The system of thought which we have thus sketched is neither Greek nor Jewish. It is, strictly speaking, not a doctrine at all, but a kind of atmosphere, the theoretical reflex of a mystical religion. It is to be noted that kindred ideas recur with infinite variety of form and emphasis among all the religious communities of later antiquity. They range from magic concreteness and mythical fancy to the most abstract speculation. They emerge in the formulæ of the magicians, in the symbolic rites of the Mystery-Religions (from which Philo borrowed many terms), in the fantastic rhapsodies of the Gnostics, in the lofty teachings of the philosophic schools, and in the esoteric ramblings of the Christian theologians. They are the changing face of a catholic religiosity, the last and most fascinating creation of the religious genius of pagan antiquity, begotten of the dualistic consciousness of later Greece and the Orient—not the Old East with its realistic imagination, but a Hellenized Orient which has gone through a fruitful crisis of self-examination. As this new body of thoughts was not a definite system but the spontaneous expression of a new sense of reality, it possesses neither a distinct native country nor a genealogical tree; it has only representatives who try to give expression to this common mysticism. Philo of Alexandria is one of its earliest known spokesmen; and since it was Alexandria that produced the most conspicuous members of this community of the spirit—Gnostics, Hermetics, Fathers of the Church, and, later, the greatest of them all, Plotinus—we are bound to suppose that this city, the melting-pot of cultures and creeds, was one of the main centres of this religious movement. Like the other religious communities of this time, Judaism also felt the impact of this spiritual force, which did not succeed in penetrating into the central position (the monistic citadel resisted firmly), but which settled down on the borders of its domain. There is no doubt that in the time of Philo something like a Jewish Gnosticism began to appear and that its secret teachings had much in common with those of the Alexandrine theosopher. The sects of the Essenes and even more the Therapeutæ, with which Philo had strong sympathies, belonged to this group. We do not know if there was any personal exchange of ideas between them. In any case, Philo is linked indirectly with the main trend of Jewish mysticism which was carried on by esoteric tradition until the Middle Ages, when the 'Cabbalah' used the remains of that tradition for the building up of its own systems of theosophy.

Only if we view Philo under this broader aspect are we in a position to determine with some precision the traits of his mental physiognomy. To begin with we note that his attachment to Greek philosophy was due to something more than missionary zeal. Only transcendental philosophy could provide him—as many of his kind—with the dialectical instruments for an appropriate expression of his transcendental mood. This is the deepest reason of his affection for Platonism, which in his time and perhaps in his surroundings, had already begun, under the influence of the atmosphere prevailing there to establish itself as a form of spiritual religion. This Platonism accounts also for the affinity between Philo and Plotinus, and, less directly for the correspondence between many of Philo's views and those of Jewish medieval philosophers who were influenced by Neoplatonic ideas. In this wider sense we may accept the well-known saying of the Church Fathers, 'either Philo platonizes or Plato philonizes'.

Philo's mystical yearning received concrete shape through its combination with Jewish ideas. As is well known, mysticism tends to run off into the abstractions of an unconditioned deity. For Philo this impersonal concept had to give way to the Jewish idea of a personal God. He infuses into the abstract schemes of metaphysics the Biblical faith in the 'Living God'. By so doing he deprived the philosophical differentiation between transcendence and immanence of much of its relevance. Philo was able to find in such divergent systems as Platonism and Stoicism the formulas appropriate to the description of the same personal God. The Jewish concept of Infinite Perfection has room for both classes of precepts. This personalization of the Divine Reality is the first contribution of Judaism to the mysticism of the age.

The Divine omnipresence operates through a constant supervision of individual life. This ethical aspect of supreme activity leads Philo to a fundamental transformation of the Platonic doctrine of the Ideas. He populates the realm of the Eternal Forms (viz. the Logos in which they are all contained) with the Jewish circle of Divine Virtues: Creative Goodness, and Majesty, Justice and Mercy. The Philonic mystic who rises to the apprehension of God is not able to behold His Face, but can grasp the virtues into which as it were, He expands. This concrete image of the Divine emanations becomes the object of meditation which ranges from the humble reverence due to the Supreme Judge to the affectionate love of a child for its father. The ethical description of the Divine character is the second contribution of Judaism to mystical thought.

The Supreme Being as the embodiment of every moral attribute satisfies by his manifold nature every human aspiration. Accordingly, Philo invests the Platonic World of Forms not only with the images of the Divine, but also with the models of human virtues: piety, love of mankind and the other norms of moral discipline. These ethical additions to the Ideas make possible a sanctification of earthly conduct, while at the same time, the intuitive perception of them becomes the summit of moral achievement. In this way spiritual progress is linked with morality and moral guidance with spirituality. The mystic is obliged to be a worker of righteousness, as the recognition of moral obligation forms an indispensable component of spiritual self-fulfilment. This gradual passage from pure introspection to concrete ethical practice is the third contribution of Judaism to this new spirituality. It prevents Philo from losing himself in vague mystical meditations and leads him back from the self-indulgent enjoyment of heavenly rapture to the actual performance of the Moral Law.

These and other Jewish concepts, recast through a mystical interpretation, form the leading ideas which serve Philo as inner directives for his selection of Greek doctrines. Often the Jewish element in them acts only negatively, showing itself in the tacit elimination of opposite concepts (e.g. on the one side, of Stoic materialism, and on the other side of the mystic credo of self-deification), or in a predilection for cognate precepts (for instance, to the principles of Stoic asceticism), but in its most intensive moment it rises to a direct statement of its own experiences. Yet Jewish thought nowhere works isolated, but appears always as the compelling force in the creation of a new synthesis which is Philonic piety.

We have dwelt upon the mystical side of Philo's nature, not only because it appears to us as the key to the understanding of his mode of thought, but also because it shows him as the earliest example of a religious type which was destined to become one of the most familiar forms of piety among the professors of the monotheistic creeds. It is the glory of Philo that he leads the choir of the religious contemplative writers to whom humanity owes its insight into hidden domains of that spiritual universe which is 'the fountain of Reason and the root of Soul'.

Jerusalem, 1945.   HANS LEWY

SELECTIONS FROM PHILO

I

GOD AND WORLD

THE CREATION OF THE WORLD IN ACCORDANCE WITH THE LAW OF NATURE

WHILE among other law-givers some have nakedly and without embellishment drawn up a code of the things held to be right among their people, and others, dressing up their ideas in much irrelevant and cumbersome matter, have befogged the masses and hidden the truth under their fictions, Moses, disdaining either course, the one as devoid of the philosopher's painstaking effort to explore his subject thoroughly, the other as full of falsehood and imposture, introduced his laws with an admirable and most impressive exordium. He refrained, on the one hand, from stating abruptly what should be practised or avoided, and on the other hand, in face of the necessity of preparing the minds of those who were to live under the laws for their reception, he refrained from inventing myths himself or acquiescing in those composed by others. His exordium (Gen. i), as I have said, is one that excites our admiration in the highest degree. It consists of an account of the creation of the world, implying[1] that the world is in harmony with the Law, and the Law with the world, and that the man who observes the law is constituted thereby a loyal citizen of the world, regulating his doings by the purpose and will of Nature, in accordance with which the entire world itself also is administered.

On the Creation of the World, 1–3 (i, p. 7)

GOD'S UBIQUITY

God fills all things; He contains but is not contained. To be everywhere and nowhere is His Property and His alone. He is nowhere, because He Himself created space and place

---

[1] The following is a basic doctrine of Stoic philosophy. The identification of Mosaic law with the law of nature implies the philosophical meaning of the Biblical precepts.

coincidently with material things, and it is against all right principle to say that the Maker is contained in anything that He has made. He is everywhere, because He has made His powers extend through earth and water, air and heaven, and left no part of the universe without His presence, and uniting all with all has bound them fast with invisible bonds, that they should never be loosed . . .[1]

The Confusion of Tongues, 136–7 (IV, pp. 83–4)

ON PRAYER

When, my mind, thou wishest to give thanks to God for the creation of the universe, give it both for the sum of things and for its principal parts, thinking of them as the limbs of a living creature of the utmost perfection. Such parts are heaven and sun and moon and the planets and fixed stars; then again earth and the living creatures or plants thereon, then the sea, the rivers, whether spring-fed or winter courses, and all they contain; then the air and its phases, for winter and summer, spring and autumn, those seasons which recur annually and are so highly beneficial to our life, are different conditions in the air which changes for the preservation of sublunar things. And if thou givest thanks for man, do not do so only for the whole genus but for its species and most essential parts, for men and women, for Greeks and barbarians, for dwellers on the mainland and those whose lot is cast in the islands. And if it is for a single person, divide the thanksgiving as reason directs, not into every tiny part of him down to the very last, but into those of primary importance, first of all into body and soul of which he is composed, then into speech and mind and sense. For thanks for each of these will by itself be not unworthy to obtain audience with God.[2]

The Special Laws, I, 210–I (VII, p. 219 ff.)

[1] Remark the adaptation of the philosophical formulas to the idea of a personal God.

[2] Philo reproduces here the scheme of a Jewish-Hellenistic prayer from which large parts have been preserved.

II

GOD AND MAN

ON THE LIBERTY OF MEN

THE special prerogative which man has received is mind, habituated to apprehend the natures both of all material objects and of things in general. For as sight holds the leading place in the body, and the quality of light holds the leading place in the universe, so too in us the dominant element is the mind. For mind is the sight of the soul, illuminated by rays peculiar to itself, whereby the vast and profound darkness, poured upon it by ignorance of things, is dispersed. This branch of the soul was not formed of the same elements, out of which the other branches were brought to completion, but it was allotted something better and purer, the substance in fact out of which divine natures were wrought.[1] And therefore it is reasonably held that the mind alone in all that makes us what we are is indestructible. For it is mind alone which the Father who begat it judged worthy of freedom, and loosening the fetters of necessity, suffered it to range as it listed, and of that free-will which is His most peculiar possession and most worthy of His majesty gave it such portion as it was capable of receiving. For the other living creatures in whose souls the mind, the element set apart for liberty, has no place, have been committed under yoke and bridle to the service of men, as slaves to a master. But man, possessed of a spontaneous and self-determined will, whose activities for the most part rest on deliberate choice, is with reason blamed for what he does wrong with intent, praised when he acts rightly of his own will. In the others, the plants and animals, no praise is due if they bear well, nor blame if they fare ill: for their movements and changes in either direction come to them from no deliberate choice or volition of their own. But the soul of man alone has received from God the faculty of voluntary movement, and in this way especially is made like to Him, and thus

---

[1] The 'divine natures' are the stars, their substance the ether.

being liberated, as far as might be, from that hard and ruthlest mistress, necessity, may justly be charged with guilt, in thas it does not honour its Liberator. . . . For God had made man free and unfettered, to employ his powers of action with voluntary and deliberate choice for this purpose, that, knowing good and ill and receiving the conception of the noble and the base, and setting himself in sincerity to apprehend just and unjust and in general what belongs to virtue and what to vice, he might practise to choose the better and eschew the opposite.[1]   *The Unchangeableness of God*, 45–9 (III, p. 33 ff.)

'THE LORD SHEPHERDS ME . . .'

'The Lord shepherds me and nothing shall be lacking to me' (Ps. xxiii. 1). It well befits every lover of God to rehearse this Psalm. But for the Universe it is a still more fitting theme. For land and water and air and fire, and all plants and animals which are in these, whether mortal or divine, yea and the sky, and the circuits of sun and moon, and the revolutions and rhythmic movements of the other heavenly bodies, are like some flock under the hand of God its King and Shepherd. This hallowed flock He leads in accordance with right and law, setting over it His true Word and Firstborn Son[2] Who shall take upon Him its government like some viceroy of a great king; for it is said in a certain place: 'Behold I am, I send MY Angel before thy face to guard thee in the way' (Ex. xxiii. 20). Let therefore even the whole universe, that greatest and most perfect flock of the God who IS, say, 'The Lord shepherds me, and nothing shall fail me'. Let each individual person too utter this same cry, not with the voice that glides forth over tongue and lips, not reaching beyond a short space of air, but with the voice of the understanding that has wide scope and lays hold on the ends of the universe. For it cannot be that there should be any lack of a fitting portion, when God rules, whose wont it is to bestow good in fullness and perfection on all that is. Magnificent is the call to holiness

---

[1] The whole argument is a characteristic mixture of Platonic and Biblical (*cf.* Gen. iii. 22) teaching.   [2] Wisdom, or the Logos.

sounded by the psalm just quoted; for the man is poor and incomplete in very deed, who, while seeming to have all things else, chafes at the sovereignty of One; whereas the soul that is shepherded of God, having the one and only thing on which all depend, is naturally exempt from want of other things for it worships no blind wealth, but a wealth that sees and that with vision surpassingly keen.

On Husbandry, 51–4 (III, p. 135 ff.)

GOD IS NEAR US

God, since His fullness is everywhere, is near us, and since His eye beholds us, since He is close beside us, let us refrain from evil-doing. It were best that our motive should be reverence, but if not, let us at least tremble to think of the power of His sovereignty, how invincible it is, how terrible and inexorable in vengeance, when He is minded to use His power of chastisement. Thus may the divine spirit of wisdom not lightly shift His dwelling and be gone, but long, long abide with us, since He did thus abide with Moses the wise . . . For we read 'stand thou here with Me' (Deut. v. 31). Here we have an oracle vouchsafed to Moses; true stability and immutable tranquillity is that which we experience at the side of God, who Himself stands always immutable.

On the Giants, 47 ff. (II, p. 469)

GOD THE POSSESSOR OF ALL, MAN ITS USURER

God claimed the sovereignty of all for Himself; to His subjects He assigned the use and enjoyment of themselves and each other . . . For I am formed of soul and body, I seem to have mind, reason, sense, yet I find that none of them is really mine. Where was my body before birth, and whither will it go when I have departed? What has become of the changes produced by life's various stages in the seemingly permanent self? Where is the babe that once I was, the boy and the other gradations between boy and full-grown man? Whence came the soul, whither will it go, how long will it be our mate and comrade? Can we tell its essential nature? When did we get it? Before birth? But then there was no 'ourselves'. What of it after death? But then we who are here joined to the body, creatures of composition and quality, shall be no more. . . . Even now in this life, we are the ruled rather than the rulers, known rather than knowing. The soul knows us, though we know it not; it lays on us commands, which we must fain obey, as a servant obeys his mistress. And when it will, it will claim its divorce in court and depart, leaving our home desolate of life. Press it as we may to stay, it will escape from our hands. So subtle is it of nature, that it affords no grip or handle to the body. Is my mind my own possession? That parent of false conjectures, that purveyor of delusion, the delirious, the fatuous, and in frenzy or melancholy or senility proved to be the very negation of mind. Is my utterance my own possession, or my organs of speech? A little sickness is a cause sufficient to cripple the tongue and sew up the lips of the most eloquent, and the expectation of disaster paralyses multitudes into speechlessness. Not even of my sense-perception do I find myself master, rather, it may well be, its slave, who follows it where it leads, to colours, shapes, sounds, scents, flavours, and the other material things.

All this surely makes it plain that what we use are the possessions of another, that nor glory, nor wealth, nor honours, nor offices, nor all that makes up body or soul are our own, not even life itself. And if we recognize that we have but their use, we shall tend them with care as God's possessions, remembering from the first, that it is the master's custom, when he will, to take back his own. The thought will lighten our sorrow when they are taken from us. But as it is, with the mass of men, the belief that all things are their own makes their loss or absence at once a source of grief and trouble.

On the Cherubim, 113-8 (ii, p. 75 ff.)

ON GOD'S GRACE

'Noah ("the righteous man") found grace in the sight of the Lord' (Gen. vi. 8). '*Finding grace*' is not as some suppose equivalent only to being well-pleasing, but something of this kind besides. The righteous man exploring the nature of existence, makes a surprising find, in this one discovery, that all things are a *grace* of God, and that creation has no gift of grace to bestow, for neither has it any possession, since all things are God's possession, and for this reason grace too belongs to Him alone as a thing that is His very own. Thus to those who ask what the origin of creation is the right answer would be: that it is the goodness and grace of God, which He bestowed on the race that stands next after Him. For all things in the world and the world itself is a free gift and act of kindness and grace on God's part.

Allegorical Interpretation III, 77–8 (I, pp. 351–3)

MAN OFFERS WHAT GOD HAS GIVEN HIM

The most sacred ordinance of Moses runs, 'My gifts, My offerings, My fruits ye shall observe to bring to Me' (Num. xxviii. 2).[1] For to whom should we make thank-offering save to God? and wherewithal save by what He has given us? for there is nothing else whereof we can have sufficiency. God needs nothing, yet in the exceeding greatness of His beneficence to our race He bids us bring what is His own. For if we cultivate the spirit of rendering thanks and honour to Him, we shall be pure from wrong-doing and wash away the filthiness which defiles our lives in thought and word and deed. For it is absurd that a man should be forbidden to enter the temples save after bathing and cleansing his body, and yet should attempt to pray and sacrifice with a heart still soiled and spotted. The temples are made of stones and timber, that is of soulless matter, and soulless too is the body in itself. And can it be that while it is forbidden to this soulless body to touch the soulless stones, except it have first been subjected to lustral and purificatory consecration, a man will not shrink from approaching with his soul impure the absolute purity of God and that too when there is no thought of repentance in his

---

[1] It may be remembered that the Greek translation of the Bible used by Philo often differs from the Hebrew original.

heart? He who is resolved not only to commit no further sin, but also to wash away the past, may approach with gladness: let him who lacks this resolve keep far away, since hardly shall he be purified. For He shall never escape the eye of Him who sees into the recesses of the mind and treads its inmost shrine.

On the Unchangeableness of God, 6-9 (III, p. 15)

ON GIVING THANKS TO GOD

The gifts which God can give are not such as man in his turn can receive, since for Him it is easy to bestow gifts, ever so many, ever so great, but for us it is no light matter to receive the proffered boons. For it is enough for us to obtain the good fruits of toil and effort, those more familiar gifts which grow up with us, but such as spring up independently without art of any form of human devising, which come ready-made to the recipient, we cannot even hope to attain. These are gifts of God, and therefore to discover them is the inevitable destiny of natures closer to God and undefiled and released from the mortal body. Yet Moses taught us to make our acknowledgements of thanks according to the power of our hands (Num. vi. 21), the man of sagacity dedicating his good sense and prudence, the master of words consecrating all the excellences of speech in praises to the Existent in poem or prose, and from other offerings after their kind, natural philosophy, ethical philosophy, the lore of the arts and sciences from the several students of the same. In this way the sailor will dedicate success of voyage, the husbandman fruitfulness of crops, the herdsman the teeming increase of his livestock, the physician the health of his patients, or again the general his victory in war, the statesman or crowned head his lawful pre-eminence, or sovereignty, and in short he who is not self-centred will vow as the cause of all goods of the soul or body or outside the body Him who in very truth is the one sole Cause of aught. Let none then of the lowly or obscure in repute shrink through despair of the higher hope from thankful supplication to God, but even if he no longer expects any greater boon, give thanks according to his power for the gifts which he has already received. Vast is the number of such gifts, birth, life, nurture, soul, sense-perception, mental picturing, impulse, reasoning. Now 'reasoning' as a name is but a little word, but as a fact it is something most perfect and most divine, a piece torn off from the soul of the universe,[1] or, as it might be put more reverently following the philosophy of Moses, a faithful impress of the divine image.

On the Change of Names, 218–23 (v, p. 255 ff.)

WORLD AND SOUL AN OFFERING TO GOD

The whole heaven and the whole world is an offering dedicated to God, and He it is who has created the offering; and all God-beloved souls, citizens of the world, consecrate themselves, allowing no mortal attraction to draw them in the opposite direction, and they never grow weary of devoting and sanctifying their own imperishable life.

On Dreams, 1, 243 (v, p. 425)

THE LEVITE

'I am thy portion and inheritance' (Num. xviii. 20): for in reality the mind, which has been perfectly cleansed and purified, and which renounces all things pertaining to creation, is acquainted with One alone, and knows but One, even the Uncreate, to Whom it has drawn nigh, by Whom also it has been taken to Himself. For who is at liberty to say 'God Himself is alone (and all) to me', save one who has no welcome for aught that comes after Him? And this is the Levite attitude of mind, for the name means 'He (is precious) to me',[2] the thought conveyed being that while different things have been held precious by different people, he is alone in holding precious the highest and worthiest Cause of all things.

On Noah's Work as a Planter, 64–5 (III, pp. 245–7)

---

[1] This is a Platonic tenet.

[2] The explanation of the name 'Levite' is one of the artificial etymologies which Philo borrowed from his predecessors.

III

MAN AND WORLD

THREE KINDS OF MEN

SOME men are earth-born, some heaven-born, and some God-born. The earth-born are those who take the pleasures of the body for their quarry, who make it their practice to indulge in them and enjoy them and provide the means by which each of them may be promoted. The heaven-born are the votaries of the arts and of knowledge, the lovers of learning. For the heavenly element in us is the mind, as the heavenly beings are each of them a mind. And it is the mind which pursues the learning of the schools and the other arts one and all, which sharpens and whets itself, aye, and trains and drills itself solid in the contemplation of what is intelligible by mind. But the men of God are priests and prophets who have refused to accept membership in the commonwealth of the world and to become citizens therein, but have risen wholly above the sphere of sense-perception and have been translated into the world of the intelligible and dwell there registered as freemen of the commonwealth of Ideas, which are imperishable and incorporeal. *On the Giants*, 60–1 (II, p. 475)

MAN A STRANGER IN THIS WORLD

(*a*) 'All the land is mine (which is the same as "all creation is mine"), but ye are strangers and sojourners before me' (Lev. xxv. 23). . . . For each of us has come into this world as into a foreign city, in which before our birth we had no part, and in this city he does but sojourn, until he has exhausted his appointed span of life. And there is another lesson of wisdom that he teaches in these words, even this—God alone is in the true sense a citizen, and all created being is a sojourner and alien, and those whom we call citizens are so called only by a licence of language. But to the wise it is a sufficient bounty, if when ranged beside God, the only citizen, they are counted as aliens and sojourners, since the fool can in no wise hold such a rank in the city of God, but we see him an outcast from it and nothing more.   *On the Cherubim,* 120–1 (II, p. 79)

(*b*) All whom Moses calls wise are represented as sojourners. Their souls are never colonists leaving heaven for a new home. Their way is to visit earthly nature as men who travel abroad to see and learn. So when they have stayed awhile in their bodies, and beheld through them all that sense and mortality has to show, they make their way back to the place from which they set out at first. To them the heavenly region, where their citizenship lies, is their native land; the earthly region in which they became sojourners is a foreign country.

On the Confusion of the Tongues, 77–8 (IV, p. 51)

ON PRACTICAL AND CONTEMPLATIVE LIFE

Do you affect the life that eschews social intercourse with others, and courts solitary loneliness? Well, what proof did you ever give before this of noble social qualities? Do you renounce money-making? When engaged in business, were you determined to be just in your dealings? Would you make a show of paying no regard to the pleasures of the belly and the parts below it—say, when you had abundant material for indulging in these, did you exercise moderation? Do you despise popular esteem? Well, when you held posts of honour, did you practise simplicity? State business is an object of ridicule to you people. Perhaps you have never discovered how serviceable a thing it is. Begin, then, by getting some exercise and practice in the business of life both private and public; and when, by means of the sister virtues, household-management and statesmanship, you have become masters in each domain, enter now, as more than qualified to do so, on your migration to a different and more excellent way of life. For the practical comes before the contemplative life;[1] it is a sort of prelude to a more advanced contest, and it is well to have fought it out first. By taking this course you will avoid the

[1] This view goes back to Plato and Aristotle.

imputation of shrinking from it through sheer laziness. It was on this principle too that the Levites were charged to perform their active service until the age of fifty (Num. iv, 3 ff.), but, when released from their practical ministry, to make everything an object of observation and contemplation; receiving as a prize for duty well done in the active life a quite different way of life whose delight is in knowledge and study of principles alone. And apart from this, it is a vital matter that those who venture to make the claims of God their aim and study should first have fully met those of men; for it is sheer folly to suppose that you will reach the greater while you are incapable of mastering the lesser. Therefore first make yourselves familiar with virtue as exercised in our dealings with men, to the end that you may be introduced to that also which has to do with our relation to God.

On Flight and Finding, 35–9 (v, p. 29 ff.)

PHILO ON HIS OWN LIFE

There was a time[1] when I had leisure for philosophy and for the contemplation of the universe and its contents, when I made its spirit my own in all its beauty and loveliness and true blessedness, when my constant companions were divine themes and verities, wherein I rejoiced with a joy that never cloyed or sated. I had no base or abject thoughts nor grovelled in search of reputation or of wealth or bodily comforts, but seemed always to be borne aloft into the heights with a soul possessed by some God-sent inspiration, a fellow-traveller with the sun and moon and the whole heaven and universe. And then I gazed down from the upper air, and straining the mind's eye beheld, as from some commanding peak, the multitudinous world-wide spectacles of earthly things, and blessed my lot in that I had escaped by main force from the plagues of mortal life. But, as it proved, my steps were dogged by the deadliest of mischiefs, the hater of good, envy, which

[1] Philo wrote these lines after he had been forced to interrupt his literary work in order to take over the political leadership of his community. See the Introduction.

suddenly set upon me and ceased not to pull me down with violence till it had plunged me in the ocean of political cares, in which I am swept away, unable even to raise my head above the water. Yet amid my groans I hold my own, for, planted in my soul from my earliest days, I keep the yearning for culture which ever has pity and compassion for me, lifts me up and relieves my pain. To this I owe that sometimes I raise my head and with the soul's eyes—dimly indeed because the mist of external affairs has clouded the clear vision—I yet make shift to look around me in my desire to inhale a breath of life pure and unmixed with evil. And if unexpectedly I obtain a spell of fine weather and a calm from civil turmoils, I get my wings and ride the waves and almost tread the lower air, wafted by the breezes of knowledge which often urge me to come to spend my days with her, a truant as it were from merciless masters in the shape not only of men but of affairs, which pour in upon me like a torrent from different sides. Yet it is well for me to give thanks to God even for this, that though submerged I am not sucked down into the depths, but can also open the soul's eyes, which in my deepest despair of comforting hope I thought had now lost their sight, and am irradiated by the light of wisdom, and am not given over to lifelong darkness. So behold me daring, not only to read the sacred messages of Moses, but also in my love of knowledge to peer into each of them and unfold and reveal what is not known to the multitude.

On the Special Laws, III, 1–6 (VII, p. 475 ff.)

AGAINST SECLUSION

The prophet (Moses) says 'Who led thee through that great and terrible wilderness, where there was biting serpent and scorpion' (Deut. viii. 15). You see that the soul falls in with the serpents, also when it is in a wilderness and it is bitten by pleasure, that subtle and snake-like passion. And pleasure's mode of action has received a most appropriate name, for it is here called a biting. But not those in a wilderness only are bitten by pleasure, but those also who are a prey to scattering.[1] For many a time have I myself forsaken friends and kinsfolk and country and come into a wilderness, to give my attention to some subject demanding contemplation, and derived no advantage from doing so, but my mind scattered or bitten by passion has gone off to matters of the contrary kind. Sometimes, on the other hand, amid a vast throng I have a collected mind. God has dispersed the crowd that besets the soul and taught me that a favourable and unfavourable condition are not brought about by differences of place, but by God who moves and leads the car of the soul in whatever way He pleases.

Allegorical Interpretation, II, 84–5 (I, p. 277 ff.)

SOUL AND BODY OF THE DIVINE LAWS

(The following section is important for the understanding of Philo's relation to positive religion. In spite of his allegorical interpretations he maintains the literal meaning of the Mosaic Laws, and sticks at their strict observance.)

There are some who, regarding laws in their literal sense in the light of symbols of matters belonging to the intellect, are over punctilious about the latter, while treating the former with easy-going neglect. Such men I for my part should blame for handling the matter in too easy and off-hand a manner: they ought to have given careful attention to both aims, to a more full and exact investigation of what is not seen and in what is seen, to be stewards without reproach. As it is, as though they were living alone by themselves in a wilderness, or as though they had become disembodied souls, and knew neither city nor village nor household nor any company of human beings at all, overlooking all that the mass of men regard, they explore reality in its naked absoluteness. These men are taught by the sacred word to have thought for good repute, and to let go nothing that is part of the customs fixed by divinely empowered men greater than those of our time. It is quite true that the Seventh Day

[1] Philo derives the name of the scorpion from the Greek verb meaning 'scatter'.

is meant to teach the power of the Unoriginate and the non-action of created beings.[1] But let us not for this reason abrogate the laws laid down for its observance, and light fires or till the ground or carry loads or institute proceedings in court or act as jurors or demand the restoration of deposits or recover loans, or do all else that we are permitted to do as well on days that are not festival seasons. It is true also that keeping of festivals is a symbol of gladness of soul and of thankfulness to God, but we should not for this reason turn our backs on the general gatherings of the year's seasons. It is true that receiving circumcision does indeed portray the excision of pleasure and all passions, and the putting away of the impious conceit, under which the mind supposed that it was capable of begetting by its own power: but let us not on this account repeal the law laid down for circumcising. Why, we shall be ignoring the sanctity of the Temple and a thousand other things, if we are going to pay heed to nothing except what is shown us by the inner meaning of things. Nay, we should look on all these outward observances as resembling the body, and their inner meaning as resembling the soul. It follows that, exactly as we have to take thought for the body, because it is the abode of the soul, so we must pay heed to the letter of the laws. If we keep and observe these, we shall gain a clearer conception of those things of which these are the symbols; and besides that we shall not incur the censure of the many and the charges they are sure to bring against us.

On the Migration of Abraham, 89–93 (IV, p. 183 ff.)

ON ASCETICISM

Disciples of the holy Word are only those who are really men, enamoured of moderation, propriety, and self-respect: men who have laid down as the foundations, so to speak, of their whole life self-control, abstemiousness, endurance, which are safe roadsteads of the soul, in which it can lie firmly moored

---

[1] The sabbatical rest reminds us that all our labouring is ineffectual compared with the eternal activity of God.

and out of danger; men superior to the temptations of money, pleasure, popularity, regardless of meat and drink and of the actual necessaries of life, so long as lack of food does not begin to threaten their health; men perfectly ready for the sake of acquiring virtue to submit to hunger and thirst and heat and cold and all else that is hard to put up with; men keen to get things most easily procured, who are never ashamed of an inexpensive cloak, but on the contrary regard those which cost much as matter for reproach and a great waste of their living. To these men a soft bit of ground is a costly couch; bushes, grass, shrubs, a heap of leaves, their bedding; their pillow some stones or mounds rising a little above the general level. Such a mode of life as this the luxurious call hard fairing, but those who live for what is good and noble describe it as most pleasant; for it is suited to those who are not merely called but really are men.[1]

On Dreams, I, 124-5 (v, p. 363)

ON THE LIFE OF THE THERAPEUTAE

The following excerpt is taken from Philo's work *On the Contemplative Life*. He describes there the life of the Therapeutae, a Jewish sect of monks and nuns living in the neighbourhood of Alexandria. This description is important not only because it shows one of the roots of later Christian monasticism, but also because it demonstrates Philo's personal affinity to mystical recluse.

The vocation of these philosophers is at once made clear from their title of Therapeutae . . . a name derived from a verb[2] used in the sense of 'worship', because nature and the sacred laws have schooled them to worship the Self-existent who is better than the good, purer than the One and more primordial than the Monad.[3] Who among those who profess piety deserve to be compared with these?

They settle in a certain very suitable place which . . . is

---

[1] Philo's precepts conform to those of the Cynics.

[2] Philo gives two explanations of the Greek verb, but the first 'to cure' can be omitted, because it is based upon an artificial symbolism ('curing the soul').

[3] For these Pythagorean terms see p. 63, n. 2.

situated above the Mareotic Lake[1] on a somewhat low-lying hill very happily placed both because of its security and the pleasantly tempered air. The safety is secured by the farm buildings and villages round about and the pleasantness of the air by the continuous breezes which arise both from the lake which debouches into the sea and from the open sea hard by. . . . The houses of the society thus collected are exceedingly simple, providing protection against two of the most pressing dangers, the fiery heat of the sun and the icy cold of the air. They are neither near together as in towns, since living at close quarters is troublesome and displeasing to people who are seeking to satisfy their desire for solitude, nor yet at a great distance because of the sense of fellowship which they cherish, and to render help to each other if robbers attack them. In each house there is a consecrated room which is called a sanctuary or closet,[2] and closeted in this they are initiated into the mysteries of the sanctified life. They take nothing into it, either drink or food or any other of the things necessary for the needs of the body, but laws and oracles delivered through the mouth of prophets, and psalms and anything else which fosters and perfects knowledge and piety. They keep the memory of God alive and never forget it, so that even in their dreams the picture is nothing else but the loveliness of divine excellences and powers. Indeed, many when asleep and dreaming give utterance to the glorious verities of their holy philosophy. Twice every day they pray, at dawn and at eventide; at sunrise they pray for a fine bright day, fine and bright in the true sense of the heavenly daylight which they pray may fill their minds. At sunset they ask that the soul may be wholly relieved from the press of the senses and . . . pursue the quest of truth. The interval between early morning and evening is spent entirely in spiritual exercise. They read the Holy Scriptures and seek wisdom from their ancestral philosophy by taking it as an allegory, since they think that the words of the literal text are symbols of something whose hidden nature is revealed

[1] On the south of Alexandria.

[2] This is the first occurrence of the term 'monastery' in Greek literature.

by studying the underlying meaning. They have also writings of men of old, the founders of their way of thinking, who left many memorials of the form used in allegorical interpretation and these they take as a kind of archetype and imitate the method in which this principle is carried out. And so they do not confine themselves to contemplation but also compose hymns and psalms to God in all sorts of metres and melodies which they write down with the rhythms necessarily made more solemn. For six days they seek wisdom by themselves in solitude in the closets mentioned above, never passing the outside door of the house or even getting a distant view of it. But every seventh day they meet together as for a general assembly and sit in order according to their age in the proper attitude, with their hands inside the robe, the right hand between the breast and the chin and the left withdrawn along the flank. Then the senior among them who also has the fullest knowledge of the doctrines which they profess comes forward and with visage and voice alike quiet and composed gives a well-reasoned and wise discourse. . . . All the others sit still and listen, showing their approval merely by their looks or nods. This common sanctuary in which they meet every seventh day is a double enclosure, one portion set apart for the use of the man, the other for the women. For women, too, regularly make part of the audience with the same ardour and the same sense of their calling. The wall between the two chambers rises up from the ground to three or four cubits built in the form of a breastwork, while the space above up to the roof is left open. This arrangement serves two purposes; the modesty becoming to the female sex is preserved, while the women sitting within earshot can easily follow what is said since there is nothing to obstruct the voice of the speaker.

They lay self-control to be as it were the foundation of their soul and on it build the other virtues. None of them would put food or drink to his lips before sunset since they hold that philosophy finds its right place in the light, the needs of the body in the darkness, and therefore they assign the day to the one and some small part of the night to the other.

Some in whom the desire for studying wisdom is more deeply implanted even only after three days remember to take food, others . . . hold out for twice that time and only after six days do they bring themselves to taste such sustenance as is absolutely necessary. . . . But to the seventh day as they consider it to be sacred and festal in the highest degree they have awarded special privileges as its due. . . . Still they eat nothing costly, only common bread with salt for a relish flavoured further by the daintier with hyssop, and their drink is spring water. . . .

(After Philo has drawn, for the sake of contrast, a very realistic picture of the 'follies and vices' of Greek banquets, he continues)

I will now describe the festal meetings of those who have dedicated themselves to knowledge and the contemplation of the verities of nature, following the truly sacred instructions of the prophet Moses. First of all these people assemble after seven sets of seven days have passed. . . . This is the eve of the chief feast which Fifty takes for its own (i.e. the feast of Pentecost). . . . So then they assemble, white-robed and with faces in which cheerfulness is combined with the utmost seriousness, but before they recline, at a signal from a member of the Rota, which is the name commonly given to those who perform these services, they take their stand in a regular line in an orderly way, their eyes and hands lifted up to Heaven . . . and pray to God that their feasting may be acceptable and proceed as He would have it. After the prayers the seniors recline according to the order of their admission, since by senior they do not understand the aged and grey-headed . . . but those who have spent their prime in pursuing the contemplative branch of philosophy, which indeed is the noblest and most god-like part. The feast is shared by women also, most of them aged virgins, who have kept their chastity . . . of their own free will in their ardent yearning for wisdom. Eager to have her for their life mate they have spurned the pleasures of the body and desire no mortal offspring but those immortal children which only the soul that is dear to God can bring to the birth unaided because the Father has sown in her spiritual rays enabling her to behold the verities of wisdom. The order of reclining is so apportioned that the men sit by themselves on the right and the women by themselves on the left. . . . Their seats are plank beds of the common kinds of wood, covered with quite cheap strewings of native papyrus, raised slightly at the arms to give something to lean on. . . . They do not have slaves to wait upon them as they consider that the ownership of servants is entirely against nature. For nature has borne all men to be free, but the wrongful and covetous acts of some who pursued that source of evil, inequality, have imposed their yoke and invested the stronger with power over the weaker. In this sacred banquet there is as I have said no slave, but the services are rendered by free men who perform their tasks as attendants not under compulsion not yet waiting for orders, but with deliberate goodwill anticipating eagerly and zealously the demands that may be made. For it is not just any free men who are appointed for these offices, but young members of the association chosen with all care for their special merit who as becomes their good character and nobility are pressing on to reach the summit of virtue. They give their services gladly and proudly like sons to their real fathers and mothers, judging them to be the parents of them all in common, in a closer affinity than that of blood, since to the right-minded there is no closer tie than noble living. And they came in to do their office ungirt and with tunics hanging down, that in their appearance there may be no shadow of anything to suggest the slave. . . . No wine is brought (abstinence from wine is enjoined to them for their lifetime), but only water of the brightest and clearest, cold for most of the guests but warm for such of the older men as live delicately. The table, too, is kept pure from the flesh of animals; the food laid on it is loaves of bread with salt as a seasoning, sometimes also flavoured with hyssop as a relish for the daintier appetites. . . . Such are the preliminaries. But when the guests have laid themselves down arranged in rows, as I have described, and the attendants have taken their stand with everything in order ready for their ministry, the President of the company, when a general silence is established . . . discusses some question

arising in the Holy Scriptures or solves one that has been
propounded by someone else. . . . His instruction proceeds in
a leisurely manner; he lingers over it and spins it out with
repetitions, thus permanently imprinting the thoughts in the
souls of the hearers. . . . His audience listens attentively . . .
signifying comprehension and understanding by nods and
glances, praise of the speaker by the cheerful change of expression . . . difficulty by a gentler movement of the head
and by pointing with a finger-tip of the right hand. The young
men standing by show no less attentiveness than the occupants
of the couches. The exposition of the sacred scriptures treats
the inner meaning conveyed in allegory. For to these people
the whole law book seems to resemble a living creature with
the literal ordinances for its body and for its soul the invisible
mind laid up in its wording. It is in this mind especially that
the rational soul begins to contemplate the things akin to
itself and looking through the words as through a mirror
beholds the marvellous beauties of the concepts, unfolds and
removes the symbolic coverings and brings forth the thoughts
and sets them bare to the light of day for those who need but
a little reminding to enable them to discern the inward and
hidden through the outward and visible. When then the
President thinks he has discoursed enough and both sides feel
sure that they have attained their object . . . universal applause
arises showing a general pleasure in the prospect of what is
still to follow. Then the President rises and sings a hymn
composed as an address to God, either a new one of his own
composition or an old one by poets of an earlier day who
have left behind them hymns in many measures and melodies
. . . After him all the others take their turn as they are arranged
and in the proper order, while all the rest listen in complete
silence except when they have to chant the closing lines or
refrains, for then they all lift up their voices, men and women
alike. When everyone has finished his hymn the young men
bring in the tables mentioned a little above on which is set
the truly purified meal of leavened bread seasoned with
salt mixed with hyssop, out of reverence for the holy table

enshrined in the sacred vestibule of the temple on which lie loaves and salt without condiments, the loaves unleavened and the salt unmixed. . . .[1]

After the supper they hold the sacred vigil which is conducted in the following way. They rise up all together and standing in the middle of the refectory form themselves first into two choirs, one of men and one of women, the leader and precentor chosen for each being the most honoured amongst them and also the most musical. Then they sing hymns to God composed of many measures and set to many melodies, sometimes chanting together, sometimes taking up the harmony antiphonally, hands and feet keeping time in accompaniment, and rapt with enthusiasm reproduce sometimes the lyrics of the procession, sometimes of the halt and of the wheeling and counter-wheeling of a choric dance. Then when each choir has separately done its own part in the feast, having drunk as in the Bacchic rites of the strong wine of God's love, they mix and both together become a single choir, a copy of the choir set up of old beside the Red Sea in honour of the wonders there wrought.[2] For at the command of God the sea became a source of salvation to one party and of perdition to the other. As it broke in twain and withdrew under the violence of the forces which swept it back there rose on either side, opposite to each other, the semblance of solid walls, while the space thus opened between them broadened into a highway smooth and dry throughout on which the people marched under guidance right on until they reached the higher ground on the opposite mainland. But when the sea came rushing in with the returning tide, and from either side passed over the ground where dry land had appeared, the pursuing enemy were submerged and perished. This wonderful sight and experience, an act transcending word and thought and hope, so filled with ecstasy both men and women that forming a single choir they sang hymns of thanksgiving to God their Saviour, the men

[1] *Cf.* Exod. xxv, 30, etc.

[2] The dancing of the Therapeutae is a kind of re-enactment of the Passage of the Red Sea.

led by the prophet Moses and the women by the prophetess
Miriam. It is on this model above all that the choir of the
Therapeutae of either sex, note in response to note and voice
to voice, the treble of the women blending with the bass of
the men, create an harmonious concert, music in the truest
sense. Lovely are the thoughts, lovely the words and worthy
of reverence the choristers, and the end and aim of thoughts,
words and choristers alike in piety. Thus they continue till
dawn, drunk with this drunkenness in which there is no shame,
then not with heavy heads or drowsy eyes but more alert
and wakeful than when they came to the banquet, they stand
with their faces and whole body turned to the East and when
they see the sun rising they stretch their hands up to heaven
and pray for bright days and knowledge of the truth and the
power of keen-sighted thinking. And after the prayers they
depart each to his private sanctuary once more to ply the
trade and till the field of their wonted philosophy. So much
then for the Therapeutae, who have taken to their hearts the
contemplation of nature and what it has to teach, and have
lived in the soul alone, citizens of Heaven and the world,
presented to the Father and Maker of all by their faithful
sponsor Virtue, who has procured for them God's friendship
and added a gift going hand in hand with it, true excellence
of life, a boon better than all good fortune and rising to the
very summit of felicity.

On the Contemplative Life, 3, 22–37, 64–90 (end) (IX, p. 113 ff.)

ON THE LIFE OF THE ESSENES

This quotation follows here as a counterpart to Philo's description of the
life of the Therapeutae. Philo deals more briefly with the Essenes also in
another treatise, but our main source about this sect is Josephus. In the
subsequent description Philo emphasizes the practical side of the life of the
Essenes, as they serve him as example of a 'practical life dedicated to God'.

The name Essenes[1] is awarded to them doubtless in recognition
of their holiness. They live in many cities of Judea and in many

---

[1] The name 'Essene' means in Aramaic 'holy'.

villages and grouped in great societies of many members. Their persuasion is not based on birth . . . but on their zeal for virtue and desire to promote brotherly love. Thus no Essene is a mere child nor even a stripling or newly bearded, since the characters of such are unstable with a waywardness corresponding to the immaturity of their age, but full grown and already verging on old age, no longer carried under by the tide of the body nor led by the passions, but enjoying the veritable, the only real freedom. This freedom is attested by their life. None of them allows himself to have any private property, either house or slave or estate or cattle or any of the other things which are amassed and abundantly procured by wealth, but they put everything together into the public stock and enjoy the benefit of them all in common. They live together formed into clubs, bands of comradeship with common meals, and never cease to conduct all their affairs to serve the general weal. But they have various occupations at which they labour with untiring application and never plead cold or heat or any of the violent changes in the atmosphere as an excuse. Before the sun is risen they betake themselves to their familiar tasks and only when it sets force themselves to return. . . . Some of them labour on the land skilled in sowing and planting, some as herdsmen taking charge of every kind of cattle and some superintend the swarms of bees. Others work at the handicrafts to avoid the sufferings which are forced upon us by our indispensable requirements and shrink from no innocent way of getting a livelihood. Each branch when it has received the wages of these so different occupations gives it to one person who has been appointed as treasurer. He takes it and at once buys what is necessary and provides food in abundance and anything else which human life requires. Thus having each day a common life and a common table they are content with the same conditions, lovers of frugality who shun expensive luxury as a disease of both body and soul. And not only is their table in common but their clothing also. For in winter they have a stock of stout coats ready and in summer cheap vests, so that he who wishes may easily take any

garment he likes, since what one has is held to belong to all
and conversely what all have one has. Again if anyone is sick
he is nursed at the common expense and tended with care and
thoughtfulness by all. The old men, too, even if they are child-
less are treated as parents of a not merely numerous but very
filial family and regularly close their life with an exceedingly
prosperous and comfortable old age. . . . Furthermore they
eschew marriage because they clearly discern it to be the sole
or the principal danger to the maintenance of the communal
life, as well as because they particularly practise continence.
For no Essene takes a wife, because a wife is a selfish creature,
excessively jealous and an adept at beguiling the morals of her
husband and seducing him by her continued impostures. For
by the fawning talk which she practises and the other ways in
which she plays her part like an actress on the stage she first
ensnares the sight and hearing, and when these subjects as it
were have been duped she cajoles the sovereign mind. And if
children come, filled with the spirit of arrogance and bold
speaking she gives utterance with more audacious hardihood
to things which before she hinted covertly and under disguise,
and casting off all shame she compels him to commit actions
which are all hostile to the life of fellowship. For he who is
either fast bound in the love-lures of his wife or under the
stress of nature makes his children his first care, ceases to be
the same to others and unconsciously has become a different
man and has passed from freedom into slavery.

Fragment of the Apology for the Jews, XI, 1–17 (IX, p. 437 ff.)

IV

THE KNOWLEDGE OF GOD

THE WAY OF WISDOM

WISDOM is a straight high road, and it is when the mind's
course is guided along that road that it reaches the goal which
is the recognition and knowledge of God. Every comrade of
the flesh hates and rejects this path and seeks to corrupt it. For
there are no two things so utterly opposed as knowledge and
pleasure of the flesh.

On the Unchangeableness of God, 143 (III, p. 81 ff.)

WHY HEAVEN WAS CREATED AFTER EARTH

On the fourth day, the earth being now finished, God ordered
the heaven in varied beauty. Not that He put the heaven in a
lower rank than the earth, giving precedence to the inferior
creation, and accounting the higher and more divine worthy
only of the second place; but to make clear beyond all doubt
the mighty sway of His sovereign power. For being aware
beforehand of the ways of thinking that would mark the men
of future ages, how they would be intent on what looked
probable and plausible, with much in it that could be supported
by argument, but would not aim at sheer truth; and how they
would trust phenomena rather than God, admiring sophistry
more than wisdom; and how they would observe in time to
come the circuits of sun and moon, on which depend summer
and winter and the changes of spring and autumn, and would
suppose that the regular movements of the heavenly bodies are
the causes of all things that year by year come forth and are
produced out of the earth; that there might be none who owing
either to shameless audacity or to overwhelming ignorance
should venture to ascribe the first place to any created thing,
'let them,' said He, 'go back in thought to the original creation
of the universe, when, before sun or moon existed, the earth
bore plants of all sorts and fruits of all sorts; and having contemplated this let them form in their minds the expectation

that hereafter too shall it bear these at the Father's bidding, whensoever it may please Him'. For He has no need of His heavenly offspring on which He bestowed powers but not independence: for, like a charioteer grasping the reins or a pilot the tiller, He guides all things in what direction He pleases as law and right demand, standing in need of no one besides: for all things are possible to God. This is the reason why the earth put forth plants and bore herbs before the heaven was furnished.

On the Creation of the World, 45–6 (i, p. 35 ff.)

THE CREATION OF THE HEAVEN AND THE RISING OF PHILOSOPHY

Its Maker arrayed the heaven on the fourth day with a most divine adornment of perfect beauty, namely the light-giving heavenly bodies; and, knowing that of all things light is best, He made it the indispensable means of sight, the best of the senses; for what the intellect is in the soul, this the eye is in the body; for each of them sees, one the things of the mind, the other the things of sense; and they have need, the mind of knowledge, that it may become cognisant of incorporeal objects, the eye of light, for the apprehending of bodily forms. Light has proved itself the source of many other boons to mankind, but pre-eminently of philosophy, the greatest boon of all. For man's faculty of vision, led upwards by light, discerned the nature of the heavenly bodies and their harmonious movement. He saw the well-ordered circuits of fixed stars and planets, how the former moved in unchanging orbit and all alike, while the latter sped round in two revolutions out of harmony with each other. He marked the rhythmic dances of all these, how they were marshalled by the laws of a perfect music, and the sight produced in his soul an ineffable delight and pleasure.[1] Banqueting on sights displayed to it one after another, his soul was insatiate in beholding. And then, as usually happens, it went on to busy itself with questionings, asking What is the essence of these visible objects? Are they

[1] This is a famous topic of Pythagorean philosophy.

in nature unoriginate, or had they a beginning of existence? What is the method of their movement? And what are the principles by which each is governed? It was out of the investigation of these problems that philosophy grew, than which no more perfect good has come into the life of mankind.

On the Creation of the World, 53–4 (I, p. 41)

ON MAN'S CREATION AFTER THE IMAGE OF GOD

Moses tells us that man was created after the image of God and after His likeness (Gen. i. 26). Right well does he say this, for nothing earth-born is more like God than man. Let no one represent the likeness as one to a bodily form; for neither is God in human form, nor is the human body God-like. No, it is in respect of the Mind, the sovereign element of the soul, that the word 'image' is used; for after the pattern of a single Mind, even the Mind of the Universe as an archetype, the mind in each of those who successively came into being moulded. It is in a fashion a god to him who carries and enshrines it as an object of reverence; for the human mind evidently occupies a position in men precisely answering to that which the great Ruler occupies in all the world. It is invisible while itself seeing all things, and while comprehending the substances of others, it is as to its own substance unperceived; and while it opens by arts and sciences roads branching in many directions, all of them great highways, it comes through land and sea investigating what either element contains. Again, when on soaring wing it has contemplated the atmosphere and all its phases, it is borne yet higher to the ether and the circuit of heaven, and is whirled round with the dances of planets and fixed stars, in accordance with the laws of perfect music, following that love of wisdom which guides its steps. And so, carrying its gaze beyond the confines of all substance discernible by sense, it comes to a point at which it reaches out after the intelligible world, and on descrying in that world sights of surpassing loveliness, even the patterns and the originals of the things of sense which it saw here, it is seized by a sober intoxication, like those filled with Corybantic frenzy, and is inspired, possessed by a longing far other than theirs and a nobler desire. Wafted by this to the topmost arch of the things perceptible to mind, it seems to be on its way to the Great King Himself; but, amid its longing to see Him, pure and untempered rays of concentrated light stream forth like a torrent, so that by its gleams the eye of the understanding is dazzled. *On the Creation of the World,* 69–71 (1, p. 55 ff.)

WHY MAN CAME LAST IN THE WORLD'S CREATION

It is obvious to inquire why man comes last in the world's creation; for, as the sacred writings show, he was the last whom the Father and Maker fashioned. Those, then, who have studied more deeply than others the laws of Moses and who examine their contents with all possible minuteness, maintain that God, when He made man partaker of kinship with Himself in mind and reason best of all gifts, did not begrudge him the other gifts either, but made ready for him beforehand all things in the world, as for a living being dearest and closest to Himself, since it was His will that when man came into existence he should be at a loss for none of the means of living and of living well. The means of living are provided by the lavish supplies of all that makes for enjoyment; the means of living well by the contemplation of the heavenly existences, for, smitten by their contemplation, the mind conceives a love and longing for the knowledge of them. And from this philosophy took its rise, by which man, mortal though he be, is rendered immortal. Just as givers of a banquet do not send out the summonses to supper till they have put everything in readiness for the feast; and those who provide gymnastic and scenic contests, before they gather the spectators into the theatre or the stadium, have in readiness a number of combatants and performers to charm both eye and ear; exactly in the same way the Ruler of all things, like some provider of contests or of a banquet, when about to invite man to the enjoyment of a feast and a great spectacle, made ready beforehand the material for both. He desired that on coming into the world man might at once find both a banquet and a most sacred display, the one full of all things that earth and rivers and sea and air bring forth for use and for enjoyment, the other of all sorts of spectacles, most impressive in their substance, most impressive in their qualities, and circling with most wondrous movements, in an order fitly determined always in accordance with proportion of numbers and harmony or evolutions. In all these one might rightly say that there was the real music, the original and model of all other,[1] from which the men of subsequent ages, when they had painted the images in their own souls, handed down an art most vital and beneficial to human life.

On the Creation of the World, 77–8 (1, p. 61 ff.)

'KNOW THYSELF'

The information that Terah left the land of Chaldea and migrated to Haran, taking with him his son Abraham and his kindred, (Gen. xi. 31) is given us not with the object that we may learn as from a writer of history, that certain people became emigrants, leaving the land of their ancestors, and making a foreign land their home and country, but that a lesson well suited to man and of great service to human life may not be neglected. What is this lesson? The Chaldeans are astronomers, while the citizens of Haran busy themselves with the place (or topic) of the senses. Accordingly Holy Writ addresses to the explorer of the facts of nature certain questions —'Why do you carry on investigations about the sun, as to whether it is a foot in diameter, whether it is larger than the whole earth, whether it is many times its size? And about the illuminations of the moon, whether it has a borrowed light, or whether it employs one entirely its own? And why do you search into the nature of the other heavenly bodies, or into their revolutions or the ways in which they affect each other

---

[1] Human music is, according to Pythagorean belief, only a dim copy of the heavenly music of the spheres.

and affect earthly things? And why, treading as you do on earth
do you leap over the clouds? And why do you say that you are
able to lay hold of what is in the upper air, when you are
rooted to the ground? Why do you venture to determine the
indeterminate? And why are you so busy with what you
ought to leave alone, the things above? And why do you extend even to the heavens your learned ingenuity? Why do you
take up astronomy and pay such full and minute attention to
the higher regions? Mark, my friend, not what is above and
beyond your reach but what is close to yourself, or rather
make yourself the object of your impartial scrutiny. What
form, then, will your scrutiny take? Go in spirit to Haran,
"excavated" land,[1] the openings and cavities of the body, and
hold an inspection of eyes, ears, nostrils, and the other organs
of sense, and engage in a course of philosophy most vital and
most fitting to a human being. Try to find out what sight is,
what hearing is, what taste, smell, touch are, in a word what
sense-perception is. Next, ask what it is to see and how you see,
what it is to hear and how you hear, what it is to smell or
taste or handle, and how each function is habitually performed.
But before you have made a thorough investigation into your
own tenement, is it not an excess of madness to examine that
of the universe? And there is a weightier charge which I do not
as yet lay upon you, namely to see your own soul and the
mind of which you think so proudly: I say, "see", for to
comprehend it you will never be able. Go to! Mount to
heaven and brag of what you see there, you who have not yet
attained to the knowledge of that of which the poet speaks in
the line

> All that existeth of good and of ill in the halls of thy
> homestead. (*Odyssey*, iv, 392.)

But bring the explorer down from heaven and away from these
researches draw the "Know thyself", and then lavish the same
careful toil on this, too, in order that you may enjoy the happiness proper to man.' This character Hebrews call 'Terah,'

---

[1] On the etymological meaning of 'Haran' see below.

Greeks 'Socrates'. For they say that 'Know thyself' was likewise the theme of life-long pondering to Socrates, and that his philosophy was concerned exclusively with his own self. Socrates, however, was a human being, while Terah was self-knowledge[1] itself, a way of thinking set before us as a tree of great luxuriance, to the end that lovers of virtue might find it easy, as they pluck the fruit of moral knowledge, to take their fill of nourishment saving the most sweet. Such do we find those to be whose part it is to explore good sense: but more perfect than theirs is the nature with which those are endowed who train themselves to engage in the contest for it. These, when they have thoroughly learned in all its details the whole study of the sense-perceptions, claim it as their prerogative to advance to some other greater object of contemplation, leaving behind them those lurking-places of sense-perception, to which the name of Haran is given. Among these is Abraham who gained much progress and improvement towards the acquisition of the highest knowledge: for when most he knew himself, then most did he despair of himself, in order that he might attain to an exact knowledge of Him Who in reality is. And this is nature's law: he who has thoroughly comprehended himself, thoroughly despairs of himself, having as a step to this ascertained the nothingness in all respects of created being. And the man who has despaired of himself is beginning to know Him that is.

On Dreams, I, 52–62 (v, p. 323 ff.)

ON THE APPREHENSION OF GOD

Doubtless hard to unriddle and hard to apprehend is the Father and Ruler of all, but that is no reason why we should shrink from searching for Him. But in such searching two principal questions arise which demand the consideration of the genuine philosopher. One is whether the Deity exists, a question necessitated by those who practise atheism, the worst form of wickedness, the other is what the Deity is in

[1] Terah means, according to the supposed Hebrew etymology, 'explorer'.

essence. Now to answer the first question does not need much labour, but the second is not only difficult but perhaps impossible to solve. Still, both must be examined. We see[1] then, that any piece of work always involves the knowledge of a workman. Who can look upon statues or painting without thinking at once of a sculptor or painter? Who can see clothes or ships or houses without getting the idea of a weaver and a shipwright and a housebuilder? And when one enters a well-ordered city in which the arrangements for civil life are very admirably managed, what else will he suppose but that this city is directed by good rulers? So then he who comes to the truly Great City, this world, and beholds hills and plains teeming with animals and plants, the rivers, spring-fed or winter torrents, streaming along the seas with their expanses, the air with its happily tempered phases, the yearly seasons passing into each other, and then the sun and moon ruling the day and night, and the other heavenly bodies fixed or planetary and the whole firmament revolving in rhythmic order, must he not naturally or rather necessarily gain the conception of the Maker and Father and Ruler also? For none of the works of human art is self made, and the highest art and knowledge is shown in this universe, so that purely it has been wrought by one of excellent knowledge and absolute perfection. In this way we have gained the conception of the existence of God.

As for the divine essence,[2] though in fact it is hard to track and hard to apprehend, it still calls for all the inquiry possible. For nothing is better than to search for the true God, even if the discovery of Him eludes human capacity, since the very wish to learn, if earnestly entertained, produces untold joys and pleasures. We have the testimony of those who have not taken a mere sip of philosophy but have feasted abundantly on its reasonings and conclusions. For with them the reason soars away from earth into the heights, travels through the

[1] This first argument is borrowed from the Stoics.

[2] This second argument is based upon later Platonistic doctrines, but changes them in accordance with Biblical tradition and mystical experiences.

upper air and accompanies the revolutions of the sun and moon and the whole heaven and in its desire to see all that is there finds its powers of sight blurred, for so pure and vast is the radiance that pours therefrom that the soul's eye is dizzied by the flashing of the rays. Yet it does not therefore faint-heartedly give up the task, but with purpose unsubdued presses onwards to such contemplation as is possible, like the athlete who strives for the second prize since he has been disappointed of the first. Now second to the true vision stands conjecture and theorizing and all that can be brought into the category of reasonable probability. So then just as, though we do not know and cannot with certainty determine what each of the stars is in the purity of its essence, we eagerly persist in the search because our natural love of learning makes us delight in what seems probable, so too, though the clear vision of God as He really is is denied us, we ought not to relinquish the quest. For the very seeking, even without find-ing, is felicity in itself, just as no one blames the eyes of the body because when unable to see the sun itself they see the emana-tion of its rays as it reaches the earth, which is but the extremity of the brightness which the beams of the sun give forth.

It was this which Moses, the sacred guide, most dearly beloved of God, had before his eyes when he besought God with the words, 'Reveal Thyself to me' (Ex. xxxiii. 13). In these words we may almost hear plainly the inspired cry: 'This universe has been my teacher, to bring me to the knowledge that Thou art and dost subsist. As Thy son, it has told me of its Father, as Thy work, of its contriver. But what Thou art in Thy essence I desire to understand, yet find in no part of the All any to guide me to this knowledge. Therefore I pray and beseech Thee to accept the supplication of a suppliant, a lover of God, one whose mind is set to serve Thee alone; for as knowledge of the light does not come by any other source but what itself supplies, so too Thou alone canst tell me of Thyself. Wherefore I crave pardon, if, for lack of a teacher, I venture to appeal to Thee in my desire to learn of Thee.' He replies, 'Thy zeal I approve as praiseworthy, but the request cannot fitly be granted to any that are brought into being by creation. I freely bestow (cf. Ex. xxxiii, 19) what is in accordance with the recipient; for not all that I can give with ease is within man's power to take, and therefore to him that is worthy of My grace I extend all the boons which he is capable of receiving. But the apprehension of Me is something more than human nature, yea even the whole heaven and universe will be able to contain. Know thyself, then, and do not be led away by impulses and desires beyond thy capacity, nor let yearning for the unattainable uplift and carry thee off thy feet, for of the obtainable nothing shall be denied thee.' When Moses heard this, he addressed to Him a second petition and said, 'I bow before Thy admonitions, that I never could have received the vision of Thee clearly manifested, but I beseech Thee that I may at least see the glory that surrounds Thee (cf. Ex. xxxiii. 18), and by Thy glory I understand the powers that keep guard around Thee, of whom I would fain gain apprehension, for though hitherto that has escaped me, the thought of it creates in me a mighty longing to have knowledge of them.' To this He answers, 'The powers which thou seekest to know are discerned not by sight but by mind even as I Whose they are, am discerned by mind and not by sight, and when I say "they are discerned by mind" I do not mean that they are now discerned by mind, but mean that if these other powers could be apprehended it would not be by sense but by mind at its purest. But while in their essence they are beyond your apprehension, they nevertheless present to your sight a sort of impress and copy of their active working. You men have for your use seals which when brought into contact with wax or similar material stamp on them any number of impressions while they themselves are not docked in any part thereby but remain as they were. Such you must conceive My powers to be, supplying quality and shape to things which lack either and yet changing or lessening nothing of their eternal nature. Some among you[1] call them not inaptly "forms" or "ideas", since they bring

[1] Plato and his school are meant here.

form into everything that is, giving order to the disordered, limit to the unlimited, bounds to the unbounded, shape to the shapeless, and in general changing the worse to something better. Do not, then, hope to be ever able to apprehend Me or any of My powers in Our essence. But I readily and with right goodwill will admit you to a share of what is attainable. That means that I bid you come and contemplate the universe and its contents, a spectacle apprehended not by the eye of the body but by the unsleeping eyes of the mind. Only let there be the constant and profound longing for wisdom which fills its scholars and disciples with verities glorious in their exceeding loveliness.' When Moses heard this, he did not cease from his desire but kept the yearning for the invisible aflame in his heart.

All of like sort to him, all who spurn idle fables and embrace truth in its purity, whether they have been such from the first or through conversion to the better side have reached that higher state, obtain His approval, the former because they were not false to the nobility of their birth, the latter because their judgement led them to make the passage to piety. These last he calls 'proselytes', or newly-joined, because they have joined the new and godly commonwealth.[1] Thus, while giving equal rank to all in-comers with all the privileges which he gives to the native-born, he exhorts the old nobility to honour them not only with marks of respect, but with special friendship and with more than ordinary goodwill.[2] And surely there is good reason for this; they have left, he says, their country, their kinsfolk and their friends for the sake of virtue and religion. Let them not be denied another citizenship or other ties of family and friendship, and let them find places of shelter standing ready for refugees to the camp of piety. For the most effectual love-charm, the chain which binds indissolubly the goodwill which makes us one is to honour the one God.   *The Special Laws*, 1, 32–52 (VII, pp. 117–29)

[1] *Cf.* Lev. xix. 33, 34; Deut. x. 18, 19.
[2] Thou shalt love him as thyself. Lev. xix. 34.

ISRAEL, THE SEER OF GOD

Those, if such there be, who have had the power to apprehend God through Himself without the co-operation of any reasoning process to lead them to the sight, must be recorded as holy and genuine worshippers and friends of God in very truth. In their company is he who in the Hebrew is called Israel but in our tongue the God-seer[1] who sees not His real nature, for that, as I said, is impossible—but that He is. And this knowledge he has gained not from any other source, not from things on earth or things in Heaven, not from the elements or combinations of elements mortal or immortal, but at the summons of Him alone who has willed to reveal His existence as a person to the suppliant. How this access has been obtained may well be seen through an illustration. Do we behold the sun which sense perceives by any other thing than the sun, or the stars by any others than the stars, and in general is not light seen by light; in the same way God too is His own brightness and is discerned through Himself alone, without anything co-operating or being able to co-operate in giving a perfect apprehension of His existence. They then do but make a happy guess, who are at pains to discern the Uncreated, and Creator of all from His creation, and are on the same footing as those who try to trace the nature of the monad from the dyad, whereas observation of the dyad should begin with the monad which is the starting-point.[2] The seekers for truth are those who envisage God through God, light through light.

On Rewards and Punishments, 43–6 (VIII, pp. 337–9)

ON SEEKING AND FINDING GOD

When the prophet (Moses) sought to know the cause of successful achievement, he found that it was the presence with

[1] 'Israel' means, according to an artificial etymology adopted by Philo, 'the seer of God'.

[2] According to Pythagorean teaching, the monad is equated to the maker, the dyad to the things made.

him of the only God. For when he asked in doubt, 'Who am I, and what is there in me that I should deliver the race of vision (Israel) from the character which . . . sets itself up against God?' he is instructed by a message from God, 'I will be with thee' (Ex. iii. 11 ff.). It is true, of course, that the seeking of partial and subordinate objects calls out in us the exercise of delicate and profound thought; but the seeking of God, best of all existences, incomparable Cause of all things, gladdens us the moment we begin our search, and never turns out fruitless, since by reason of His gracious nature He comes to meet us with His pure and virgin graces, and shows Himself to those who yearn to see Him, not as He is, which is a thing impossible, since even Moses 'turned away his face, for he was afraid to look upon God' (Ex. iii. 6), but so far as it was allowable that created nature should direct its gaze towards the Power that is beyond conception.

On Flight and Finding, 140–1 (v, p. 85)

'SEE THAT I AM'

In the great Song there come these words as from the lips of God, 'See, see that I AM' (Deut. xxxii. 39), showing that He that actually is apprehended by clear intuition rather than demonstrated by arguments carried on in words. When we say that the Existent One is visible, we are not using words in their literal sense, but it is an irregular use of the word by which it is referred to each one of His powers. In the passage just quoted He does not say 'See Me,' for it is impossible that the God who is should be perceived at all by created beings. What he says is 'See that I AM', that is 'Behold My subsistence'. For it is quite enough for a man's reasoning faculty to advance as far as to learn that the Cause of the Universe is and subsists. To be anxious to continue his course yet further, and inquire about essence or quality in God, is a folly fit for the world's childhood. Not even to Moses, the all-wise, did God accord this, albeit he had made countless requests, but a divine communication was issued to him, 'Thou shalt behold that which is behind Me, but My Face thou shalt not see' (Ex. xxxiii. 23). This meant, that all that follows in the wake of God is within the good man's apprehension, while He Himself alone is beyond it, beyond, that is, in the line of straight and direct approach, a mode of approach by which (had it been possible) His quality would have been made known; but brought within ken by the powers that follow and attend Him; for those make evident not His essence but His subsistence from the things which He accomplishes.[1]

On the Posterity of Cain, 167–9 (II, p. 427)

THE SYMBOL OF THE BURNING BUSH

The prophet (Moses), led on by his love of acquiring knowledge, was seeking after the causes by which the most essential occurrences in the universe are brought about; for observing all created things wasting away and coming to the birth, perishing and yet remaining, he is smitten with amazement and cries out saying, 'Why is it that the bush is burning and not being consumed?' (Ex. iii. 2 ff.), for his thoughts are busy over the untrodden place,[2] familiar only to Divine natures. But when now on the point of engaging in an endless and futile labour, he is relieved of it by the kindness and providence of God the Saviour of all men, who from out of the hallowed spot warned him 'Draw not nigh hither' (*ibid.* 5), as much as to say 'Enter not on such an inquiry'; for the task argues a busy, restless curiosity too great for human ability; marvel at all that has come into being, but as for the reasons for which they have either come into being or are decaying, cease to busy thyself with them. For 'the place on which thou standest is holy ground,' it says (*ibid.* 5). What kind of place or topic is meant? Evidently that of causation, a subject which He has assigned to Divine natures only, deeming no human being capable of dealing with the study of causation. But the

[1] On these Divine powers see p. 69.

[2] Philo combines the Greek word for bush (βάτος) with ἄβατος, 'untrodden place'.

prophet owning to desire of knowledge lifts his eyes above the whole universe and becomes a seeker regarding its Creator, asking of what sort this Being is so difficult to see, so difficult to conjecture. Is He a body or incorporeal, or something exalted above these? Is He a single Nature, a Monad as it were?[1] Or a composite Being? What among all that exists? and seeing that this is a problem hard to pursue, hard to take in by thought, he prays that he may learn from God Himself what God is: for he had no hope of being able to ascertain this from another, from one of those that are inferior to Him. Nevertheless he did not succeed in finding anything by search respecting the essence of Him that Is. For he is told 'What is behind Me thou shalt see, but my face thou shalt by no Means see' (Ex. xxxiii. 23). For it amply suffices the wise man to come to a knowledge of all that follows on after God and in His wake, but the man that wishes to set his gaze upon the Supreme Essence, before he sees Him will be blinded by the rays that beam forth all round Him.

On Flight and Finding, 161–6 (v, p. 97 ff.)

'MANIFEST THYSELF TO ME'

So unceasingly does Moses yearn to see God and to be seen by Him, that he implores Him to reveal clearly His own nature (Ex. xxxiii. 13), which is hard to divine, hoping thus to obtain at length a view free from all falsehood, and to exchange doubt and uncertainty for a most assured confidence. Nor will he abate the intensity of his desire, but although he is aware that he is enamoured of an object which entails a hard quest, nay, which is out of reach, he will nevertheless struggle on with no relaxation of his earnest endeavour, but honestly and resolutely enlisting all his faculties to co-operate for the attainment of his object. So see him enter into the thick darkness where God was (Ex. xx. 21), that is into conceptions regarding the Existing Being that belong to the unapproachable region where there are no material forms. For the Cause

[1] On the Monad see p. 63, n. 2.

of all is not in the thick darkness, nor locally in any place at all, but high above both place and time. For He has placed all creation under His control, and is contained by nothing, but transcends all. But though transcending and being beyond what He has made, none the less He filled the universe with Himself; for He has caused His powers to extend themselves throughout the Universe to its outmost bounds, and in accordance with the laws of harmonies has knit each part to each. When therefore the God-loving soul probes the question of the essence of the Existent Being, he enters on a quest of that which is beyond matter and beyond sight. And out of this quest there accrues to him a vast boon, namely to apprehend that the God of real Being is apprehensible by no one, and to see precisely this, that He is incapable of being seen. But the holy Guide seems to me even before he began this search to have discerned its futility. That he did so is evident from his imploring the Existent One to be His own Interpreter and reveal His own Nature. He says 'Manifest thyself to me' (Ex. xxxiii. 13), showing quite clearly by so saying that there is not a single created being capable of attaining by his own efforts the knowledge of the God Who verily exists. This must be borne in mind if we are to under-stand what we read about Abraham, how, on reaching the place of which God has told him, he looked up on the third day and 'seeketh the place from afar' (Gen. xxii. 3 ff.). What place? The one which he had reached? And how can it be far off if he is already there? It may be that what we are told under a figure is to this effect. The wise man is ever longing to discern the Ruler of the Universe. As he journeys along the path that takes him through knowledge and wisdom, he comes into contact first with divine words, and with these he makes a preliminary stay, and though he had meant to go the remainder of the way, he comes to a stop. For the eyes of his understanding have been opened, and he sees perfectly clearly that he has engaged in the chase of a quarry hard to capture, which always eludes its pursuers and is off to a dis-tance leaving them ever so far behind. Rightly does he reflect that all the fleetest things under the sky would be seen standing still, if their motion were compared with that of the sun and moon and the other heavenly bodies. And yet (he ponders) all heaven is God's handiwork, and that which makes it ever ahead of the things made it follows, then, that not only other things with which we are familiar, but that whose movement surpasses them all in swiftness, the mind, would come short of the apprehension of the First Cause by an immeasurable distance. But the strangest thing of all is, that whereas the heavenly bodies as they go past moving objects are themselves in motion, God who outstrips them all is motionless. Yea, we aver that remaining the same He is at once close to us and far from us. He takes hold of us by those forming and chastening powers which are so close to each one of us; and yet He has driven created being far away from His essential Nature, so that we cannot touch it even with the pure spiritual contact of the understanding.

On the Posterity of Cain, 13–20 (II, p. 335 ff.)

THE CLOUD OF UNKNOWING

(*a*) Moses entered into the darkness where God was, that is into the unseen, invisible, incorporeal and archetypal essence of existing things. Thus he beheld what is hidden from the sight of the mortal nature, and, in himself and his life displayed for all to see, he has set before us, like some well-wrought picture, a piece of work beautiful and godlike, a model for those who are willing to copy it. Happy are they who imprint that image in their souls.

The Life of Moses, I, 158 (VI, p. 358 ff.)

(*b*) Moses entered into the darkness (Ex. xx. 21), the invisible region, and there abode, initiated into the most sacred mysteries. And he came to be not only an initiate, but the hierophant of rites and teacher of divine things which he will expound to those whose ears have been purified.

On the Giants, 54 (II, p. 473)

ON GOD'S POWERS

(*a*) We must now examine what is symbolized by the Cherubim and the sword of flame which turns every way (Gen. iii. 24) . . . A higher thought (on this question) comes from a voice in my own soul, which oftentimes is god-possessed and divines where it does not know. This thought I will record in words if I can. The voice told me that while God is indeed one, His highest and chiefest powers are two, even goodness and sovereignty. Through His goodness He begat all that is, through His sovereignty He rules what He has begotten. And in the midst between the two there is a third which unites them, Reason (the Logos), for it is through reason that God is both ruler and good. Of these two potencies sovereignty and goodness the Cherubim are symbols, as the fiery sword is the symbol of the Logos. For exceeding swift and of burning heat is reason and chiefly so the reason of the (Great) Cause, for it alone preceded and outran all things, conceived before them all, manifest above them all.

O then, my mind, admit the image unalloyed of the two Cherubim, that having learnt its clear lesson of the sovereignty and beneficence of the Cause, thou mayest reap the fruits of a happy lot. For straightway thou shalt understand how these unmixed potencies are mingled and united, how, where God is good, yet the glory of His sovereignty is seen amid the beneficence, how, where He is sovereign, through the sovereignty the beneficence still appears. Thus thou mayest gain the virtues begotten of these potencies, a cheerful courage and a reverent awe towards God. When things are well with thee, the majesty of the sovereign king will keep thee from high thoughts. When thou sufferest what thou wouldest not, thou wilt not despair of betterment, remembering the loving-kindness of the great and bountiful God.

On the Cherubim, 21, 29 (II, pp. 21, 25)

(*b*) The purest and most prophetic mind receives knowledge and understanding of God not from himself, for the mind is not great enough to compass His magnitude, but from His primary and guardian Powers. One must be content with the fact that beams are borne from these in the soul, so that one may be able to perceive the Elder and Brighter by means of the secondary illumination.

> *Questions and Answers to Exodus,* ii, p. 67
> (translation from the Greek fragment, after E. R. Goodenough. By Light, Light. New Haven, 1939, p. 26).

(c) Oh Mind, receive the uncounterfeited impression in order that as you are instructed concerning the Rulership and Goodness of the Cause you may win the blessed heritage and may at once know as well the blending and mixture of the supreme Powers. In these Powers together (*sc.* Rulership and Goodness), God is good by the fact that His dignity as ruler is made manifest, while He rules by the fact that his goodness is made manifest. This is all so in order that you may possess the virtues that arise from them, love and piety towards God, and that in your contact with these you may not, by exalting yourself, suffer because of the greatness of the Rulership of the King, and similarly you may not, by despairing of your better hopes, experience what is undesirable through the kindliness of the great and bountiful God.

> Fragment from a lost work, translation from Greek after Goodenough. By Light, Light, p. 35.

V

THE MYSTIC WAY

THE WITHDRAWAL OF THE MIND

'GOD led Abraham forth abroad and said, Look up to heaven and count the stars' (Gen. xv. 5). . . . He led forth the mind to the outermost bound. For what advantage would it have been for it to leave the body behind and take refuge in sense-perception? What gain in renouncing sense-perception and taking shelter under the uttered word? For it behoves the mind that would be led forth and let go free to withdraw itself from the influence of everything, the needs of the body, the organs of sense, specious arguments, the plausibilities of reasoning, last of all itself. For this reason he glories elsewhere saying 'The Lord, the God of heaven, and the God of the earth, who took me out of my father's house' (Gen. xxiv. 7); for it is not possible that he whose abode is in the body and the mortal race should attain to being with God; this is possible only for him whom God rescues out of the prison. . . . When the soul in all utterances and all actions has attained to perfect sincerity and godlikeness, the voices of the senses cease and all those abominable sounds that used to vex it. For the visible calls and summons the sense of sight to itself, and the voice calls the sense of hearing, and the perfume that of smell, and all round the object of sense invites the sense to itself. But all these cease when the mind goes forth from the city of the soul and finds in God the spring and aim of its own doings and intents. . . . For everyone that sought the Lord went out to it.[1] Right finely is this said. For if thou art seeking God, O mind, go out from thyself and seek diligently; but if thou remainest amid the heavy encumbrances of the body or the self-conceits with which the understanding is familiar, though thou mayest have the semblance of a seeker, not thine is the quest for the

---

[1] Philo had before referred to Gen. xxiv. 63 (on Isaac), Ex. ix. 29 (on Moses) and Num. xx. 25 (on Aaron).

things of God. But whether thou wilt find God when thou seekest is uncertain, for to many He has not manifested Himself, but their zeal has been without success all along. And yet the mere seeking by itself is sufficient to make us partakers of good things, for it always is the case that endeavours after noble things, even if they fail to attain their object, gladden in their very course those who make them.

Allegorical Interpretation, III, 39–48 (I, pp. 327–33)

THE FLIGHT FROM THE BODY

Depart out of the earthly matter that encompasses thee: escape, man, from the foul prison-house thy body, with all thy might and main, and from the pleasures and lusts that act as its jailers; every terror that can vex and hurt them, leave none of them unused; menace the enemy with them all united and combined. Depart also out of sense-perception thy kin. For at present thou hast made a loan of thyself to each sense, and art become the property of others, a portion of the goods of those who have borrowed thee, and hast thrown away the good thing that was thine own. Yes, thou knowest, even though all men should hold their peace, how eyes draw thee, and ears, and the whole crowd of thine kinsfolk, towards what they themselves love. But if thou desire to recover the self that thou hast lent and to have thine own possession about thee, letting no portion of them be alienated and fall into other hands, thou shalt claim instead a happy life, enjoying in perpetuity the benefit and pleasure derived from good things not foreign to thee but thine own.

On the Migration of Abraham, 9–11 (IV, p. 137 ff.)

ON INSPIRATION

The harvest of spontaneous good things is called 'Release', inasmuch as the Mind is released from the working out of its own projects,[1] and is, we may say, emancipated from

---

[1] An allusion to the ordinance of Ex. xxiii, 11, by which in the Sabbatical year the land (here compared with the mind) is to be left fallow.

self-chosen tasks, by reason of the abundance of the rain and ceaseless shower of blessings. And these are of a most marvellous nature and passing fair. For the offspring of the soul's own travail are for the most part poor abortions, things untimely born; but those which God waters with the snow of heaven come to the birth perfect, complete and peerless. I feel no shame in recording my own experience, a thing I know from its having happened to me a thousand times. On some occasions, after making up my mind to follow the usual course of writing on philosophical tenets, and knowing definitely the substance of what I was to set down I have found my understanding incapable of giving birth to a single idea, and have given it up without accomplishing anything, reviling my understanding for its self-conceit, and filled with amazement at the might of Him that is to Whom is due the opening and closing of the soul-wombs.[1] On other occasions, I have approached my work empty and suddenly become full, the ideas falling in a shower from above and being sown invisibly, so that under the influence of the Divine possession I have been filled with corybantic frenzy and been unconscious of anything, place, persons present, myself, words spoken, lines written. For I obtained language, ideas, an enjoyment of light, keenest vision, pellucid distinctness of objects, such as might be received through the eyes as the result of clearest shewing.

On the Migration of Abraham, 32–5 (IV, p. 151)

ON ECSTASY

(*a*) 'He who shall come out of thee', Scripture says, 'shall be thy heir' (Gen. xv. 4). Therefore, my soul, if thou feelest any yearning to inherit the good things of God, leave not only thy land, that is the body, thy kinsfolk, that is the senses, thy father's house (Gen. xii. 1), that is speech, but be a fugitive from thyself also and issue forth from thyself. Like persons possessed and corybants, be filled with inspired frenzy, even as the prophets are inspired. For it is the mind which is under

[1] A Biblical image, see Gen. xx. 18 and often.

the divine afflatus, and no longer in its own keeping, but is stirred to its depths and maddened by heavenward yearning, drawn by the truly existent and pulled upward thereto, with truth to lead the way and remove all obstacles before its feet, that its path may be smooth to tread—such is the mind, which has this inheritance. To that mind I say, 'Fear not to tell us the story of thy departure from the first three. For to those who have been taught to give ear to the things of the mind, thou ever repeatest the tale.' 'I migrated from the body', she answers, 'when I had ceased to regard the flesh; from sense, when I came to view all the objects of sense as having no true existence, when I denounced its standards of judgement as spurious and corrupt and steeped in false opinion, and its judgements as equipped to ensnare and deceive and ravish truth away from its place in the heart of nature; from speech, when I sentenced it to long speechlessness, in spite of all its self-exaltation and self-pride. Great indeed was its audacity, that it should attempt the impossible task to use shadows to point me to substances, words to point me to facts. And, amid all its blunders, it chattered and gushed about, unable to present with clear expression the distinctions in things. . . . Thus through experience, as a foolish child learns, I learnt that the better course was to quit all these three, yet dedicate and attribute the faculties of each to God, who compacts the body in its bodily form, who equips the senses to perceive, and extends to speech the power of speaking.' Such is the mind's confession, and to it I reply, 'even as thou hast quitted the others, quit thyself, depart from thyself'. And what does this 'departing' mean? It means 'do not lay up a treasure for thyself, thy gifts of thinking, purposing, apprehending, but bring them and dedicate them to Him Who is the source of accurate thinking and unerring apprehension.'

Who is the Heir? 69–74 (IV, p. 317 ff.)

(*b*) Admirably does Moses describe the inspired (Abraham) when he says 'about sunset there fell on him an ecstasy'[1]

---

[1] The Hebrew word means 'deep sleep', but the Greek translation allows the above explanation.

(Gen. xv, 12). 'Sun' is his name under a figure for our mind. For what the reasoning faculty is in us, the sun is in the world, since both of them are light-bringers, one sending forth to the whole world the light which our senses perceive, the other shedding mental rays upon ourselves through the medium of apprehension. So while the radiance of the mind is still all around us, when it pours as it were a noonday beam into the whole soul, we are self-contained, not possessed. But when it comes to its setting, naturally ecstasy and divine possession and madness fall upon us. For when the light of God shines, the human light sets; when the divine light sets, the human dawns and rises. This is what regularly befalls the fellowship of the prophets. The mind is evicted at the arrival of the divine Spirit, but when that departs the mind returns to its tenancy. Mortal and immortal may not share the same home. And therefore the setting of reason and the darkness which surround it produce ecstasy and inspired frenzy. To connect what is coming with what is here written he says 'it was said to Abraham' (Gen. xv. 13). For indeed the prophet even when he seems to be speaking, really holds his peace, and his organs of speech, mouth and tongue, are wholly in the employ of Another, to show forth what He wills. Unseen by us that Other beats on the chords with the skill of a master-hand and makes them instruments of sweet music, laden with every harmony.

Who is the Heir? 263–6 (IV, p. 417 ff.)

ON PROPHETISM

No pronouncement of a prophet is ever his own; he is an interpreter prompted by Another in all his utterances, when knowing not what he does, he is filled with inspiration, as the reason withdraws and surrenders the citadel of the soul to a new visitor and tenant, the Divine Spirit which plays upon the vocal organism and raises sounds from it, which clearly express its prophetic message.

On the Special Laws, iv, 49 (VIII, p. 37 ff.)

ON GRACE

Samuel's name means 'appointed or ordered to God', and
Hannah, his mother, means 'grace'. For without divine grace
it is impossible either to leave the ranks of mortality, or to stay
for ever among the immortal. Now when grace fills the soul,
that soul thereby rejoices and smiles and dances, for it is
possessed and inspired, so that to many of the unenlightened it
may seem to be drunken, crazy and beside itself. And therefore
she is addressed . . . in these words: 'How long wilt thou be
drunken? put away thy wine from thee' (1 Sam. i. 14). For
with the God-possessed not only is the soul wont to be stirred
and goaded as it were into ecstasy but the body also is flushed
and fiery, warmed by the overflowing joy within which passes
on the sensation to the outer man, and thus many of the foolish
are deceived and suppose that the sober are drunk. Though,
indeed, it is true that these sober ones are drunk in a sense, for
all good things are united in the strong wine on which they
feast, and they receive the loving-cup from perfect virtue. . . .
Fitly, then, does she answer the reckless one who thinks to
mock her stern and austere life, 'I . . . have drunk no wine or
strong drink, and I will pour out my soul before the Lord'
(1 Sam. i. 15). How vast is the boldness of the soul which is
filled with the gracious gifts of God! . . . what else was
meant by these words but 'I will consecrate all my soul to
him, I will loosen all the chains that bound it tight, which the
empty aims and desires of mortal life had fastened upon it; I
will send it abroad, extend and diffuse it, so that it shall touch
the bounds of the All, and hasten to that most glorious and
loveliest of visions—the Vision of the Uncreated'?

On Drunkenness, 144 ff. (III, p. 395 ff.)

DELIGHT IN GOD

The name of 'Eden' means 'luxuriance', symbol of a soul
whose eyesight is perfect, disporting itself in virtues, leaping
and skipping by reason of abundance of great joy, having set

before it, as an enjoyment outweighing thousands of those that men deem sweetest, the worship and service of the Only Wise. One, after taking a sheer draught of this bright joy, a member indeed of Moses' fellowship, not found among the indifferent, spake aloud in hymns of praise, and addressing his own mind cried, 'Delight in the Lord' (Ps. xxxvii. 4), moved by the utterance to an ecstasy of the love that is heavenly and Divine, filled with loathing for those interminable bouts of softness and debauchery amid the seeming and so-called good things of mankind, while his whole mind is snatched up in holy frenzy by a Divine possession, and he finds his gladness in God alone.

Noah's Work as a Planter, 38–9 (III, p. 231)

ON VISION

If we close the eye of our soul and either will not take the trouble or have not the power to regain our sight, do thou thyself, O Sacred Guide, be our prompter and preside over our steps and never tire of anointing our eyes, until conducting us to the hidden light of hallowed words thou display to us the fast-locked loveliness invisible to the uninitiate. Thee it beseems to do this; but all ye souls which have tasted divine loves, rising up as it were out of a deep sleep and dispelling the mist, hasten towards the sight to which all eyes are drawn; put away the heavy-footed lingering of hesitation, that you may take in all that the Master of the contests has prepared in your behoof, for you to see and hear.

- *On Dreams*, 164–5 (v, p. 383)

THE THEOPHANY ON SINAI

It was natural that the place should be the scene of all that was wonderful, claps of thunder louder than the ears could hold, flashes of lightning of surpassing brightness, the sound of an invisible trumpet reaching to the greatest distance, the descent of a cloud which like a pillar stood with its foot planted on the earth, while the rest of its body extended to the height of the upper air, the rush of heaven-sent fire which shrouded all around in dense smoke. For when the power of God arrives, needs must be that no part of the world should remain inactive, but all move together to do Him service. Near by stood the people. . . . Then from the midst of the fire that streamed from heaven there sounded forth to their utter amazement a voice, for the flame became articulate speech in the language familiar to the audience, and so clearly and distinctly were the words formed by it that they seemed to see rather than hear them. What I say is vouched for by the law in which it is written, 'All the people saw the voice' (Ex. xx. 18), a phrase fraught with much meaning, for it is the case that the voice of men is audible, but the voice of God truly visible. Why so? Because whatever God says is not words but deeds, which are judged by the eyes rather than the ears. Admirable, too, and worthy of the Godhead, is the saying that the voice proceeded from the fire, for the oracles of God have been refined and assayed as gold is by fire. And it conveys, too, symbolically, some such meaning as this: since it is the nature of fire both to give light and to burn, those who resolve to be obedient to the divine utterances will live for ever as in unclouded light with the laws themselves as stars illuminating their souls, while all who are rebellious will continue to be burnt, aye, and burnt to ashes, by their inward lusts, which like a flame will ravage the whole life of those in whom they dwell.

On the Decalogue, 44–9 (VII, p. 29 ff.)

THE REFORMATION OF MAN

'Ye shall eat the old and older yet, but also bear out the old from the face of the new' (Lev. xxvi. 10). The meaning is this. We must not indeed reject any learning that has grown grey through time, nay, we should make it our aim to read the writings of the sages and listen to proverbs and old-world stories from the lips of those who know antiquity, and ever seek for knowledge about the men and deeds of old. For truly it is sweet to leave nothing unknown. Yet when God causes the young shoots of self-inspired wisdom to spring up within the soul, the knowledge that comes from teaching must straightway be abolished and swept off. Ay, even of itself it will subside and ebb away. God's scholar, God's pupil, God's disciple, call him by whatever name you will, cannot any more suffer the guidance of men.

On the Sacrifices of Abel, 79 (ii, p. 155)

THE DEATH OF MOSES

Afterwards the time came when he (Moses) had to make his pilgrimage from earth to heaven (*cf.* Deut. xxxiii and xxxiv), and leave this mortal life for immortality, summoned thither by the Father Who resolved his twofold nature of soul and body into a single unit, transforming his whole being into mind, pure as the sunlight. Then, indeed, we find him possessed by the spirit, no longer uttering general truths to the whole nation but prophesying to each tribe in particular the things which were to be and hereafter must come to pass. Some of these have already taken place, others are still looked for, since confidence in the future is assured by fulfilment in the past. It was very fitting that persons so different in the history of their birth, particularly in their descent on the mother's side and in the manifold varieties of their thoughts and aims and the endless diversities of their practices and habits of life, should receive as a sort of legacy a suitable apportionment of oracles and inspired sayings. This was indeed wonderful, but most wonderful of all is the conclusion of the Holy Scriptures, which stands to the whole law-book as the head to the living creature; for when he (Moses) was already being exalted and stood at the very barrier, ready at the signal to direct his upward flight to heaven, the divine spirit fell upon him and he prophesied with discernment while still alive the story of his own death;[1] told ere the end how the end came; told how he was buried with none present, surely by no mortal hands but by immortal

[1] As Moses composed the whole Pentateuch, he also wrote down before his departure the last lines describing his own death.

powers; how also he was not laid to rest in the tomb of his forefathers but was given a monument of special dignity which no man has ever seen; how all the nation wept and mourned for him a whole month and made open display, private and public, of their sorrow, in memory of his vast benevolence and watchful care for each one of them and for all. Such, as recorded in the Holy Scriptures, was the . . . end of Moses, King, law-giver, high priest, prophet.

Life of Moses, II, 288–91 (VI, p. 593 ff.)

VI

THE SOUL AND HER GOD

'THE CITY OF GOD'

THERE is a psalm which runs thus: 'The strong current of the river makes glad the city of God' (Ps. xlvi (xlv). 4). . . . God's city is the name in one sense for the world which has received the whole bowl, wherein the divine draught is mixed, and feasted thereon and exultingly taken for its possession the gladness which remains for all time never to be removed or quenched. In another sense he uses this name for the soul of the Sage, in which God is said to walk as in a city. For 'I will walk in you', he says, 'and will be your God' (Lev. xxvi. 12). And, when the happy soul holds out the sacred goblet of its own reason, who is it that pours into it the holy cupfuls of true gladness, but the Word (Logos), the Cup-bearer of God and Master of the feast, who is also none other than the draught which he pours—his own self free from all dilution, the delight, the sweetening, the exhilaration, the merriment, the ambrosian drug (to take for our own use the poet's terms) whose medicine gives joy and gladness? Now the city of God is called in the Hebrew Jerusalem and its name when translated is 'vision of peace'.[1] Therefore, do not seek for the city of the Existent among the regions of the earth, since it is not wrought of wood or stone, but in a soul, in which there is no warring, whose sight is keen, which has set before it as its aim to live in contemplation and peace. For what grander or holier house could we find for God in the whole range of existence than the vision-seeking mind, the mind which is eager to sell all things and never even in its dreams has a wish for faction or turmoil? I hear once more the voice of the invisible spirit, the familiar secret tenant, saying, 'Friend, it would seem that there is a matter great and precious of which thou knowest nothing, and this I will ungrudgingly show thee, for many other well-timed lessons have I given thee. Know them, good friend, that

[1] This is, of course, an artificial etymology.

God alone is the real veritable peace, free from all illusion, but the whole substance of things created only to perish is one constant war. For God is a being of free will; the world of things is Fatality. Whosoever then has the strength to forsake war and Fatality, creation and perishing, and cross over to the camp of the uncreated, of the imperishable, of free-will, of peace, may justly be called the dwelling-place and city of God. Let it be then a matter of indifference that you should give to the same object two different names, vision of God and vision of peace. For indeed the Potencies of the Existent have many names, and of that company peace is not only a member but a leader.'

On Dreams, II, 246–54 (v, p. 553 ff.)

THE WISE MAN THE HOME OF GOD

His mind it is . . . in which God, so says the prophet (Moses), 'walks'[1] as in a palace, for in truth the wise man's mind is a palace and house of God. This it is which is declared to possess personally the God who is the God of all, this again is the chosen people, the people not of particular rulers, but of the one and only true ruler, a people holy even as He is holy.

On Rewards and Punishments, 122–3 (VIII, p. 387 ff.)

ON GOD'S VISIT

Wicked men think that the eye of God sees nothing but the outer world through the co-operation of the sun. They do not know that He surveys the unseen even before the seen, for He Himself is His own light. For the eye of the Absolutely Existent needs no other light to effect perception, but He Himself is the archetypal essence of which myriads of rays are the effluence, none visible to sense, all to the mind. And therefore they are the instruments of that same God alone, who is apprehended by mind, not of any who have part and lot in the world of creation. . . . Seeing then that our souls are a region open to His invisible entrance, let us make that place as beautiful as

[1] *Cf.* Lev. xxvi. 12 (according to the Greek translation).

we may, to be a lodging fit for God. Else He will pass silently into some other home, where He judges that the builder's hands have wrought something worthier. When we think to entertain kings we brighten and adorn our own houses. We despise no embellishment, but use all such freely and ungrudgingly, and make it our aim that their lodging shall have every delight and the honour withal that is their due. What house shall be prepared for God the King of kings, the Lord of all, who in His tender mercy and loving-kindness has deigned to visit created being and come down from the boundaries of heaven to the utmost ends of earth, to show His goodness to our race? Shall it be of stone or timber? Away with the thought, the very words of blasphemy. For though the whole earth should suddenly turn into gold, or something more precious than gold, though all that wealth should be expended by the builder's skill on porches and porticoes, on chambers, vestibules, and shrines, yet there would be no place where His feet could tread. One worthy house there is—the soul that is fitted to receive Him. Justly and rightly then shall we say that in the invisible soul the invisible God has His earthly dwelling-place.

On the Cherubim, 96–100 (II, p. 67 ff.)

ALL THINGS BELONG TO GOD

'All things', God says, 'are Mine'. And these 'all things' are the 'bounties, and gifts and fruits which ye shall observe and offer to Me at My feasts' (Num. xxviii. 2). Here Moses clearly shows that among existing things there are some which . . . are fruit meet for eating, even that one and only fruit which feeds the soul of him whose quest is the Vision. He who has learned this lesson, and can keep and ponder it in his heart, will offer to God the blameless and fairest sacrifice of faith at feasts which are no feasts of mortals. For God has claimed the feasts for Himself, and herein He lays down a principle which they who belong to the company of the philosophers must not fail to know. The principle is this. God alone in the true sense keeps festival. Joy and gladness and rejoicing are His alone; to Him alone it is given to enjoy the peace which has no element of war. He is without grief or fear or share of ill, without faint-heartedness or pain or weariness, but full of happiness unmixed. Or rather since His nature is most perfect, He is Himself the summit, end and limit of happiness. He partakes of nothing outside Himself to increase His excellence. Nay He Himself has imparted of His own to all particular beings from that fountain of beauty—Himself. For the good and beautiful things in the world could never have been what they are, save that they were made in the image of the archetype, which is truly good and beautiful.

On the Cherubim, 84–6 (II, p. 59 ff.)

ON SPIRITUAL OFFERINGS

God does not rejoice in sacrifices even if one offer hecatombs, for all things are His possession, yet though He possesses He needs none of them, but He rejoices in the will to love Him and in men that practise holiness, and from these He accepts plain meal or barley, and things of least price, holding them most previous rather than those of highest cost. And indeed though the worshippers bring nothing else, in bringing them-selves they offer the best sacrifices, the full and truly perfect oblation of noble living, as they honour with hymns and thanksgivings their Benefactor and Saviour, God, sometimes with the organs of speech, sometimes without tongue or lips, when within the soul alone their minds recite the tale or utter the cry of praise. These one ear only can apprehend, the ear of God.

The Special Laws, I, 271–2 (VII, p. 257)

THE PRAISE OF MIND

It is not possible genuinely to express our gratitude to God by means of buildings and oblations and sacrifices, as is the custom of most people, for even the whole world were not a temple adequate to yield the honour due to Him. Nay, it must be expressed by means of hymns and praise, and these not such as the audible voice shall sing, but strains raised and re-echoed by the mind too pure for eye to discern.

On Noah's Work as a Planter, 126 (III, p. 277)

THE SOUL AN ALTAR TO GOD

The true altar of God is the thankful soul of the Sage, compacted of perfect virtues. . . . On this soul-altar the sacred light is ever burning and carefully kept unextinguished, and the light of the mind is wisdom. . . .

On the Special Laws, I, 287 (VII, p. 267)

VII

ON MAN'S HUMILITY, HOPE, FAITH AND JOY

ON MAN'S NOTHINGNESS

HE who says (like Abraham), 'Master, what wilt thou give me?' (Gen. xv. 2) virtually says no less than this, 'I am not ignorant of Thy transcendent sovereignty; I know the terrors of Thy power; I come before Thee in fear and trembling, and yet again I am confident. For Thou has vouchsafed to bid me fear not; Thou hast given me a tongue of instruction that I should know when I should speak (Isaiah, l. 4), my mouth that was knitted up Thou hast unsewn, and when Thou hadst opened it, Thou didst strengthen its nerves for speech; Thou hast taught me to say what should be said, confirming the oracle "I will open thy mouth and teach thee what thou shalt speak" (Ex. iv. 12). For who was I, that Thou shouldst impart speech to me, that Thou shouldst promise me something which stood higher in the scale of goods than "gift" or grace, even a "reward"? Am I not a wanderer from my country, an outcast from my kinsfolk, an alien from my father's house? Do not all men call me excommunicate, exile, desolate, disfranchised? But Thou, Master, art my country, my kinsfolk, my paternal hearth, my franchise, my free speech, my great and glorious and inalienable wealth. Why then shall I not take courage to say what I feel? Why shall I not inquire of Thee and claim to learn something more? Yet I, who proclaim my confidence, confess in turn my fear and consternation, and still the fear and the confidence are not at war within me in separate camps, as one might suppose, but are blended in a harmony. I find then a feast which does not cloy in this blending, which has schooled my speech to be neither bold without caution, nor cautious without boldness. For I have learnt to measure my own nothingness, and to gaze with wonder on the transcendent heights of Thy loving-kindness. And when I perceive that I am earth and cinders or whatever is still more worthless, it is just then that

I have confidence to come before Thee, when I am humbled, cast down to the clay, reduced to such an elemental state, as seems not even to exist. And the watchful pen of Moses has recorded this my soul's condition in his memorial of me. For Abraham, he says, drew near and said, "Now I have begun to speak to the Lord, and I am earth and ashes" (Gen. xviii. 27), since it is just when he knows his own nothingness that the creature should come into the presence of his Maker.'

Who is the Heir? 24–31 (IV, p. 297 ff.)

'And forget the Lord thy God' (Deut. viii. 12–14). When then wilt thou not forget God? Only when thou dost not forget thyself. For if thou rememberest thine own nothingness in all things, thou wilt also remember the transcendence of God in all things.

On the Sacrifices of Abel, 55 (II, p. 137)

ON MAN'S IGNORANCE

What then, is the end of right-mindedness? To pronounce on himself and all created being the verdict of folly; for the final aim of knowledge is to hold that we know nothing, He alone being wise, who is also alone God. . . . Come forward now, you who are laden with vanity and gross stupidity and vast pretence, you that are wise in your own conceit and not only declare (in every case) that you perfectly know what each object is, but go so far as to venture in your audacity to add the reasons for its being what it is, as though you had either been standing by at the creation of the world, and had observed how and out of what materials its several parts were fashioned, or had acted as advisers to the Creator regarding the things He was forming—come, I say, and then, letting go all other things whatever, take knowledge of yourselves, and say clearly who you are, in body, in soul, in sense-perception, in reason and speech, in each single one, even the most minute, of the sub-divisions of your being. Declare what sight is and how you see, what hearing is and how you hear, what taste, touch, smelling are, and how you act in accordance with each of them, or what are the springs and sources of these, from which is derived their very being. For pray do not, O ye senseless ones, spin your airy fables about moon or sun or the other objects in the sky and in the universe so far removed from us and so varied in their natures, until you have scrutinized and come to know your-selves. After that, we may perhaps believe you when you hold forth on other subjects: but before you establish who you yourselves are, do not think that you will ever become capable of acting as judges or trustworthy witnesses in the other matters.

On the Migration of Abraham, 134–8 (iv, p. 209 ff.)

ON HOPE

The most vital form of seed which the Creator sowed in the rich soil of the rational soul . . . is hope, the fountain head of the lives which we lead. In hope of gain the tradesman arms him-self for the manifold forms of money getting. In hope of a successful voyage the skipper crosses the wide open seas. In hope of glory the ambitious man chooses political life and the charge of public affairs. The hope of prizes and crowns moves the training athlete to endure the contests of the arena. The hope of happiness incites also the devotees of virtue to study wisdom, believing that thus they will be able to discern the nature of all that exists and to act in accordance with nature and so bring to their fullness the best types of life, the con-templative and the practical, which necessarily make their possessor a happy man. Now some have acted like enemies in war to the germs of hope, and consumed them in the fire of the vices which they have kindled in the soul or like careless husbandmen have through their laziness allowed them to perish. There are others who seem to have guarded them well but have clung to self-assertion rather than piety and regarded themselves as the source of the achievements. All these are to be condemned. He alone is worthy of approval who sets his hope on God both as the source of his coming into existence itself is due and as the sole power which can keep him free from harm and destruction. What reward then is offered to the winner of the Crown in this contest? It is that living being whose nature is a mixture of the mortal and immortal, even man, not the same man nor yet another than the winner. The Hebrew name for him is Enos, and Enos translated is man.[1] He takes the name which is common to the whole race as his personal name, a reward of special distinction implying that no one should be thought a man at all who does not set his hope on God.

On Rewards and Punishments, 10–14 (VIII, p. 319 ff.)

ON FAITH

(*a*) 'Abraham trusted in God' (Gen. xv. 6). 'To trust in God alone and join no other with Him is no easy matter, by reason of our kinship with our yokefellow, mortality, which works upon us to keep our trust placed in riches and repute and office and friends and health and strength and many other things. To purge away each of these, to distrust created being, which in itself is wholly unworthy of trust, to trust in God, and in Him alone, even as He alone is truly worthy of trust—this is a task for a great and celestial understanding which has ceased to be ensnared by aught of the things that surround us.'

Who is the Heir? 92–3 (IV, p. 32 f.)

(*b*) Abraham 'trusted in God' (Gen. xv. 6). Now that is a little thing if measured in words, but a very great thing if made good by action. For in what else should one trust? In high offices or fame and honours or abundance of wealth and noble birth? . . . But office is wholly precarious, beset by countless foes who lie in wait for it, and if by chance it is secured the security is accompanied by countless ills in which those in high positions

---

[1] *Cf.* Gen. iv. 26, according to the Greek translation 'He called his name Enos, he hoped to call on the name of the Lord God'. Philo argues that Enos' reward for his hopefulness was that he received the name of man.

are either the agents or the victims. Fame and honour are a most precarious possession, tossed about on the reckless tempers and flighty words of careless men: . . . As for wealth and high birth, they attach themselves even to the most worthless of men, and even if they were confined to the virtuous they would be a compliment not to the actual possessors but to their ancestors and to fortune. . . . Faith in God, then, is one sure and infallible good, consolation of life, plenitude of bright hopes, dearth of ills, harvest of goods, inacquaintance with misery, acquaintance with piety, heritage of happiness, all-round betterment of the soul which is fairly stayed on Him Who is the cause of all things and can do all things yet only wills the best. For, just as those who walk on a slippery road are tripped up and fall, while others on a dry highway tread without stumbling, so those who set the soul travelling along the path of the bodily and the external are but learning it to fall, so slippery and utterly insecure are all such things; while those who press onward to God along the doctrines of virtue walk straight upon a path which is safe and unshaken, so that we may say with all truth that belief in the former things is disbelief in God, and disbelief in them belief in God.

On Abraham, 262–9 (VI, p. 129 ff.)

ON JOY

(*a*) After faith comes the reward set aside for the victorious champion who gained his virtue through nature and without a struggle. That reward is joy. For his name was in our speech 'laughter', but as the Hebrews call it, Isaac. Laughter is the outward and bodily sign of the unseen joy in the mind, and joy is in fact the best and noblest of the higher emotions. By it the soul is filled through and through with cheerfulness, rejoicing in the Father and Maker of all, rejoicing too in all His doings in which evil has no place, even though they do not conduce to its own pleasure, rejoicing because they are done for good and serve to preserve all that exists. . . . He never knows gloom and depression; his days are passed in happy freedom from fears and grief; the hardships and squalor of life never touch him even in his dreams, because every spot in his soul is already tenanted by joy.

On Rewards and Punishments, 31–5 (VIII, p. 331)

(*b*) The name of Isaac is translated into our language, Laughter. But the laughter here understood is not the laughter which amusement arouses in the body, but the good emotion of the understanding,[1] that is joy. This (Isaac) the Sage (Abraham) is said to sacrifice as his duty to God (Gen. xxii), thus showing in a figure that rejoicing is most closely associated with God alone. For mankind is subject to grief and very fearful of evils either present or expected, so that men are either distressed by disagreeables close at hand or are agitated by troublous fear of those which are still to come. But the nature of God is without grief or fear and wholly exempt from passion of any kind, and alone partakes of perfect happiness and bliss. The frame of mind which has made this true acknowledgement to God, Who has banished jealousy from His presence in His kindness and love for mankind, fitly rewards by returning the gift in so far as the recipient's capacity allows. And indeed we may almost hear His voice saying: 'All joy and rejoicing I know well is the possession of none other save Me alone, the Father of All. Yet I do not grudge that this My possession should be used by such as are worthy, and who should be worthy save one who should follow Me and My will, for he will prove to be most exempt from distress and fear if he travels by this road which passion and vice cannot tread, but good feelings and virtue can walk therein.' But let no one suppose that joy descends from heaven to earth pure and free from any mixture of grief. No, it is a mixture of both, though the better element is the stronger, just as light too in heaven is pure from any mixture of darkness but in regions below the moon is clearly mixed with dusky air.

On Abraham, 201–5 (VI, p. 99 ff.)

[1] This is the Stoic definition of joy as a reasonable form of affect.

(c) The countenance of wisdom is not scowling and severe, contracted by deep thought and depression of spirit, but on the contrary cheerful and tranquil, full of joy and gladness, feelings which often prompt a man to be sportive and jocular in a perfectly refined way. Such sportiveness is in harmony with a dignified self-respect, a harmony like that of a lyre tuned to give forth a single melody by a blending of answering notes.

On Noah's Work as a Planter, 167 (III, p. 299)

VIII

ON VICES AND VIRTUES

ON SENSUAL DESIRE

THE words 'I am the Lord' are full of beauty and fraught with
much instruction. Weigh, friend, he says, the good as the flesh
sees it against the good as it exists in the soul and in the All.
The first is irrational pleasure, the second is the mind of the
universe, God. . . . Honour bids you not to steal away from
that rank in God's array where they that are so posted must all
seek to be the bravest, nor desert to pleasure, the cowardly
and invertebrate, pleasure, who harms her friends and helps her
enemies. Her nature is a paradox indeed. On those to whom she
would fain impart of the boons which she has to give she
inflicts loss in the very act. On those from whom she would
take away, she bestows the greatest blessings. She harms when
she gives, she benefits when she takes. Therefore, my soul, if
any of the love-lures of pleasure invite thee, turn thyself aside,
let thine eyes look else-whither. Look rather on the genuine
beauty of virtue, gaze on her continually, till yearning sink
into the marrow, till like the magnet it draw thee on and bring
thee nigh and bind thee fast to the object of thy desire.

On the Giants, 40 ff. (II, p. 465 ff.)

ON HYPOCRISY

To rant and boast of evil doings is a double sin. But what
regularly happens with the multitude is this: they are ever
addressing words of friendship and fairness to the maiden
Virtue, but they let no occasion slip without using it to outrage
and maltreat her if they can. What city is not crowded with
those who hymn virtue the ever virgin? They tear to pieces the
ears of all they meet with such disquisitions as these, prudence
is necessary, imprudence is harmful, temperance deserves our
choice, intemperance our hatred; courage is worthy of per-
severance therein, cowardice of avoidance; justice is profitable,

injustice unprofitable; holiness is honourable, unholiness disgraceful; piety is praiseworthy, impiety blameworthy; right purposing, speaking and acting is most conformable to man's nature, wrong purposing, speaking and acting most alien to the same. With a perpetual string of this or suchlike talk they deceive the law courts, the theatres, the council chambers and every gathering and group of men, like people who set handsome masks on the ugliest of faces to prevent the ugliness being detected by the eyes of others. But it is all useless. The vindicators will come strong and doughty, inspired with zeal for virtue. They will strip off all this complication of wraps and bandages which the perverted art of the talkers has put together, and beholding the soul naked in her very self will know the secrets hidden from sight in the recesses of her nature; and then exposing to every eye in clear sunlight her shame and all her disgraces they will point the contrast between her real character, so hideous, so despicable, and the spurious comeliness which, disguised in her wrappings, she counterfeited.

On the Change of Names, 196–9 (v, p. 243 ff.)

ON THE DIFFERENCE BETWEEN HEARING AND
HEARKENING

Abraham, it says, 'hearkened to the voice of Sarah' (Gen. xvi. 2), for the learner must needs obey the commands of Virtue (symbolized by Sarah). Yet all do not obey, only those in whom the strong longing for knowledge has become ingrained. Hardly a day passes but the lecture-halls and theatres are filled with philosophers discoursing at length, stringing together without stopping to take breath their disquisitions on virtue. Yet what profit is there in their talk? For instead of attending, the audience dismiss their minds else whither, some occupied with thoughts of voyaging and trading, some with their farming and its returns, others with honours and civic life, others of the profits they get from their particular trade and business, others with the vengeance they hope to wreak on their enemies, others with enjoyments of their amorous passions, the class of thought in fact differing with the class of person. Thus, as far as what is being demonstrated is concerned, they are deaf, and while they are present in the body are absent in mind, and might as well be images or statues. And any who do attend sit all the time merely hearing, and when they depart they remember nothing that has been said, and in fact their object in coming was to please their sense of hearing rather than to gain any profit; thus their soul is unable to conceive or bring to the birth, but the moment the cause which stirred up pleasure is silent their attention is extinguished too. There is a third class, who carry away an echo of what has been said, but prove to be sophists rather than philosophers. The words of these deserve praise, but their lives censure, for they are capable of saying the best, but incapable of doing it. Rarely then shall we find one who combines attention, memory and the valuing of deeds before words, which three things are vouched for in the case of Abraham, the lover of learning, in the phrase 'He hearkened to the voice of Sarah', for he is represented not as hearing, but as hearkening, a word which exactly expresses assent and obedience.

The Preliminary Studies, 63–8 (IV, p. 491 ff.)

ON KINSHIP

For we should have one of the affinity, one accepted sign of goodwill, namely the willingness to serve God and that our every word and deed promotes the cause of piety. But as for these kinships, as we call them, which have come down from our ancestors and are based on blood-relationship, or those derived from intermarriage or other similar causes, let them all be cast aside if they do not seek earnestly the same goal, namely, the honour of God, which is the indissoluble bond of all the affection which makes us one. For those who are so minded will receive in exchange kinships of greater dignity and sanctity. This promise of mine is confirmed by the law, where it says that they who do 'what is pleasing' to nature and what is 'good' are sons of God (Deut. xiii. 18). For it says, 'Ye are sons to your Lord God', clearly meaning that He will think fit to protect and provide for you as would a father. And how much this watchful care will exceed that of men is measured, believe me, by the surpassing excellence of Him who bestows it.

The Special Laws, I, 317–8 (VII, p. 283 ff.)

ON NOBILITY OF BIRTH

Those who hymn nobility of birth as the greatest of good gifts and the source of other great gifts deserve no moderate censure, if only because they think that those who have many generations of wealth and distinction behind them are noble, though neither did the ancestors from whom they boast descent find happiness in the superabundance of their possessions. For the true good cannot find its home in anything external, nor yet in things of the body, and further not even in every part of the soul, but only in its sovereign part, reason. . . . And, therefore, I think, that if God had so formed nobility as to take a human shape, she would stand to face the rebellious descendants and address them thus: 'In the court where truth presides, kinship is not measured only by blood, but by similarity of conduct and pursuit of the same objects. But your practice has been the opposite. What I hold dear you regard as hostile and my enemies you love. In my sight, modesty and truth and control of the passions and simplicity and innocence are honourable, in your eyes dishonourable. Shamelessness, falsehood, passion uncontrolled, vanity, vices are my enemies, but to you they are the closest friends. You have done your best by your actions to make yourselves strangers, why do you hypocritically assume a specious name and call yourselves kinsmen?

On the Virtues, 187, 195, 196 (VIII, p. 279 ff.)

ON FATHER AND MOTHER

'Father and mother' is a phrase which can bear different meanings. For instance we should rightly say and without further question that the Architect who made this universe was at the same time the father of what was thus born, whilst its mother was the knowledge possessed by its Maker. With His Knowledge [1] God had union, not as men have it, and begat created being. And knowledge, having received the divine seed, when her travail was consummated, bore the only beloved son who is apprehended by the senses, the world which we see. Thus in the pages of one of the inspired company, wisdom is represented as speaking of herself after this manner: 'God obtained me first of all his works and founded me before the ages' (Prov. viii. 22). True, for it was necessary that all that came to the birth of creation should be younger than the mother and nurse of the All. If *these* parents accuse, who is able to withstand their accusation, or even a mild threat or the lightest chiding? Why, even their gifts are so boundless in number that no one, not even, one may say, the world, can contain them, but like some small cistern it will quickly be filled to the brim by the influx from the fountain of God's gracious boons, and discharge the rest in an overflow.

On Ebriety, 30–2 (III, p. 333)

ON THE DISPERSION OF THE SOUL

Those who would imitate the examples of good living . . . are bidden not to despair of changing for the better or of a restoration to the land of wisdom and virtue from the spiritual dispersion [2] which vice has wrought. For when God is gracious He makes all things light and easy, and He does become gracious to those who depart with shame from incontinence to self-restraint and deplore the deeds of their guilty past . . . and first earnestly strive to still the storm of the passions, then seek to lead a life of serenity and peace. So then just as God with a single call may easily gather together from the ends of the earth to any place that He wills the exiles dwelling in the utmost parts of the earth, so too the mind which has strayed everywhere

[1] i.e. Wisdom, the personified attribute of God.

[2] An allegorization of Deut. xxx. 4: 'If thy dispersion be from one end of heaven to the other, the Lord will gather thee thence'.

in prolonged vagrancy, maltreated by pleasure and lust . . .
may well be brought back by the mercy of its Saviour from
the pathless wild into a road wherein it is resolved to flee
straight on, a flight not the discredited flight of the outcast, but
a flight of one banished from evil to salvation, a banishment
which may be truly held to be better than a recall.

On Rewards and Punishments, 115–7 (VIII, p. 381 ff.)

THE REWARD OF THE PENITENTS[1]

If the penitents, shamed into a whole-hearted conversion,
reproach themselves for going astray, and make a full confession and acknowledgment of all their sin[2] . . . then they will
find favour with God the Saviour, the Merciful, who has
bestowed on mankind that peculiar and chiefest gift of kinship
with His own Word, from whom as its archetype the human
mind was created. For[3] even though they dwell in the uttermost parts of the earth, in slavery to those who led them away
captive, one signal, as it were, one day will bring liberty to all.
This conversion in a body to virtue will strike awe into their
masters, who will set them free, ashamed to rule over men
better than themselves. When they have gained this unexpected
liberty, those who but now were scattered in Greece and the
outside world over islands and continents will arise and post
from every side with one impulse to the one appointed place,
guided in their pilgrimage by a vision divine and superhuman unseen by others but manifest to them as they pass
from exile to their home. Three intercessors they have to
plead for their reconciliation with the Father. One is the
clemency and kindness of Him to whom they appeal, who
ever prefers forgiveness to punishment. The second is the
holiness of the founders of the race because with souls
released from their bodies they show forth in that naked
simplicity their devotion to their Ruler and cease not to make
supplication for their sons and daughters, supplications not

---

[1] According to Lev. xxvi. 40 ff., and Deut. xxx. 1 ff.   [2] Lev. xxvi. 40.
[3] For the following see Deut. xxx. 3–5.

made in vain, because the Father grants to them the privilege
that their prayers should be heard.[1] The third is one which
more than anything else moves the loving kindness of the
other two to come forward so readily, and that is the reforma-
tion working in those who are being brought to make a
covenant of peace, those who after much toil have been able
to pass from the pathless wild to the road which has no other
goal but to find favour with God, as sons may with their
father. When they have arrived, the cities which but now
lay in ruins, will be cities once more; the desolate land will
be inhabited; the barren will change into fruitfulness; all the
prosperity of their fathers and ancestors will seem a tiny
fragment, so lavish will be the abundant riches in their possession, which flowing from the gracious bounties of God as
from a perennial fountain will bring to each individually
and to all in common a deep stream of wealth leaving no
room for envy.[2] Everything will suddenly be reversed. God
will turn the curses against the enemies of these penitents,[3]
the enemies who rejoiced in the misfortunes of the nation and
mocked and railed at them, thinking that they themselves
would have a heritage which nothing could destroy and which
they hoped to leave to their children and descendants in due
succession; thinking, too, that they would always see their
opponents in a firmly established and unchanging adversity
which would be reserved for the generations that followed
them. In their infatuation they did not understand that the
short-lived brilliance which they had enjoyed had been given
them not for their own sakes but as a lesson to others, who had
subverted the institutions of their fathers, and therefore grief—
the very painful feeling aroused by the sight of their enemy's
good fortune—was devised as a medicine to save them from
perdition. So then those of them who have not come to utter
destruction, in tears and groans lamenting their own lapse, will
make their way back with course reversed to the prosperity of

[1] *Cf.* Lev. xxvi. 42.
[2] Deut. xxx. 5. He will make thee abundant beyond thy father.
[3] Deut. xxx. 7.

the ancestral past. But these enemies who have mocked at their lamentations, proclaimed public holidays on the days of their misfortunes, feasted on their mourning, in general made the unhappiness of others their own happiness, will, when they begin to reap the rewards of their cruelty, find that their misconduct was directed not against the obscure and unmeritable but against men of high lineage retaining sparks of their noble birth, which have to be but fanned into a flame, and from them shines out the glory which for a little while was quenched. For just as when the stalks of plants are cut away, if the roots are left undestroyed, new growths shoot up which supersede the old, so too if in the soul a tiny seed be left of the qualities which promote virtue, though other things have been stripped away, still from that little seed spring forth the fairest and most precious things in human life, by which States are constituted manned with good citizens, and nations grow into a great population.

On Rewards and Punishments, 163–72 (VIII, pp. 417–23).

IX

ISRAEL AND THE NATIONS

THE LEGACY OF ISRAEL

The Jewish nation is to the whole inhabited world what the priest is to the State. For the holy office in very truth belongs to the nation because it carries out all the rites of purification and both in body and soul obeys the injunctions of the Divine laws . . . setting reason to guide the irrational senses, and also check and rein in the wild and extravagant impulses of the soul, sometimes through gentler remonstrances and philosophical admonitions, sometimes through severer and more forcible condemnations and the fear of punishment which they hold over it as a deterrent. But not only is the legislation in a sense a lesson on the sacred office, not only does a life led in conformity with the laws necessarily confer priesthood or rather high priesthood in the judgement of truth, but there is another point of special importance. There is no bound or limit to the number of deities, male and female, honoured in different cities, the vain inventions of the tribe of poets and of the great multitude of men to whom the quest for truth is a task of difficulty and beyond their powers of research. Yet instead of all peoples having the same gods, we find different nations venerating and honouring different gods. The gods of the foreigner they do not regard as gods at all. They treat their acceptance by the others as a jest and a laughing-stock and denounce the extreme folly of those who honour them and the failure to think soundly shewn thereby. But if He exists Whom all Greeks and barbarians unanimously acknowledge, the supreme Father of gods and men and the Maker of the whole universe, whose nature is invisible and inscrutable not only by the eye, but by the mind, yet is a matter into which every student of astronomical science and other philosophy desires to make research and leaves nothing untried which would help him to discern it and do it service— then it was the duty of all men to cleave to Him and not introduce new gods . . . to receive the same honours. When they went wrong in what was the most vital matter of all, it is the literal truth that the error which the rest committed was corrected by the Jewish nation which passed over all created objects because they were created and naturally liable to destruction and chose the service only of the Uncreated and Eternal, first because of its excellence, secondly because it is profitable to dedicate and attach ourselves to the elder rather than to the younger, to the ruler rather than to the subject, to the maker rather than to the thing created. And therefore it astonishes me to see that some people venture to accuse of inhumanity[1] the nation which has shewn so profound a sense of fellowship and goodwill to all men everywhere, by using its prayers and festivals and first-fruit offerings as a means of supplication for the human race in general and of making its homage to the truly existent God in the name of those who have evaded the service which it was their duty to give, as well as of itself.

The Special Laws, ii, 163–7 (vii, p. 407 ff.)

THE SCOPE OF THE MOSAIC LAW

What our most holy prophet through all his regulations especially desires to create is unanimity, neighbourliness, fellowship, reciprocity of feeling, whereby houses and cities and nations and countries and the whole human race may advance to supreme happiness. Hitherto, indeed, these things live only in our prayers, but they will, I am convinced, become facts beyond all dispute, if God, even as He gives us the yearly fruits, grants that the virtues should bear abundantly. And may some share in them be given to us, who from well-nigh our earliest days have carried with us the yearning to possess them.

On the Virtues, 119–20 (viii, p. 235)

---

[1] A widespread accusation raised against the Jews because of their exclusiveness.

ON THE SPREAD OF THE JEWISH LAWS AMONG
THE GENTILES

Not only Jews but almost every other people, particularly those which take more account of virtue, have so far grown in holiness as to value and honour our laws. In this they have received a special distinction which belongs to no other code. Here is the proof. Throughout the world of Greeks and barbarians, there is practically no State which honours the institutions of any other. Indeed, they can scarcely be said to retain their own perpetually as they adapt them to meet the vicissitudes of times and circumstances. The Athenians reject the customs and institutions of the Lacedæmonians, and the Lacedæmonians those of the Athenians; nor, in the world of the barbarians, do the Egyptians maintain the laws of the Scythians nor the Scythians those of the Egyptians—nor, to put it generally, Europeans those of Asiatics nor Asiatics those of Europeans. We may fairly say that mankind from East to West, every country and nation and State, shew aversion to foreign institutions, and think that they will enhance the respect for their own by shewing disrespect for those of other countries. It is not so with ours. They attract and win the attention of all, of barbarians, of Greeks, of dwellers on the mainland and islands, of nations of the East and the world from end to end, of nations of the East and the West, of Europe and Asia, of the whole inhabited world from end to end. For, who has not shewn this high respect for that sacred seventh day, by giving rest and relaxation from labour to himself and his neighbours, freeman and slaves alike, and beyond these to his beasts? For the holiday extends also to every herd, and to all creatures made to minister to man, who serve like slaves their natural master. It extends also to every kind of tree and plant; for it is not permitted to cut any shoot or branch, or even a leaf, or to pluck any fruit whatsoever. All such are set at liberty on that day, and live as it were in freedom, under the general edict that proclaims that none should touch them. Again, who does not every year shew awe and reverence for the fast, as it is called (the Day of Atonement), which is kept more strictly and solemnly than the 'holy month' of the Greeks.[1] For in this last the untempered wine flows freely, and the board is spread sumptuously, and all manner of food and drink are lavishly provided, whereby the insatiable pleasures of the belly are enhanced, and further cause the outburst of the lusts that lie below it. But in our fast man may not put food and drink to their lips, in order that with pure hearts, untroubled and untrammelled by any bodily passion, such as is the common outcome of repletion, they may keep the holy day, propitiating the Father of All with fitting prayers, in which they are wont to ask that their old sins may be forgiven and new blessings gained and enjoyed.

Life of Moses, II, 17–24 (VI, p. 459 ff.)

THE PREFECT AND THE SABBATH

Not long ago I knew one of the ruling class who when he had Egypt in his charge and under his authority, purposed to disturb our ancestral customs and especially to do away with the law of the Seventh Day, which we regard with most reverence and awe. He tried to compel men to do service to him on it and perform other actions which contravene our established custom, thinking that if he could destroy the ancestral rule of the Sabbath it would lead the way to irregularity in all other matters, and a general backsliding. And when he saw that those on whom he was exercising pressure were not submitting to his orders, and that the rest of the population instead of taking the matter calmly, were intensely indignant and shewed themselves as mournful and disconsolate as they would were their native city being sacked and razed, and its citizens being sold into captivity, he thought good to try to argue them into breaking the law. 'Suppose', he said, 'there was a sudden inroad of the enemy or an inundation caused by the river rising and breaking through the dam, or a blazing conflagration or a thunderbolt or famine, or

[1] A period in which hostilities or legal processes were forbidden in certain Greek States.

plague, or earthquake, or any other trouble either of human or Divine agency, will you stay at home perfectly quiet? Or will you appear in public in your usual guise, with your right hand tucked inside and the left held close to the flank under the cloak lest you should even unconsciously do anything that might help to save you? And will you sit in your conventicles and assemble your regular company and read in security your holy books, expounding any obscure point and in leisurely comfort discussing at length your ancestral philosophy? No, you will throw all these off and gird yourselves up for the assistance of yourselves, your parents and your children, and the other persons who are nearest and dearest to you, and indeed also your chattels and wealth to save them too from annihilation. See then', he went on. 'I who stand before you am all the things I have named. I am the whirlwind, the war, the deluge, the lightning, the plague of famine or disease, the earthquake which shakes and confounds what was firm and stable, I am constraining destiny, not its name but its power, visible to your eyes and standing at your side.' What shall we say of one who says or even merely thinks these things? Shall we not call him an evil thing hitherto unknown . . . he who dared to liken to the All-blessed his all-miserable self? Would he delay to utter blasphemies against the sun, moon and the other stars, if what he hoped for at each season of the year did not happen at all, or only grudgingly, if the summer visited him with scorching heat or winter with a terrible frost, if the spring failed in its fruit-bearing or the autumn shewed fertility in breeding diseases? Nay, he will loose every reef of his unbridled mouth and scurrilous tongue and accuse the stars of not paying their regular tribute, and scarce refrain from demanding that honour and homage be paid by the things of heaven to the things of earth, and to himself more abundantly inasmuch as being a man he conceives himself to have been, made superior to other living creatures. Such is our description of leaders of vainglory.[1]   *On Dreams*, II, 123–33 (v, p. 497 ff.)

[1] The name of this Roman prefect of Egypt is not known. It was *not* Flaccus.

ISRAEL THE ORPHAN AMONG THE NATIONS

When Moses has hymned the excellence of the Self-existent in this manner (Deut. x. 17, 18) : 'God the great and powerful, Who has no respect to persons, will receive no gifts and executes judgement', he proceeds to say for whom the judgement is executed—not for satraps and despots and men invested with power by land and sea, but for the 'incomer (stranger), for the orphan and widow.' For the incomer, because he has turned his kinsfolk, who in the ordinary course of things would be his sole confederates, into mortal enemies, by coming as a pilgrim to truth and the honouring of One who alone is worthy of honour, and by leaving the mythical fables and multiplicity of sovereigns, so highly honoured by the parents and grandparents and ancestors and blood relations of this immigrant to a better home. For the orphan, because he has been bereft of his father and mother, his natural helpers and champions, deserted by the sole force which was bound to take up his cause. For the widow because she has been deprived of her husband who took over from the parents the charge of guarding and watching over her, since for the purpose of giving protection the husband is to the wife what the parents are to the maiden.

One may say that the whole Jewish race is in the position of an orphan compared with all the nations on every side. They when misfortunes fall upon them which are not by the direct intervention of heaven are never, owing to international intercourse, unprovided with helpers who join sides with them. But the Jewish nation has none to take its part, as it lives under exceptional laws which are necessarily grave and severe, because they inculcate the highest standard of virtue. But gravity is austere, and austerity is held in aversion by the great mass of men because they favour pleasure. Nevertheless, as Moses tells us, the orphan-like desolate state of his people is always an object of pity and compassion to the Ruler of the Universe whose portion it is, because it has been set apart out of the whole human race as a kind of first fruits to the Maker and Father.

On the Special Laws, IV, 177–80 (VIII, pp. 117–21)

SOME REMARKS ON THE ARRANGEMENT OF THE SELECTION AND A BIBLIOGRAPHICAL NOTE

THE principles on which the preceding selection has been made have been explained in the Introduction. Preference has been given to those passages in which Philo tries to express what appears to be his peculiar mood of religious contemplation. Consequently, those passages in which this tendency is obscured by exegetical subtleties, rhetorical effusions, sweeping generalizations or mechanical borrowings have been excluded. This arrangement often necessitated the separation of his deductions from their exegetical framework. Philo's exegesis is not always easy to follow and in threading his way through its intricacies the reader may often lose sight of the central idea. Hence it has sometimes seemed advisable to break up the text for the sake of rendering it more intelligible.

No attempt has been made in this work to compare Philo with the sources from which he derived his ideas. On the other hand it is hoped that the Introduction will provide the reader with all the information required for the understanding of the selected passages. Special difficulties are dealt with in the notes, which have been kept as brief as possible. If we give Philo himself a hearing, we shall find that he is able to express his case with sufficient clearness.

A few bibliographical hints may be added for readers who wish to obtain further knowledge of this author. The majority of Philo's writings are easily accessible to the English reader in the Loeb Classical Library. This work was begun by F. H. Colson and G. H. Whitaker and is being carried on since the latter's death by Colson. It will contain all the writings of Philo extant in Greek. Already nine volumes have appeared and the remaining tenth volume may be expected before long. It is an admirable translation accompanied by an equally excellent text.

The rather inaccurate English translation of Philo's works by C. D. Yonge (printed 1854–5 in the Bohn Library series, 4 vols.) no longer requires mention. There is an excellent German translation with a useful commentary. It was begun by L. Cohn (who, together with P. Wendland, published the critical edition of the Greek Philo in 6 vols.) and continued by I. Heinemann (Breslau 1900–37. One volume is missing.) No translation has yet been published of the writings of Philo preserved only in Armenian though the present writer has an English one in preparation, along with a critical edition of these texts.

As regards books on Philo, the best are written for the specialist, but a few years ago, E. R. Goodenough, known for various contributions to research on Philo, published an *Introduction to Philo Judaeus* (New Haven 1940) which contains an excellent introductory chapter of personal interest, though the author adopts certain hypotheses which for the major part are still far from being accepted by the critics, and which are at variance with many of the views expressed (or better, hinted at) in the short Introduction to the present selection. There is no other book on Philo in English which can be recommended for the general reader. The work of J. Drummond (*Philo Judaeus*, London 1880, 2 vols.) is antiquated and that of N. Bentwich (*Philo Judaeus*, Philadelphia 1910), though containing many fine glimpses, is unsatisfactory from a critical point of view. We are, therefore, obliged to have recourse to non-English literature. By far the best work on Philo is E. Bréhier, *Les Idées philosophiques et religieuses de Philon d'Alexandrie* (Paris, 2nd ed. 1925). His views require supplementing only as regards the question of the religious background of Philo. The student of philosophy will, besides, consult the chapter in the standard work of Ed. Zeller, *Geschichte der Philosophie der Griechen*, vol. iii, sect. 2, pp. 385–467 (5th ed., Leipzig 1923). The question of Philo's debt to Greek and Jewish erudition has been dealt with in the important work of I. Heinemann, *Philons griechische and jüdische Bildung* (Breslau 1932), whose results have not been shaken by the criticism of more recent researches. Much has been written in the last decades on the relationship between Philo and the religious movements of contemporary paganism, but a comprehensive study on this important subject is still lacking. Meanwhile, the reader may be referred to the magnificent work of F. Cumont, *Les religions orientales dans le paganisme romain* (ed. 4, Paris 1929; 2nd ed. translated by G. Showerman) and to supplement it to H. Lietzmann, *History of the Church* (translated by B. L. Woolf 1936), who deals also with Jewish Hellenism. A treatment of this subject unbiased by religious prejudice is still to seek. The two standard works, Schürer, *History of the Jewish People at the time of Jesus Christ*, and Juster, *Les Juifs dans l'Empire romain*, give only the material without any attempt at a critical valuation. Mention may be made in this connection of the forthcoming work of A. D. Nock, *The Hellenistic*

Religion. The reader who wishes to follow up the brief remarks given at the conclusion of the Introduction will find abundant material and illuminating criticism in the famous work of E. Underhill, *Mysticism* (London 1926). For further information on Philo research the excellent (although not always complete) bibliography composed by H. L. Goodhart, New York, the possessor of the most ample collection of Philo literature at the time, and E. R. Goodenough, the author of the *Introduction* mentioned above, will be of invaluable help (*The Politics of Philo Judaeus*, together with a general bibliography of Philo, by H. L. Goodhart and E. R. Goodenough, New Haven 1938).

ABBREVIATIONS USED FOR THE REFERENCES

The references to Philo's works are given according to the Loeb edition. The first number following the title designates at the paragraphs, the numbers in the brackets volume and page. A short list of the various works of Philo may be added:

ESOTERIC WRITINGS

(*a*) Allegorical Commentary to Genesis i–xx

  1. Allegorical Interpretation of Genesis ii. iii. (in 3 vols.)
  2. On the Cherubim (on Gen. iii. 24 and iv. 1)
  3. On the sacrifices of Abel and Cain (on Gen. iv. 2–4)
  4. That the worse is wont to attack the better (on Gen. iv. 8–15)
  5. On the posterity of Cain (on Gen. iv. 16–25)
  6. On the Giants (on Gen. vi. 1–4)
  7. On the unchangeableness of God (on Gen. vi. 5–12)
  8. On husbandry (on Gen. ix. 20)
  9. On Noah's work as a planter (continued)
 10. On ebriety (Gen. ix. 21)
 11. On sobriety (on Gen. ix. 24–27)
 12. On the confusion of tongues (on Gen. xi. 1–9)
 13. On the migration of Abraham (on Gen. xii. 1–6)
 14. Who is the heir? (on Gen. xv. 2–18)
 15. On preliminary studies (on Gen. xvi. 1–6)
 16. On flight and finding (on Gen. xvi. 6–14)
 17. On the change of names (on Gen. xvii. 1–22)
 18. On dreams i–ii (on Gen. xxviii. 12 ff. and xxxi. 10 ff. xxxvii. xl–xli)

(b) Questions and answers to Genesis and Exodus (6 books)
  1. On the creation of the world (on Gen. i)
  2. Life of Abraham
  3. Life of Joseph
  4. Life of Moses, i–ii
  5. On the decalogue
  6. On the special laws, i–iv
  7. On virtues
  8. On rewards and punishments
  9. On the contemplative life
  10. Apology for the Jews (fragments)

Writings on contemporary events (1) Against Flaccus and The Embassy to Gaius (omitted from the Selection). Philosophical writings (omitted). On the eternity of the world. (2) On the virtuous being also free. (3) On Providence. (4) Alexander, or On the question whether dumb animals have the power of reason.

NOTE ON THE EDITOR

The proofs of this volume came too late to be read by its editor. They were corrected by Dr. H. J. Polotsky, Lecturer in Egyptology at the Hebrew University, who was a close friend of Lewy's, and by the undersigned, with the assistance of two of his students, Mr. A. Fuchs, M.A., and Mr. A. Rabinowitz. Our cordial thanks are tendered to the publishers of the Loeb Classical Library and to the translator of Philo's works, Mr. F. H. Colson, for their kind permission to use the English text of the Loeb edition of Philo.

Dr. Hans Lewy, the editor of this volume of selections from Philo's works, died on 22 July 1945. In him classical philology in general and research in Jewish Hellenism in particular have lost an outstanding scholar. Though Lewy was only forty-four at the time of his death, he already had unusual achievements to his credit and far-reaching plans for future work, which the shortness of his life prevented him from executing.

Born in Berlin, Lewy received his early education and the distinctive direction of his interests in a classical secondary school in his native city; but while still very young he was greatly attracted to the problems of Jewish life, past and present. At the University of Berlin he studied under Wilamowitz, Jaeger, Norden and Eduard Meyer, and at the same time attended the Hochschule für die Wissenschaft des Judentums in Berlin;

*he acquired a thorough mastery of ancient and modern Hebrew, and strove in
life, as in scholarship, for a synthesis of classical and Jewish culture. Early
in his student days his interest was aroused in Philo and his religious
philosophy, which remained ever after the focus of all his work. His introduction to the present volume, which was written not long ago, reflects the
depth and originality of his understanding of Philo which he attained in the
course of two decades of continuous research.*

*Lewy began by investigating a central idea in Philo's doctrine of the union
of men with God, that of Sobria Ebrietas, 'drunken sobriety'. In the so-
called state of ecstasy, according to Lewy, the spiritual element in man is
merged into God, thanks to the divine grace which, however, vouchsafes
such union only to those who dedicate themselves to the ascetic life and to
Gnosis.[1] In a book published in 1929,[2] he investigates the Philonic conception in its strictly original aspects, and shows that it was derived from
the Greek doctrine of the Pneuma and is rooted in the early development of
Gnosis. In the second part of the book Lewy traces the influence of Philo's
ideas upon Christian literature down to the fourth century. Philo was
always the central theme of his researches. When, as a young scholar, Lewy
realized that those portions of Philo's works which have come down to us
only in the Armenian version are extant in an incomplete form, he embarked on the study of the Armenian language and was enabled by the
Prussian Academy to visit the Near East, Armenia and Russia, where he
examined the Armenian manuscripts of Philo in order to gather material
for a critical first edition of those works. A specimen of this material is given
in his edition of the pseudo-Philonic homily on the prophet Jonah, an
Armenian critical text of which was published in America in 1939. A
commentary by Lewy on this homily is now in the press.*

*Lewy's study of Philo's writings led him to investigate the spiritual
environment of the Jewish philosopher, that is to say, the Jewish-Hellenistic
culture and the religious syncretism of the Hellenized Orient. In his very
extensive reading, Lewy gathered a vast amount of material on all that was
known of Judaism in the Graeco-Roman world, with the object of super-
seding Th. Reinach's* Textes d'auteurs grecs et romains rélatifs au
Judaisme *by a more comprehensive work which, unfortunately, he did not
live to complete. Specimens of the material as edited by Lewy appear in a
series of monographs which he wrote. The essay on Cicero's speech in
defence of Flaccus, in which the section on the Jews is given a wholly new*

---

[1] *See* Lewy's Introduction, p. XIX, seq.

[2] *Sobria Ebrietas, Untersuchungen zur Geschichte der antiken Mystik,* Giessen,
1929. Beihefte zur Zeitschrift f. neut. Wissenschaft, Bd. 9.

interpretation, and another on the excursus in Tacitus's Historiae[1] which contains an account of Jewish history and customs, convey a notion of the manner in which Lewy planned to write his commentary.

The works of Josephus claimed much of Lewy's attention, and his writings reveal a profound knowledge of this author, with whose survival in the Middle Ages he dealt in an illuminating essay fertile in its conclusions. An important contribution to our knowledge of the Slavonic Josephus was made by Lewy in his criticism of B. Eisler's book on Jesus in the Deutsche Literaturzeitung,[2] *which attracted much attention in learned circles. Lewy also wrote many shorter essays, all dealing with Jewish Hellenism and the sources to that subject.*

Lewy's acuteness of method and breadth of vision distinguish, in particular, his essay on Aristotle and the Jewish Sage according to Clearchus of Soli,[3] in which the Jewish sage who converses with Aristotle is shown to be a fictitious figure and a typical representative of the Oriental priest-sage.

With his study on Julian and the building of the Jewish temple,[4] which portrays Julian's attitude towards the Jewish religion and its centre in a new light within a larger religious-historical setting, Lewy entered the second major field of his researches. His knowledge of the sources of the Jewish, Christian and Hellenistic-Roman religions and their reciprocal effects upon one another was extensive and profound, and led him to investigate further the religious syncretism of the Hellenized Orient. The later sources, to which scholars have hitherto devoted too little attention, and in which Platonic, neo-Platonic, Orphic and Hellenistic-Roman ideas are merged with Gnostic-Philonic elements, had a special attraction for him. To those sources he devoted his last work, the monumental Chaldean Oracles and Theurgy, *which is now in the press.*

A career rich in scholarly achievement has been abruptly cut off by Fate. Many of Lewy's researches were left unfinished, but during his twelve years at the Hebrew University in Jerusalem he taught his methods to students who will carry on the work of their revered teacher. The Classic Department of the Hebrew University had intended this very year to introduce his favourite subject, Jewish Hellenism, into its curriculum, with Lewy himself giving the principal course. The Department feels in honour bound to include in its programme Jewish Hellenism, which cannot be taught at present without Lewy, as soon as other teachers of the subject can be found.

Jerusalem, Hebrew University.   M. SCHWABE.
23-10-45

[1]V. 2-5.   [2]1930, p. 481.   [3]Harv. Theol. Rev. 1938.   [4]'Zion', 1941.

SAADYA GAON:
BOOK OF DOCTRINES AND BELIEFS

Abridged edition translated from the Arabic
with an introduction and notes
by Alexander Altmann

PREFACE

SAADYA's *magnum opus*, the *Book of Doctrines and Beliefs*, which inaugurated the medieval school of Jewish philosophy, has so far not been accessible in an English rendering. Apart from the totally inadequate German version by Julius Fürst (published in Leipzig exactly a hundred years ago, in 1845), it has not been translated into any European language. The millenary of Saadya's death in 1942 produced a host of publications on almost every aspect of the many literary and communal activities of this epoch-making Jewish thinker. No less than five Anniversary Volumes have appeared, adding to the wealth of material and knowledge which since J. L. Rapoport's famous biographical essay on Saadya (1828) has been accumulated by the inspired efforts of the 'Wissenschaft des Judentums'. But whilst Saadya's work has thus become an object of penetrating and detailed research amongst scholars, it has remained, more or less, *terra incognita* to the larger public. It is indeed a matter of surprise that, of all Jewish classics, the *Book of Doctrines and Beliefs* should not have been edited in any modern language, seeing that most of the other classical works of medieval Jewish philosophy have been published in several languages. The Translator therefore feels that by presenting Saadya's book in a comprehensive Selection translated from the Arabic original he is satisfying a long-felt need. His thanks are due to Dr. B. Horovitz, Director of the East and West Library, whose creation of a Jewish Classical Library, of which Saadya's book is to be the first in the Series, has made the publication possible. He also wishes to tender sincere thanks to Prof. Mahdi Allam, of Kairo, at present Special Lecturer in Arabic at Manchester University, for his unfailing courtesy and readiness to advise in matters of translation, and to Mr. Maurice Simon, M.A., for many helpful suggestions, by which this volume has profited.

Manchester
25th Iyar, 5705
8th May, 1945

To
Professor Isaak Heinemann
Guide, Philosopher and Friend

TRANSLATOR'S INTRODUCTION

As Saadya[1] makes it clear in the very opening of his book, the reason which prompted him to write this work was not a mere desire for self-expression. As the leader of his nation and as a member of the 'Human Race', he felt the urge to guide and inspire his people in an age which he so movingly describes as one of moral, intellectual and spiritual confusion. He could have named his book, like Maimonides over two hundred years later, a *Guide of the Perplexed*, for this is how he describes the purpose of his endeavour. We have it on the testimony of Abū'l-Ala, a contemporary of his, that the epoch must indeed have been one of bewilderment and waning faith in the standards of Truth: 'Muslims, Jews, Christians and Magians, they all are walking in error and darkness; there are only two kinds of people left in the world; the one group is intelligent, but lacking in faith; the other has faith, but is lacking in intelligence'.[2] This verdict may be rather too harsh, but there can be little doubt that Baghdād, where Saadya wrote his book in the year 933, was a place torn between the extremes of conflicting religious and philosophical creeds.

There is, however, a marked difference between the perplexity from which Maimonides sought to rescue his people and that which Saadya encountered. In the case of Maimonides the problem was summed up in the question: Aristotle or the Bible? Aristotle, that is to say, the neo-platonic Aristotle of al-Fārābī and Ibn Sīnā, had conquered their minds, and the problem which Maimonides had to solve was the harmonization of Aristotle and the Bible. In the case of Saadya the situation was different. The neo-platonic Aristotle with his

---

[1] Sa'adya ben Josef al-Fayyūmī was born 892 in Fayyūm, Upper Egypt. He left his native country in 915, travelled in Palestine, Syria and 'Irak, became a leading member ('Alūf) of the famous Academy in Sura (922) and finally Gaon (Head of the Academy) in 928. After a period of enforced retirement owing to a controversy with the Exilarch (the political Head of Babylonian Jewry) he was reinstated, and died in 942. For details of his life and work cf. Henry Malter, *Saadia Gaon, His Life and Works*, Philadelphia, 1921. For a full bibliography see Malter, *loc. cit.*, pp. 305-419, and the additions by A. Freimann in *Saadya Anniversary Volume*, published by the American Academy for Jewish Research, New York, 1943, pp. 327-39, and I. Werfel in *Rab Saadya Gaon*, ed. J. L. Fishman, Jerusalem, 1943, pp. 644-57.

[2] Quoted by Graetz in his *Geschichte der Juden*, Vol. V, p. 285.

doctrine of the Active Intellect, Emanation, Matter and Form, did not yet dominate the intellectual strata of his generation. Although he is a contemporary of al-Fārābī (died 950) and in spite of the fact that a Jewish contemporary of his, the famous physician Isaac Israeli (855-955) wrote in the neo-platonic fashion, Saadya himself shows no trace of neo-platonic influence, but he bears eloquent witness to the impress which Greek philosophy and science, in general, had left upon him and his environment. The 'bewilderment' which characterized his own age is due not so much to the conflict between one particular creed of philosophy and the traditional faith, as to the impact of so many rival creeds and philosophies upon the minds of his contemporaries.

The fact is not surprising. The tenth century began to absorb the rich and variegated heritage of classical Greek and Hellenistic philosophy which had been made accessible by the translations of the ninth. Under the patronage of the Caliph al-Ma'mūn (813-33) a school for translations had been established in Baghdād. Most of the writings of Hippocrates and Galen, and many works of Plato and Aristotle had been rendered in the Syriac and Arabic vernaculars by Ḥunayn ibn Ishāḳ and his disciples.[1] The period of the 'Renaissance of Islam'[2] had thus been initiated. The blending of the ancient Hellenistic civilization with the new faith of Islam was a process which had only reached its first stage, and this was, by necessity, one of bewilderment. Sects and schools sprang up in mushroom-like fashion. The book of the famous Arabic historian al-Shahrastānī (died 1153) with its detailed account of the various sects and philosophic schools gives an idea of the great variety of opinions which prevailed. Islamic theology could not fail to be deeply influenced by the changed cultural outlook. Whereas the orthodox school of *Ash'ariyya* clung to the literal interpretation of the *Kur'ān*, the *Mu'tazilites*, the 'Free thinkers of Islam', introduced the method of *ta'wīl* (allegorical interpretation) as a means of harmonizing Faith and Reason.[3] But these main schools were again sub-divided into

---

[1] Cf. *The Legacy of Islam*, ed. Sir Thomas Arnold and Alfred Guillaume, Oxford, 1931, pp. 250 ff., 316 ff.
[2] Cf. A. Mez, *Die Renaissance des Islâms*, 1922.
[3] Cf. I. Goldziher, *Vorlesungen über den Islam*, 1925; A. J. Wensinck, *The Muslim Creed*, 1932.

numerous branches, which differed in regard to important doctrines of theology. In addition, Christianity exercised an important influence, notably through John of Damascus (died 749), the spokesman of Eastern Christianity. Saadya shows himself intimately acquainted with the various formulations of Christian dogma from the orthodox creed down to the Spanish school of adoptianism.[1] To round off the picture, Zoroastrianism, Manichaeanism and Indian philosophy were also well represented in the intellectual circles of Baghdād and the Near East in general. If we take the evidence of a Muslim historian, al-Ḥum'aydī, who records a personal experience of another Muslim in the Baghdād of the tenth century, we can appreciate Saadya's account of the spiritual confusion in his generation:

One of the Spanish theologians — Abū Omar Aḥmad ibn Muḥammad ibn Sā'dī — visited Baghdād ... Upon his return he met the famous scholar of Kairuwan, Abū Muḥammad ibn Abī Za'yd, who asked him whether he had an opportunity of attending, during his stay in Baghdād, one of the assemblies of the *Kalām*.[2] Yes, he answered, I attended twice, but I refused to go there for a third time. —Why? — For this simple reason, which you will appreciate: At the first meeting there were present not only people of various (Islamic) sects, but also unbelievers, Magians, materialists, atheists, Jews and Christians, in short, unbelievers of all kinds. Each group had its own leader, whose task it was to defend its views, and every time one of the leaders entered the room, his followers rose to their feet and remained standing until he took his seat. In the meanwhile, the hall had become overcrowded with people. One of the unbelievers rose and said to the assembly: we are meeting here for a discussion. Its conditions are known to all. You, Muslims, are not allowed to argue from your books and prophetic traditions since we deny both. Everybody, therefore, has to limit himself to rational arguments. The whole assembly applauded these words. So you can imagine,

[1] Cf. M. Ventura, *La Philosophie de Saadia Gaon*, Paris, 1934, pp. 184-5.

[2] *Kalām* ('speech') means, in a technical sense, 'theology'. The *Mutakallimūn* (from sing. *Mutakallim*) are theologians, notably *Mu'tazilites* as distinguished from the orthodox theologians, the mystics and the philosophers.

Ibn Sā'dī concluded, that after these words I decided to withdraw. They proposed to me that I should attend another meeting in a different hall, but I found the same calamity there.[1]

Within the Jewish Communities under Islamic rule disruption was likewise spreading. Towards the end of the eighth century, the Karaite sect had arisen and had won a considerable following. With its blunt rejection of Talmudic Judaism and with its reformative zeal to establish a tradition-less Judaism on the pure basis of Scripture (*mikra*'), it constituted a grave danger to the continuance of historic Judaism. There existed, in addition, some minor sects, which are described in the *Kitāb al-Anwār* ('Book of Lights') by the Karaite Kirkisānī, such as the Maghariyya sect, which seems to have owed its existence to the influence of Philonic tradition. Their angel doctrine echoes in some ways the Logos conception of Philo, and they indulge, like Philo, in an allegorical interpretation of the Bible. Another group of Jews had strong leanings towards the Manichaean religion. It seems that Ḥiwi ha-Balkhi was the spokesman of this group. This strange and mysterious figure, the Jewish Marcion of the age, upon whom some light has been thrown for the first time by I. Davidson's discovery of part of Saadya's polemic against him,[2] sharply criticized the Bible from a Gnostic point of view.

A considerable part of Saadya's literary activities were devoted to combating the Karaite and other sectarian views, which dangerously undermined the spiritual foundations of Judaism.[3] Although personally he may have recognized the stimulating effect which the Karaite emphasis on the Scriptures undoubtedly had on his own thinking — he had valuable conversations with the Karaite Solomon b. Yeruḥam as testified by the chronicler al-Hītī[4] — he became the Rabbanite protagonist in the struggle against the Karaite sect. His literary work was, however, by no means of a purely polemical nature. As we have seen, he wrote his philosophical book with the

---

[1] Quoted from *Journal Asiatique* (1852), p. 93, by M. Ventura, in *Raḥ Saadya Gaon*, ed. J. L. Fishman, p. 311.
[2] Cf. Israel Davidson, *Saadia's Polemic against Ḥiwi Al-Balkhi*, New York, 1915.
[3] Cf. A. Harkavy, 'Anti-Karaite Writings of Saadya', *JQR*, Vol. 13 (1901); I. Davidson, *loc. cit.*
[4] Cf. *JQR*, Vol. 9 (1897), p. 434.

aim of offering guidance to his people. In fact, his whole literary work is devoted to the same end. There is a single purpose and design running through all the extensive writing which he did, and which, incidentally, made him the pioneer of the 'Scientific' Jewish Learning in the Middle Ages. At the time when he wrote the opening chapter of his great book in which he deplored the spiritual confusion of his generation, he had already performed an act which was destined to save the Jewries of the Arabic-speaking world from falling into spiritual decay: he had written and published his Arabic translation (*Tafsīr*) of the Bible. He had also written an extensive Commentary (*Sharḥ*) on the Bible for more learned readers. Unfortunately, the latter work is lost except for small fragments and excerpts,[1] but his *Tafsīr* has remained 'the standard Arabic Bible for all Arabic-speaking Jews ... down to the present time'.[2] This epoch-making achievement, comparable in importance to the historic rendering of the Bible in the Greek Septuagint, was prepared for and made possible by his researches in the field of Hebrew grammar and lexicography, which laid the foundations of Hebrew philology.[3] Another important production was his *Siddur*, the first Jewish Prayer Book of which we know.[4] Here too Saadya's purpose is in the main educational and pedagogical. He recognizes the need of supplying the Communities with a textbook of prayer instead of the mere halachic rules of prayer, with which his predecessors in the field of Jewish liturgy, R. Natronai and R. 'Amram Gaon, were chiefly concerned.[5]

Important and far-reaching though these literary achievements were, they could not hope to change, fundamentally, the outlook of those of his people who had 'lost their way' or

[1] Cf. the recent article by Boaz Cohen, 'Quotations from Saadia's Arabic Commentary on the Bible from Two Manuscripts of Abraham ben Solomon' in *Saadya Anniversary Volume*, New York, pp. 75-139.

[2] Cf. Malter *loc. cit.*, p. 142; for an appreciation see Edward Robertson, 'Saadya Gaon as Translator and Commentator' in *Melilah*, ed. Edward Robertson and Meir Wallenstein, Manchester University Press, 1944, pp. 178-84.

[3] Saadya wrote a Hebrew dictionary ('*Agron*), a grammatical work called 'Books on Languages', and gave in his 'Explanation of the 70 Hapaxlegomena' the first indication that Biblical Hebrew can be interpreted and augmented by Mishnaic Hebrew. Cf. S. Krauss' article in *Saadya Studies*, ed. E. I. J. Rosenthal, Manchester University Press, 1943, p. 47.

[4] Ed. by I. Davidson, S. Assaf, B. I. Joel, Jerusalem, 1940.

[5] Cf. I. Elbogen, 'Saadya's Siddur' in *Saadya Anniversary Volume*, New York, pp. 249-50.

were 'lacking in faith' or tormented by 'doubts'. To them he had to offer religious guidance in the language of philosophy. So he used the years of his enforced retirement from public life for writing, first (in 931), his *Commentary on the Sefer Yeṣīrah* ('Book of Creation'),[1] then, two years later (933), his *magnum opus*, 'The Book of Doctrines and Beliefs' (Arab. *Kitāb al-'Amānāt wa'l-'I'tiḳādāt*; known, in Yehudah ibn Tibbon's Hebrew translation, as *Sefer ha-'Emūnōt we-ha-Deōt*).[2] The two books stand in close relation to each other. The cosmological theory, the theory of knowledge, the doctrine of the soul and, to some extent, the theory of Revelation are identical in both. The books are nevertheless different in character. The *Sefer Yeṣīrah* with its neo-pythagorean play on numbers and letters gives Saadya a great opportunity for displaying his linguistic and mathematical knowledge.[3] But the Commentary fails to develop a metaphysical system of its own. Saadya may have crystallized his ideas on the main subjects of philosophy and theology in the process of writing it, but, compared with the major work, it is of small significance. It has, nevertheless, attained to fame in the circles of the so-called 'German Ḥasīdīm' (R. Yehudah the Ḥasīd; R. Eleazar of Worms), who borrowed their theory of Revelation ('Created Glory' and 'Created Speech') from it.[4] The 'Book of Doctrines and Beliefs', however, fulfills all the requirements set out by Saadya in the opening of the book. It gives a full and comprehensive answer to all the problems which agitated the minds of his contemporaries. It is not a work of academic

---

[1] Arab. *Tafsīr Kitāb al-Mabādī*, ed., with a French translation, by M. Lambert, Paris, 1891.

[2] An earlier anonymous Hebrew paraphrase, which is extant in several MSS, bears the title, *Pitron Sefer ha-'Emūnōt*.

[3] A recent study by S. Gandz in *Saadya Anniversary Volume*, New York, 'Saadya Gaon as a Mathematician', pp. 141-95, has assessed Saadya's attainments in mathematics. It shows that Saadya was proficient as a *ḥāsib*, an arithmetician and calculator; that he had a fair knowledge of the theory of numbers, as it was taught in the arithmetic of Nicomachus of Gerara (about 100 c.e.); that he knew the Arabic treatises dealing with the arithmetic of inheritance; and that he was most likely familiar with the astronomy of al-Farghānī. — In this connection mention may also be made of the fact that 'The earliest known Jewish writing on music' is contained in the tenth chapter of Saadya's *Book of Doctrines and Beliefs* (not included in this selection). He appears to have depended on Arabic sources, al-Kindī being his chief authority. Down to the twelfth century Saadya is the only Jewish writer of whom any fragment on the theory of music is extant. Cf. H. G. Farmer, *Sa'adyah Gaon on the Influence of Music*, London, 1943, pp. 2, 6.

[4] Cf. G. G. Scholem, *Major Trends in Jewish Mysticism*, Jerusalem, 1946, pp. 112 ff.

research and speculation, but a collection of living answers to living questions. The phrase which so often occurs in it, 'Someone may ask', is never a rhetorical phrase designed to introduce the author's own trend of argument, but the echo of some real question or objection, which Saadya had met either in a book or in a personal discussion.

The answer which Saadya's book evolves is not that of any particular philosophical system, but the interpretation of Judaism in the light of 'Reason' ('akl). It is Saadya's firm conviction, eloquently expressed, that Judaism teaches nothing contrary to 'Reason', and that, furthermore, its fundamental principles, such as Creation, Unity of God, the rational character of the Law, Freedom of the Will, the Future Life, can be demonstrated by the 'speculation' (nazar) of Reason. For his conception of Reason, and indeed, his basic principle of the conformity of Revelation to Reason, he is indebted to the Mu'tazilite schools, on whose teachings he frequently draws. But it would be wrong to assume that he is, like the Karaite Josef al-Baṣir and other Karaites, a pure Mu'tazilite clothed in a Jewish garb. His dependence on the Mu'tazila, though far from inconsiderable, has often been overstated. The Mu'tazilite schools and their controversies with the Ash'ariyya have, no doubt, stimulated his thought. But often he gives Talmudic answers to problems posed by these schools. Thus, the nature of the Law — a problem on which Mu'tazila and Ash'ariyya fought violent battles — is defined in accordance with an earlier Talmudic distinction between purely rational and purely revelational laws.[1] The question of Reward and Punishment, again a major topic of Islamic controversy, is solved in accordance with a Talmudic dictum.[2] This is not surprising, for it should be borne in mind that many of the problems with which Islamic theology was confronted for the first time as a consequence of the influx of Hellenistic thought had already been answered in a previous epoch, when Judaism had its first encounter with the Hellenistic civilization. The process of rationalization through which Islam was passing had long before left its mark on the body of Jewish theological thought.

[1] Cf. the Translator's articles in *Rab Saadya Gaon*, ed. J. L. Fishman, pp. 658-73, and in *Bulletin of the John Rylands Library*, Manchester, Vol. 28, No. 2 (1944), pp. 320-39.
[2] Cf. Jakob Guttmann, *Die Religionsphilosophie des Saadia*, Göttingen, 1882, p. 180.

The 'purification of the idea of God'[1] had, in Judaism, already resulted in the Targumic avoidance of anthropomorphic expressions, and in elaborating the idea of the Unity of God and other Jewish concepts Saadya had only to link up with the Jewish theological tradition. Moreover, rationality is a prominent feature of the Jewish faith with its stress on the Unity and Justice of God. Thus, Saadya had no great difficulty in demonstrating that the dogmas of Revelation as embodied in the Torah plus the Oral Tradition were in basic agreement with Reason. Such an irrational Talmudic and Midrashic notion as that of the pre-existent Torah — the *locus classicus* for the Torah mysticism — finds no place in his system of Jewish doctrine. The only part of his system which is definitely mystical is his theory of Revelation, where he draws on the Jewish mystical tradition.[2] Also in his conception of the Messianic Future faith, pure and simple, takes the place of rational argumentation. But otherwise, the weight of the 'reasonableness of Judaism' is so decisive that the real problem, to him, is not so much the question whether or not Revelation conforms to Reason, but rather why Revelation has been necessary at all. His answer is that without Revelation mankind would have had to struggle some time until Reason prevailed. Revelation is not essentially superior, but historically prior to Reason and has an educational function in the evolution of humanity.

The real conflict, as Saadya sees it, is thus not one between Faith and Reason, but one between Faith and pseudo-Reason. Saadya insists, and his book is intended as proof for this thesis, that intellectual speculation, if properly and patiently carried to its final conclusion, confirms the doctrines of the Jewish faith. The trouble is, he asserts, that so few people care to complete their research and speculation. They pretend to follow their Reason, but in fact they only follow their Nature, that is to say, the irrational factors which impede the progress of true speculation, such as indolence, prejudice, resentment, etc. In a paragraph not included in this selection, Saadya enters into a psychological analysis of the reasons for unbelief.[3] He

[1] Cf. Simon Rawidowicz, 'Saadya's Purification of the Idea of God', in *Saadya Studies*, ed. E. I. J. Rosenthal, pp. 139-65.
[2] Cf. the Translator's article, 'Saadya's Theory of Revelation: its origin and background', in *Saadya Studies*, ed. E. I. J. Rosenthal, pp. 4-25.
[3] Cf. *Amānāt*, pp. 26-9 (13-14).

shows himself a keen and observant student of psychology on more than one occasion.[1]

In the light of what has been said above we can see the real meaning of the title which Saadya gave to his book, and which has been an object of controversy amongst scholars. As B. Klar has pointed out in a study published a few years ago,[2] no less than twenty different translations have in turn been suggested. The matter has again been dealt with in two more recent publications.[3] A fresh investigation of the usage of the terms 'Amānah and 'I'tikād throughout the book has led the translator to substantially the same result as indicated in the two last-mentioned articles. 'Amānah denotes a doctrine which is accepted by an act of religious faith. (The verb 'āmana signifies the act of religious faith; cf. below, p. 106, n. 4.) Thus the doctrines of Creation and Resurrection are called 'amānat. (Cf. (Cf. below, pp. 62, 180.) Ibn Tibbon translates it by 'emūnah. 'I'tikād, on the other hand, signifies an attitude of firm belief as the result of a process of speculation. Saadya gives a clear definition of this term. (Cf. below, pp. 26–7.) Ibn Tibbon usually translates it likewise by 'emūnah, except in the title of the book, where he renders it (in the plural) by de'ōt. One sympathizes with his difficulty in finding suitable Hebrew terms to express the difference between 'amānāt and 'i'tikādāt, but, unfortunately, neither of these Hebrew terms adequately conveys the meaning of the Arabic original. Neither does 'emūnōt express the objective quality of 'doctrine', nor does de'ōt denote the subjective character of 'belief' in the sense of 'conviction'.[4] To reverse the order of the Hebrew terms in the title would come

[1] Especially in his Commentary on Proverbs; see the Translator's article, 'Saadya's Conception of the Law', in *Bulletin of the John Rylands Library*, Manchester, Vol. 28, No. 2 (1944), pp. 327–8.

[2] Cf. B. Klar, *Kiryat Sefer*, XVI (1939–40), pp. 241–5.

[3] Cf. I. Efros' and A. Heschel's articles in *Saadya Studies*, published by the *Jewish Quarterly Review* (1943).

[4] As has recently been shown by S. Rawidowicz, Maimonides and his translators were faced with a similar difficulty. Maimonides clearly distinguished between 'i'tikād and 'ilm ('knowledge') and used 'i'tikād for 'belief' in the sense of faith based on Reason, sometimes also in the general sense of faith. The Hebrew translator of the *Sefer ham-miṣwōt* renders it by 'emūnah, ha'amanah; Samuel ibn Tibbon, in his translation of the *Moreh*, uses the same Hebrew terms. Maimonides himself, in his *Mishneh Torah*, employs the Hebrew madda', as distinct from de'ah, as an equivalent for the Arabic 'i'tikād. Rawidowicz rightly emphasizes the necessity of interpreting Maimonides' use of madda' in the light of the underlying Arabic term 'i'tikād which points in the direction of 'emūnah rather than de'ah. Cf. Meṣudah, ed. S. Rawidowicz (1943), pp. 132–43; *Essays Presented to Dr. J. H. Hertz*, pp. 331–9.

nearer the truth. The title of the book thus epitomizes the whole purpose which the author had in mind, namely, to enable the reader to reach a stage where the '*Amānāt* ('doctrines', i.e. of Judaism) become the object of '*I'tiḳādāt* ('conviction', i.e. faith based on speculation).

The style in which the book is written is a true expression of Saadya's mind and character. It is a matter-of-fact style, lucid and precise, sometimes of an abrupt brevity which the translator often had to paraphrase. There is lacking in Saadya's style the tranquil solemnity of Maimonides' neo-platonic pathos and the beauty of Yehudah Hallewi's mystical yearning. But at times even Saadya's cool and symmetrical prose rises to heights of inspiration. Passages such as those describing the future Redemption of Israel or setting out the reasons for our belief in the Future Life have a beauty of their own. Another point worth remembering is Saadya's mastery of Biblical quotations. His skill in finding Scriptural support for almost every detail of argument, let alone doctrine, is truly amazing. The whole of the Bible becomes, as it were, enmeshed in the network of his system of thought, and special use is made of the Psalms, Proverbs, Job and Ecclesiastes. The translator quotes the Scriptural text according to the Authorized Version except in cases when Saadya's own exegesis is divergent. Full use has been made in this respect of Saadya's Commentaries on the various books of the Bible. Whether the reader will share Saadya's fondness of numerical classification may be doubtful; but it certainly makes for lucidity in emphasizing the different points of the arguments advanced and of the doctrines expounded.

As to the principle of selection which guided the translator in the presentation of the text, his main consideration was to give the reader a faithful and well proportioned picture of the book as a whole. The selection has been made from all chapters of the 'Amānāt except chapter 10, which, according to the unanimous opinion of the experts, must be regarded as a kind of appendix added later. It does not fit in with the general structure and trend of the book since it reopens, after the climax is reached in the last three eschatological chapters, the problem of ethical conduct which has already been dealt with in chapter 3. Naturally, not all the arguments advanced in favour of, or against, a particular view have been included, as must be the case in any Selection, but a constant endeavour has been made to present in their entirety passages or sequences of passages forming a single whole, and not to give a distorted view by cutting out sentences from the context. A novel feature introduced by the translator is the sub-division of the main chapters into minor chapters with distinct titles. The rich content of the book becomes thereby manifest from a glance at the table of contents.

The Translation is based throughout on S. Landauer's edition of the Arabic text (Leiden, 1880), which follows, in the main, the so-called Oxford Recension. Wherever there were strong reasons on logical grounds, preference was given to the readings of the Leningrad Recension — the only other extant MS. of the *'Amānāt* — as indicated in Landauer's marginal notes. Special consideration had to be given to chapter 7. Here the texts of the two Recensions differ very considerably. Landauer was of opinion that the Leningrad Recension had not originated from Saadya himself, but from a second hand. He therefore omitted all reference to its readings from his marginal notes. W. Bacher, who edited the Leningrad Recension of chapter 7 (in the M. Steinschneider Festschrift, Leipzig, 1896, pp. 219-26; hebr. pp. 98-112) was able to disprove Landauer's arguments against Saadya's authorship, and showed that the Leningrad Recension represented a revised version of the chapter, undertaken by Saadya himself, with the purpose of publishing it as a separate polemical treatise. As to the question whether Saadya himself substituted this new version for the original chapter 7 as part of the *'Amānāt*, Bacher thought that this may have been the case. If this assumption were true, a translation of chapter 7 would have to base itself on the text of the Leningrad Recension as Saadya's authorized revised text of the chapter. But it appears that such an assumption cannot be accepted. As Bacher himself emphasized, the text of the Leningrad Recension does not fit in with the character of the other chapters of the book. Its lengthy title, opening laudation and different method of presentation render it unsuitable for inclusion as a chapter amongst the other chapters of the book. It can only be considered as a separate treatise. The Translator therefore felt justified in following the Oxford Recension as presented in Landauer's edition. He made, however, ample reference to the Leningrad Recension in the notes.

A word must be said in regard to Yehudah ibn Tibbon's Hebrew rendering, of which, needless to say, full use has been made. Unfortunately, as is well known, the extant text of Tibbon's version abounds in mistakes.[1] It would have been very welcome to the Translator if the critical edition of this text as prepared by Malter and announced as early as 1921 (in his book on Saadya, p. 372) had already appeared. According to an announcement contained in the Bibliography of the *Saadya Volume*, ed. J. L. Fishman, Jerusalem, 1943 (p. 653), this critical edition is now to appear under the editorship of Malter's disciple, Dr. Yehudah ibn Shmuel Kaufmann. The hope may be expressed that this longstanding promise will be at last fulfilled. In the absence of a critical edition of Ibn Tibbon's text, the various corrections suggested by M. Wolff, D. Kaufmann, S. H. Margulies, M. Ventura and B. Klar proved most helpful. Of particular value were the two standard works on Saadya's philosophy, Jakob Guttmann's *Die Religionsphilosophie des Saadia* (1882) and M. Ventura's *La Philosophie de Saadia Gaon* (1934).

---

[1] For a history of the editions of the Hebrew text see B. Klar, *Tarbiṣ*, XII (1940), pp. 51 ff. — The references to Tibbon's Hebrew translation in this book are quoted according to D. Slucki's edition, Leipzig, 1864.

LIST OF ABBREVIATIONS

A. Initials

EI — Encyclopaedia of Islam. Leiden-London. 4 vols.

EJ — Encyclopaedia Judaica. Berlin, 1928 ff.

HUCA – Hebrew Union College Annual. Cincinnati, 1924 ff.

JQR — Jewish Quarterly Review, New Series. Philadelphia, 1910 ff.

MGWJ – Monatsschrift für die Geschichte und Wissenschaft des Judentums. Breslau, 1851-1938.

REJ — Revue des Études Juives. Paris, 1880 ff.

B. Abbreviated Titles

Amānāt — Saadya's Kitāb al-'Amānāt wa'l-'I'tiḳādāt, ed. S. Landauer. Leiden, 1880. (Bracketed figures refer to Slucki's edition of the Hebrew text. Cf. p. 22, n. 1).

Comm. Yeṣ. — Saadya's Commentaire sur le Séfer Yesira, Publié et traduit par M. Lambert. Paris, 1891. (Bracketed figures refer to the French translation included in the same edition).

Comm. Pent. — J. Dérenbourg, Les Œuvres complètes de Saadia. Vol. I (1893).

Comm. Isa. — J. Dérenbourg, Les Œuvres complètes de Saadia. Vol. III (1896).

Comm. Prov. — J. Dérenbourg — M. Lambert, Les Œuvres complètes de Saadia. Vol. VI (1894).

Guttmann — J. Guttmann, Die Religionsphilosophie des Saadia, 1882.

Judaica — 'Judaica', Festschrift zu Hermann Cohen's 70. Geburtstag, 1912.

Kaufmann — D. Kaufmann, Gesammelte Schriften. Vol. III, pp. 432 ff. (reprinted from 'Zeitschrift der Deutschen Morgenländischen Gesellschaft'. Vol. 37 (1883), pp. 230 ff.).

Kaufmann, Attrib.-Lehre — D. Kaufmann, Geschichte der Attributenlehre in der jüdischen Religionsphilosophie des Mittelalters von Saadja bis Maimûni, 1877.

Klatzkin-Zobel — Thesaurus Philosophicus Linguae Hebraicae et Veteris et Recentioris, Auctore Jac. Klatzkin, Operis Collaborator M. Zobel, 1928.

Malter — Henry Malter, Saadia Gaon, His Life and Works. Philadelphia, 1921.

Margulies — S. H. Margulies, Kritische Bemerkungen zum Wortlaut der Emunot wedeot in 'Magazin für die Wissenschaft des Judentums', ed. A. Berliner and D. Hoffmann. Vol. 17 (1890).

Pines — S. Pines, Beiträge zur Islamischen Atomenlehre. Berlin, 1936.

Scholem — G. G. Scholem, Major Trends in Jewish Mysticism. Jerusalem, 1941.

al-Shahrastānī — 'Schahrastani's Religionspartheien und Philosophen-Schulen', translated by T. Haarbrücker. 2 vols. (1850-51).

Theodor-Albeck — Bereschit Rabba mit Kritischem Apparat und Kommentar, ed. J. Theodor and Ch. Albeck. Berlin, 1912 ff.

Ventura — M. Ventura, La Philosophie de Saadia Gaon. Paris, 1934.

Wensinck — A. J. Wensinck, The Muslim Creed, 1932.

Wolff — M. Wolff, Bemerkungen zum Wortlaut der Emunot we Deot in 'Magazin für die Wissenschaft des Judentums', ed. A. Berliner and D. Hoffmann. Vol. 7 (1880).

PROLEGOMENA[1]

1. The Purpose of the Book

> (ed. Landauer 1.1-6.20;
> ed. Slucki   1.1-4.10)

Blessed be the Lord, the God of Israel, to whom the truth is known with absolute certainty;[2] who confirmeth to men the certainty of the truths which their souls experience[3] — finding as they do through their souls their sense perceptions to be trustworthy; and knowing as they do through their souls their rational knowledge to be correct;[4] thereby causing their errors to vanish, their doubts to be removed, their proofs to be clarified, and their arguments to be well-grounded. Glory unto Him who is exalted above all attributes and praise.[5]

After this brief opening in praise and eulogy of our Lord, I will begin this book, which it is my intention to write, with an exposition of the reason why men, in their search for Truth, become involved in errors, and how these errors can be removed so that the object of their investigations may be fully attained; moreover, why some of these errors have such a powerful hold on some people that they affirm them as the truth, deluding themselves that they know something. May God help me to dispel errors from my mind and thereby reach the stage of obedience towards Him, even as His Faithful Servant prayed that He might grant him perfection, saying, 'Open

---

[1] For a full treatment of this chapter cf. the articles by I. Efros, 'Saadia's Theory of Knowledge', and A. Heschel, 'The Quest for Certainty in Saadya's Philosophy', in *Saadya Studies*, published by the *Jewish Quarterly Review* (1943).

[2] Lit. 'Who is competent in regard to the matter (*ma'nā*) of clear truth'. Tibbon translates *ma'nā* by hebr. '*eyn*, essence. Bacher suggests the reading '*inyan*, which should be adopted in view of the fact that Tibbon translates *ma'nā* throughout the book in numberless instances by '*inyan*. The range of meaning in which Saadya employs the word corresponds exactly to the meaning of '*inyan*: sense, meaning, idea, fact, aspect, circumstance, matter.

[3] Prophecy confirms the truth of sense perception and sound reasoning. Cf. *Amānāt*, p. 14 (7).

[4] Sound sense perception and sound reason are able to establish the truth. Cf. below, p. 38-9.

[5] A short introductory laudation of God is customary in Arabic works. Jewish authors adopted this practice, for which Steinschneider has collected numerous instances. Cf. Malter, p. 180, n. 411. — Saadya expresses in the above prayer the essential concern of his book: the conquest of error and doubt.

Thou mine eyes, that I may behold wondrous things out of Thy Law' (Ps. 119.18). My intention is to place the subject matter throughout the book within the grasp of the reader and not beyond it; to speak a language which is easy and not difficult; to adduce only the principal proofs and arguments, not their ramifications, so that the reader may find his way about without too great difficulty; that his study may be made straightforward, and through it he may attain his object: Justice and Truth, even as the Faithful Servant said with regard to wisdom when placed within easy grasp, 'Then thou shalt understand righteousness and justice, and equity, yea, every good path' (Prov. 2.9).

I will first explain the reason why men are involved in doubts. I say then that all 'knowledge of Reason'[1] is based on knowledge derived from sense perception. Now the information afforded by the senses is liable to doubts in one of two ways: either because the person who is inquiring has an inadequate idea of the object of the investigation, or, alternatively, because he is perfunctory in his observation and does not take sufficient pains with it. Take the case of a person who is looking for someone called Reuben ben Jacob. He may be in doubt whether he has found him for one of two reasons: either because his knowledge of Reuben is inadequate, since he never met him before and therefore does not know him, or else because seeing some other person he may wrongly assume him to be Reuben, taking the line of least resistance and neglecting to make proper inquiries. He has no claim to be forgiven since he takes things too easily and conducts his search carelessly. The result will be that his doubts will never be cleared up.

The same applies to the 'knowledge of Reason'. Here again doubts arise from one of two causes: either because the person who seeks such knowledge may be unfamiliar with the methods of demonstration, and therefore discard a correct proof and accept a false proof as correct; or, alternatively, he may know the right methods of investigation, but is neglectful in applying them, and hasty in arriving at conclusions before having completed the work of investigation with regard to the matter he seeks to know. All the more is this the case if both deficiencies

[1] For a definition of this term cf. below, p. 36.

26

are combined in the same person, that is to say, if the person is not acquainted with the art of investigation, and, in addition, lacks patience to proceed even as far as his proper knowledge would carry him. He will remain far removed from the object of his investigation, or despair of attaining it. Concerning the first of the two kinds of people we have mentioned the prophet says, 'Everyone that knoweth, understandeth' (Neh. 10.29);[1] concerning the latter[2] it is said, 'They know not, neither do they understand' (Ps. 82.5).[3] There may even be a third deficiency in addition to these two, namely, where the one who carries on an investigation has no clear idea as to what he actually wants to know. Then he will be still further removed from attaining true knowledge, so much so that even if the truth should occur to him and strike his mind, he would not notice it. He resembles a man who is unacquainted with the art of weighing and with the shape of the scales and weights, and who, in addition, does not know how much money he has a right to claim from his debtor. Even if his debtor had paid the full amount of the debt, he would not know that he had received the full payment; and if he took less from the debtor than was owing to him, he would, nevertheless, think that he had treated him unjustly. If this will be the position when one of the two people has a claim on the other, a similar thing will happen if one wants to weigh money for himself, but does not understand the instruments of weighing, and is unable to determine the exact weight they indicate.[4] To use yet another simile: He resembles a man who in accepting money for himself or somebody else sorts out the coins himself although he is ignorant of the art of testing coins, and, therefore, frequently accepts a worthless coin and refuses a good one. The result will be the same if though well able to test he nevertheless acts carelessly.[5] Scripture has already compared the test which is applied to the words of righteousness to the testing of money. It says, 'The tongue of the righteous is as choice silver; the heart

---

[1] i.e. Only one that knows the right methods of investigation is able to arrive at the truth.

[2] Who combine both deficiencies.

[3] They neither possess the methods of investigation, nor do they try to understand by patient effort.

[4] Here the only deficiency is lack of knowledge.

[5] The two alternatives of this simile illustrate the two points made above: deficiency of knowledge and lack of patience are the causes of doubt.

of the wicked is little worth' (Prov. 10.20).[1] Those who have only little skill in the art of testing, or, alternatively, have only little patience in applying it, are regarded as oppressors because they do violence to the truth, as is said, 'The heart of the wicked is little worth',[2] whereas those who practice the art of testing are considered righteous on account of their knowledge and patience, as stated in the preceding words, 'The tongue of the righteous is as choice silver'. The wise are praiseworthy, and their doubts vanish only if they persevere in carrying through their investigation to the end, in addition to knowing how to conduct it,[3] as the wise said, 'Behold, I waited for your words, I listened for your reasons, until I searched out what to say' (Job 32.11), and as has been said by another wise man, 'Take not the final word of truth out of my mouth' (Ps. 119.43).[4]

I have been led to make these introductory remarks by my observation of the state of many people in regard to their doctrines and beliefs. Some there are who have arrived at the truth and rejoice in the knowledge that they possess it; of them the prophet says, 'Thy words were found, and I did eat them, and Thy words were unto me a joy and the rejoicing of my heart' (Jer. 15.16). Others have arrived at the truth, but doubt it; they fail to know it for a certainty and to hold on to it; of these the prophet says, 'Though I write for him ever so many things of My law, they are accounted as a stranger's' (Hosea 8.12). Still others confidently affirm that which is false in the belief that it is true; they hold on to falsehood, and abandon that which is right; of them it is said, 'Let him not trust in vanity, deceiving himself; for vanity shall be his recompense' (Job 15.31). Others again base their conduct on a certain belief for a time, and then reject it on account of some defect they find in it; then they change over to another belief and renounce it in turn because of something in it which seems questionable to them; then they go over to yet another belief for a while, and drop it because of some point which, in their opinion, renders it invalid. These

---

[1] The words of truth are the result of a testing process, i.e., that of investigation, similar to the testing of silver. Cf. *Comm. Prov.*, p. 59.

[2] i.e. Small in knowledge and patience.

[3] Doubt vanishes only after the completion of the whole process of investigation. The process of cognition is later described as a successive elimination of doubts.

[4] The final word in the process of cognition contains the truth and is free from doubt and uncertainty.

people are changing continually all their life. They resemble a person who desires to go to a town, but does not know the road that leads to it; he travels a parasang[1] on one road and becomes perplexed, returns and travels a parasang on another road, becomes again perplexed and returns, and so a third and fourth time. Of such a man Scripture says, 'The labour of fools wearieth everyone of them, he knoweth not how to go to the city' (Eccl. 10.15), that is to say *because* he knoweth not.[2]

When I considered these evils both in their own nature and in their particular manifestations, my heart grieved for my race, the race of mankind, and my soul was moved on account of our own people Israel, as I saw in my time many of the believers clinging to unsound doctrines and mistaken beliefs while many of those who deny the faith boast of their unbelief and despise the men of truth, although they are themselves in error. I saw men sunk, as it were, in a sea of doubt and covered by the waters of confusion,[3] and there was no diver to bring them up from the depths and no swimmer to come to their rescue. But as my Lord has granted unto me some knowledge which I can use for their support, and endowed me with some ability which I might employ for their benefit, I felt that to help them was my duty, and guiding them aright an obligation upon me, as the Prophet says, 'The Lord God hath given me the tongue of them that are taught, that I should know how to sustain with words him that is weary' (Isa. 50.4), although I confess to the shortcomings of my knowledge, which is far from being perfect, and admit the deficiency of my understanding, which is far from being complete, realizing as I do that I am not superior in knowledge to my contemporaries, but can offer my contribution only to the best of my ability and according to my lights, as the prophet says, 'But as for me, this secret is not revealed to me for any wisdom that I have

[1] A parasang is three miles.

[2] Saadya classifies his contemporaries on the basis of the distinction between doubt and certainty, error and truth: (1) Some possess both truth and certainty; (2) others possess truth, but lack certainty; (3) others lack truth, but possess certainty; (4) still others lack both truth and certainty. It is Saadya's endeavour to offer them both truth and certainty. Cf. Heschel *loc. cit.*, p. 291.

[3] No doubt, Saadya alludes to Isa. 11.9 (Hab. 2.14), 'For the earth shall be full of the knowledge of the Lord, as the waters cover the sea'. Cf. below, p. 31, where the verse is quoted to illustrate the state of man's perfection in contrast to his state of error and doubt as described in the above passage.

more than any living' (Dan. 2.30). Nevertheless, I maintain
the hope that He who knoweth my intentions and the desire
of my heart will grant me success and sustain me according to
my purpose, not according to my gifts and abilities, as has been
said by another prophet, 'I know, my God, that Thou searchest
the heart, and hast pleasure in uprightness' (1 Chron. 29.17).

In the name of God, the Creator of the universe, I implore
any learned man who may read this book and find in it some
mistake, to correct it, or if he finds a doubtful letter,[1] to put it
right. Let him not be prevented from doing so by the fact that
the book is not his, or because I preceded him in shedding
light on matters which were not clear to him. For the wise
have compassion on wisdom and feel kindness for it as members
of one family feel kindly towards each other, as is said, 'Say
unto wisdom: thou art my sister' (Prov. 7.4); the ignorant
have likewise compassion on their ignorance, and do not forsake it, as is said, 'Though he spare it, and will not let it go, but
keep it still within his mouth' (Job 20.13).

I further implore in the name of God (may He be exalted)
all those of my readers who strive after wisdom to read this
book with an open mind, to try honestly to see my point of
view, and to clear their minds of partiality, hasty judgment and
confused thinking so that they may derive from it the maxi-
mum of profit and advantage with the help of Him who has
taught us wherein our benefit lies and on what it depends, as
the prophet said, 'I am the Lord thy God, who teacheth thee
for thy profit, who leadeth thee by the way that thou shouldest
go' (Isa. 48.17). If both the scholar and the learner follow this
path in reading this book, the certainty of him that feels certain will increase; the doubt of him that is in doubt will vanish;
the believer who blindly relies on tradition,[2] will turn into one
basing his belief on speculation and understanding; those who
put forward erroneous arguments will be silenced; those who
are obstinate and defy evidence will be ashamed; and the
righteous and upright will rejoice, as is said, 'The upright see

---

[1] Kaufmann (p. 440) sees here an allusion to the fact that Saadya wrote his book in
Arabic characters whose diacritical points are apt to cause misreading and confusion.
Cf. also Attrib.-Lehre, p. 89, n. 150.

[2] Arab. *taklīd*, a term which denotes 'the adoption of the utterances or actions of
another as authoritative with faith in their correctness without investigating reasons'.
Cf. *EI*, Vol. IV, p. 630.

it and are glad; and all iniquity stoppeth her mouth. Whoso is wise, let him observe these things, and let them consider the mercies of the Lord' (Ps. 107.42-3). In this way the innermost thoughts of a man will be purified and brought into conformity with his outward behaviour; his prayer will be sincere as there will be enshrined in his heart an inner voice rebuking and summoning him to right conduct, as the prophet says, 'Thy words have I laid up in my heart, that I might not sin against Thee' (Ps. 119.11). Their faith will show itself in their dealings with each other; jealousy between them in matters of this world will diminish; all will turn towards the Master of wisdom and not to anything else. He will be for them salvation, mercy and happiness, as God (be He praised and sanctified) has said, 'Look unto Me, and be ye saved, all the ends of the earth, for I am God, and there is none else' (Isa. 45.22). All this will result from the disappearance of doubts and the removal of errors. The knowledge of God and His Law will spread in the world like the spreading of water in all parts of the sea, as is said, 'For the earth shall be full of the knowledge of the Lord, as the waters cover the sea' (Isa. 11.9).

2. THE NATURE OF DOUBT AND BELIEF

(ed. Landauer 7.1-17; 9.15-12.17;
ed. Slucki 4.11-26; 5.19-7.2)

One might ask: 'How can it be reconciled with the wisdom of the Creator (be He exalted and glorified) that He allowed errors and doubts to arise in the minds of His creatures?' We may answer this question at once by saying that the very fact that they are created beings causes them to be subject to error and delusion. For according to the order of Creation they require for every work which they undertake a certain measure of time in which to complete it stage after stage. Cognition being one of their activities, it undoubtedly comes under the same rule. In its initial stage, their knowledge proceeds from a complex, vague and confused idea of things, but by their faculty of Reason they purify and clarify it in a continual process until, after a certain measure of time, their errors are removed, and a clear idea is formed without any admixture of doubt.[1] And just as every productive art is carried out by successive operations and remains incomplete if those performing it desist from it prior to its completion — such as sowing, building, weaving and the other kinds of productive work which can only be accomplished by the worker's persisting in it patiently until the end — so the work of acquiring knowledge demands that one should start from the beginning and proceed chapter after chapter until the final stage is reached. At the beginning there may be, for example, ten doubts; at the second stage they will be reduced to nine, at the third to eight, and if a man continues to reason and to reflect, his doubts will in this way be further reduced until, at the final stage, there will emerge in full clarity the one proposition which formed the object of his search, and which stands out clearly defined, with no error or doubt attached to it . . . Now were he to abandon his speculation when he arrived at the fifth or fourth or any other stage, the doubts which attended the preceding stages of his reflection would be removed, but there would still remain with him the doubts attached to the remaining stages in front of him. If he retains in his mind the result of his speculation up to the point which he reached, he may hope to return to this point and complete the inquiry. If he fails to retain it, he will have to start his inquiry afresh. For this reason many people have gone astray and spurned wisdom. Some of them are ignorant of the road that leads to it, others whilst taking the road fail to complete the journey and get lost, as Scripture says, 'The man that strayeth out of the way of understanding shall rest in the congregation of the shades' (Prov. 21.16).

With regard to those who fail to reach the goal of wisdom the Sages of Israel have said, 'With the increase in numbers of the disciples of Shammai and Hillel, who did not advance far

---

[1] Saadya describes the process of cognition as a successive elimination of doubts. It consists of three stages: (a) the complex impression, which gives only a vague idea as to the nature of the object of enquiry; (b) the act of analysing this idea; (c) the acceptance of the final truth by an act of belief which is free from doubt. In his *Comm. Yeṣ.* (pp. 36-7, transl. p. 59), Saadya speaks of the three operations of synthesis, analysis and belief which constitute the three stages in the process of cognition. He finds these three faculties expressed in the formula used by the *Sefer Yeṣirah*, 'Know, reflect, preserve' (*da' we-ḥashōḇ u-neṣōr*). The faculty of synthesis presents the object in its concrete entirety; the faculty of analysis eliminates what is faulty and confirms what is correct in the impression; the faculty of belief adopts and conserves the knowledge established by the two preceding faculties. Saadya's definition of Belief (see below, p. 34) follows the same pattern.

enough in their studies, the controversies increased'.[1] This utterance of theirs shows that if the disciples carry through their studies to the end, no controversy or discord arises amongst them. Let not therefore the fool in his impatience lay the blame for his own fault on the Creator (be He exalted and glorified) by saying that He implanted these doubts in him, whereas it is his own ignorance or impatience which threw him into confusion, as we have explained. Nor is it possible that any action of his can, by a single stroke, remove all doubt. For if it could, it would transcend the sphere of created beings, to which he belongs. Another person may not attach any blame for this fault of his to God,[2] but desires God to impart to him the ability to know with a knowledge that is free from doubt. Such a one asks for nothing less than to be like God. For the one who possesses immediate knowledge[3] is the Creator of the universe (be He blessed and sanctified) as we shall explain later when we come to this matter again.[4] The knowledge of all created beings, however, is only possible through the intermediacy of causes, i.e. through inquiry and speculation, which require time as we have described. From the first until the last moment of this period of time they must remain in doubt as we have explained, and they are the praiseworthy ones who persist until they have cleansed the silver from the dross, as is said, 'Take away the dross from the silver, and there cometh forth a vessel for the refiner' (Prov. 25.4); and until their churning has produced butter, as is said, 'For the churning of milk bringeth forth curd' (Prov. 30.33); and until their seed sprouts and can be reaped, as is said, 'Sow to yourselves according to righteousness, reap according to mercy' (Hosea 10.12); and until the fruit has ripened on their tree and turned into nourishing food, as is said, '. . . A tree of life to them that lay hold upon her' (Prov. 3.18).

Having thus dealt sufficiently with the origin of error and

[1] b. Sanh. 88b; the passage is also quoted by R. Sherira Gaon in his famous Letter where he gives an historical account of the origin and development of Rabbinic controversies. He explains that the Hadrianic persecutions made it impossible for the disciples to complete their studies. Cf. Iggeret de-Rabbenu Sherira Gaon, ed. A. Hyman, London, 1910, p. 22.

[2] Kaufmann, p. 443, misunderstood this sentence. Saadya now turns to those who, whilst not blaming God for their own fault, nevertheless, act stupidly by desiring a kind of knowledge which is peculiar to God.

[3] Lit. 'Knowledge without cause', i.e. without the effort of inquiry and speculation.

[4] Cf. Amānāt, p. 108 (56).

doubt, it is now fitting that we should explain the nature of Belief.[1] We affirm that this is an idea[2] arising in the soul as to what an object of knowledge really is: when the idea is clarified by speculation,[3] Reason comprehends it, accepts it, and makes it penetrate the soul and become absorbed into it; then man believes this idea which he has attained, and he preserves it in his soul for another time or other times, as is said, 'Wise men lay up knowledge' (Prov. 10.14), and as is further said, 'Receive, I pray thee, instructions from His mouth, and lay up His words in thy heart' (Job 22.22).

Belief is of two kinds, true or false. True belief means believing a thing to be as it really is, the large as large, the small as small, the black as black, the white as white, the existing as existing, the non-existing as non-existing. False belief means believing a thing to be the opposite of what it really is, the large as small, the small as large, the white as black, the black as white, the existing as non-existing, and the non-existing as existing. The wise man, who deserves praise, is the one who fixes his attention on the realities of things, and adapts his belief to them. Thanks to his wisdom he relies on that which can indeed be relied on and guards against that which must be guarded against. The fool, who is blameworthy, is the one who makes his belief the standard, and decrees that the realities of things must follow his belief. Thanks to his folly he relies on

[1] Arab. *'itiḳād*; Tibbon translates it here and elsewhere rightly by *'emūnah*, whereas in the title of the book he renders *'i'tiḳādāt* by *deōt*. Saadya's definition given above makes it clear beyond doubt that he uses the word in the sense of 'belief'. Cf. Translator's Introduction, p. 19.

[2] Arab. *ma'nā*; hebr. *'inyan*; it means 'idea', 'thought', not 'process' as Ventura (p. 81, n. 13) suggests, since the word occurs twice in the above definition and undoubtedly denotes 'idea' in the second place. The difficulty involved in the statement by Saadya that belief is an idea, is not solved by substituting 'process' for 'idea', since belief is not described as a process, but as an attitude of mind. The process of speculation which leads to Belief is not identical with Belief. Saadya's way of expression is inaccurate, and what he means to say is that Belief *starts* from an idea arising in the soul, etc. The above definition describes Belief as the final stage in the process of cognition much in the same way as the passage of *Comm. Yeṣ.* quoted above, p. 32, n. 1. One must compare the above definition with the passage in *Comm. Yeṣ.* in order to see that Belief represents only the final stage in the process of knowledge: First an impression (idea) arises as to the quality of a thing (faculty of synthesis); then examination clarifies the impression (faculty of analysis); finally Reason adopts the knowledge and makes it the object of belief (faculty of Belief). A different interpretation has been suggested by Heschel, *loc. cit.* p. 300 ff. Heschel is of opinion that Saadya discriminates between 'two types of belief or two stages in the process of belief'. As we have shown, *Comm. Yeṣ.* does not support this interpretation.

[3] Lit. 'When the butter of speculation emerges', a reference to the metaphor used before as a description of the process of speculation.

34

that which should be guarded against, and guards against that which can be relied on, as is said, 'A wise man feareth, and departeth from evil, but the fool behaveth overbearingly, and is confident' (Prov. 14.16).

In this connection I should like to refer to certain people who cause me astonishment. Though really servants they think they have no master, and they feel confident that what they reject is false and what they affirm is correct. These people are sunk in the depths of foolishness and stand on the brink of the abyss. If they are right, let the poor man believe that his boxes and baskets are full of money, and let him see what it will profit him. Or let one believe that he is seventy years of age when he is forty, and let him see what that will benefit him. Or let him believe that he is well fed whilst he is starving or that he has drunk his fill whilst he is thirsty, or that he is well clothed whilst he is naked. Let him see in what condition he will find himself. Another one belonging to this sort of people, who has a dangerous enemy, may believe that his enemy has already died and perished, and he fears him no more. How quickly there will come upon him the evil that he apprehends not! The height of folly, however, is reached by those people who think that because they do not believe in Divine authority they are free from God's commandments and prohibitions, from His promise and warning, and all that these imply. Scripture describes such people as saying, 'Let us break His bonds asunder, and cast away His cords from us' (Ps. 2.3).

Some people in India try to make themselves insensitive to fire, but it still burns them whenever they touch it. Others laying claim to self-denial inure themselves to be flogged and whipped, but they nevertheless suffer pain every moment they are beaten. How much more severe will be the lot of those who brazenly defy the Creator of the universe. Apart from their ignorance, they will not escape what His wisdom had imposed on them, as is said, 'He is wise in heart, and mighty in strength; who hath hardened himself against Him and prospered?' (Job 9.4).

3. The Four Roots of Knowledge

(ed. Landauer 12.17-14.6; 15.13-17.14; 18.16-20.18;
ed. Slucki 7.3-30; 8.12-9.8; 9.29-10.33)

Having completed the inquiry with which we were first concerned, it is desirable that we should now mention the sources[1] of truth and certainty, which are the origin of all knowledge and the fountain of all cognition.[2] We shall discuss the matter so far as it has a bearing on the subject of this book. We affirm then that there exist three sources of knowledge:[3] (1) The knowledge given by sense perception;[4] (2) the knowledge given by Reason; (3) inferential knowledge.[5] We proceed now to give an explanation of each of these Roots.

By the knowledge of sense perception we understand that which a man perceives by one of the five senses, i.e. sight, hearing, smell, taste, and touch.[6] By the knowledge of Reason we understand that which is derived purely from the mind,[7] such as the approval of truth and the disapproval of falsehood. By inferential knowledge we understand a proposition which a man cannot deny without being compelled to deny at the same time some proposition obtained from Reason or sense perception. Where there is no way of denying these propositions, the previous proposition must of necessity be accepted. E.g. we are compelled to admit that man possesses a soul, although we do not perceive it by our senses, so as not to deny its obvious functions. Similarly, we are compelled to admit that the soul is endowed with Reason, although we do not perceive it by our senses, so as not to deny its (Reason's) obvious function.

We have found many people who reject these three Roots of

[1] Lit. 'matters' (Arab. *mawādd*, from sing. *mādda*, matter), a term used by Saadya in the sense of source, origin. Tibbon copies the Arabic noun which is derived from the verb *madda*, to spread, extend, by using the Biblical noun, *meshek*, which is derived from *mashak*, to extend. Cf. Ps. 126.6; Job 28.18. See Kaufmann, Attrib.-Lehre, p. 1, n. 2; Klatzkin-Zobel, Vol. II, p. 293.

[2] Having dealt with the origin of error and doubt, Saadya now turns to a discussion of the origin of their opposites, i.e. truth and certainty.

[3] An additional fourth source of knowledge, that of reliable Tradition, will be mentioned further below.

[4] Lit. 'the knowledge of the eye witness'.

[5] Lit. 'knowledge arrived at by (logical) necessity'.

[6] This is the order in which the senses are enumerated by Aristotle, and following him, by most Arabic and Jewish philosophers. Cf. Kaufmann, *Die Sinne*, p. 44 ff. Tibbon's translation changes the order slightly.

[7] i.e. unaided by sense perception. Saadya refers to self-evident axioms of Reason. See Kaufmann, pp. 445-6; Heschel *loc. cit.*, p. 277, n. 65.

Knowledge. A few of them deny the first root. I shall deal with them in chapter 1 of this book and refute their arguments.[1] By denying the first root they (implicitly) deny the second and third as well since these are based on it. A larger group of people admit the first root, but deny the second and third. I shall deal with their view as well in chapter 1 and refute their arguments. Most people, however, admit the first two roots and deny the third one. The reason of this unequal distribution of views lies in the fact that the second type of knowledge is more hidden[2] than the first, and likewise the third more hidden than the second. Naturally, one is more readily inclined to deny what is hidden than what is obvious. There are also people who alternately deny a type of knowledge and approve another just as it suits them in their opposition to other people's views.[3] Each group of these affirms what their opponents reject, and claims that it is driven by inexorable logic to its own view. Some people, for instance, affirm that all things are in a state of rest, and deny that there is any movement, whereas others affirm that all things move, and deny that there is any rest.[4] Each group stigmatizes the arguments put forward by its opponents as inconclusive and erroneous. But we, the Congregation of the Believers in the Unity of God, accept the truth of all the three sources of knowledge,[5] and we add a fourth source, which we derive from the three preceding ones, and which has become a Root of Knowledge for us, namely, the truth of reliable Tradition.[6] For it is based on the knowledge of sense perception and the knowledge of Reason, as we shall explain in chapter 3 of this book.

These four Roots of Knowledge having been specified, we have now to explain in which way we may rely on them for evidence of truth.

[1] In a passage not included in this Selection. See, however, below, p. 62, n. 4; p. 110, n. 3.

[2] i.e. less obvious and evident.

[3] The version given above is based on the reading of the Leningrad recension.

[4] Saadya refers to the well-known controversy between Parmenides and Heraclitos, which was resumed by the Mutakallimūn. Cf. Ventura, p. 83.

[5] The distinction between the three sources of knowledge as stated by Saadya was also upheld by the 'Faithful Brethren of Basra', but they defined Reason as that which is acquired by speculation, not as the axioms of self-evident truth. Cf. Heschel *loc. cit.*, p. 280, n. 73; Ventura p. 83.

[6] Arab. *al-chabar aṣ-ṣādiḳ*. The Arabic term denotes both Kur'ān and Tradition. Saadya comprises in this term the written and oral traditions of Judaism.

First with regard to the knowledge of sense perception, whenever an object makes an impression on our normal sense organ by coming into contact with it,[1] we may safely believe without any doubt that it is in reality as we perceived it, provided we are sufficiently expert not to be misled by illusions, like the people who believe that the image which appears in the mirror is an image which has been actually created there, the truth being that it is the property of polished bodies to reflect the image of an object that faces them; or like those people who regard the image of a man's stature which appears in the water reversed as real and created in that moment, not knowing that the reason for this is that the depth of the water exceeds the height of the stature. If we are careful to avoid these and similar mistakes, the belief in sense perception will prove sound, and we shall not be misled by illusions, as is said, 'And they rose up early in the morning, and the sun shone upon the water, and the Moabites saw the water some way off as red as blood; and they said: This is blood' (2 Kings 3.22-3).

As to the knowledge of Reason we hold that every conception formed in our mind (Reason) which is free from defects is undoubtedly true knowledge, provided we know how to reason, complete the act of reasoning and guard against illusions and dreams. For there are people who affirm that the images one sees in a dream are real things which are created.[2] They are driven to this assumption in order not to have to reject the testimony of the senses. They do not know that some dreams are produced from the thoughts of yesterday which pass through the mind; of these it is said, 'For a dream cometh through a multitude of business' (Eccl. 5.2); or that other dreams are due to the food they have eaten, which may have been too hot or too cold, too much or too little; in regard to these Scripture says, '. . . As when a hungry man dreameth, and, behold, he eateth . . . or as when a thirsty man dreameth, and, behold, he drinketh . . .' (Isa. 29.8); or that still other dreams are caused by the preponderance of one of the humours

[1] Saadya holds, with Aristotle, that perception comes about when a particular element in an object comes in contact with the same element in the sense organ. Cf. *Amānāt*, p. 60 (32); Aristotle, *De sensu*, 2.

[2] Ibn Ḥazm reports that in the opinion of Ṣāliḥ Kubba, one of the disciples of the Muʻtazilite al-Naẓẓām, everything one sees in dreams conforms to reality: an inhabitant of Andalusia who sees himself in China whilst dreaming must have been actually transferred by God to China during that moment. Cf. Ventura, p. 84.

in the temperament[1] — the hot and the moist create the illusion of joy and pleasure, while the dry produces the illusion of grief and sorrow; of this the suffering Job[2] said, 'When I say: my bed shall comfort me, my couch shall ease my complaint; then Thou scarest me with dreams, and terrifiest me through visions' (Job 7.13-14). But dreams also contain a flash of inspiration from above in the form of illuminating hints and images, as is said, 'In thoughts from the visions of the night, when deep sleep falleth on men' (Job 4.13).

As to inferential knowledge the position is this: if we perceive a certain object with our senses and accept it as actually existing, but are unable to believe firmly that this object exists unless we believe that some other things co-exist with it, then it is necessary for us to believe in the existence of all those things be they a few or many. For the sense perception concerned could not have come to us without them. There may be one such inferred object or there may be two, three, four or more. Whatever the conclusion may be, it must be upheld because neither the sense perception nor any of these inferential notions can be denied.

An example of the inference of a single object is the following: if we see smoke without seeing the fire which produces the smoke, it is necessary for us to believe in the existence of the fire on account of the existence of the smoke because the one could not be accounted for without the other. Similarly, if we hear the voice of a man from behind a wall, it is necessary for us to believe in his presence there, for there could be no voice of a man unless from one who was present. An example of more than one single inference is the case when we see food being absorbed into the stomach of an animal in solid form and re-emerge in the form of waste. If we do not believe in the performance of four different functions, our sense perception could not be accounted for. These functions are performed (1) by the power of attracting nourishment into the body; (2) the power of retaining the food until it is thoroughly softened; (3) the power of digestion and assimila-

---

[1] Cf. H. A. Wolfson, *JQR*, Vol. 33 (1942-43), p. 237, n. 103; see also the Translator's article in *Melilah* (ed. E. Robertson and M. Wallenstein), 1944, p. 11, n. 65. The four humours correspond to the four qualities (warm, cold, dry, moist) and to the four temperaments.

[2] Lit. 'the suffering man smitten with illness'.

tion; and (4) the power of expelling from the body what has become waste.[1] Since our sense perception can only be accounted for by the performance of these four functions, it is necessary to believe that they actually take place.

The character of inferential knowledge having been explained, it is necessary for us to draw attention to certain mistakes against which one must guard, for most of the controversies between men and most of their differences in methods of argument arise from these mistakes.

(1) If someone declares that he believes in such and such a thing, because otherwise he would have to deny some sense perception, it is necessary for us to consider whether the sense perception could occur without that other thing which he believes. If this is the case, his belief is invalidated. Some people, for instance, believe that the whiteness of the Milky Way, which is testified by sense perception, is due to the fact that originally the rotation of the sun followed that course.[2] But if we examine the facts we find that other explanations are possible. The phenomenon may be caused by rising vapours or by fixed luminous particles or by an accumulation of small stars or similar causes. Thus their statement is invalidated.

(2) If someone declares that he believes in such and such a thing because, otherwise, he would have to deny some proposition furnished by Reason, it is necessary for us to consider whether this proposition would be true without the thing which he believes. In such case his belief would be invalidated. Some people, for instance, assert that there exists more than one earth.[3] They argue that fire must occupy the centre of the universe since the most precious thing is invariably placed in the centre so as to be well guarded.[4] But in our opinion this belief[5] is equally safeguarded by our acknowledgment that man

---

[1] A detailed description of these four faculties and their functions is given by Josef b. Yehudah, the disciple of Maimonides, in his *Sefer Mussar* (ed. W. Bacher), pp. 43-6.

[2] Cf. Aristotle, *Meteorologica*, I, 8, in the name of some Pythagoreans.

[3] Cf. below, p. 53, n. 2.

[4] Cf. Aristotle, *De Caelo*, II, 13, 293a, in the name of the Pythagoreans. The assumption is that the fire is the most precious element and must therefore be surrounded by a circle of earths since 'the most precious place befits the most precious thing'. Cf. below, pp. 115-6.

[5] i.e. the proposition derived purely from the reason that the most precious thing is always placed in the centre.

40

lives upon this earth which is the centre of the universe.[1] Thus their assertion is invalidated.

(3) If someone declares that he believes that such and such an inference must be drawn from some sense perception, but this belief of his is inconsistent with some other sense perception, we have to weigh which is the more decisive of the two sense perceptions and judge accordingly. Some people, for instance, assert that all things originated from water[2] because all living beings come from a moist substance.[3] But they ignore another testimony of their senses, namely the fact that water is fluid and flows off. It is impossible to assume that it is the basic element[4] seeing that it cannot stay by itself. If two arguments like these clash, it is proper that we should give preference to the more decisive one.

(4) If someone declares that he believes that such and such an inference must be drawn from some sense perception, but his statement involves a contradiction, it must be considered as false. Some people, for instance, assert that the good is identical with the pleasant,[5] because this is what sense perception suggests to them. But they fail to remember that to kill them affords pleasure to their enemies in much the same way as killing their enemies affords pleasure to them. Thus good and evil will be present in the same act, which is self-contradictory.[6]

(5) If someone declares that he believes such and such a thing for such and such a reason, and, upon examining his reason, we find that it necessitates something different which he does not believe, his belief is rendered invalid.[7] Those, for instance, who affirm the pre-existence of the world, declare that they believe the universe to be without beginning in time,

---

[1] If we assign central importance to the human race, we must assume that the earth is placed in the centre of the universe.

[2] The well-known view of Thales of Milet.

[3] Arab. *'unsur;* element, origin.

[4] Lit. 'root'.

[5] The hedonistic view of the Epicureans, which dominates also Plato's earlier dialogues.

[6] Saadya uses this argument again below, pp. 99-100, where he is concerned with the rational character of the Law and combats the hedonistic view on grounds of Reason.

[7] In other words, a belief which does not conform to the principle on which it is assumedly based is inadmissible.

because they want to accept as true only what they perceive with their senses.[1] But if they accept as true only what their senses perceive, this principle should also preclude their view that the world is without beginning in time, since it is impossible for them to perceive with their senses the timeless in its original state.

Likewise, if someone declares that he rejects such and such a thing for such and such a reason, but we find that in fact he involves himself in an even greater difficulty than the one he tried to avoid, his assertion will be invalid. Thus some of those who affirm the Unity of God refuse to admit that God is unable to bring back yesterday, so as not to attribute to him any lack of power, but they involve themselves in an even more serious difficulty in that they attribute to Him something absurd, as will be pointed out, please God, in part of chapter 2.[2]

In endeavouring to establish the truth of inferential know-ledge we shall henceforth be on guard against these five possible forms of mistakes, namely, (1) that it does not conflict with knowledge established by sense perception; (2) that it does not conflict with knowledge established by Reason; (3) that it should not conflict with some other truths; (4) that it should not be self-contradictory, still more that it should not (5) involve a difficulty more serious than the one intended to avoid. The first and primary condition, however, is that we should carefully apply our experience[3] to our interpretation of sense perceptions and of the dictates of Reason as described. In addition, we have to persevere in the work of rational inquiry until its final completion so that altogether seven con-ditions have to be fulfilled in order to bring out the clear truth. If, therefore, someone who is not a member of our people comes forward with certain arguments based on inferential knowledge we have to examine his statement in the light of the above seven conditions. If it stands their test and is proved correct when weighed in their balances, it is the clear truth which we, too, have to accept.

We shall employ similar rules in dealing with the reliable

---

[1] Cf. above, p. 37.
[3] Cf. *Amānāt*, p. 108 (56).
[2] Which teaches us to guard against illusions and dreams. Cf. above, p. 38.

Tradition, that is to say the Books of the Prophets. But this is not the place to explain the conditions peculiar to them. I have explained them at length in the Introduction to the Commentary on the Torah.[1]

4. REASON AND FAITH

(ed. Landauer 20.18-22.8; 24.14-26.17;
ed. Slucki 10.33-11.24;12.26-13.26)

It may be objected: 'How can we undertake to pursue knowledge by means of speculation and inquiry with the object of attaining mathematical certainty seeing that our people reject this manner of speculation as leading to unbelief[2] and the adoption of heretical views[3]?' Our answer is that only the ignorant speak thus.[4] Similarly one will find that the ignorant people in our town[5] are of opinion that every one who goes to India becomes rich. So, too, some of the ignorant people in our nation are said to think that the eclipse of the moon occurs whenever something resembling a dragon swallows the moon.[6] Some of the ignorant people in Arabia are said to hold the opinion that unless a man's camel is slaughtered over his grave, he will have to appear on foot on Judgment Day.[7] There exist many more ridiculous opinions like these. Another objection is that the greatest of the Sages of Israel prohibited this, and particularly the speculation on

[1] Saadya obviously refers to his extensive Commentary on the Pentateuch which he wrote for learned readers and from which only fragments have survived. The Introduction to his Translation (*tafsir*), which he wrote for the general public, contains no reference such as mentioned above. Cf. *Comm. Pent.*, pp. 1-4. Below, pp. 157-8, Saadya lays down four Rules for the interpretation of Scripture. There can be little doubt that this exegetical canon is identical with the rules mentioned in the above passage.

[2] Arab. *kufr*.

[3] Arab. *zandaka*

[4] Saadya's sharp rebuff of those who condemn philosophical speculation is matched by the equally sharp hostility towards him on the part of those who held that view. Moses Taku (1250-90) selected Saadya as his chief target of attack in denouncing philosophical speculation. Cf. J. Sarachek, *Faith and Reason*, 1935, p. 136.

[5] Baghdād.

[6] An Arabic folklore belief, which also occurs in Jewish sources. For the literature see Kaufmann, p. 449.

[7] Instead of riding on his camel. Cf. Pococke, *Specimen*, p. 65, quoted by Kaufmann, ibid.

the origin of Time and Space, when they declared, 'Whosoever speculates on four things should better not have been created: on what is above and what is below, what was in the beginning, and what will be in the end'.[1] Our answer is this: it cannot be thought that the Sages should have wished to prohibit us from rational inquiry seeing that our Creator has commanded us to engage in such inquiry in addition to accepting the reliable Tradition. Thus He said, 'Know ye not? Hear ye not? Hath it not been told you from the beginning? Have ye not understood the foundations of the earth?' (Isa. 40.21)[2]. The pious men said to each other, 'Let us choose for us that which is right; let us know among ourselves what is good' (Job 34.4), and, indeed, the five men, namely Job, Eliphaz, Bildad, Zopher and Elihu, had long discussions on this subject.

What, however, our Sages did try to prevent us from doing was to brush aside the prophetic Scriptures and to rely on our own personal judgments in our speculations on the origin of Space and Time. For one who speculates after this manner may sometimes find the truth and sometimes go astray; until he has found the truth, he will be without religion[3]; and even if he finds the truth of religion and clings to it, he is never sure that he will not depart from it should doubts arise in his mind and weaken his belief. All of us agree that one who acts in this way is a sinner, even though he may be a genuine philosopher. But we, the Congregation of the Children of Israel, have a different way of investigation and speculation, and it is this which I want to mention and explain with the help of God.

The reader of this book should know that we inquire and speculate in matters of our religion for two reasons: (1) in

[1] Ḥagigah 2.1. As Scholem (*EJ*, Vol. 9, col. 635) has pointed out, this Mishnah passage echoes the definition of Gnosis in the 'Excerpta ex Theodoto'. There can be no doubt that it was directed against the mounting tide of Gnostic speculation in Jewish circles, without, however, achieving much result. The Rabbis continued to engage in speculations on the subjects indicated in the above formula, as testified by the innumerable utterances on these matters scattered throughout Talmud and Midrash.

[2] Saadya emphasizes the necessity of knowing, hearing and understanding in addition to the acceptance of Tradition. He declares that philosophical speculation is a religious duty. Maimonides holds the same view. Cf. Leo Strauss, *Philosophie und Gesetz*, pp. 76 ff. In his *Comm. Yeṣ.*, p. 1 (14), Saadya describes Philosophy as 'comparable to that which is best amongst the works of the Creator'.

[3] Arab. *dīn*. Cf. *EI*, Vol. I, p. 975. In Saadya's terminology *dīn* denotes the sum total of revealed truths or the true revealed religion. Tibbon translates it by *dat*, sometimes by *Torah*. Cf. below, p. 47, n. 2; p. 95, n. 1.

order that we may find out for ourselves[1] what we know in the way of imparted knowledge from the Prophets of God; (2) in order that we may be able to refute those who attack us on matters connected with our religion. For our Lord (be He blessed and exalted) instructed us in everything which we require in the way of religion, through the intermediacy of the Prophets after having established for us the truth of prophecy by signs and miracles. He commanded us to believe these matters and to keep them. He also informed us that by speculation and inquiry we shall attain to certainty on every point in accordance with the Truth revealed through the words of His Messenger.

In this way we speculate and search in order that we may make our own[1] what our Lord has taught us by way of instruction. There is, however, another objection which we have to consider. It may be asked: If the doctrines of religion can be discovered by rational inquiry and speculation, as God has told us, how can it be reconciled with His wisdom that He announced them to us by way of prophetic Revelation and verified them by proofs and signs of a visible character, and not by rational arguments? To this we will give a complete answer with the help of God. We say: God knew in His wisdom that the final propositions which result from the labour of speculation can only be attained in a certain measure of time.[2] Had he, therefore, made us depend on speculation[3] for religious knowledge, we should have existed without religion for some time until the work of speculation was completed and our labour had come to an end. Perhaps many of us would never have completed the work because of their inability[4] and never have finished their labour because of their lack of patience;[5] or doubts may have come upon them, and confused and bewildered their minds. From all these troubles God (be He exalted and glorified) saved us quickly by sending us His Messenger, announcing through him the Tradition, and allowing us to see with our own eyes signs in support of it and

[1] Lit. 'that it may become a matter of actual (*bi-l-fi'l*) knowledge to us'. For the term 'actual' cf. below, p. 57, n. 6.
[2] Cf. above, pp. 31–2.
[3] Lit. 'transferred our debt to it', i.e. to speculation; Tibbon's translation uses the Talmudic term *himḥah*, 'to give an order'.
[4] Because of their deficiency of skill in the art of speculation. Cf. above, pp. 26–8.
[5] Cf. above, pp. 26–8.

proofs which cannot be assailed by doubts, and which we can find no ground for rejecting, as is said, 'Ye yourselves have seen that I have talked with you from heaven' (Ex. 20.22). He spoke to His Messenger in our presence, and He based on this fact our obligation to believe him for ever, as He said, 'That the people may hear when I speak with thee, and may also believe thee for ever' (Ex. 19.9). So we were immediately obliged to accept the teaching of religion with all that it implies since it was verified by the testimony of sense perception, and its acceptance is obligatory on the strength of the reliable Tradition which has been handed down to us as we shall explain.[1] He commanded us to inquire patiently until the truth of Tradition was brought out by speculation, and not to depart from our religious position before its truth was verified, since we are obliged to believe in it on account of what we saw with our eyes and heard with our ears. In the case of some of us it may take a very long time until our speculation is completed, but we shall be none the worse for that, and if another one is held up in his studies on account of some hindrance, he will nevertheless not remain without religion. Even women and children and people incapable of speculation will possess a complete religion and be aware of its truths, for all human beings are equal so far as the knowledge of the senses is concerned. Praise unto Him Whose wisdom guideth man! This is why we find that the Torah mentions in many passages children and women in addition to the men when speaking of signs and miracles.

To make the matter clearer, let us suppose that someone who possesses 1000 dinar distributes this money in the following way:[2]

$$5 \text{ persons receive each } 20\tfrac{2}{5} \text{ dinar,} = 102$$
$$6 \text{ persons receive each } 16\tfrac{2}{3} \text{ dinar,} = 100$$
$$7 \text{ persons receive each } 14\tfrac{2}{7} \text{ dinar,} = 100$$
$$8 \text{ persons receive each } 12\tfrac{3}{8} \text{ dinar,} = 99$$
$$9 \text{ persons receive each } 11 \quad \text{dinar,} = 99$$

$$500$$

[1] Cf. below, pp. 108-11.
[2] The following account is one of the numerous instances in which Saadya indulges 'in his favourite hobby of arithmetical calculations'. Cf. Gandz, 'Saadia Gaon as a Mathematician', in *Saadya Anniversary Volume*, New York, 1943, p. 187.

He wishes to show his friends without delay how much of the money is left in his hands. He, therefore, tells them that the balance left amounts to 500 dinar and proves it by weighing the gold that is left in his hands. After he has weighed it in their presence, and the amount of 500 dinar has been established, his friends are obliged to believe what he told them. They are now at leisure to arrive at the same knowledge by a different method, namely, by working it out arithmetically, each according to his capacity and understanding, provided no hindrance arises through adverse conditions.[1] Another illustration: One may diagnose rapidly a certain malady on the evidence of some obvious symptom long before another reaches the same conclusion after an exhaustive examination.

It is desirable that we should further believe that even prior to the existence of the children of Israel God imparted our religion[2] to humanity[3] by means of prophecy, wondrous signs, miracles and manifestations.[4] Those who were present were convinced by what they had perceived with their own eyes; those who received a tradition in regard to it were convinced by what they had perceived with their own ears, as the Torah says, with reference to some of them, 'For I have known him (Abraham), to the end that he may command his children' (Gen. 18.19).

[1] Saadya speaks of two kinds of tests for the verification of truth: one is the quick and easy one, and the other the slow and difficult one. One who wants to know how much money he has distributed and how much is left, may simply weigh the gold that was left in his hand, which is the easy and quick way. The other slow and difficult test is to figure out the sums of all the shares, add them and deduct the sum total from the original sum. Cf. Gandz, *loc. cit.*

[2] Arab. *din*; Tibbon translates it here by *Torah.* cf. above, p. 44, n. 3;

[3] Lit. 'To His creatures'.

[4] Saadya obviously refers to the Revelations to Adam, Noah and Abraham.

CHAPTER I

CREATIO EX NIHILO[1]

1. The Nature of the Problem

(ed. Landauer 30.8-32.10;
ed. Slucki 15.1-16.13)

THE problem dealt with in this chapter is one on which we have no data from actual observation or from sense-perception, but conclusions on which can be derived only from postulates of the pure Reason. We mean the problem of the origin of the world.[2] The ultimate proposition which we seek to establish is of a very subtle nature. It cannot be grasped by the senses, and one can only endeavour to comprehend it by thought. This being the nature of the subject, one who inquires into it must necessarily expect to arrive at results of a corresponding nature, and one ought not to reject such results, or try to obtain results of a different character. It is quite certain that the origin of things is a matter concerning which no human being was ever able to give evidence as an eye-witness. But we all seek to probe this distant and profound matter which is beyond the grasp of our senses, and regarding which it has been said by the wise king, 'That which was[3] is far off, and exceeding deep; who can find it out?' (Eccl. 7.24). Should, therefore, our inquiry lead us to the conclusion that all things were created *ex nihilo* — a thing the like of which was never experienced by sense perception — we have no right to reject it out of hand on the ground that we never experienced the like of it, so how can we believe it; for what we tried to find from the very outset of our inquiry was precisely something the like of which we never experienced. We must welcome this solution and rejoice in it, since it presents a success on our part in attaining the object of our inquiry.

I thought it necessary to make the above introductory remark in order to warn the reader of this book not to expect

[1] For a full discussion of this chapter cf. Guttmann, pp. 33-84; Ventura, pp. 92-171.
[2] Lit. 'How the things were prior to us'.
[3] i.e. in the beginning.

49

me to demonstrate the *creatio ex nihilo* by way of sense perception. I have made it clear in my Introduction that if this
were possible there would be no need for argument or speculation or logical inferences. Furthermore, there would be agreement between us and all other people in regard to its truth,[1]
and opinions would not be divided on any point connected
with this problem. But in fact we do depend on speculation to
reveal to us the truth of the matter, and on arguments to clarify
it, since it in no way comes within the domain of experience
or sense perception.

We are, in fact, not the only ones who have agreed to accept
a cosmological theory which has no basis in sense perception.[2]
All those who discuss this problem and seek a solution are
agreed on this point. Those, for instance, who believe in the
eternity of the world[3] seek to prove the existence of something
which has neither beginning nor end. Surely, they never came
across a thing which they perceived with their senses to be
without beginning or end, but they seek to establish their
theory by means of postulates of Reason. Likewise, the
Dualists exert themselves to prove the co-existence of two
separate and opposing principles, the mixture of which caused
the world to come into being.[4] Surely they never witnessed
two separate and opposing principles, nor the assumed process
of mixture, but they try to produce arguments derived from
the pure Reason in favour of their theory. In a similar way,
those who believe in an eternal Matter[5] regard it as a *Hyle*,[6]
i.e. something in which there is originally no quality of hot
or cold, moist or dry, but which becomes transformed by a
certain force and thus produces those four qualities.[7] Surely
their senses never perceived a thing which is lacking in all those
four qualities, nor did they ever perceive a process of trans-

---

[1] Lit. 'existence', i.e. of the *creatio ex nihilo*.
[2] Lit. 'to admit something in the beginning, the like of which we have never seen'.
[3] Arab. *ashāb al-dahr*. Saadya refers to the theory of contemporary sensualists who professed to accept the verdict of their senses only. Their view, called *dahriyya*, is mentioned by many Arabic writers. Cf. Ventura, pp. 148 ff.
[4] Saadya refers to the doctrine of the Manichaeans. See below, pp. 69–73.
[5] Arab. *ashāb al-tīna al-kadīma*. On the use of *tīna*, clay, in the sense of matter, which is copied by the Hebrew term *hōmer*, clay, for matter, see Pines, p. 39, n. 2.
[6] Arab. *hayūlā*; Hebr. *hayyūlē*.
[7] The Platonic view. Cf. *Timaeus* 52 D. Plato himself did not employ the word ὕλη in the sense of 'raw material' of any process of construction or 'matter' in the Aristotelian sense. Cf. A. E. Taylor, *A Commentary on Plato's Timaeus* (1928), p. 493.

formation and the generation of the four qualities such as is suggested. But they seek to prove their theory by means of arguments drawn from the pure Reason. And so it is with all other opinions, as I shall explain later. This being so, it is clear that all have agreed to accept some view concerning the origin of the world which has no basis in sense perception. If, therefore, our treatment of the subject produces something similar, namely, the doctrine of the *creatio ex nihilo*, let the reader of this book who inquires into this problem not be hasty in rejecting our theory, since from the very outset of his inquiry he was virtually asking for some result similar to this, and every student of this problem is asking for such a result. But the reader may be assured that our arguments are stronger than theirs, and that, moreover, we are in a position to disprove their arguments, whatever their school of thought. We have, too, the advantage of being supported in our doctrine by the signs and miracles of Scripture which were intended to confirm our belief. I would ask the reader to bear in mind these three facts which will meet him in every part of this book, namely, (1) that our arguments are stronger than theirs; (2) that we are able to disprove the arguments of our opponents; and (3) that we have in the bargain the testimony of the miracles narrated in Scripture.

2. FOUR ARGUMENTS FOR CREATION[1]

(ed. Landauer 32.10-37.9;
ed. Slucki 16.14-20.10)

From these introductory remarks I go on to affirm that our Lord (be He exalted) has informed us that all things were created in time, and that He created them *ex nihilo*, as it is said, 'In the beginning God created[2] the heaven and the earth' (Gen.

[1] For an analysis of the following exposition cf. in particular H. A. Wolfson, 'The Kalam Arguments for Creation in Saadya, Averroes, Maimonides and St. Thomas,' in *Saadya Anniversary Volume*, New York, 1943, pp. 197 ff.

[2] The verb *bara'*, by which Gen. 1.1 denotes the act of creation, is used only with reference to God. It implies the totally new and unprecedented. Cf. B. Jacob, *Genesis* (1934), pp. 20-2. Doubt has been expressed as to whether *bara'* necessarily implies the idea of a *creatio ex nihilo*. Cf. S. R. Driver, *The Book of Genesis*, p. 3. Saadya asserts that this is the case. Cf. his *Comm. Isaiah*, p. 123; Ventura, p. 110. He is followed by Naḥmanides (*Comm. Gen.* 1.21), Maimonides (*Moreh* II.30; III.10), and others, whereas Abraham ibn Ezra holds that *bara'* does not necessarily convey this meaning. Cf. A. Schmiedl. *Studien* (1869), p. 94.

1.1), and as it is further said, 'I am the Lord that maketh all things; that stretched forth the heavens alone; that spread abroad the earth by Myself' (Isa. 44.24). He verified this truth for us by signs and miracles, and we have accepted it. I probed further into this matter with the object of finding out whether it could be verified by speculation as it had been verified by prophecy. I found that this was the case for a number of reasons, from which, for the sake of brevity, I select the following four.[1]

(1) The first proof is based on the finite character of the universe. It is clear that heaven and earth are finite in magnitude,[2] since the earth occupies the centre and the heaven revolves round it. From this it follows that the force residing in them is finite in magnitude.[3] For it is impossible for an infinite force to reside in a body which is finite in magnitude. This would be contradictory to the dictates of Reason. Since, therefore, the force which preserves[4] heaven and earth is finite, it necessarily follows that the world has a beginning and an end.[5] Being struck by the force of this argument, I subjected it to a close examination, taking good care not to be hasty in drawing definite conclusions before having scrutinized it. I, therefore, asked myself: Perhaps the earth is infinite in length, breadth and depth? I answered: If this were the case, the sun could not encompass it and complete his revolution once every day and night, rising again in the place in which he rose the day before, and setting again in the place in which he set the

---

[1] All the four proofs are borrowed from the Kalam. Maimonides' list of seven Kalam proofs includes three of Saadya's four. Cf. Wolfson, *loc. cit.*, pp. 197-8.

[2] Cf. Aristotle, *De caelo* I, 5-7.

[3] Cf. Aristotle, *Physica* VIII, 10.

[4] Aristotle speaks of the force which causes the *motion* of the world. Saadya, who describes the force in question as one which *preserves* the world, i.e. keeps it from corruption, follows a line of argument reported in the name of John Philoponos, who argued that the force which keeps the world from corruption must be finite. Cf. Wolfson, *loc. cit.*, p. 201-3.

[5] John Philoponos concluded from the corruptibility of the world its createdness on the basis of the Aristotelian principle that 'Whatever is corruptible must be generated'. Cf. *De caelo* I, 12, 282 b, 2. Saadya's argument must be interpreted in the light of this original version of the idea. Aristotle's own view is that beyond the finite force which is within the body of the world there must be an external bodiless force which causes motion to continue during an *infinite* time. Cf. *Physica* VIII, 10, 266 a, 10-11; 267 b, 17-26. John Philoponos rejects this assumption on the grounds of Aristotle's own principle, 'That it is impossible that that which is capable of corruption should not at some time be corrupted'. Cf. *De caelo* 283 a, 24-5. Saadya omits this essential proposition. See Wolfson, *loc. cit.*

day before; and so with the moon and the stars. Then I asked myself: Perhaps the heaven is infinite? To this I answered: How could this be the case seeing that all celestial bodies are moving and continually revolving round the earth?[1] For it cannot be supposed that only the sphere that is next to us performs this rotation, whereas the others are too large to perform any movement. For by 'heaven' we understand the body which revolves, and we are not aware of anything else beyond it, far less do we believe it to be the heaven and not revolving. Then I explored further and asked: Perhaps there exists a plurality of earths and heavens, each heaven revolving round its earth. This would involve the assumption of the co-existence of an infinite number of worlds,[2] a thing in its nature[3] impossible. For it is inconceivable that, nature being what it is, some earth should exist above the fire, or that air should be found beneath the water. For both fire and air are light, and both earth and water are heavy. I cannot doubt that if there were a clod of earth outside our earth, it would break through all air and fire until it reached the dust of our earth. The same would happen if there were a mass of water outside the waters of our oceans. It would cut through air and fire until it met our waters. It is, therefore, perfectly clear to me that there exists no heaven apart from our heaven, and no earth except our earth; moreover, that this heaven and this earth are finite, and that in the same way as their bodies are limited, their respective force, too, is limited and ceases to exist once it reaches its limit. It is impossible that heaven and earth should continue to exist after their force is spent, and that they should have existed before their force came into being. I found that Scripture testifies to the finite character of the world by saying, 'From the one end of the earth, even unto the other end of the earth' (Deut. 13.8), and, 'From the one end of heaven unto the other' (Deut. 4.32). It further testifies that the sun revolves round the earth and

[1] Cf. Aristotle, *De caelo* I, 5, 271 b, 26: 'The body which moves in a circle must necessarily be finite in every respect'.

[2] Cf. Aristotle, *De caelo* I, 6, 274 a, 26-8; II, 13, 293 a, 24-5; Plato, *Tim.* 31 A, B. Saadya mentions this view also in his *Comm. Yeṣ.*, p. 5 (19). Crescas discusses it in connection with his criticism of Maimonides' proofs of the existence of God. Cf. H. A. Wolfson, *Crescas' Critique of Aristotle* (1929), p. 472.

[3] Lit. 'in a natural way'. This does not mean 'according to the laws of Nature', as Fürst translates, but 'in its natural place'. Every body has its natural place towards which it tends and moves unless impeded by force. Cf. Aristotle, *Physica* IV, 5, 212 b, 29; Ventura, p. 97.

completes its circle every day by saying, 'The sun also ariseth, and the sun goeth down, and hasteneth to his place where he ariseth' (Eccl. 1.5).

(2) The second proof is derived from the union of parts and the composition of segments. I saw that bodies consist of combined parts and segments fitted together. This clearly indicated to me that they are the skilful work of a skilful artisan and creator.[1] Then I asked myself: Perhaps these unions and combinations are peculiar to the small bodies only, that is to say the bodies of the animals and plants. I, therefore, extended my observation to the earth, and found the same was true of her. For she is a union of soil and stone and sand, and the like.[2] Then I turned my mental gaze to the heavens and found that in them there are many layers of spheres,[3] one within another, and that there are in them also groups of luminaries called stars which are distinguished from one another by being great or small, and by being more luminous or less luminous, and these luminaries are set in those spheres.[4] Having noted these clear signs of the union and composition which has been created in the body of the heaven and the other bodies, I believe also, on the strength of this proof, that the heaven and all it contains are created. I found that Scripture also declares that the separateness of the parts of the organisms and their combination prove that they

[1] As Wolfson has shown, Saadya's argument is from design, not from the mere fact of composition. Aristotle proved the existence of God from the composite nature of the world, but held that the world was eternal and determined by an immutable order. Cf. *Physica* I, 7; *Metaphysica* I, 3, 984 a, 21-5; XII, 3, 1096 b, 35-1070 a, 2. Saadya's argument is directed against Aristotle in that it emphasizes not the immutable order of the world, but the fact that the composition of heaven and earth exhibits a certain degree of arbitrariness and deviation from order, which can only be explained by reference to the design of a creator. Cf. Wolfson, *loc. cit.*, pp. 204-8.

[2] Saadya makes no mention of the world being composed of matter and form, according to Aristotle, or of atoms and accidents, according to the Kalam, since he wishes to emphasize the aspect of arbitrary design, not the one of order, as explained in the preceding note. Cf. Wolfson, *loc. cit.* Apart from this motive, he adopts neither the Aristotelian distinction between matter and form, nor the Kalam notion of the atom. Cf. Ventura, p. 102.

[3] The spheres of the planets were considered to be set one within another like the 'coats of an onion'. Cf. Maimonides, *Yes. ha-Torah* 3.2; Dieterici, *Philosophie der Araber*, vol. I, p. 179; M. Sachs, *Die religiöse Poesie der Juden in Spanien* (1845), p. 230.

[4] Since Saadya shares the Aristotelian view that the heavens consist of a subtle ether which is wholly homogeneous (cf. below, pp. 145-6), he speaks of the composite nature of the heavens only with reference to their size, form and movements. Cf. *Amānāt*, p. 282 (144); *Comm. Yeṣ.*, p. 33 (53-54); Guttmann, p. 38; Ventura, p. 99, n. 29. By stressing the difference of the stars in size and degree of light, Saadya clearly shows that his argument is one from design.

are created. In regard to man it is said, 'Thy hands have made me and fashioned me' (Ps. 119.73); in regard to the earth it is said, 'He is God, that formed the earth and made it, He established it' (Isa. 45.18); in regard to the heaven it is said, 'When I behold Thy heavens, the work of Thy fingers, the moon and the stars, which Thou hast established' (Ps. 8.4).

(3) The third proof[1] is based on the nature of the accidents.[2] I found that no bodies are devoid of accidents which affect them either directly or indirectly.[3] Animals, e.g. are generated, grow until they reach their maturity, then waste away and decompose. I then said to myself: Perhaps the earth as a whole is free from these accidents? On reflection, however, I found that the earth is inseparable from plants and animals which themselves are created, and it is well known that whatsoever is inseparable from things created must likewise be created.[4] Then I asked myself: Perhaps the heavens are free from such accidents?[5] But, going into the matter, I found that this was not the case. The first and principal accident affecting them is their intrinsic movement which goes on without pause. There are, however, many different kinds of movement. If you compare them, you will find that some planets move slowly, others quickly. And another kind of accident is the transmission of light from one celestial body to another one, which becomes illumined by it, like the moon. The colours of the various stars also differ. Some are whitish, some reddish, others yellowish and greenish.[6] Having thus established that these bodies are affected by accidents which are coeval with them, I

[1] Averroes ascribes this argument to the Ash'arites. There exist two versions of it, an earlier and a later one. Saadya uses the earlier version. Cf. Wolfson, *loc. cit.*, p. 211-4.
[2] Arab. *'arad*, Hebr. *mikreh*. The Arabic philosophers restrict the use of the term to the 2-10 Aristotelian categories, whereas the Mutakallimūn use it in a very wide sense for everything that is not substance (*djawhar*). Cf. *EI*, I, 417. According to some Mu'tazilites, the term includes movement and rest, standing and sitting, composition and separation, length and breadth, colours, tastes, and smells, speech and silence, etc. Ibn al-Murtaba compiled a list of 19 accidents. Cf. Pines, pp. 19-20. Saadya employs the term in this wide sense, but he does not follow the Mu'tazilite view, which combines the doctrine of the accidents with the doctrine of the atoms.
[3] Directly, like generation and corruption; indirectly, like reflected light, or animals and plants as they affect the earth. Cf. Ventura, p. 103.
[4] Cf. *Kuzari*, V, 18; *Moreh*, I, 74.5.
[5] According to Aristotle, the celestial bodies are not affected by accidents; their circular motion being eternal, the spheres which perform those motions are likewise eternal. Cf. *Metaphysica*, XII, 7; *Moreh*, I, 74.4; Guttmann, p. 39.
[6] As to the coloration of the stars, cf. Plato, *Rep.* 616 e-617 b; Plotinus, *En.* II, 1.7.

firmly believe that everything which has accidents coeval with it must be created like the accident, since the accident enters into its definition.[1] Scripture also uses the accidents of heaven and earth as argument for their beginning in time by saying, 'I, even I, have made the earth and created man upon it; I, even My hands, have stretched out the heavens, and all their hosts have I commanded' (Isa. 45.12).

(4) The fourth proof is based on the nature of Time.[2] I know that time is threefold: past, present and future. Although the present is smaller than any instant, I take the instant as one takes a point[3] and say: If a man should try in his thought to ascend from that point in time to the uppermost point, it would be impossible for him to do so, inasmuch as time is now assumed to be infinite and it is impossible for thought to penetrate to the furthest point of that which is infinite.[4] The same reason will also make it impossible that the process of generation should traverse an infinite period down to the lowest point so as ultimately to reach us. Yet if the process of generation did not reach us, we would not be generated, from which it necessarily follows that we, the multitude of generated beings, would not be generated and the beings now existent would not be existent. And since I find myself existent, I know that the process of generation has traversed time until it has reached us, and that if time were not finite, the process of generation would not have traversed it. I profess unhesitatingly the same belief with regard to future time as with regard to past time.[5] I find

[1] The definition of the celestial bodies includes both their substance and their accidents, such as motion, colour, etc.

[2] Cf. Aristotle, *Metaphysica*, I, 2, 994 a, 18-19; *Physica*, VIII, 5, 256 a, 11-12; Themistius, *De caelo*, I, 1; Baḥya, *Ḥoḇōt hal-Leḇaḇōt*, I, 5; *Kuzari*, V, 18; *Moreh*, I, 73 (2); 74 (2); Spinoza, *Cogitata metaphysica*, II.10; Wolfson, *Crescas' Critique of Aristotle*, pp. 492-3; Z. Diesendruck, 'Saadya's Formulation of the Time-Argument for Creation', in *Jewish Studies in Memory of George A. Kohut* (1935), pp. 145-58; Wolfson, *Kalam Arguments*, etc., pp. 214-29.

[3] The present is a mere geometrical point. Cf. Klatzkin-Zobel, Vol. III, p. 65.

[4] The first part of the argument is based on Aristotle's definition of the infinite as 'that which cannot be traversed'. Saadya paraphrases Aristotle's statement that 'It is impossible to traverse infinites by thought: consequently there are infinites neither upwards nor downwards' (*Anal. Post.*, I, 22, 83 b, 6-7). The term 'Uppermost point' (*suʿd*) used by Saadya corresponds to the 'Beginning' (ἀρχή) and 'First' (πρῶτον) in Aristotle. Like Aristotle, Saadya holds that in an infinite series there is no beginning and no first which thought could reach. Cf. Wolfson, *Kalam Arguments*, etc., p. 215.

[5] The basis of this argument is the principle that 'If there is no first there is no cause at all'. Cf. Aristotle, *Metaphysica*, II, 2, 994 a, 18-19. Aristotle himself, however, combines the principle of the impossibility of an infinite series with the principle of the eternity of the world by distinguishing between an essential causal series and an

that Scripture speaks in similar terms of the far distant time by saying, 'All men have looked thereon; man beholdeth it afar off' (Job 36.25); and the faithful one says, 'I will fetch my knowledge from afar' (Job 36.3).

It has come to my notice that a certain heretic in conversation with one of the Believers in the Unity (of God) objected to this proof. He said: 'It is possible for a man to traverse that which has an infinite number of parts by walking. For if we consider any distance which a man walks, be it a mile, or an ell, we shall find that it can be divided into an infinite number of parts.'[1] To answer this argument some thinkers resorted to the doctrine of the indivisible atom.[2] Others spoke of *tafra* (the leap).[3] Others again asserted that all the parts (in space) are covered by corresponding parts (in time).[4] Having carefully examined the objection raised I found it to be a sophism for this reason: the infinite divisibility of a thing is only a matter of imagination,[5] but not a matter of reality.[6] It is too subtle to be a matter of reality, and no such division occurs. Now if the process of generation had traversed the past in the imagination, and not in reality, then, by my life, the objection raised would be valid. But seeing that the process of generation has traversed the real time and reached us, the argument cannot invalidate our proof, because infinite divisibility exists only in the imagination.

In addition to these four proofs, there are some more, part

---

[1] The well-known argument of Zeno.

[2] Ibn Ḥazm in the first of his five proofs for the existence of the atom argues: If there were no indivisible atom one would traverse an infinite space by walking any distance. Cf. Pines, p. 11.

[3] According to Naẓẓām, a moving body does not touch all the parts of the space in which it moves, but leaps over some of them. Cf. Pines, ibid.; Guttmann, p. 43, n. 1.

[4] Cf. Aristotle, *Physica*, Vi, 1, 233 a, 21-3.

[5] Arab. *wahm*; Tibbon translates it by *maḥshaḫah*. The Arabic philosophers sometimes use the term *bi'-l-wahm* in the sense of 'potentially'. Cf. Pines, p. 12.

[6] Arab. *fi'l*; hebr. *pō'al*; actuality, reality. Naẓẓām seems to have assumed the actual existence of infinite parts. Ibn Sinna rejects this view. Cf. Pines, *ibid*. In admitting an infinite divisibility *in potentia*, Saadya follows Aristotle, *Physica*, III, 6, 206 b, 12-13; Ventura, p. 108.

---

accidental causal series. An infinite causal series is possible, according to him, when the causes and effects exist in succession to each other, which is the case with the relation of the successive revolutions of the spheres and with the successive generations of man. This 'accidental' series can go on to infinity. On the difference between Aristotle and the Kalam, which Saadya does not discuss, see Maimonides, *Moreh*, I, 73 (11); Wolfson, *loc. cit.*, pp. 222 ff.

of which I have adduced in my Commentary on Genesis,[1] others in my Commentary on Hilkōt Yeṣīrah,[2] and in my Refutation of Ḥiwi al-Balkhi,[3] in addition to more details which the reader will find in other books of mine. Moreover, the arguments employed by me in the present chapter in refutation of the various opponents of our belief, are all sources[4] of this belief, and strengthen and confirm it.

3. THE TRANSCENDENCE OF THE CREATOR; ARGUMENTS FOR THE CREATIO EX NIHILO

(ed. Landauer 37.11-41.10;
ed. Slucki 20.12-22.18)

Having made it perfectly clear to myself that all things are created, I considered the question whether it was possible that they had created themselves, or whether the only possible assumption is that they were created by someone external to them. In my view it is impossible that they should have created themselves, for a number of reasons of which I shall mention three. The first reason is this: Let us assume that an existing body has produced itself. It stands to reason that after having brought itself into existence that particular body should be stronger and more capable of producing its like than before. For if it was able to produce itself when it was in a relatively weak state, it should all the more be able to produce its like now that it is relatively strong. But seeing that it is incapable of creating its like now when it is relatively strong, it is absurd to think that it created itself when it was relatively weak. The second reason is: If we imagine that a thing has created itself, we shall find that the question of the time when it did so presents an insuperable difficulty. For if we say that the thing created itself before it came into being, then we assume that it

---

[1] In an extract from Saadya's lost Commentary on Genesis, which is extant in R. Yehudah b. Barzillai's Commentary on the *Sefer Yeṣīrah* (ed. S. J. Halberstam, Berlin, 1885), p. 89, reference is made to the argument for Creation from the fact that the created beings require time, space and a preserving force.

[2] Cf. *Comm. Yeṣ.*, pp. 3-4 (16-17); 11-12 (27-8).

[3] Cf. I. Davidson, *Saadia's Polemic against Ḥiwi al-Balkhi*, New York (1913), pp. 74-5, where it is said, 'Through them (i.e. the accidents) we learn that it (the world) is new (i.e. *creata ex nihilo*)'. See note 241 by Davidson.

[4] Arab. *mawādd*. Cf. above, p. 36, n. 1.

was non-existent at the time when it created itself, and obviously something non-existent cannot create a thing. If, on the other hand, we say that it created itself after it had come into being, the obvious comment is that after a thing has come into existence there is no need for it to create itself. There is no third instant between 'before' and 'after' except the present which, however, has no duration in which an action can take place.[1] The third reason is: If we assume that a body is able to create itself, we must necessarily admit that at the same time it is likewise capable of abstaining from the act of self-creation.[2] Under this assumption we shall find that the body is both existent and non-existent at the same time. For in speaking of the body as *capable*, we take it to be existent, but in going on to speak of it as being capable of abstaining from the act of self-creation, we assume it to be non-existent. Obviously, to attribute existence and non-existence to the same thing at the same time is utterly absurd. I found that Scripture had already anticipated the refutation of this belief, namely, that things created themselves, by saying, 'It is He that hath made us, not we' (Ps. 100.3),[3] and by rebuking the one who said, 'My river is mine own, and I have made it for myself' (Ez. 39.3).[4]

Having proved by these arguments that things can on no account have created themselves, and that they must necessarily be regarded as created by a Creator who is external to them, I tried to reason out an answer to the question whether the Creator made them from something (*prima materia*) or from nothing (*ex nihilo*) as revealed in the Scriptures.[5] I found that it is wrong to assume that things were created from something already existent. Such a view is self-contradictory, because the term *creation* implies that the substance[6] of the thing is created and has a beginning in time, whilst the qualifying statement, 'From something' implies that its substance was eternal, uncreated and without beginning in time. If we

[1] Cf. above, p. 56, n. 3.
[2] 'Capability' as distinct from necessity implies freedom of choice. Necessity of creation is incompatible with creation in time. Cf. *Moreh*, II, Prop. 18.
[3] Cf. the passage *Gen. R.* 100.1, which, after quoting Ps. 100.3, continues, 'R. Yehudah b. Simon said, "Ye shall know that the Lord God hath made us, and that we have not made ourselves".'
[4] Referring to Pharaoh and the Nile.
[5] Cf. above, p. 51, n. 2.
[6] Arab. *'ayn*; Hebr. *eṣem*.

assume that things were created *ex nihilo*, there is no self-contradiction.

Someone may raise the following objection: 'You have affirmed as a conclusion acceptable to Reason that things have a Creator because in the realm of sense perception you have witnessed that nothing is made without a maker. But you likewise find in the realm of sense perception that nothing comes from nothing.[1] Why, then, have you made use of the proposition that nothing is made except by a maker, and have ignored the proposition that everything comes from something already existent,[2] seeing that the two propositions are equally valid?' My answer is: The problem which forms the object of my inquiry, and to the solution of which my arguments are directed, is the question whether or not the world is created *ex nihilo*. Obviously it is inadmissible that a proposition which is under examination should be adduced as evidence in favour of itself against an alternative proposition.[3] We must seek evidence on its behalf from elsewhere; and since the principle that nothing is made except by a maker has a bearing on the subject-matter of our inquiry, I applied this to the solution of our problem, and it led to the conclusion that the world is created *ex nihilo*. I followed this procedure although I found that in certain cases it is permissible to use a proposition in this way as evidence;[4] but this is a subtle matter which lies outside the province of this book.[5] I, therefore, decided to leave it alone and to follow the plain course.

Another point which I made clear to myself is this: Whatever we imagine to be the thing from which the existent

---

[1] Lit. 'That everything comes into being from something'.

[2] Cf. Kaufmann, Attrib.-Lehre, p. 6, and Ventura, *loc. cit.*, p. 110, both of whom explain the sentence in the sense of 'Why did you accept as decisive the one sense experience and not the other?'

[3] Arab. *manzila*; Hebr. *ma'alah*; degree, rank, here used in the sense of proposition, conclusion. Cf. also *Amānāt*, p. 73 (39); Ventura, p. 111, n. 77. — Saadya's answer is that his aim is the solution of the problem whether or not the world is created *ex nihilo*. It would, therefore, have been a *petitio principii*, had he allowed the sense experience which testifies that nothing comes from nothing, to influence his rational argument.

[4] In the interpretation of this obscure sentence we follow Ventura (p. 111) against Kaufmann (Attrib.-Lehre, p. 7), although we admit that even Ventura's suggestion is not wholly satisfactory. According to Ventura, Saadya refers to the logical possibility of using the proposition as a premise on condition that the sense of the term is more comprehensive in the premise than in the conclusion.

[5] A distinction of this kind, Saadya means to say, is out of place in a book which is not a treatise on logic.

beings were created, it must necessarily be assumed to have existed from all eternity.[1] But if it were pre-existent, it would be equal to the Creator in regard to its eternity. From this it follows that God would not have had the power to create things out of it, since it would not have accepted His command, nor allowed itself to be affected according to His wish and shaped according to His design,[2] except if we were to imagine, in addition to these two, the existence of a third cause which intervened between the two with the result that the one of the two became the Maker, and the other the thing made. But such a view would postulate the existence of something which does not exist; for we have never found anything except a maker and the thing made.

I remembered further that the principal object of our inquiry was to find out who created the substance of things. Now it is well known to us that the maker must necessarily be prior to the thing made by him, and that, by virtue of his being prior to the substance of the thing, the thing becomes one that is created in time. Should we, however, believe the substance to be eternal, the maker would not be prior to the thing created by him, and neither of the two could claim priority so as to be the cause of the other's existence, which is completely absurd.

There is another point which I remembered: The assertion that God created the world from something already existent must inevitably lead to the conclusion that He created nothing at all. For the reason which causes us to think that the world originated from something (*prima materia*) is the fact that such is the way we find the objects of sense perception come into being. Now it is common ground that the objects of sense perception are also found to exist in Space and Time, in shape and form, in measured quantity, in a fixed position and mutual relation, and other similar conditions.[3] All of these experiences are on the same footing[4] as the experience that everything comes from something. Now if we are going to allow all these experiences their full weight and say that things were

---

[1] Arab. *ḳadīm*.
[2] Saadya advances the same argument in *Comm. Yeṣ.*, p. 4 (18). Cf. al-Sharastānī, I, p. 135; Guttmann, p. 44, n. 1.
[3] A reference to the ten Aristotelian Categories.
[4] Lit. 'have the same title'; Arab. *ḥaḳ*.

created from something which existed in Time, Space, form, quantity, position, relation, etc., all this would have to be considered as eternal, and nothing would remain to be created. Creation would become meaningless altogether.[1]

I went still further, arguing that if we fail to admit the existence of something which has nothing prior to it, it is impossible for us to accept the fact that there exists anything at all. For if we consider in our mind that one thing comes from another thing, we have to predicate the same thing of the second as of the first, and say that it could only have come into being from a third thing; the same predicate again must be made of the third thing, namely that it could only have come into being from a fourth thing, and so *ad infinitum*. Since, however, an infinite series cannot be completed, it follows that we are not in existence. But, behold, we are in existence, and unless the things which preceded us were finite (in number), they could not have been completed so as to reach us.[2]

What we have deduced from the postulates of Reason, has also been intimated in the Books of the Prophets, namely, that material bodies originate from the design of the Creator, as is said, 'Before the mountains were brought forth, or ever Thou hadst formed the earth and the world, even from everlasting to everlasting, Thou art God' (Ps. 90.2).

Having thus succeeded in demonstrating by argument these three principles, viz. that the things are created, that their Creator is external to them, and that He created them *ex nihilo*, as it has been verified by the Tradition of the Prophets and by miracles, and this opinion being the first one discussed in this chapter (which is devoted to a speculation on the origin of things) I will now proceed to deal, in the following, with twelve opinions which are held by those who disagree with us in regard to this doctrine.[3] Thus there are altogether thirteen opinions. I shall explain both the arguments put forward by the advocates of these opinions, and their refutation. Whenever their opinion seems to find support in Scripture, I shall elucidate the Scriptural passages concerned, with the help of God.[4]

[1] The same argument is found in *Comm. Yeṣ.*, p. 4 (18).
[2] Cf. above, p. 56.
[3] Arab. *'amānat*; Tibbon translates it by *'emunah*.
[4] The thirteen cosmological theories which Saadya discusses in this book are the following: (1) *Creatio ex nihilo* (cf. above); (2) Plato's Cosmology; (3) Theory of

4. A Refutation of Plato's Cosmology

(ed. Landauer 41.10-43.16;
ed. Slucki 22.19-23.27)

The Second Theory[1] is held by those who declare that the creator of material bodies had at his disposal incorporeal and eternal substances[2], from which he created composite bodies. They base their view on the principle that nothing comes from nothing. When they indulged in further flights of fancy and tried to picture to themselves how the creator made the composite things from incorporeal substances, they said: We imagine that he collected from them small points, i.e. indivisible particles — they assumed them to be finer than dust — and he formed of them a straight line. Then he split that line into two halves. Then he laid one half across the other at right angles in the form of the Greek letter χ[3] which resembles the form of the Arabic ﻻ (Lam Alif) without the base. Then he fastened them at the point of their meeting. After that he cut them from the point of their fastening, and made the one of them the great outer sphere, and the other the smaller spheres. Then he formed from these incorporeal particles a cone-shaped figure, and created from it the sphere[4] of fire. After that he formed from them an octahedron, and made from it the sphere

---

[1] Saadya refers here and in *Comm. Yeṣ.*, p. 4 (17 ff.) to Plato's Cosmology as outlined in the *Timaeus*, not to the Atomists, as Guttmann and Lambert suggested. Cf. Ventura, p. 116.

[2] Lit. 'Spiritual and eternal things'. The Arabs seem to have interpreted Plato's *prima materia* as 'fine particles'. Cf. al-Shahrastānī, II, p. 123; Guttmann, *loc. cit.*, p. 45. In *Comm. Yeṣ.* Saadya uses also the Platonic terms matter, mother, the simple thing, the simple principle, element besides *Hyle*. For a discussion of the Platonic view see F. M. Cornford, *Plato's Cosmology* (1937).

[3] The Arab. text reads, 'the Greek letter Sīn', which is obviously a copyist's mistake. The Hebrew edition of Constantinople has the figure χ as in *Timaeus*. Cf. Guttmann, p. 46, n. 2; Ventura, p. 116, n. 93.

[4] Arab. *dā'ir*; Hebr. *'agullah*; circle, sphere. Cf. Klatzkin-Zobel, Vol. III, pp. 123-5.

[5] Plato takes the pyramid as the element of fire. Cf. *Tim.*, 56 B.

---

emanation according to the Upanishads; (4) the Indian system of *Sankyo*; (5) the dualistic cosmogony of the Manichaeans; (6-7) two aspects of the Hippocratic system; (8) Aristotle's view; (9) the theory of the Atomists; (10) the system of the Sensualists who professed the eternity of the world (*dahriyya*); (11) the Sophistic view; (12) the view of empirical scepticism; (13) the view of absolute scepticism. — In *Comm. Yeṣ.* Saadya enumerates and discusses nine cosmological theories by following a different way of arrangement and leaving out a number of theories. For the identification of these theories see, in particular, Ventura, *loc. cit.*, pp. 113-71. — In the present Selection we shall present only Saadya's discussion of the Platonic (second) and dualistic (fifth) theories.

of the earth. Then he formed from them a dodecahedron, and produced from it the rotation of the air.[1] Then he formed from them an icosahedron, and created from it all the water.[2] They affirm all this as certain and believe it as a religious doctrine.[3] What has led them to this theory is the determination not to admit anything which contradicts our experience,[4] and these figures which they have elaborated are chosen because they bear a certain resemblance to the existing elements.[5]

I shall now set forth what has to be said against them in regard to these points. There are altogether twelve answers to their propositions, namely, the four arguments which we mentioned first, and which proved to us that all things are created; then the other four arguments which proved to us that the Creator created the world *ex nihilo*; and when they have digested these eight answers, I find four more which apply to them.

(1) They believe something the like of which cannot be found in our experience, viz. the existence of incorporeal things which they imagine to be like dust and hair, indeed finer than anything, and like indivisible particles. This is something which Reason cannot accept.[6]

(2) We find that those things, the existence of which they affirm, cannot be warm or cold or moist or dry because, according to their opinion, these four (qualities) are created from them. We further find that they cannot have colour, taste, smell, limit and quantity, nor be large in number or small in number, nor exist in Space and Time, because all these categories[7] are the attributes[8] of material bodies, and these things,

---

[1] According to Plato, the cube corresponds to the element of earth, and the octahedron to the element of air. Cf. *Tim.*, 55 D-56 B.

[2] This agrees with Plato's description. Plato also makes a mysterious reference to a fifth construction, the dodecahedron; 'And the God used it for the whole, making a pattern of animal figures thereon'. Cf. *Tim.*, 55 C. — It is possible that Saadya's account of the Cosmology of the *Timaeus* goes back to a version which differed from the original. Cf. Ventura, p. 119.

[3] The two terms ('doctrine' and 'belief') used in the title of the book appear here combined in the construction of the sentence. Cf. Translator's Introduction, pp. 19-20.

[4] Such as the statement that something comes from nothing.

[5] Cf. *Tim.*, 58 A, 61 C, 78 A, 54 E-56 E.

[6] Cf. above, p. 57.

[7] Lit. 'matters' (*ma'ānī*).

[8] Arab. *ṣifa*.

according to their opinion, are prior to material bodies. This is an additional point which Reason cannot accept.[1] In trying to avoid the admission that things were created *ex nihilo*, they have involved themselves in assumptions still more remote and improbable.

(3) I consider it improbable, nay, impossible, that something which possesses no shape or form should change in such a way as to transform itself into fire, water, air and earth; or that something which has neither length nor breadth nor depth should be shaped in such a way as to acquire length, breadth and depth; or that something which is not conditioned in any way[2] should change in such a way as to become subject to all the conditions experienced by us now.[3] If they hold that these changes and transformations are conceivable because the Creator is wise and capable of changing and transforming, then his wisdom and power must be equally capable of creating things *ex nihilo*, and we can dismiss this absurd notion of incorporeal substances.

(4) There is no evidence for their elaborate theory of the cutting, joining, crossing, fastening, second cutting and the other operations (of the Creator), because none of these things is susceptible of proof. They are mere conjectures and opinions. Nay, I find that they actually involve a self-contradiction. For if, according to their view, the Maker (*Demiurge*) is capable of transforming the incorporeal substances into bodies, he should be capable of performing the operation at one stroke, so that all their subdivisions are useless. But if, according to their opinion, he is incapable of working upon them otherwise than step by step, like the work of the created beings which proceeds from stage to stage,[4] then he should indeed be incapable altogether of transforming incorporeal substances into corporeal substances.[5] They have to bear with all these absurdities

---

[1] Similarly, Aristotle argues that matter cannot exist without form. Cf. *De Gen.*, I, 5, 320 b, 14-18.
[2] As by position in time and space, etc.
[3] Cf. Aristotle's argument in *De caelo*, III, 299 b, 14-15; *De Gen.*, I, 315 b, 30-31
[4] Cf. above, pp. 31-3.
[5] Seeing that they conceive the work of the *Demiurge* in an anthropomorphic fashion according to the rules of experience.

in addition to ignoring the signs and miracles, and yet cannot free themselves from the necessity of admitting something which is contrary to sense perception.[1]

5. A REFUTATION OF THE THEORY OF EMANATION

(ed. Landauer 45.20-48.3;
ed. Slucki 24.27-25.27)

The Third Theory[2] is held by those who maintain that the Creator of the physical universe created it from His own substance.[3] These, it seems to me, are people who found it impossible to deny the existence of the Maker, but whose Reason would not allow them to believe that something can come out of nothing. And since there existed nothing except the Creator, they believe that He created the things out of Himself. These people are more foolish than those first mentioned. I will now proceed to expose their foolishness by thirteen arguments. Four of these are identical with those advanced against the adherents of the doctrine of incorporeal substances;[4] then there are four proofs for Creation;[5] then there are four more proofs for the *creatio ex nihilo*.[6] The four methods of refuting those who assume the eternity of incorporeal substances do

[1] In a subsequent passage, Saadya mentions that some Jewish people explained the passages Prov. 8.22, and Job 28.23 as referring to the doctrine of 'incorporeal substances' from which God created the world. He has no difficulty in refuting this exegesis by pointing out that both passages clearly refer to God's Wisdom. At the same time, he explains that the passages quoted do not imply a pre-existent Wisdom in the sense of an instrument of Creation, but merely express the idea that the Creator's Wisdom becomes manifest through the order and harmony of the universe. He makes the same point in *Comm. Prov.*, p. 49; see also below, p. 93, n. 4. Cf. the Translator's article, 'Saadya's Theory of Revelation', in *Saadya Studies* (ed. E. I. J. Rosenthal), pp. 13-14.

[2] According to Guttmann (p. 50), Saadya refers here to the doctrine of the Magians. Neumark, who disproved this interpretation, held that Saadya refers to the Neoplatonic doctrine of the 'Faithful Brethren of Baṣra'. Cf. *Toldōt hap-pilosofia be-Yisrael*, Vol. II, p. 153. As Ventura has shown, Saadya most probably refers to the doctrine of the Upanishads as expounded in the Vedanta. This teaches that the one, single, eternal, infinite and formless substance (*ātman*) is manifested in the world as its body. It creates the world out of its own substance and takes it back again into itself, not by necessity, but by its free will, like a spider which produces its web and takes it back into itself. Cf. Ventura, pp. 123-5.

[3] Arab. *min-dātihu*; *dāt* denotes the 'essence' of God as distinct from His attributes (*sifāt*).

[4] Cf. above, pp. 64-5.

[5] Cf. above, pp. 52-7.

[6] Cf. above, pp. 59-62.

not, however, apply to the adherents of this theory, and therefore we substitute for them five methods which do apply to them, and each of which disproves this view.

(1) Reason rejects the idea that the nature[1] of the Eternal Being[2] to whom is not attached any form, quality,[3] quantity, limit, space and time, should be transformed in such a way that part of His being becomes a body to which is attached form, quantity, quality, space, time, and all the other general characteristics of existent things. One cannot consider this but as in the highest degree improbable.

(2) Reason rejects the idea that the Wise whom no suffering can befall, whom no influence can affect and whom no perception can perceive, should make part of Himself into a body so that He can be perceived by the senses and affected by external influence; that He should become ignorant after having been wise, suffer pain after having been at ease, endure hunger, thirst, sadness and fatigue, and be exposed to all the other evils from which He had been free from all eternity. He did not require them for any useful purpose, nor is it possible to suppose that He could have attained His purpose through them. All this is utterly absurd.[4]

(3) How could the Just who does no injustice decree that part of His being be subjected to these calamities? To this question I find, on close consideration, that only two answers can be given: This came upon Him either because He deserved it, and He could have deserved it only on account of some wrong committed or some evil done; or it happened without His having deserved it, in which case He would have inflicted injustice and oppression upon Himself. Whichever theory is accepted, we find it completely absurd.

(4) Why should part (of His being), having accepted the command of the remaining part so as to become subject to physical affections, allow itself to be shaped and formed, and

[1] Arab. *ma'nā*.
[2] Arab. *al-'azalī*.
[3] Lit. 'state', 'condition' (*ḥāl*).
[4] In his rigorously rationalistic attitude, which does not conceive the possibility of a suffering God, Saadya seems to ignore the Jewish conception of *Galut Shekinah*, according to which God voluntarily shares the exile of His people and is in need of redemption like His people.

enter into a state of suffering? Did this happen because of some fear or of some hope on its part? Whichever of these two conditions we assume, one conclusion must inevitably be drawn: Either it is the manner of the entire being (of God) to fear or to hope, or it is the manner of part of His being only. If it is the manner of His entire being, I fail to know what it could fear and what it could hope for, seeing that there exists nothing besides Him. If it is the manner of part of His being, for what reason should this part become subject to hope and fear seeing that the remainder is not subject to hope and fear? If the (minor) part accepted the command of the major part without hope or fear, this would be wicked since there would be no conceivable reason for it. All this is absolutely false.

(5) One who is capable of saving part of his being from pain, if he is wise, could not possibly fail to do so. If we imagine that He acts in this way, then created beings will cease to exist, and if they are necessary in the end as they were in the beginning, these parts will enter into bodily existence in succession as their turn comes, each of them assuming form and shape for some while, then being delivered and removed, whilst another part would take its place and be affected. Yet it cannot be supposed that the succession of these turns is finite, since the total from which they come is infinite. This is something which Reason rejects as intrinsically illogical.[1] I compare these people who foolishly try to escape the assumption that the world was created *ex nihilo* by adopting these irrational beliefs to those who jump from a hot place to heated stones and from the rain to the gutter — not to mention the fact that they reject the tradition which testifies to the signs and miracles.[2]

---

[1] Because an infinite series is impossible. Cf. above, p. 56.

[2] Saadya's spirited rejection of the theory of emanation clearly shows how far he is removed from any mystical tendencies. In Jewish mysticism, too, the idea of 'Creation out of nothing' is firmly upheld, but this Nothing is interpreted as the supreme reality, the Divine. As Scholem (*loc. cit.*, p. 26) points out, '*Creation out of nothing* means to many mystics just *creation out of God*', it becomes 'the symbol of emanation'.

6. A REFUTATION OF GNOSTIC DUALISM

(ed. Landauer 48.12-50.8; 51.19-52.9; 53.6-20; 54.14-55.6;
ed. Slucki 26.3-37; 27.26-28.8; 28.23-29.2; 29.15-26)

The Fifth Theory[1] is held by those who maintain the existence of two eternal agents.[2] In following this opinion, they surpass in foolishness all those previously mentioned. For they reject the possibility that two (opposite) actions should originate from one single agent, and they assert that they never saw such a thing. They are all agreed on this and say: We find that in everything there is contained good and evil, the harmful and the useful. It is, therefore, necessary to assume that the good contained in it comes from a principle[3] which is entirely good, and that the evil contained in it comes from a principle which is entirely evil. This has led them to the assumption that the source[4] of the good is unlimited in five directions, namely, upward and in the east, west, south, and north, but is limited below where it touches the source of the evil. Likewise, the source of the evil is unlimited in five directions, namely, downward and in the east, west, south, and north, but is limited above where it touches the source of the good. They further assert that these two principles were originally separated, then became mixed, and that the physical universe was created as a result of their mixture.[5] They are divided as to the cause of their mixture. Some assert that the good was its cause, as it

---

[1] Saadya describes and discusses here the view of Gnostic dualism as expressed in the system of the Manichaean religion, which, in his time, was one of the great world religions and exercised a far-reaching influence. See H. Jonas, *Gnosis und spätantiker Geist*, I, pp. 284 ff.; F. Cumont, *La cosmogonie manichéenne*; H. H. Schaeder, *Urform und Fortbildungen des manichäischen Systems*.

[2] Arab. *ṣāni'āni ḳadīmāni*.

[3] Arab. *'aṣl*; root, principle.

[4] Arab. *ma'din*; mine, origin, source.

[5] The view that this world resulted from the mixture of good and evil, light and darkness, is common to all Gnostic systems. The world, according to Gnosis, is a 'world of mixture'. The above account is a faithful record of the Manichaean Cosmogony. It paraphrases it in terms similar to the report given by En-Nadîm, *Fihrist* (ed. Fluegel), p. 86, which reads: 'In the beginning of the world there existed two beings, light and darkness, which were separated from each other. The light is the first supreme sovereign, unlimited in number, God, King of the paradise of light. He has five elements: gentleness, knowledge, understanding, secret, intelligence . . . The other being is darkness, with the five elements of mist, fire, storm, poison and darkness. Mani taught: the world of light borders immediately upon the world of darkness without a dividing wall between them. The light touches the darkness below, but is unlimited above and at its right and left flanks. Likewise, the darkness is unlimited below and at its right and left flanks.'

wanted to pacify the upper part of the evil which it met on its border. Others assert that the evil was the cause, as it coveted the good and wanted to enjoy the sweetness contained in it.[1] They agree that this mixture will last for a certain period and that, when it dissolves, the good will triumph, and the evil will be subdued and its activities brought to an end.[2]

I shall now set forth the arguments by which the assertions of these people can be refuted on every point. To begin with, I say that we can adduce against them the four arguments on which we based our proofs for the creation of the physical world.[3] Then there are the four arguments on which we based our proofs for the *creatio ex nihilo*.[4] Then there are the five considerations which we brought forward against those who assert that the Creator created the world from His substance.[5] This makes a total of thirteen. In addition there will be given in this chapter fifteen answers directed against them particularly, apart from what I have to say against them in Chapter II. For I took the salient points[6] of their statement, and probed them to the bottom[7] with the result that they were completely eliminated and nothing remained of them.

First I examined their assertion that, according to experience, two opposite actions do not originate from one single agent. I found that the emanation of two such actions from one single agent can be confirmed in many ways: (1) We see that a man is angry and enraged, then becomes calm and friendly, and says, 'I am pacified, I have forgiven'. Now if the good is that which forgives, it is also that which is angry; and if the evil is that which forgives, it acts beneficently in so far as it forgives. In viewing both aspects together, we find that the two actions belong to one agent. (2) Furthermore, we see that a man commits the crime of murder or of theft, and when caused to confess, confesses his sin. Now if the evil is that which confesses, it tells the truth, and the truth is good; if, however, the good is that which confesses, it is at the same time that which killed and committed theft. In viewing both conditions

---

[1] Cf. Jonas, *loc. cit.*, pp. 289-95.
[2] The Manichaean 'Drama of Redemption' is described and analysed by H. Jonas, *loc. cit.* On the Iranian sources of the Manichaean eschatology, see H. Junker, *Üeber iranische Quellen der hellenistischen Aion-Vorstellung, Vorträge der Bibliothek Warburg,* 1921-2.
[3] Cf. above, pp. 52-7.   [4] Cf. above, pp. 59-62.   [5] Cf. above, pp. 67-8.
[6] Lit. 'axis', 'poles'.   [7] Lit. 'Applied the spiral screw to them'.

together, it becomes clear that the two actions belong to one single agent. (3) Furthermore, if the faculty of being angry[1] is separate from the faculty of being pacified, and, likewise, the faculty of committing theft is different from the faculty of making confession, it would be fitting that one who is pacified should not remember, in his state of pacification, what happened to him in his state of anger; nor should one who desires to make confession remember, in his state of confession, what happened to him in his state of sin. But we find that the experience of our senses contradicts all this.[2]

Then I examined the two causes which, according to their opinion, led to the mixture (of the two principles). I found both to be invalid. For if the action (of mixture), as some of them maintain, sprang from a tendency on the part of the good, the good must already have become evil in that it intended to mix with the evil.[3] And if it sprang from a tendency on the part of the evil, the evil must already have changed into the good in that it intended the good.[4] Whichever of the two statements is accepted, the principle which took the initiative must have changed its substance, but this they refuse to admit. Moreover, if the mixture is due to the action of the good, the good has not achieved what it intended, namely, to pacify the

---

[1] For the same term in its technical sense (Plato's Θυμοειδές) cf. below, p. 147, n. 3. (*Amānāt*, p. 195.)

[2] Saadya's point in this argument is that unless we split the human personality into the two domains of the good and the evil, its good and evil actions must be attributed to one and the same source. The continuity of memory and consciousness proves to him that there is only one centre of the personality, a view which is open to debate from the aspect of modern psychology. Cf. C. G. Jung, *The Integration of the Personality*, transl. by S. M. Dell (1940). In the Gnostic view, the Psyche is essentially different from the spiritual Self (*Pneuma*) of man. It is of an evil and demonic character. Cf. Jonas, *loc. cit.*, pp. 199, 210-4.

[3] This argument only applies to those systems of Gnosis which admit that there is an element of guilt in the 'Fall' of the Light. (Syriac, Valentinian, and Hermetic Gnosis.) The Manichaean cosmogony absolves the Light from any guilt in that it describes the process of 'mixture' as a result of the attack made by the powers of darkness upon the realm of light. Being of a peaceful nature, the light had no other weapon than its self-sacrifice: By entering the domain of evil it hoped to soften and mitigate its harshness. This is what Saadya apparently alludes to when he speaks of the tendency of the good to 'pacify' the evil. (See above, p. 70.) It is strange that he should call such a tendency an evil one, unless his argument in the above passage refers to those branches of Gnosis which admit the initiative and guilt of the Light. Cf. Jonas, *loc. cit.*, p. 283.

[4] Saadya rightly stresses the ambiguity involved in the initiative of the evil according to the Manichaean conception. The powers of darkness are attracted by the beauty of light and long for its possession. There is greed and a destructive tendency in their onslaught upon the light, but at the same time, self-hatred and a realization of the superiority of the light. Cf. Jonas, *loc. cit.*, pp. 289-91.

part (of the evil) upon which it bordered. On the contrary, we see that having entered into the evil, its suffering is more intense than what it was when it only bordered upon it. If, however, the action (of mixture) is due to the evil, it has indeed achieved its purpose, for we find that it enjoys the good, eats and drinks and smells and embraces it. In either case it appears that we must despair of the triumph of the good over the evil.

Having said so much on this subject,[1] I still cannot leave it without pointing out that the thing which these people put forward (as a separate principle), namely Darkness, is, in fact, not a principle in opposition to Light, but the absence (privation)[2] of Light.[3] If I am asked: On what grounds do you assert that the Darkness is not a principle in opposition to the Light, I can offer three proofs: (1) A man is unable to produce a 'principle', but we find that when he stands in the sun and puts the palms of his hands one upon another like a dome, the space between them will be dark. Not that man produces the 'principle' of darkness; he merely shuts the light out from the space between his palms, and causes darkness because the light is absent. (2) We find that a man casts a shadow when standing in front of a lamp. If we surround him by a number of lamps, the shadow disappears. Surely, it is not within the power of man to annihilate any 'principle'. What he has done has been to admit the light which had been absent from part of the space which surrounded the person. (3) We do not find two bodies of opposite characters change in such a way that the one becomes completely the other. Thus water does not change into fire, nor fire into water. Our observation that the dark atmosphere (of the night) brightens up (in the morning) teaches us that the darkness is not the opposite of the light, but its absence.

I know that God describes Himself in the words, 'I form the

---

[1] i.e. the fifteen arguments against Manichaean dualism, of which only five have been included in the above Selection.

[2] Arab. *'adam*; Hebr. *he'der*; στέρησις.

[3] Gnosis, and, under its influence, Jewish mysticism conceive of the evil not as a mere 'privation' (absence) of the good, but as a positive reality and potency of its own. On this point medieval Jewish philosophy and mysticism are fundamentally divided. Cf. the Translator's article, 'Maimunis Verhältnis zur jüdischen Mystik' in *MGWJ* (1936), pp. 322-30. Saadya makes it clear that in his view evil has no positive existence of its own, but is identical with the absence of the good.

light, and create darkness' (Isa. 45.7).[1] But I explain this to mean, in accordance with the experience of our senses,[2] that He created the air which receives light and darkness in the way of existence and privation.[3] Similarly, it is said afterwards, 'I make peace and create evil' (*ibid.*), and we are agreed that the Wise has not created evil, but He created the things which allow peace and evil to occur to man according to his free will. If he eats food according to his need, and drinks water according to his need, he will have peace; but if he partakes of them in larger measure than is permissible, he will experience evil, as we shall explain in Chapter IV on the subject of God's Justice.[4] The reason, however, why He ascribes both the light and the darkness to His own act of creation, is in order to combat the view of those who proclaim dualism. For this reason He said, 'I form the light, and create the darkness'.[5] He further informed us that light and darkness are finite and limited, and provided us with a refutation of these people by saying, 'He hath described a boundary upon the face of the waters, unto the confines of light and darkness' (Job 26.10).

---

[1] The expression, 'and *create* darkness' seems to imply that darkness has a positive reality.

[2] i.e. the experience that darkness is merely the absence of light.

[3] God created the air as the vehicle of light and darkness, the one being positive and real, the other being a mere absence of the light.

[4] Cf. below, p. 121-2.

[5] Saadya means to say that as a protest against (Iranian) dualism, Isaiah uses an emphatic way of expression, which, however, must not be taken literally. The purpose of this verse is merely to reject the idea that darkness and light are the creations of two opposing principles. Saadya frequently employs the exegetical rule that emphatic expressions must not be taken literally.

CHAPTER II

THE UNITY OF THE CREATOR[1]

1. The Abstract Character of the Knowledge of God

(ed. Landauer 72.9-76.5; 76.14-78.10;
ed. Slucki 39.1-40.23; 40.31-41.27)

I wish to preface this chapter by the following remarks. (1) The starting point of knowledge[2] is invariably of a concrete nature,[3] and its final result is some abstract idea.[4] (2) When knowledge reaches the final stage, no further knowledge beyond it is possible. (3) Man in his pursuit of knowledge progresses from one stage to another. (4) Each conclusion[5] at which he arrives is by necessity more abstract and subtle than the preceding one, so that (5) the last and final conclusion is more abstract and subtle than all the rest. (6) When a man has arrived at this abstract knowledge, it is this which he aimed at, and it would be wrong on his part if he wished it to be of a concrete nature. If he desired that, he would, in fact, desire to retrogress to the first stage of his knowledge from which he started, or to its second stage, notwithstanding the fact that he thereby violates and transgresses the principles of knowledge. In proportion as he seeks to 'coarsen' ultimate knowledge,[6] he seeks the destruction of his speculation, nay, the destruction of his knowledge, and retrogresses to his condition of ignorance in regard to it.

It is proper that I should explain on what grounds I have made these six statements. Later on I will give the reasons for having placed them at the opening of this chapter.

First as to the statement that the starting point of knowledge

---

[1] Chapter II deals with the doctrine of the Divine attributes. The Mu'tazilites call this part of their theological system the 'Confession of Unity' (*Tawḥīd*). Saadya uses a similar title as seen above. The chapter has found its classical treatment in D. Kaufmann's *Geichichte der Attributenlehre*, pp. 1-90.

[2] Lit. 'That which is known'; in Saadya's terminology, this denotes the knowledge of Reason.

[3] Lit. 'Something coarse'.

[4] Lit. 'Something subtle'.

[5] Arab. *manzila*; degree, rank, here used in the sense of proposition, conclusion. Cf. above, p. 60, n. 3.

[6] i.e. seeking to obtain final knowledge in concrete terms.

is of a concrete nature. This I say on account of the fact that knowledge starts from sense perception,[1] and all information conveyed by the senses is open to all alike, and in regard to it no man is superior to his fellow-men, nor, for that matter, to the animals, for we find that he sees and hears through sense perception in exactly the same way as they do, and, surely, there can be no knowledge more gross than one which man shares with the animal. Now when a man examines the object of his sense perception, he knows that it is a body. By the abstractive faculty of his Reason, he finds that the body is affected by accidents, for he sees that it is sometimes black and sometimes white, sometimes warm and sometimes cold. Then, continuing the process of abstraction, he discovers features[2] in it which suggest the idea of quantity,[3] namely, by examining the features of length, breadth and depth. Then, continuing still further the process of abstraction, he finds that the body has one feature due to its position, namely its meeting (with another body), out of which arises (the aspect of) space.[4] Proceeding with his abstractive speculation, he arrives at the knowledge that the body has yet another feature attached to it, namely, duration, out of which arises (the idea of) time.[5] Thus he goes on, driving forward from one observation to another until he reaches the final point within his grasp. This ultimate knowledge will be more abstract than anything which occurred to him before, in the same way as his knowledge at its starting point was more concrete than anything which occurred to him afterwards. Hence I judge that the final stage of knowledge is the most abstract of all.

I further remarked that man progresses from knowledge to knowledge until he reaches a point beyond which no further knowledge is possible. There are three reasons for this. (1) Since the body of man is limited and finite, it necessarily follows that all his faculties, including the faculty of knowledge, are also finite just as with regard to the heaven, as I have already stated, the time of its duration must necessarily be assumed to be

---

[1] Cf. pp. 36 ff.   [2] Arab. *ma'nā*.   [3] Arab. *kam*.

[4] Arab. *makān*. — Following Themistius' interpretation of Aristotle, Saadia defines space as 'the meeting of two contiguous bodies'.   Cf. *Amānāt*, p. 51 (37); 102 (52); see Wolfson, *Crescas' Critique of Aristotle*, pp. 364-5.

[5] Following a Greek tradition reported in the names of Plato and Zeno, Saadia defines time as 'the extension of the duration of the bodies'. Cf. *Amānāt*, p. 102 (52). See Wolfson, *loc. cit.*, pp. 638-40.

finite.[1] (2) Knowledge can be acquired by man only because it is of a finite nature. If thought were to entail an infinite process, it would be impossible to master it, and if this were impossible, man would not know anything. (3) Since the root from which all knowledge springs, i.e., sense perception, is undoubtedly finite in character, it is impossible that its offspring should be infinite, and the branch different from the root.

I further said that man in his pursuit of knowledge progresses from one stage to another. This point is based on the fact that all knowledge has a root from which it springs, whereas ignorance has no root from which to spring, but is merely the absence (privation)[2] of knowledge in the same way as we have explained with reference to darkness that it is the absence of light, not its opposite.[3] One of our arguments also was that if darkness were the opposite of light, the dark atmosphere (of the night) could not change into the brightness (of daylight). In the same way we contend here that if ignorance had a root like knowledge, it would be impossible for the ignorant to become knowing; for knowledge and ignorance, if combined in the same person,[4] would destroy each other On these grounds I said that man progresses in knowledge from stage to stage, seeing that knowledge springs from a root and branches out, whereas it is impossible to suppose that one progresses in ignorance from one stage to another, because in ignorance there are no conclusions towards which one could travel, ignorance being merely the abandoning, step by step, of knowledge, and its disappearance.

I further said that the ultimate conclusion reached is more abstract and subtle than all previous discoveries. This can be shown from a physical example: Snow, as it drops from the air, has the appearance of a solid crystal.[5] If we examine it more closely, we shall find that it originates from water. If we probe still more deeply, we shall learn that this water could not have been lifted up except in the form of rising vapour. Thus we conclude that snow originates from vapour.[6] Then

---

[1] Cf. above, p. 52.   [2] Cf. above, p. 72, n. 3.
[3] Cf. Saadya's argument against Dualism, pp. 72-3.
[4] Lit. 'part', 'element'.   [5] Lit. 'Like the stone'.
[6] The above explanation of the origin of snow is borrowed from Aristotle, *Meteorologica*, I, 10-12; the 'Faithful Brethren of Basra' also accepted it. Cf. Dieterici, *Naturanschauung*, p. 80.

we go still deeper into the matter and assert that there must be some cause for the rising of vapour. It should already be clear that the final cause which we shall discover will be more subtle than vapour, which, in turn, is more subtle than water, which, in turn, is again more subtle than snow. It is this subtle cause which formed the real object and the goal of our inquiries. For this reason I said that one who desires this final knowledge to be similar to his initial knowledge does violence to the very nature of knowledge, as I have made clear from my description of its laws and methods.

Having completed these explanations, it is desirable that I should now state the reason which prompted me to enunciate them here at the beginning of this chapter. It is that, when I came to deal with the subject of the Creator,[1] I found that people rejected this whole inquiry, some because they could not see God; others on account of the profundity and extreme subtleness of His nature; still others claim that beyond the knowledge of God there is some other knowledge; others again go so far as to picture Him as a body; others, while not explicitly describing Him as a body, assign to Him quantity or quality or space or time, or similar things, and by looking for these qualities they do in fact assign to Him a body, since these attributes belong only to a body. The purpose of my introductory remarks is to remove their false ideas, to take a load from their minds, and to point out that the extreme subtleness which we have assigned to the nature of the Creator is, so to speak, its own warrant, and the fact that, in our reasoning, we find the notion of God to be more abstract than other knowledge shows that reasoning to be correct. Those who declare that they only hold true what they perceive with their own eyes, and deny all knowledge (of Reason), I refuted already when discussing the theories of the Sensualists,[2] the Subjectivists,[3] and the Sceptics.[4] Those who reject the conception

---

[1] i.e. the doctrine of the Divine attributes, having proved the existence of the Creator in Chapter I.

[2] Lit. 'Those who profess the eternity of the world' (*dahriyya*). Cf. above, p. 62, n. 4.

[3] Lit. 'The people of obstinacy' (*'anūd*), according to whom the reality of things depends on subjective opinion. This group, also called *indiyya,* follows the Sophistic view (Protagoras) which makes man the measure of all things. Cf. Ventura, pp. 154-7.

[4] Lit. 'The people of abstention' (*wukūf*), who insist on the suspension of judgment (ἐποχή) on all matters which involve reasoning. Cf. Ventura, pp. 157-9. — The three above-mentioned views figure as No. 10, 11 and 12 in Saadya's list of cosmological theories and are not included in the Selection presented in Chapter I.

of God on account of its subtleness and profundity fail to proceed to their second objective after attaining the first,[1] for the
reader will remember what I have already explained in regard
to the Creation of the world, namely, that our aim in this
respect was something deep, subtle, fine and profound the
like of which cannot be met in our experience. I noted that
Scripture says with reference to such a thing, 'That which is
far off, and exceeding deep; who can find it out?' (Eccl. 7.24).[2]
I have met some thinkers who are not of our Faith and who
imagined this object to be something subtle like dust and hair,
or like the indivisible atom.[3] But we have arrived at the
result that the world was created from nothing, and this being
the character of the object investigated at that stage, it is
necessary that the character of the object investigated at the
next stage, namely, the Creator (be He exalted and glorified)
should be more abstract than anything abstract, more profound
than anything profound, more subtle than anything subtle,
deeper than anything deep, more powerful than anything
powerful, and higher than anything high, so that it becomes
impossible to probe His quality.[4] With regard to this Scripture
has said, 'Canst thou find out the deep things of God? Canst
thou attain unto the purpose of the Almighty? It is high as
heaven; what canst thou do? Deeper than the nether-world;
what canst thou know? The measure thereof is longer than the
earth, and broader than the sea' (Job 11.7-9).

As to those who wish us to imagine God as a body, they
should wake up from their illusions. Is not the conception of
the body the first stage arrived at in our pursuit of knowledge?
Was not the body the first stage in the process of our knowledge, and was it not from this starting-point that we reached
the conception of the Maker of the body? How, then, do these
people go back to the A B C and seek to conceive God as a
body? Is the body whose Maker we endeavour to find some
specific person so that it might be assumed that his Maker

---

[1] They have reached the first objective, namely, the doctrine of Creation which
implies the existence of the Creator, but they are reluctant to pursue the second
objective, namely, the doctrine of the Divine attributes.

[2] Cf. above, p. 49.

[3] Saadya obviously refers to the theories of the Greek and Islamic atomists.

[4] The crescendo of epithets describing the absolute transcendence and unfathomable
depth of the *Deus Absconditus* bears eloquent testimony to Saadya's religious fervour.

[5] Arab. *āṯār*; traces, signs. The reference is to the Aristotelian categories.

was some other person? No, what we endeavoured to find was the Creator of all bodies which we can perceive and imagine, and every body which can be grasped in our thought must be the work of that Maker who is external to all the bodies.

In regard to those who seek to find something beyond God, we have already declared such a desire to be inadmissible from the point of view of the person who knows, seeing that his knowledge is necessarily limited by his faculties; of the object of knowledge, for that which does not reach a limit and stop cannot be comprehended by the soul; and finally of the root from which all knowledge is derived.[1]

2. THE ATTRIBUTES OF GOD

(ed. Landauer 79.12–81.2; 84.14–86.2;
ed. Slucki 42.8–35; 44.31–45.18)

Our Lord (be He exalted and glorified) has informed us through the words of His prophets that He is One, Living, Powerful and Wise, and that nothing can be compared unto Him or unto His works. They established this by signs and miracles, and we accepted it immediately. Later, speculation led us to the same result. In regard to His Unity, it is said, 'Hear O Israel, the Lord our God, the Lord is One' (Deut. 6.4); furthermore, 'See now that I, even I, am He, and that there is no god with Me' (Deut. 32.39), and also, 'The Lord alone did lead him, and there was no strange god with Him' (Deut. 32.12). In regard to His Life, it is said, 'For who is there of all flesh, that hath heard the voice of the living God speaking out of the midst of the fire, as we have, and lived?' (Deut. 5.23); furthermore, 'But the Lord God is a true God, He is the living God, and the everlasting King' (Jer. 10.10). As to His Power, it is said, 'I know that Thou canst do every thing, and that no purpose can be withholden from Thee' (Job 42.2); and furthermore, 'Thine, O Lord, is the greatness, and the power, and the glory, and the victory, and the majesty' (1 Chron. 29.11). As to His Wisdom, it is said, 'He is wise in heart, and mighty in strength; who hath hardened himself

---

[1] i.e. Sense perception, which is finite in character.

against Him, and prospered?' (Job 9.4); and furthermore, 'His discernment is past searching out' (Isa. 40.28). In regard to the incomparability of God and His works, it is said, 'There is none like unto Thee among the gods, O Lord; and there are no works like Thine' (Ps. 86.8).

Having accepted these six attributes[1] from the Books of the Prophets, we endeavoured to confirm them by way of speculation, and found them in agreement with Reason. At the same time, we discovered the arguments with which to refute the attacks of our opponents who disagree with us in regard to some of these attributes. Their attacks arise from two sources only: (1) from their practice of drawing analogies[2] between God and His creatures; (2) from their tendency to blame us on account of the terms by which we express His attributes,[3] because they take the anthropomorphic expressions which occur in Scripture not in a metaphorical[4] sense, but literally. We hope to make all this clear in our exposition of this doctrine.[5]

(a) *The Unity of God.* — My first argument for the Unity of God is based on the proofs which I have given before, to the effect that God is the Maker of the physical world. As the Maker of corporeal bodies, He cannot be of their kind.[6] Since there exist many bodies, he must necessarily be One. For if He were more than One, the category of number would apply to Him, and He would enter the realm of the physical world.[7]

---

[1] In the course of his later exposition, Saadya omits the last-mentioned attribute (that of God's incomparability) since it expresses only a formal aspect of God's essence.

[2] Arab. *kiyās*; deduction by analogy. Cf. *EI*, Vol. II, p. 1051 ff. — Tibbon translates it by *hakashah*.

[3] Arab. *sifa*.

[4] Arab. *majāz*.

[5] i.e. the doctrine of the Divine attributes.

[6] Saadya follows the Mutakallimūn whose arguments for the incorporeality of God included one which was based on the principle of the 'impossibility of comparison', i.e. the belief that God cannot be compared to any of His creatures, and that He would be comparable to other corporeal objects if He were conceived of as corporeal. The anthropomorphists, however, believed that the substance of God differed from the substances of all bodies created by Him, but that it was none the less of a corporeal nature. It was sublime, perfect, simple, constant and immutable. Cf. *Moreh*, I, 76, 2.

[7] Saadya obviously accepts Aristotle's statement that 'all things that are many in number have matter'. Cf. *Metaphysica*, XII, 8, 1074 a, 33-4. Maimonides also accepted this view. Cf. *Moreh*, II, Introd., XVI. See Guttmann, p. 95; Wolfson, *loc. cit.*, p. 666,

My second argument is: Reason decides that a Maker exists only because it cannot avoid this assumption. But what it cannot avoid is only the assumption of one Maker. If, however, anything is added to Him, this further assumption is not an unavoidable, but an unnecessary, one.[1]

My third argument is: The existence of the One Maker has been established by the first proof, i.e. the proof for Creation.[2] Anything added to Him requires a second proof in addition to this one in order to demonstrate it. But no further proofs can be brought beyond those given for Creation.

(b) *The three attributes of God.* — Considering the subject further I found that the conception of God as Creator, which we established, implies the attributes of Life, Power, and Wisdom. By means of our faculty of ratiocination[3] it becomes clear to us that creation is impossible without power, and that power is impossible without life, and that a well-ordered creation presupposes an intelligence which knows in advance the result of its activities. Our Reason discovers these three aspects of the notion of a Creator in a single flash of intuition,[4] as one reality. For the very idea that God is the Creator involves the attribution to Him of Life, Power, and Wisdom, as I explained. Reason can in no way find one of these three aspects prior to the other, but arrives at all of them at one stroke, since it cannot possibly conceive of God as Creator without conceiving of Him as endowed with Life and Power, and it cannot think of a complete and well-ordered creation otherwise than as the product of an intelligence capable of knowing in advance the result of its activities. For the work of a mind lacking in such knowledge cannot be well-ordered and skilfully designed. Now these three aspects of God, which occur to our Reason in combination, cannot be expressed by one single word in our language. For we do not find a word

---

[1] Cf. the Mu'tazilite argument quoted by Maimonides, *Moreh*, I, 75, 4, 'The existence of an action is necessarily positive evidence of the existence of an *agens*, but does not prove the existence of more than one *agens*'. Baḥya, *Hoḫōt Hal-leḫaḫōt* 7, III, elaborates this argument, which is of Aristotelian origin. Cf. *Physica*, I, 6, 189 b, 17-20; cf. also Spinoza, *Cog. met.*, II, 2; Guttmann, p. 95; Ventura, pp. 177-8.

[2] Saadya refers to the set of Four Proofs for Creation in Chapter I, which demonstrate the existence of a Creator.

[3] Arab. *fī-fiṭari'aḵlinā;* Tibbon: *be-koaḥ siḵlenū.* The Arabic term *fiṭra* denotes 'man's natural gifts, his mental equipment by birth'. Cf. H. Malter, 'Mediaeval Hebrew terms for Nature', in *Judaica*, p. 253; Wensinck, pp. 214-5, 261.

[4] Arab. *badīḥā*, which is insufficiently rendered by Tibbon's Hebr. *pit'om*, suddenly.

in language which covers all these three aspects. We must needs express them by three different words, but it should be well understood that Reason conceived them as one single idea. Let nobody assume that the Eternal (blessed be He) contains a plurality of attributes. For all the attributes which we assign to Him are implied in the one attribute of Creator, and it is merely the deficiency of our language which makes it necessary for us to express our notion of God in three different words, since there exists no word in our vocabulary which covers all the three aspects. Nor would it be advisable to create a special term for this conception, because that new term would convey no meaning by itself, and it would still be necessary to explain it, so that it would lead us back to a plurality of words in place of one term. If someone imagines that these attributes imply a diversity[1] within God, i.e. some difference between the various attributes, I will show him his mistake by pointing out the real truth of the matter, viz. that diversity and change can take place in bodies and their accidents only, but the Creator of all bodies and accidents is above diversity and change.[2] Nor should I be satisfied until I had made the matter perfectly clear to him by saying that in the same way as the attribute of 'Creator' does not imply something in addition to the essence[3] of God, but merely implies that there exists a world created by Him, so the attributes of Life, Power and Wisdom, which explain the term Creator — it being

[1] Arab. *taghayyur*, change, diversity.

[2] In a subsequent passage not included in the present Selection (*Amānāt*, 86-7; Hebr. 45-6), Saadya elaborates this argument by pointing out that in the case of man life and wisdom are distinct and separate from his self (essence) seeing that he dies and is liable to ignorance. Unless we witnessed the changes which take place in regard to man — the changes from life to death and from ignorance to wisdom — we should have assumed that he is living and wise by virtue of his essence. God in whom no change takes place is living, wise and powerful by virtue of His essence. In other words, these three attributes are identical with His essence. Saadya stresses this point in his treatment of the Christian doctrine of Trinity, which, in his opinion (cf. also al-Sharastānī, I, 260, 266, who mentions particularly the Nestorians), interpreted the three attributes of Existence, Wisdom and Life in the sense of the three separate persons of Father, Son (*Logos*) and Holy Spirit. Saadya's view that the three attributes are not separate aspects of God follows in the footsteps of Mu'tazilite theology, particularly Abū-l-Hudail's school of thought, who insisted that the three attributes of Life, Wisdom and Power are identical with the essence of God. Cf. Kaufmann, *loc. cit.*, pp. 33 ff. The Mu'tazilites combated the orthodox Islamic doctrine of *Sifa Dhātiyya* (Attributes of Essence) because of its christological implications. Cf. the Translator's article, 'Saadya's Theory of Revelation' in *Saadya Studies* (ed. E. I. J. Rosenthal), p. 12 ff.

[3] Arab. *ḏāt*.

understood that there can be no Creator unless He possesses these aspects simultaneously – add nothing to His essence but merely denote the existence of a world created by Him.[1]

Having thus established this conception by force of reason, I turned to Scripture and found that it precludes any notion of plurality within God: 'There is none else beside Him' (Deut. 4.35); furthermore, 'Lo, these are but the outskirts of His ways; and how small a whisper is heard of Him (Job. 26.14); furthermore, 'In that day shall the Lord be One, and His name One' (Zech. 14.9).

3. THE MEANING OF THE ANTHROPOMORPHIC EXPRESSIONS IN THE BIBLE[2]

(ed. Landauer 92.10-93.18; 94.9-20; 95.3-98.1; 99.4-101.9; ed. Slucki 48.19-49.5; 49.17-27; 49.30-50.42; 51.20-52.16)

Having established the above principles, I will now specify most of the attributes and deal with the questions which are asked in connection with this matter.[3] I refer both to the attributes which naturally occur to one's mind and to those which we find in Scripture and are mentioned by believers. But first I wish to make a general remark.

All such expressions as refer to God in terms of substance and accident, or, for that matter, in terms of attributes of substance and accident[4] do not really apply to Him in any degree, be it large or small. For it is established that the Creator (be He blessed and exalted) is the Creator of everything.

[1] Having refuted the idea that the three attributes describe separate aspects of God's essence, Saadya now goes further in suggesting that all that is really implied in these attributes is the notion of God as Creator. In other words, they are not 'attributes of essence' at all, but merely state the relation of God to the world, i.e. the implications of the notion of Creator. They are, in Yehudah Hallevi's and Maimonides' terminology, 'attributes of action', and leave the essence and nature of God untouched. This view amounts to the thesis of 'negative theology' and is not quite consistent with the idea previously expressed (see above p. 83, n. 2) that the three attributes are identical with God's essence. Cf. Julius Guttmann, *Die Philosophie d. Judentums*, pp. 79-80. Saadya's prime concern is to safeguard the principle of the Unity of God against any misconception.

[2] For a full treatment of this chapter cf. S. Rawidowicz, 'Saadya's Purification of the Idea of God', in *Saadya Studies* (ed. E. I. J. Rosenthal), pp. 139-65.

[3] The Mu'tazilites likewise first stated the principles of the doctrine of Divine attributes, and subsequently interpreted those Kur'ān verses which seemed to contradict these principles. Cf. al-Shahrastāni 1, 43; Kaufmann, Attrib.-Lehre, p. 55, n. 102; Guttmann, p. 115, n. 2.

[4] Such as quantity, quality, etc.

Hence there is left nothing, be it substance or accident, or any of their attributes, which could be applied to Him, it being recognized and clearly established that He, the Creator, has made everything. Obviously, it is impossible and absurd to speak of Him in terms of the things which He created.[1] With regard to the Books of the Prophets, which do speak of God in terms of substance and accident, it is indispensable that we should seek for them, according to the usage of language, some meaning other than anthropomorphic which will conform to the dictates of Reason.[2] All those attributes of an apparently anthropomorphic character which we, the Community of the Believers, use in speaking of Him, have a symbolic and figurative meaning; they must not be taken in their literal sense as one would apply them to man. After I have explained these three points,[3] I hope the reader of this book will not be misled nor left in doubt whenever he uses, or reads in Scripture, such expressions as 'He was', or 'He willed', or 'He was gracious', or 'He was in anger', and similar phrases. For these expressions are used only in conformity with the principle which we have laid down, and it is this principle to which they must be referred and on which they must be based, since a building can be built only from its foundation upwards, and never from the top downwards. For this reason one should never be confused by an attribute which he comes across in Scripture or finds in general use amongst us, nor should one begin to question the principle of the matter which is so clearly and firmly established.

I shall now discuss this principle in its relation to the ten categories,[4] giving the appropriate exposition in each case.

[1] Since created things came into existence only at the moment of their creation, they cannot possibly share in the eternity of God's existence. It is, therefore, futile to describe God by means of attributes which belong to the realm of created things.

[2] Both the Arabic original and the Hebrew version leave no alternative but the above rendering. Kaufmann's interpretation (*loc. cit.*, p. 54) ignores the double negation in the phraseology used. Cf. also the parallel passage *Amānāt*, 94.11 (49.18), 95.13 (49.40).

[3] i.e. relating to substance, accident, and their attributes.

[4] Saadya goes through the ten Aristotelian Categories for the purpose of showing that none of them can be applied to God. He uses this method already in his *Comm. Yeṣ.* (pp. 62 ff.). There is no evidence that in so doing he is following a Muʿtazilite precedent. Cf. Kaufmann *loc. cit.*, p. 55, n. 108. His fondness of numbers induced him to apply the Ten Categories even to the exposition of the Ten Commandments. Cf. S. Rawidowicz, *loc. cit.*, pp. 147 ff.; Kaufmann, *loc. cit.*, p. 55, n. 103. The present Selection includes only categories 1-3.

(a) *Substance*

Some people hold that this Being (i.e. God) is a substance, and they only differ in so far as some of them think He resembles man,[1] others that He is like fire, still others that He is like air, and again others that He has the nature of Space.[2] Others entertain still different views. But since it is established that He is the Maker of all men, fire, air and space, in short, of all being, all these opinions are repudiated by Reason. In addition to the verdict of Reason, Scripture likewise confirms this. For there exist five classes of beings, i.e. minerals, plants, animals, stars and angels,[3] and Scripture emphatically denies that these five can be likened unto the Creator or He to them . . .[4] It passes in review the whole universe and rejects the idea that anything contained in it resembles the Maker, or vice versa. The unequivocal testimony of these Scriptural passages is the principle on which we must rely, and it is our duty to refer back to it every doubtful expression in the way of metaphors until we can make it conform to the principle.[5] Take as an example the verse, 'And God created man in His own image, in the image of God created He him' (Gen. 1.27). I explain it in the sense of God bestowing dignity and honour upon man; i.e. in the same way as all lands belong unto Him, and yet He honoured one land in particular by calling it 'My Land', and in the same way as all mountains belong unto Him, and yet He conferred special honour to one particular mount by calling it 'My Mount', so, similarly, all images belong unto Him, and yet He honoured a particular one in a special way by using the expression, 'This is My Image'. This phrase must, therefore, be taken in the sense of special distinction, not as anthropomorphic.[6] — Or take as another instance the verse

[1] Kaufmann's emendation '*adamah* instead of '*adam* is mistaken, as evidenced by the Arabic text which reads '*insan*, man. Saadya may refer to the Christian doctrine of 'the Word that became flesh' (Cf. Guttmann, p. 116, n. 2), or, more likely, to the anthropomorphists in Islam (cf. Ventura, p. 187).

[2] Arab. *faḍā*'; empty space. This reading is more probable than the reading *faḍḍa*, silver, followed by Tibbon. Cf. Ventura, p. 188; Kaufmann, *loc. cit.*, p. 56. See, however, Guttmann, p. 116, n. 2.

[3] A similar classification of the universe was adopted by the 'Faithful Brethren of Baṣra'. Cf. Dieterici, *Die Philosophie der Araber im 10. Jahrhundert*, I, p. 91.

[4] In the omitted passage Saadya quotes the following Scriptural passages: Isa. 46.5-6; 40.18-20; Deut. 4.15-18; Isa. 40.25-26; Psa. 89.7.

[5] Cf. above, pp. 84-5.

[6] Saadya takes the word *ṣelem* in Gen. 1.27 not in an allegorical sense, but literally, the idea being that God calls man's image affectionately 'My image'. The Karaite Elia Haddassi accepted and elaborated this interpretation. Cf. the Translator's article in *Saadya Studies* (ed. E. I. J. Rosenthal), p. 10, n. 2.

(Deut. 4.24), 'For the Lord thy God is a devouring fire'. I explain it to mean that He acts like a burning fire against those who deny and reject Him. There are several instances of a comparison being made without the use of the comparative particle[1] ... So, too, the phrase, 'a devouring fire' means 'like a devouring fire', i.e. that He metes out punishment.

(b) *Quantity*

I next take the category of quantity. This category postulates two things which do not apply to the Creator; one, the threefold dimension of length, breadth and depth; the other, the separation and composition of things that can be separated and joined together. Nothing of this kind can be predicated of the Creator, as is proved by Reason, Scripture, and Tradition. As to Reason, it is precisely the separation and composition of things which led us to look for a Creator, whom we found by the exercise of our Reason.[2] We established the fact that there exists nothing which does not come under the category of things created by Him. As to Scripture, we have already quoted some verses such as Deut. 9.16 and others. With regard to Tradition, we find that the Sages of our people, who are the trustworthy guardians of our religious heritage,[3] whenever they came across such metaphors, never translated them in anthropomorphic terms, but paraphrased them in a manner which conformed to the fundamental principle. They were the disciples of the Prophets and understood their words. Had they thought that these words had an anthropomorphic meaning, they would have rendered them in their literal sense. But they knew on the authority of the Prophets, apart from the judgment of their own Reason, that those anthropomorphic expressions were intended to convey certain sublime and exalted ideas, and so they translated them according to what they knew was the true meaning. Thus, they translated, 'Behold, the hand of the Lord was ...' (Ex. 9.3) by 'Behold, from before the presence of God there was ...'; the verse, '... there was under His feet ...' (Ex. 24.10), they rendered

[1] Other instances of omitted comparative particles quoted by Saadya are Deut. 9.20; 1 Sam. 24.15; 1 Chron. 12.8.
[2] Cf. the Second Proof for Creation, above, pp. 54-5.
[3] Saadya makes here a veiled attack upon the Ḳaraites, who denied the validity of the Oral Tradition.

by '. . . under the throne of His glory'; the phrase 'By the mouth of God' (Ex. 17.1), they rendered by the expression, 'By the Word (*memra*) of God'; the phrase, 'in the ears of God' (Num. 11.18), they rendered by the expression 'before God', and so in many similar instances.[1]

Having explained that Reason, Scripture, and Tradition are unanimous in rejecting the 'comparison' of God (blessed be He), I will now draw up a list of these anthropomorphic expressions. There are ten of them[2]: Head, cf. Isa. 59.17 ('And a helmet of salvation upon His head'); Eye, cf. Deut. 11.12 ('The eyes of the Lord are always upon it'); Ear, cf. Num. 11.18 ('For ye have wept in the ears of the Lord'); Mouth, cf. Ex. 17.1 ('Upon the mouth of God'); Lip, cf. Ps. 89.35 ('Nor alter that which is gone out of My lips'); Face, cf. Num. 6.25 ('The Lord make His face to shine upon you'); Hand, cf. Ex. 9.3 ('Behold, the hand of the Lord'); Heart, cf. Gen. 8.21 ('And the Lord said in His heart'); Bowels, cf. Jer. 31.20 ('Therefore My bowels are stirred for him'); Foot, cf. Ps. 99.5 ('And prostrate yourselves at His footstool').

These and similar expressions show the tendency of language to broaden the meaning of words. Each of the above expressions covers a certain range of meaning, and their allegorical meaning[3] is established by their use in contexts in which there is no reference to God. We know that it is an essential feature of language to extend the meaning of words, to use metaphors and images. Thus, it does not shrink from making Heaven speak — 'The Heavens declare the glory of God' (Ps. 19.2); it makes Sea and Death speak — 'The sea hath spoken, the stronghold of the sea saying . . .' (Isa. 23.4); 'Destruction and death say . . .' (Job 28.23); it makes stones hear — 'Behold, this stone shall be a witness against us; for it hath heard . . .' (Joshua 24.27); it makes mountains exalt — 'The mountains and the

---

[1] Saadya refers to the *Targumim*, which took pains to eliminate anthropomorphic expressions by rendering them in the above-mentioned manner. Cf. A. Schmiedl, *Saadya und Onkelos, MGWJ* 46, pp. 84-8; Rawidowicz, *loc. cit.*, p. 150.

[2] The list is not complete, but Saadya only wishes to illustrate the principle of his exegesis, more examples of which can be found in his Translations and Commentaries. Cf. Rawidowicz, *loc. cit.*, p. 152.

[3] Arab. *ta'wil*; Tibbon's translation *ṣeḥarah* is inaccurate. The Arabic term *ta'wil* denotes the allegorical method of interpretation, which the Mu'tazilites employed in regard to anthropomorphic Ḳur'ān passages. Saadya introduced the method of *ta'wil* into Jewish theology and exegesis. Another term for metaphor repeatedly used in this passage is *madjās*. Cf. above p. 81, n. 4.

hills shall break forth before you into singing' (Isa. 55.13); it describes the hills as clothing themselves — 'And the hills are girded with joy' (Ps. 65.13), and so in many similar instances too numerous to mention. One may ask what a language benefits by using words so loosely as to make them liable to misunderstanding? Why does it not limit itself to a precise usage so as to save us all this trouble (of finding the correct meaning)? My answer is: If language were limited to single and precise words[1] (for each idea), it would be a poor instrument of expression and would not be able to convey even a fraction of what we think. Thus, if we wanted to speak of God in exact language, we would have necessarily to refrain from describing Him as hearing, seeing, being merciful, desirous, so that the only activity we could assign to Him would be His mere existence. [2]

Having explained this point I will now return to the ten metaphorical expressions and elucidate their meaning. I consider that the word Head is used by the prophets in the sense of excellency and elevation; thus it is said with reference to man, 'Thou art my glory, and the lifter up of my head' (Ps. 3.4). The word Eye is used in the sense of supervision; e.g. '... that I may set mine eyes upon him' (Gen. 44.21). Face means favour or anger; e.g. 'In the light of the King's countenance is life' (Prov. 16.15),[3] and 'Her countenance was no longer (sad) with her' (1 Sam. 1.18). The word Ear denotes acceptance; e.g. 'Let thy servant, I pray thee, speak a word in my Lord's ears' (Gen. 44.18). Mouth and Lip mean teaching and command; e.g. 'By the mouth of Aaron and his sons' (Num. 4.27); 'The lips of the righteous feed many' (Prov. 10.21). Hand denotes power; e.g. 'Their inhabitants were of small hand' (II Kings 19.26). Heart signifies wisdom; e.g., 'A young man void of heart' (Prov. 7.7). Bowels denote amiability; e.g. 'Thy Law is in my bowels' (Ps. 40.9). Foot denotes coercion; e.g.

---

[1] Rawidowicz infers from this passage that Saadya had some idea of a *basic language* 'employing the irreducible minimum of words as well as the most concise and adequate ones'. Cf. *loc. cit.*, p. 143.

[2] Although Saadya, in theory, rejects all positive attributes of God he, nevertheless, believes in the practical necessity of describing God in positive terms. He was aware that the religious mind cannot rest satisfied with negative attributes only. The Mu'tazilites who denied the positive attributes of God were, by their opponents, mockingly called Mu'aṭṭilites, i.e. 'Those who emptied the conception of God ' Cf. al-Shahrastānī I. 96, 222; Kauffmann, *loc. cit.*, p. 59, n. 108.

[3] The second half of the verse reads, 'And His favour is as a cloud of the latter rain'. The *parallelismus membrorum* shows that countenance is used in the sense of 'favour'.

'Until I make thine enemies thy footstool' (Ps. 110.1). — In view of the fact that, as we have seen, these words have occasionally a non-anthropomorphic meaning even when used in connection with man, how much more so must their meaning be non-anthropomorphic when used in relation to God. . . .

One might bring against us the following argument: How is it permissible to assume that the anthropomorphic expressions and their derivations bear a metaphorical sense, seeing that, according to Scripture, the form of God is shaped like the form of Man, a form which the Prophets saw speak to them, and to which they attributed His Words; moreover, that He is represented as seated upon a Throne, carried by angels above the firmament, as it is said, 'And above the firmament that was over their heads was the likeness of a throne, as the appearance of a sapphire stone; and upon the likeness of the throne was a likeness as the appearance of a man upon it above' (Ez. 1.26). This form was seen by them likewise upon the Throne with angels standing to its right and to its left, as it is said, 'I saw the Lord sitting on His throne, and all the hosts of heaven standing by Him on His right hand and on His left' (1 Kings 22.19).[1] Our answer is that this form is something created, and that likewise the Throne, the firmament, and the carriers of the Throne are

---

[1] Saadya's problem is whether or not to extend the method of allegorical interpretation (ta'wīl) to Scriptural passages which describe Divine manifestations such as Ezekiel 1.26, or Daniel 7.9. According to the Mu'tazilites and certain Karaites (notably Josef al Baṣir), the prophetic visions describing God must be explained allegorically, just as the anthropomorphic expressions like God's face and hand have to be taken in the allegorical sense of bounty and knowledge. Their argument was that a vision of God is impossible on account of His non-corporeal nature. They denied for the same reason the possibility of a *visio beatifica* in the after-life. Saadya was inclined to accept this view. Thus in the fragment of his *Refutation of Ibn Sākawaihi* (cf. *JQR*, 13, 1901, pp. 662 ff.), his answer to the Karaite assertion that the Rabbis considered the Creator to be corporeal, reads, 'Moreover, all those passages (i.e. of Midrashic, liturgical and mystical literature) have a figurative meaning, just as much as the analogous passages of the Bible'. His final answer, however, is expressed in his conception of Created Glory (*Kaḇod niḇra'*). Whilst he unhesitatingly employed the method of ta'wīl in all other respects, he held that the prophetic descriptions of Divine manifestations admit of no allegorical interpretation. They were the reports of real and true experiences. But what the prophets saw was not God himself, who is incorporeal and invisible, but an appearance of Light, called Glory of God, also *Shekinah* and *Ruah haḵ-ḵodesh*, which God formed from the Primordial Light, which, according to Rabbinic tradition, was withdrawn from the world and stored up for the righteous in the Future World. Saadya combines this conception of Created Glory with the conception of Created Speech (*Dibbur niḇra'*). The Biblical phrase, 'God spoke', means, according to Saadya, that God created a speech which, through the medium of the air, reached the ear of the prophet. For an analysis of these two conceptions and their sources in the Jewish mystical tradition, cf. the Translator's article, 'Saadya's Theory of Revelation', in *Saadya Studies* (ed. E. I. J. Rosenthal), pp. 4-25.

all created. God created them out of Light in order to verify to His prophets that it was He who inspired them with His words, as we shall explain in the third chapter.[1] This Form is more magnificent than the angels, of overpowering majesty and transcendent splendour. It is called Glory of God, and it is this Form which one of the prophets described in these words, 'I beheld till thrones were placed and one that was ancient of days did sit . . .' It is this Form which the Sages called *Shekīnah.* Sometimes there appears a light without the form of a human person. God confers distinction upon His prophet by allowing him to hear a prophetic revelation from that tremendous Form created out of Light and called the Glory of God, as we have explained. What we have said is proved by the words spoken by the prophet in regard to this Form: 'And He said unto me, "Son of man, stand upon thy feet, and I will speak with thee".' (Ez. 2.1). It is not permissible to assume that this speaker was identical with the Lord of the Universe, for, according to the Torah, the Creator never spoke to anyone without a mediator except in the case of our Teacher Moses only, as is said, 'And there hath not arisen a prophet . . .' (Deut. 34.10). In the cases of all other prophets, however, angels spoke to them.[2] If we find a Scriptural passage which definitely mentions an angel, this is clear proof that it speaks of a created being. If it speaks of the Glory of God, it likewise refers to something created. If it mentions the *Tetragrammaton* without adding to it either the word Glory or angel, but adds to it the mention of vision, Throne or Form of a human person, there is no doubt that this is an elliptical expression, and means to say, The Glory of God, or The Angel of God, a usage to which many parallels could be found.

(c) *Quality*

I will now deal with the category of quality, i.e. the accidents.[3] I maintain that it is not in fact permissible to assume

[1] Cf. *Amānāt*, pp. 123-4 (63-4).

[2] Saadya deviates here from his own theory of *dibbur-niḫra'*, which clearly states that the Created Speech and not an angel speaks to all prophets. Cf. the Translator's article quoted above, pp. 20-1.

[3] The 'qualities' of a substance are its 'accidents', although one must extend the term 'accident' to all categories except that of substance. Cf. Guttmann, p. 120, n. 1; Rawidowicz, *loc. cit.*, p. 153, n. 3; Pines, pp. 19 ff. Saadya is here chiefly concerned with the affections (love, hatred, favour, anger).

that God is affected by accidents, seeing that He is the Creator of all accidents. Whenever we find that He speaks of Himself as loving one thing and hating another, the meaning is that everything which He commands us to do He calls 'Loved by Him', since He bids us love it; e.g. 'For the Lord loveth justice' (Ps. 37.28); 'For the Lord is righteous, He loveth righteousness' (Ps. 11.7), etc.; and, after a summary of the things to be loved, it is said, 'For in those things I delight, saith the Lord' (Jer. 9.23) — and everything which He forbids us to do He terms 'Hated by Him', since He bids us hate it; e.g. 'There are six things which the Lord hateth' (Prov. 6.16); 'I hate robbery with iniquity' (Isa. 61.8); and, after a summary of the things to be hated, 'For all these are things that I hate, saith the Lord' (Zech. 8.17). Whenever we find that He speaks of himself as being pleased or wrathful, the meaning is that His bestowal of happiness and reward on some of His creatures He calls pleasure — e.g. 'The Lord taketh pleasure in them that fear Him' (Ps. 147.11); 'Lord, Thou hast been favourable unto Thy land' (Ps. 85.2) — and when He decrees suffering and punishment to others He calls it wrath — e.g. 'The face of the Lord is against them that do evil' (Ps. 34.17); 'But His power and His wrath is against all them that forsake Him' (Ezra 8.22). But wrath and pleasure, as well as love and hatred in the human sense, apply only to beings in whom there is hope and fear. In the case of the Creator of the universe it is impossible to suppose that He should hope for, or fear, anything which He has created.[1] Likewise, we have to exclude from Him all other attributes of quality that may arise in our minds.

---

[1] A vindication of Love and Wrath as essential attributes of God has been attempted by A. Heschel (*Die Prophetie*, 1936).

CHAPTER III

COMMANDMENT AND PROHIBITION[1]

1. LAW AND GRACE

(ed. Landauer 112.11–113.12;
ed. Slucki 58.1-20)

IT is desirable that I should preface this chapter by the following remarks. Since it has been established that the Creator (be He exalted and glorified) is eternal, and that there was nothing co-existent with Him,[2] His creation of the world testifies to His goodness and grace,[3] as we mentioned at the end of Chapter I in speaking of the reason for the creation of things,[4] and according to what we find in the Scriptures as well, namely, that He is good and doeth good, as is said, 'The Lord is good to all; and His tender mercies are over all His works' (Ps. 145.9).

The first of His acts of kindness towards His creatures was the gift of existence, i.e. His act of calling them into existence after they had been non-existent, as He said to the men of distinction among them, 'Everyone that is called by My name, and whom I have created for My glory' (Isa. 43.7). Thereafter He offered them a gift by means of which they are able to obtain complete happiness and perfect bliss, as is said, 'Thou makest me to know the path of life; in Thy presence is fullness of joy, in Thy right hand bliss for evermore' (Ps. 16.11). This

[1] For an analysis and appreciation of the main thesis of this chapter cf. the Translator's article, 'Saadya's Conception of the Law' in *Bulletin of the John Rylands Library*, Manchester, Vol. 28, No. 2 (1944), pp. 320-39; also his (Hebr.) article, 'Saadya's Classification of the Law' in *Rab Saadya Gaon* (ed. J. L. Fishman), Jerusalem, 1943, pp. 658-73.

[2] Cf. Saadya's refutation of the Platonic conception of a *prima materia* and of the dualistic view of two co-eternal principles, above, pp. 61-2, 69-73.

[3] Arab. *jūd wa-faḍl*; Tibbon translates it by *tobah we-hesed.* — Saadya means to say that the act of Creation sprang entirely from God's initiative, seeing that nothing existed which could have caused him to act.

[4] Saadya explains at the end of Chapter 1 (*Amānāt*, pp. 72-3; Hebr., p. 38) that God created the world for two reasons: to manifest His wisdom through the order of creation (cf. above, p. 66, n. 1) and to bestow happiness upon the beings to be created, through the medium of the Law.

gift consists of the commandments and prohibitions which He gave them.

When faced with this statement, the first impulse of Reason will be to object that God should have been able to bestow upon men perfect bliss and to grant them everlasting happiness without imposing upon them commandments and prohibitions. Moreover, it would seem that in this way His goodness would have been more beneficial to them, seeing that they would have been free from the necessity of making any laborious effort. My answer to this objection is that, on the contrary, the order instituted by God, whereby everlasting happiness is achieved by man's labours in fulfilment of the Law, is preferable. For Reason judges that one who obtains some good in return for work which he has accomplished enjoys a double portion of happiness in comparison with one who has not done any work and receives what he receives as a gift of grace. Reason does not deem it right to place both on the same level. This being so, our Creator has chosen for us the more abundant portion, namely, to bestow welfare on us in the shape of reward, thus making it double the benefit which we could expect without an effort on our part, as is said, 'Behold, the Lord God will come as a Mighty One, and His arm will rule for Him; behold, His reward is with Him, and His recompense before Him' (Isa. 40.10).[1]

2. THE TWO CLASSES OF LAW: LAWS OF REASON AND LAWS OF REVELATION

(ed. Landauer 113.13-118.11; ed. Slucki 58.21-61.13)

After these introductory remarks, I now come to the subject proper. I declare that our Lord (be He exalted and glorified) has informed us through the words of His prophets that He

---

[1] Saadya's answer is that man's happiness is greater when his own action has merited the blessings granted to him. For this reason, God, in His infinite love, gave him the Law. It enables man to feel that his happiness is due to a blend of grace and merit. In this sense, the Law is a creation of God's love. Saadya's words paraphrase the well-known saying of R. Ḥananyah b. 'Akashya (Makkot 3.16); they evidently oppose the Pauline doctrine, which considers Law and Grace as incompatibles. On the subject of reward, see A. Marmorstein, *The Doctrine of Merits in Old Rabbinical Literature*, 1920.

wishes us to lead a religious life by following the religion[1] which He instituted for us. This religion contains laws[2], which He has prescribed for us, and which it is our duty to keep and to fulfil in sincerity, as is said, 'This day the Lord thy God commanded thee to do these statutes and ordinances; thou shalt, therefore, observe and do them with all thy heart and with all thy soul' (Deut. 26.16). His messengers established these laws for us by wondrous signs and miracles, and we commenced to keep and fulfil them forthwith. Later we found that speculation confirms the necessity of the Law for us. It would, however, not have been appropriate to leave us to our own devices.[3]

It is desirable that I should explain which matters and aspects (of the Divine Law) speculation confirms as necessary. (1) I maintain that Reason bids us[4] respond to every benefactor either by returning his kindness if he is in need of it, or by offering thanks if he is not in need of recompense. Now since this is a dictate of Reason itself, it would not have been fitting for the Creator (be He exalted and glorified) to waive this right in respect of Himself, but it was necessary that He should command his creatures to worship Him and to render thanks unto Him for having created them.[5] (2) Reason further lays down that the wise man should not permit himself to be vilified and treated with contempt. It is similarly necessary that the

---

[1] Arab. *dín*; Tibbon translates it by *Torah*. Cf. above, p. 44, n. 3.

[2] Arab. *sharī'a*; Tibbon translates it by *miswah*.

[3] Saadya means to say that mankind would have been able to evolve a code of moral laws based on Reason, but such a process would have taken some considerable time. For this reason, God revealed His Law and thus enabled mankind to follow the right path immediately. In a similar way, Lessing solves the tension between Reason and Revelation by explaining the latter as a stage preparatory to, and necessary for, the 'education of the human race'.

[4] Arab. *al-'akl yuwajibu*; Hebr. *has-sekel mehayyeb*. In the subsequent passage Saadya enumerates three distinctly rational laws, those of gratitude, reverence, and social conduct, all of which are introduced by the stereotyped formula, 'Reason dictates it as necessary'. As the Translator has shown in his above quoted articles, the choice both of these three principles and of the term *'akl* for Reason reflects the Mu'tazilite background of Saadya's thought.

[5] In the controversy between Mu'tazila and Ash'ariya as to the nature of the Law, 'gratitude' is the classical example adduced by the Mu'tazila in order to demonstrate the rational character of moral cognition. It is noteworthy that Saadya bases the institution of Divine Worship on the duty of gratitude towards God. In the introduction to his Prayer Book (*Siddur*) he derives the duty of prayer from the verse, 'He is thy praise' (Deut. 10.21): *Tehilah* (praise) comprises three branches, the first of which is thanks for the past (*todah*); the two others are petitions for the future (*tefilah*) and recognition of God's might (*hoda'ah*). Cf. I. Elbogen, 'Saadya's Siddur', in *Saadya Anniversary Volume*, New York, p. 250.

Creator should forbid His servants to treat Him in this way.[1]
(3) Reason further prescribes that human beings should be forbidden to trespass upon one another's rights by any sort of aggression. It is likewise necessary that the Wise should not permit them to act in such a way. (4) Reason, furthermore, permits[2] a wise man to employ a workman for any kind of work and pay him his wages for the sole purpose of allowing him to earn something; since this is a matter which results in benefit to the workman and causes no harm to the employer.[3]

If we put together these four points, their total is tantamount to a summary of the laws which our Lord has commanded us. That is to say, he imposed upon us the duty of knowing and serving Him with a sincere heart, as the prophet said, 'And thou, Solomon, my son, know thou the God of thy father, and serve Him with a whole heart and with a willing mind' (1 Chron. 28.9). Then he forbade us to hurl at Him insult and abuse although it causes Him no harm, seeing that it would not be consonant with wisdom to permit it. Thus it is said, 'Whosoever curseth his God, shall bear his sin' (Lev. 24.15). He did not permit us to trespass upon one another's rights nor to defraud one another, as is said, 'Ye shall not steal; neither shall ye deal falsely, nor lie one to another' (Lev. 19.11). These three groups of laws and their subdivisions form the first of the Two Classes of Law.[4] The first group of the three

[1] This principle excludes blasphemy and all forms of inappropriate attributes of God. It is another product of the contemporary Islamic discussions as to whether the Faithful may invent new names and attributes of God. The Mu'tazilites held that Reason is able to decide whether or not an appellative of God amounts to blasphemy. Cf. the Translator's (Hebr.) article quoted above, p. 664.

[2] The fourth group of legal principles is not dictated, but only permitted by Reason. Although the contents of the laws concerned cannot be ratified by Reason, the very fact that they give man a chance of 'serving' God in obedience to His will renders them, in a formal sense, rational because of the promise of reward and happiness.

[3] God is the 'employer' (cf. Abot 2.21) who bids man to serve Him in the way of obedience to the Law not because He is in need of man's labour, but in order to allow him to earn the reward and happiness which flow from the service of God.

[4] The two classes of Law are those which are discovered by Reason and those based on Divine Revelation only, as Saadya explains later on. The terms used by him to denote these two types of Law are 'akliyyāt (Hebr. sikliyōt) and sam'iyyāt (Hebr. shim'iyōt). Although a similar distinction is already found in Rabbinical literature (b. Yoma' 67 b; Sifra', ed. Weiss, p. 86 a; see I. Heinemann, HUCA IV, 1927, pp. 159-66), Saadya was the first to introduce it in a philosophical form into Jewish thought. He was, no doubt, influenced by the Islamic controversies regarding the nature of the Law. Outwardly considered, his distinction between, and recognition of, the two classes of Law is a compromise between the Asha'rite and Mu'tazilite standpoints. The Asha'rites would not allow Reason to judge the Divine Law. The Mu'tazilites proclaimed Reason the sole arbiter over the validity of the Law; a law was not good

includes humbleness before God, worship, standing up in His presence, etc. All this is written in the Law.[1] The second group includes the prohibition of idolatry,[2] swearing falsely by His name, describing Him by derogatory attributes, etc. All this is written in the Law. To the third group belongs the practice of justice, truth-telling, equity, and impartiality, the avoidance of homicide, adultery, theft, tale-bearing, and trickery against one's fellowman; also the command that the Believer should love his neighbour as he loves himself, and whatever is involved in these precepts. All this is written in the Law.

In regard to all the things which He commands us to do, He has implanted approval of them in our Reason; and in regard to all the things which He forbids us to do, He has implanted disapproval of them in our Reason,[3] as is said in the Book of Wisdom — wisdom being identical with Reason — 'For my mouth shall utter truth, and wickedness is an abomination to my lips' (Prov. 8.7).

The Second Class of Law[4] consists of matters regarding which Reason passes no judgment in the way either of approval or disapproval so far as their essence is concerned. But our Lord has given us an abundance of such commandments and prohibitions in order to increase our reward and happiness through them, as is said, 'The Lord was pleased, for His righteousness' sake, to make the Law great and glorious' (Isa. 42.21).[5] That which belongs to the things commanded by God assumes the character of 'good', and that which belongs to the things forbidden by Him assumes the character of 'evil' on account of

---

[1] Lit. 'is in the text' (*naṣṣ*), i.e. of the Torah.

[2] Arab. *shirk*; association, i.e. of other gods with Him.

[3] In stating that God has implanted the cognition of moral values in man's Reason, Saadya follows the Stoic and Mu'tazilite conception of natural religion. The term Reason (*'aḳl*) used in this connection denotes man's natural moral sense. It corresponds to the notion of *fiṭra*, which expresses the Mu'tazilite doctrine of natural religion.

[4] i.e. the revelational laws.

[5] Cf. above, p. 94, n. 1.

---

because it was revealed by God, but it was revealed by God because it was good, a view clearly inspired by Greek thought. Saadya, in dividing the laws into rational and purely revelational, and recognizing both, seems to have steered a middle course in this controversy, which agitated the mind of the Islamic world. But his attitude was necessitated not so much by a tendency to compromise as by the character of the Biblical Law itself, which so clearly showed the two aspects of (rational) morality and (non-rational) ritual.

the Service thereby performed.[1] Thus the Second (Class of Law) is in fact joined to the First Class.[2] In spite of this[3] one cannot fail, upon closer examination, to find in it some slender moral benefits and rational basis to act against the greater moral benefits and firmer rational basis attached to the First Class (of Law).

It is proper that I should first and foremost discuss the rational laws.[4] Wisdom lays down that bloodshed must be prevented among human beings, for if it were allowed people would annihilate each other. That would mean, apart from the pain suffered, a frustration of the purpose which the Wise (God) intended to achieve through them. Homicide cuts them off from the attainment of any purpose He created and employs them for.

Wisdom further imposes the prohibition of adultery; for, otherwise, human beings would become similar to the animals. No person would be able to know and honour his father in return for the education he received at his hands. Nor would a father be able to bequeath to his son his means of livelihood though the son inherited his existence from him; nor would one know one's other relatives such as paternal and maternal uncles; nor would one be able to show them the kindness due to relatives.

Wisdom further imposes the prohibition of theft; for if it were permitted some people would rely on their ability to steal some other people's property, and would not do any productive work[5] nor amass wealth. But if everyone relied on

---

[1] Saadya means to say that in the case of the revelational laws the character of good and evil is not constituted by the innate moral cognition of man, but by the label of command and prohibition affixed to them by the Divine Law. Since the essence of the Divine Law is 'Service', i.e. obedience to God's will, good and evil in the realm of the Second Class of Law is conditioned by the idea of 'Service'.

[2] Since Reason 'permits' Service as a means of achieving happiness (cf. above, pp. 96-7), the Second Class of Law, i.e. that based on the idea of Service only, are nevertheless 'reasonable', though to a lesser degree than the First Class.

[3] Viz. the fact that the Second Class of Law has no rational basis in itself.

[4] Saadya starts here another line of exposition of the rational and revelational laws. He no longer adheres to the division of the rational laws into three groups as suggested above, but surveys them under different aspects. It must be assumed that this second passage represents a revised version of Saadya's treatment of the subject. As will be seen from the context, it no longer reflects Mu'tazilite influence but a background of Platonic and Aristotelian thought. Cf. the Translator's (Hebr.) article quoted above, pp. 666-71.

[5] Lit., 'cultivate the world'.

this sort of subsistence, theft itself would be rendered impossible by the abolition of property since nothing at all would be found to steal.

Wisdom further lays down, and this is perhaps its first principle, that one should speak the truth and abstain from falsehood, for truth is a statement which accords with facts and actual conditions, whereas a lie is a statement which does not accord with facts and actual conditions. When the senses perceive an object in a certain state, and the soul ascribes to it another state, then the two statements conflict in the soul, and from their contradiction the soul knows that there is something blamable.[1]

I will furthermore say this: I have met certain people who think that our selection of these four things[2] as objects of reprobation is wrong. In their opinion that is to be reprobated which causes them pain and grief, and the good, in their opinion, is that which causes them pleasure and rest.[3] To this proposition I reply at length in Chapter 4 on the subject of Justice.[4] I will here mention only part of the reply. I say that one who holds this opinion has ignored all the arguments which I have adduced[5], and one who ignores this is a fool with whom we need not trouble ourselves. Nevertheless, I shall not be content until I have compelled him to admit that his view is self-contradictory and impossible. I declare that the killing of an enemy whilst pleasing to the killer causes pain to the killed; that the seizure of any property or married woman whilst pleasing to the person who commits this act causes pain to the person who suffers it. According to the opinion of those who hold this theory it would necessarily follow from their premise that each of these acts is both wisdom and folly at the same time, wisdom because it affords pleasure to the person who commits murder, robbery and rape, and folly

---

[1] Arab. *munkar*; Tibbon translates it by *nokrī* or *muzar*. Cf. *Amānāt*, 119.9, 200.2. On the definition of the lie cf. Plato, *Republic* II, B–C 382.

[2] i.e. Homicide, adultery, theft and falsehood.

[3] The hedonistic view, which seems to have found many followers in Saadya's time since the Mu'tazilites also regarded it necessary to combat it. Cf. al-Shahrastānī I, 62. In his refutation of the hedonistic position Saadya stands solidly on Platonic ground.

[4] In a paragraph of Chapter 4 not included in this Selection (*Amānāt*, 149–50; Hebr. 77) Saadya points out that man could not exist without the desire for the satisfaction of his physical wants, but that it is his task to control his passions.

[5] i.e. the four dialectical arguments against homicide, adultery, theft and falsehood.

because it causes pain to his victim. But every theory which involves a self-contradiction is invalid.[1] The contradictory qualities may also appear combined in relation to one person as in the case of honey into which poison has been dropped. In this case the same person eats something which affords pleasure and causes death at the same time. Surely this compels them to admit that (according to their theory) wisdom and folly will exist together.[2]

The Second Class of Law concerns such matters as are of a neutral character from the point of view of Reason,[3] but which the Law has made the objects of commandment in some cases, and of prohibition in others, leaving the rest in their neutral state. Instances are the distinguishing from ordinary days of Sabbath and Festivals; the selection of certain individuals to be Prophets and Leaders;[4] the prohibition to eat certain foodstuffs; the avoidance of sexual intercourse with certain people; the abstention enforced during periods of impurity. The great motive for the observance of these principles and the laws derived and branching out from them is, of course, the command of our Lord and the promotion of our happiness resulting from it, but I find for most of them also some minor and partial motives of a useful character.[5] I wish to point out and to discuss some of them, realizing as I do

[1] Saadya's arguments against the hedonistic view follow closely the Platonic pattern. Plato demonstrated the self-contradiction involved in this theory by pointing out that the pleasant of to-day becomes the pain of to-morrow. Saadya uses the same argument elsewhere. (*Amānāt*, p. 116; Hebr. 60; *Comm. Prov.* p. 7.) Here he introduces a significant change by pointing out that what is pleasing to the evildoer is painful to his victim. The contradiction between pleasure and pain is thus established by reference to the I and the Thou, an attitude which reflects the Jewish ethical conception in contrast to the more self-centered Greek attitude.

[2] Since this is absurd, their theory that the good is identical with the pleasant is disproved.

[3] Lit., 'concerns that which is permissible (i.e. neither commanded nor prohibited) by Reason'. Saadya now turns to a discussion of the 'usefulness' of the Second Class of Law, i.e. that based entirely on Revelation.

[4] Arab. *imām*; Tibbon's translation by *kohen* (priest) obliterates the meaning of the Arabic term which denotes religious and secular leadership. Cf. S. W. Baron, 'Saadya's Communal Activities' in *Saadya Anniversary Volume*, New York, p. 59, n. 113. In his *Siddur*, Saadya uses the term Imām for the Reader (*sheliah ṣibbūr*). Cf. Elbogen, *loc. cit.*, p. 250.

[5] Saadya intends to show that in addition to the general principle of 'Service' which he established as a rational basis for the Second Class of Law (see above, pp. 96–97), there is also an aspect of practical usefulness attached to them.

that God's wisdom (be He blessed and exalted) is above all this.[1]

The distinction conferred upon certain times has these advantages: In the first place, it enables us to desist from our work at certain times and obtain a rest from our many travails; furthermore, to enjoy the pleasures of learned pursuits, and to have the benefit of additional prayer; there is also the advantage that people will be free to meet at gatherings and discuss matters concerning their religion and proclaim them in public, etc.[2]

The distinction conferred upon a certain person has these advantages: it enables the public to receive reliable instruction from him, to ask his intercession; and it enables him to inspire people with a desire for godliness that they may attain something like his own rank, and to devote his efforts to promoting piety amongst men, since he is worthy of that; and similar activities.[3]

The prohibition not to eat certain animals has this advantage: it makes it impossible to liken any of the animals to the Creator;[4] since it is unthinkable that one should permit oneself either to eat or to declare as impure what one likens to God; also it prevents people from worshipping any of the animals, since it is unthinkable that one should worship either what serves for food or what one declares as impure.[5]

[1] Saadya means to say that the rational explanation of these laws cannot claim to exhaust their deep and hidden meaning, which is only known to the wisdom of the Divine Lawgiver.

[2] In other words, the holy seasons of the year are intended to enable man to devote himself entirely to the spiritual side of life. They also help to promote human fellowship on the ground of common ideals. Saadya stresses here the moral and social value of Sabbath and Festivals.

[3] It is noteworthy that Saadya sees here the chief function of religious leadership in its social aspects. In his *Sefer ha-galui* he asserts that 'God does not leave His people in any generation without a scholar whom He inspires and enlightens so that he in turn may so instruct and teach the people as to make them prosper through him'. He leaves no doubt that he regarded himself as the chosen leader of his own generation (cf. S. W. Baron, *loc. cit.*, pp. 57-55), although he modestly mentions on another occasion (cf. above pp. 29-30) that he did not feel himself to be superior in wisdom to any of his contemporaries.

[4] i.e. to conceive God in the image of a particular animal as was the case in ancient pagan religions.

[5] Saadya's interpretation of the dietary laws is, in a sense, a striking anticipation and rejection of the theory of modern ethnologists who explain the Biblical prohibition of eating certain animals by reference to their alleged sacred character as the totems of ancient Hebrew clans. Cf. L. B. Paton, 'Early Hebrew Ethics', in *The Evolution of*

The prohibition of sexual intercourse with certain categories of women has this advantage: in the case of a married woman, I have already stated the reason before.[1] As to one's mother, sister and daughter, the reason is this: the necessities of daily life foster intimacy between the members of a family. Consequently, if marriage between them were permitted, they would indulge in sexual licence.[2] Another purpose is to prevent men from being attracted only by those women who are of beautiful appearance and rejecting those who are not, when they see that their own relatives do not desire them.[3]

The laws of defilement and purity have this advantage: they teach men humility and reverence; they strengthen in them (the desire) to pray once more after a period of neglect;[4] they make people more conscious of the dignity of the Holy Place after they have abstained from entering it for a period; and they turn their minds to the fear of God.[5]

If one examines most of these revelational laws in the above fashion, one will find for them a great number of partial motives and reasons of usefulness. But the wisdom of the Creator and His knowledge is above everything human beings can attain, as is said, 'For the heavens are higher than the earth, so are My ways higher than your ways' (Isa. 55.9).

---

[1] Cf. above, pp. 98-9, where the law forbidding adultery is rationally explained.

[2] Cf. Freud's *Totem and Taboo*, where the complicated social system of primitive society is explained by reference to the need for separation of blood relatives in order to avoid sexual licence.

[3] Saadya wrote a special treatise, *The Interpretation of the Laws of Incest*, which has been edited with an English translation and introduction by H. Hirschfeld in *JQR* Vol. 17, pp. 713-20. Cf. Malter, pp. 346-7.

[4] Cf. *b. Berakōt*, 20 b ff.; *Oṣar ha-Geonīm* (ed. B. M. Lewin), Vol. I, pp. 54-5.

[5] Saadya wrote also a special treatise, *On Defilement and Purity*, which is quoted by a number of medieval authors. Cf. Malter, p. 348.

Ethics (1927), p. 166. Saadya explains that these animals were forbidden in order to combat the view that they were of a sacred character. He wrote a *Book on Forbidden Food*, a fragment of which has survived in two different recensions. Cf. Malter, p. 347.

3. THE NECESSITY OF REVELATION

(ed. Landauer 118.11-120.3;
ed. Slucki 61.14-62.14)

Having distinguished in the preceding chapter the Two Classes of Law, namely, the rational and the revelational laws, it is now desirable that I should explain the necessity of prophetic Revelation.[1] For I have heard that there are people who contend that men do not need prophets, and that their Reason is sufficient to guide them aright according to their innate cognition of good and evil.[2] I, therefore, subjected this view to the test of true reasoning, and it showed me that if things were as they make out, God would know it better and would not have sent us prophets, for He does not do things which have no purpose. Then I reflected still more deeply and found that mankind is fundamentally in need of the prophets, not solely on account of the revelational laws, which had to be announced, but also on account of the rational laws, because their practice cannot be complete unless the prophets show us how to perform them. Thus, for instance, Reason commands gratitude towards God for the blessings received from Him, but does not specify the form, time, and posture appropriate[3]

[1] Lit. 'What is the necessity for messengers and prophets?' So far as the Second Class of Law is concerned, i.e. those based entirely on Revelation, the necessity of prophetic Revelation is no problem. Saadya's question is as to whether there was any need to include the rational laws in the Torah seeing that human Reason could have established them by its own efforts, unaided by Revelation. An answer to this question is already implied in Saadya's two previous statements, (a) that it would have taken some time for mankind to evolve a code of moral laws, and that it would have been unfair to leave a portion of humanity without it; (b) that man's happiness is greater if merited by obedience to God's will; that is to say that although the moral Law is valid in itself by virtue of Reason, reward is only possible for obedience to the revealed Law. (Cf. *Amānāt*, 155; Hebr. 79). Without Revelation, only grace is possible. For this reason God included in the Torah also the laws of Reason. He stamped them, as it were, with the seal of religious Law. In this section Saadya advances a third reason for the necessity of Revelation.

[2] Saadya refers here to the doctrine of the Brahmins (*Barāhima*) which is frequently quoted in both Islamic and Karaite sources as having rejected, on the grounds of 'natural religion', all prophetic (revealed) religion. Cf. al-Shahrastānī II, 356-7; Wensinck, p. 261; Aaron b. Elijah, *'Eṣ Ḥayyim* (ed. Delitzsch), pp. 160-1. Saadya knows also of another version of the doctrine of the Brahmins, that which accepts the Revelation to Adam, but rejects all later prophecy. Cf. *Amānāt*, 139 (71); Pines, p. 211, n. 1.

[3] In his *Siddur*, Saadya covers these three points: he offers the established texts of prayers, the rules about the hours of prayer, and the attitude at prayer. Cf. Elbogen, *loc. cit.*, p. 253.

to the expression of such gratitude. So we are in need of prophets. They gave it a form which is called 'Prayer'[1]; they fixed its times, its special formulae, its special modes and the special direction which one is to face when praying.[2] Another instance: Reason disapproves of adultery, but gives no definition of the way in which a woman can be acquired by a man so as to become his legal wife; whether this is effected merely by a form of words, or merely by means of money, or by her and her father's consent, or by the witness of two or ten people, or in the presence of the whole population of a town, or by a symbolic act, or by impressing a sign upon her.[3] So the prophets laid down the rules of dowry, contract and witness. Another instance: Reason disapproves of theft, but gives no definition of the way in which some object of value becomes a man's property; whether by means of labour, or by way of commerce, or by inheritance, or by the appropriation of un-owned articles as in the case of a hunter in the desert or on the seas; whether the purchase becomes valid by the payment of the price, or by the act of taking possession of the purchased article, or merely by repeating a form of words; and so with many other questions which arise in the wide and extensive field covered by this subject. So the prophets presented us with an equitable decision on every single point relating to these matters.[4] Another instance is the measure of punishment for crimes. Reason deems it right that every crime be punished according to its measure, but does not define its measure; whether punishment should be in the nature of a reprimand only, or should include the defamation of the evildoer, or include, in addition, corporal punishment by stripes, and if so,

[1] Arab. *ṣalāt*; Tibbon translates, *tefilah*, but according to Saadya's classification of Prayer (quoted above, p. 95, n. 5), *tefilah* denotes only one particular element of Prayer, namely, the petition. There is, in fact, another line of thought expressed in Saadya's *Siddur*, which considers *tefilah* (petition) the essential element of prayer (cf. Elbogen, *loc. cit.*, pp. 250-1), but there is no evidence for this in the above passage since it uses the comprehensive Arabic term *ṣalāt*.

[2] As in his *Siddur*, Saadya uses familiar terms of the Muslim cult to denote Jewish practices and institutions, since he wrote for Jews brought up in an Islamic environment. Here he uses the Arabic term *ḳibla* for the direction in which the prayer is to be spoken (i.e. the direction of the Temple in Jerusalem). Other expressions borrowed from the Islamic cult are *Imām* (cf. above, p. 100, n. 4) and *ṣalāt*. See Elbogen, *loc. cit.*, p. 250.

[3] Obviously some non-Jewish practice, which Saadya found in vogue.

[4] Saadya himself wrote treatises on the Laws of Inheritance, on the Laws of Pledges, on Testimony and Contracts, and on Laws regulating the acquisition of objects received by gift. Cf. Malter, pp. 344-8.

to what extent, which question applies likewise to defamation and reprimand; or whether nothing short of capital punishment would suffice; and whether the punishment of every offender should be one and the same, or whether one punishment should be different from another. So the prophets prescribed a measure of punishment for each crime according to its nature; they did not lay down the same rule for all, fixing for some a fine in money. And because of these matters which we have enumerated, and other similar ones, we are in need of prophetic Revelation.[1] If we had had to rely on our own judgment in these matters, we should have opposed each other and never agreed on anything;[2] moreover, prophetic Revelation was necessary on account of the revelational laws, as I have already explained.

4. THE CREDENTIALS OF TRUE PROPHECY

(ed. Landauer 120.3-122.14;
ed. Slucki 62.14-63.28)

Having explained the necessity for the sending of prophets, it is desirable that I should now explain how their prophetic mission was verified to the rest of the people.[3] I say then that

[1] Saadya assigns to prophetic Revelation the function of determining the details and particulars of the rational laws, which Reason is unable to establish. He must have had in mind Aristotle's distinction between natural and legal justice, the one being the universal law of nature, the other being the particular law of each country and founded on agreement. Cf. *Eth. Nic.*, V, 1134 b; *Rhetoric* I, 13.2.

[2] In echoing Aristotle's reliance on agreement for legal justice, Saadya makes the ironical remark that people never agree. Hence the authority of the revealed Law is necessary to settle the details of legislation, although Reason is able to establish the principles. In other words, the Prophet is the legislator of the ideal state. Cf. the Translator's article, *loc. cit.*

[3] Saadya explains elsewhere that the appearance of the Created Glory (*Kabod nibra'*), which accompanied, as a visible element, the audible manifestation (*dibbur nibra'*) of God's Word (see above, p. 90, n. 1), served as a criterion to the Prophet that he was in the presence of Divine Revelation. (Cf. *Amānāt*, 99-100, 123; Hebr. 51, 63). Only in the case of Moses' prophecy did the Word speak directly, without the intermediacy of a visible manifestation. (For an explanation of Saadya's complicated theory see the Translator's article, 'Saadya's Theory of Revelation', pp. 20 ff.). Saadya's problem, in the above chapter, is, however, the criterion of true prophecy, not for the prophet himself, but for the people to whom he is to convey the Divine message. Here the function of miracle comes in, as explained in the text. Although Saadya states (see *Amānāt*, 123; Hebr. 63) that the people saw in the 'Pillar of cloud' a testimony of God's self-manifestation to Moses and probably to the other prophets as well (cf. Ps. 99.7), he regards, not quite consistently, the performance of miracles as a necessary credential of true prophecy.

men know (the limits) of their power and ability, namely, the fact that they are unable to subdue the elements of nature or to change the essence of things. They realize that they are powerless in regard to these matters since this is the work of the Creator. He subdued the diverse elements of nature and combined them to form composite things in spite of their antagonistic character. He transformed their original natures so that, in their combinations, their essential characteristics disappeared and something new and different emerged, namely, man and plant and similar bodies. This is indisputably a sign that they are the work of a Creator. Now every prophet chosen by the Creator for a prophetic mission commences his career as soon as God furnishes him with one of the following signs; either he enables him to subdue the elements of nature, e.g. to prevent fire from burning or restraining water from flowing or cause the sphere to halt on its way, etc.; or He enables him to change the essence of the elements, e.g. to transform an organism into inorganic nature, or inorganic nature into an organism, or water into blood, or blood into water. And whenever such a sign is delivered into the hands of the prophet the people who see it are obliged to pay reverence to him and to hold his message to be true, for the Wise (God) does not deliver a sign into his hands unless he is trusted.[1] This fact, although discoverable by Reason, is also stated in the text of Scripture, as the reader will know from the story of our Teacher Moses and the wonders and miracles delivered into his hand, which, for the sake of brevity, I shall not mention here as these things are described in the text of the Book of Exodus and in other books and their Commentaries;[2] thus he said to his people, 'The great trials which thine eyes saw' (Deut. 7.19). Those men[3] who believed[4] in him believed the truth,[5] and they were the superior ones, as is said, 'And he did the signs in the sight of the people, and the people believed' (Ex. 4.30-31). Those who did not believe in him and did not believe the truth were lost in error, as the reader will know

---

[1] Saadya qualifies this statement later (see below, pp. 113-4) by saying that miracles produced in support of doctrines which are contrary to Reason cannot be accepted as evidence for their truth. For 'no miracle can prove the rationally impossible'. It is most remarkable that he unhesitatingly puts the judgment of Reason above any proof furnished by miracles. Cf. also Albo, 'Iḳḳarim, I, 18.

[2] Arab. tafsir.   [3] Lit. 'servants'.   [4] Arab. 'āmana.   [5] Arab. ṣaddaḳa.

from the story of those in regard to whom it is said, 'Because they believed not in God . . .' (Ps. 78.22).

I must here add a qualification to avoid misunderstanding, namely, that the Creator (be He exalted and glorified) does not change the essence of a thing before having announced to the people that He is going to change it. The reason for this[1] is that they may believe in the truth of His prophet. But without reason He does not make any change in the essence of things, for if we were to believe[2] that, we should have no certainty of anything, and none of us when returning to his home and people would be sure that the Creator had not changed their essences so that they would be different from what they were when we left them; similarly if a man acted as witness for a person or pronounced judgment on a person. But it is necessary for us to believe[2] that the existing things remain as they are, and that their Lord does not alter them except after having announced it beforehand.

I say furthermore that, in the judgment of wisdom, it is impossible that the messengers sent to mankind should have been angels,[3] because men do not know either the capabilities or the limitations of the angels. If they (the angels) had come and performed miracles which men are powerless to perform, people would have thought that such is the nature of all angels, and they would have had no clear proof that the miracle was a sign from the Creator. If, however, the prophets are men like ourselves and we find that they are doing things which we are actually powerless to do and which are entirely the work of the Creator, it becomes evident to us that they are sent by His Word. I maintain that for this very reason God placed the prophets and the rest of mankind on the same level in regard to death, so that men should not think that, in the same way as the prophets differ from the rest of mankind by being able to live

---

[1] i.e. the reason for changing the nature of things.

[2] Arab. *'i'tiḳād*.

[3] Saadya rejects the conception of angel as intermediary of Revelation. According to the *Barāhima* who denied prophecy (cf. above, p. 103, n. 2) God communicates with men through angels. Cf. al-Shahrastāni, II, 6, 42; Guttmann, p. 144, n. 2.—Saadya also repudiates the angel doctrine in the form given it by Nahawandi and the Maghāriyya sect as well as by Jewish mystics who identified the angel mentioned in Ex. 23.20 with a mediator (*meṭaṭron*), a conception closely akin to the *Logos* of Philonic tradition and bordering upon Gnostic dualism. Instead of the angel, he introduces the conception of *Kabod nibra'*, which is rooted in the Jewish mystical tradition. Cf. the Translator's article, 'Saadya's Theory of Revelation', pp. 17-19; 21-5.

for ever, so they also differ from the rest of mankind in being able to do things which others are powerless to do. For the same reason, God did not cause them to abstain from food, drink and sexual intercourse, since this might have weakened the force of their miracles, for people might have thought that such abstinence was due to their peculiar nature and that in the same way as such a nature was granted to them, so the power of working miracles was also granted to them. For the same reason, God did not assure them of lasting bodily health, or of great fortunes, or of posterity, or of protection against oppressors seeking to beat or insult or kill them; for if He had done so, it was possible that people might attribute their miracles to their peculiar condition by virtue of which they did not belong to the same class as ordinary men; they would say that since they are shown to be exceptional in those respects, it follows that they are capable of things which all other people are powerless to do. Knowing as I do that His wisdom is above everything, I nevertheless venture to declare that the reason why He left them in every respect in the same condition as the rest of mankind, and yet at the same time made them different by enabling them to do things which all other men are powerless to do, was to verify His sign and to establish His prophecy. I declare that for this reason also, He did not cause them to perform miracles continually or to know the hidden things (of the future) continually lest the people should think that they are possessed of a peculiar quality to which this power is due, but He made them do this at certain periods and to have such knowledge at certain opportune times. In this way it became clear that this originated from the Creator and not from them.[1]

5. SCRIPTURE AND TRADITION

(ed. Landauer 125.18-128.2;
ed. Slucki 65.13-66.12)

I will now explain the character of the Holy Scriptures.[2] I declare that God included in His Book a brief record of all that

[1] Whilst Saadya emphasizes the ordinary human quality of the prophet, Yehudah Hallevi raises the status of the prophet to a position similar to that of the angels. As to the background of Yehudah Hallevi's theory, cf. the article by I. Heinemann in *K'nesset*, 5702, pp. 267 ff., and the Translator's article in *Melilah*, pp. 14-17.
[2] Arab. *al-kutub al-mukaddas*.

happened in past times in the form of narratives[1] intended to instruct us in the right way of obedience towards Him. He further included His laws, and added promises of reward for their observance. Thus Scripture became a source of everlasting benefit. For all the books of the prophets and the learned books of all nations, numerous though they are, comprise only three principal elements: (1) a list of commandments and prohibitions, which forms one point; (2) the reward and punishment which are the fruits of the former; and (3) an account of those who rendered good service to their country and prospered, as well as of those who dealt corruptly and perished. For the instruction needed for a good life is only complete if these three elements are combined. Let me give an illustration: A man visits a sick person afflicted with fever and knows for certain that the cause of his illness is pressure of the blood. Now if he tells him not to eat meat nor to drink wine, he has already done something to instruct him in the right way, but his instruction is as yet incomplete. If he adds the warning, 'lest you contract pleurisy', he has increased the weight of his instruction, but it still remains incomplete until he clinches it with the example, 'As was the case with X who contracted pleurisy'. By this means he has made his instruction complete. For this reason the Scriptures comprise these three principal aspects, of which I need not give any examples as they are so familiar.

I say further that the Wise (be He exalted and glorified) knew that His laws and the stories of His wondrous signs would, through the passage of time, require people to hand them down[2] to posterity, so that they might become as evident to later generations as they were to the earlier ones. Therefore, He prepared in our minds a place for the acceptance of reliable Tradition,[3] and in our souls a quiet corner for trusting it so that His Scriptures and stories should remain safely with us.[4]

[1] Arab. 'achbār, from sing. chabar. The term chabar, story, report, is also used in the wider meaning of tradition, and occurs in this sense repeatedly throughout this chapter.

[2] Arab. nāḳil. Saadya discusses in this chapter the character of the 4th Root of Knowledge mentioned in the Prolegomena. Cf. above, p. 37.

[3] Arab. al-chabar aṣ-ṣādiḳ; Tibbon translates, ha-haggadah han-neëmenet. Cf. above, p. 37, n. 6.

[4] Saadya means to say that the faculty of belief in the truth of reports received, and tradition in general, forms an integral part of the make-up of the human soul. He illustrates this point in the exposition which follows; it stresses the paramount importance of tradition in all spheres of intellectual and practical life.

I deem it proper to mention a few points in regard to the truth of Tradition. Unless men had the confidence that there exists in the world such a thing as true report, no man would build any expectations on any report he might be told about success in any branch of commerce, or of progress in any art [which we naturally believe], since it is gain which man requires and for which he exerts his strength. Nor would he fear what he should guard against, be it the dangerous state of a road, or a proclamation prohibiting a certain action. But if a man has neither hopes nor fears,[1] all his affairs will come to grief. Unless it is established that there is such a thing as true report in this world, people will not pay heed to the command of their ruler nor his prohibition, except at such time as they see him with their own eyes, and hear his words with their own ears; and when no longer in his presence, they will cease to accept his commands and prohibitions.[2] If things were like this, all management of affairs would be rendered impossible and many people would perish. And unless there was a true tradition in this world, a man would not be able to know that a certain property was owned by his father, and that this is an inheritance from his grandfather, nor would a man be able to know that he is the son of his mother, let alone that he is the son of his father. Human affairs would be in a state of perpetual doubt, so much so that people would only hold to be true what they perceive with their own senses, and this only at the actual moment of their sense perceptions, an opinion which is akin to the view of *those who affect ignorance*,[3] which I mentioned in Chapter 1.

Scripture already declares that reliable tradition is as true as the things perceived by sight. Thus it says, 'For pass over to the isles of the Kittites, and see, and send unto Kedar, and consider diligently . . .' (Jer. 2.10).[4] Why does it add the words, 'And consider diligently' in connection with the matter of

[1] Saadya sees in Hope and Fear — the two cardinal themes of the Greek Tragedy — the prime movers in human affairs. Cf. above, pp. 68, 92, where he states that in the case of God it is impossible to assume that He should hope or fear.

[2] Saadya seems to assume that the refusal to believe in true reports entails an inability to believe oneself in regard to the testimony of one's own memory.

[3] Arab. *mutajahilun*; by this term Saadya denotes the Pyrrhonists whose standpoint is one of absolute scepticism. He deals with this view under No. 13 of his list of cosmological theories. Cf. *Amānāt*, 69 ff. (36 ff.); see above, p. 62, n. 4.

[4] The verse mentions two ways of verification, (1) to see for oneself; (2) to ask for reports. Both are put on the same level, which seems to Saadya an indication that sense perception and tradition have the same character of truth.

report? The answer is: because a report (tradition) is, unlike sense perception, liable to be falsified in two ways, either through a wrong idea or through wilful distortion. For this reason Scripture warns, 'And consider diligently'. Having considered deeply how we can have faith in tradition seeing that there are these two ways (of possible falsification) I found, by way of Reason, that wrong idea and wilful distortion can only occur and remain unnoticed if they emanate from individuals, whereas, in a large collective group, the underlying ideas of the individuals who compose it will never be in agreement with one another, and if they wilfully decide and agree on inventing a story, this will not remain unnoticed amongst their people, but whenever their story is put out, there will be related, at the same time, the story of how they came to agree upon it. And when a tradition is safe against these two possibilities (of falsification), there is no third way in which it could possibly be falsified. And if the Tradition of our Fathers is viewed from the aspect of these principles, it will appear sound and safe against any attack, and true, and firmly established.[1]

6. The Eternal Validity of the Law

(ed. Landauer 128.3-19; 132.5-133.10;
ed. Slucki 66.13-26; 68.9-32)

Having dealt with these matters (i.e. the character of Scripture and Tradition), I deem it right to add to my remarks a word on the Abrogation of the Law,[2] since this seems to be

[1] In a passage of the Prolegomena not included in this Selection (*Amānāt*, 22-3; Hebr. 11-12), Saadya quotes Isa. 44.8 ('And ye are my witnesses') with reference to the historical experience of Israel as recorded in the Scriptures. He particularly mentions the Ten Plagues, the dividing of the Red Sea, and the Sinaitic Revelation. He continues, 'I think that the most wondrous experience of all is the miracle of the Mannah; for a miracle which continues for some period is more wondrous than one which passes, for no fraudulent device can be suspected when a people of nearly a million souls is fed from nothing for a period of 40 years . . . and it cannot be assumed that the whole people should have agreed (to invent this story), for general consent is sufficient as a condition for the trustworthiness of a tradition'. The meaning of the last sentence becomes clear from the above exposition. Cf. Guttmann, p. 147-8, n. 3. Later Jewish philosophers followed the trend of this 'historical' argument. It plays a most prominent part in Yehudah Hallevi's thought. Cf. *Kuzari*, I, 86, where Saadya's remark about the miracle of Mannah is literally repeated. Cf. also I, 25, 47-8.

[2] The question whether the Biblical Law was given for all time or whether it was to be abrogated at a certain period, formed the subject of many disputes amongst Jews, Christians, and Muhammedans. The famous historian al-Mas'ūdī (died 957) reports that he had numerous discussions on this point with Abū Kathir, the teacher of Saadya. Cf. Ventura, pp. 201-2.

the proper place for it. I declare that the Children of Israel, according to an accepted tradition,[1] were told by the prophets that the laws of the Torah shall never be abrogated.[2] They assert that they heard this in clear terms which allowed no room for misunderstanding or allegorical interpretation. I thereupon searched in the Scriptures and found support for this tradition. First, in regard to most of the laws it is written that they are 'a covenant for ever'[3] and 'for your generations'. There is, furthermore, the phrase which occurs in the Torah, 'Moses commanded us a law, an inheritance of the congregation of Jacob' (Deut. 33.4). Moreover, our people, the Children of Israel, are a people only by virtue of our laws, and since the Creator has declared that our people should exist as

[1] Arab. *nakl*; Tibbon translates it by *kabbalah*.

[2] Cf. *p. Megillah*, I, 5: R. Johanan said, 'The Prophets and the Writings will be abolished in the Future World, but the Five Books of the Torah will never be abolished ... R. Shimeon b. Levi said, 'Not even the Scroll of Esther nor the laws (*halakōt*) will ever be abolished'. In some Midrashic utterances, however, the possibility of an abrogation of certain laws in the Future World is considered. Cf. *Lev. R.* 13.3; *Midr. Shoḥer Ṭob* on Ps. 146.7 ('The Lord looseth the prisoners' — *mattir 'assurim* — in the sense of *mattir 'issurim*, 'permitteth that which is forbidden'); *Yalk. Shimeoni Prov.* §944. See also *Tossafot Niddah* 61 b. In Halachic literature the view is predominant that even in the Future World not a single law nor letter of the Torah will be changed. The Midrashic passages quoted above are explained either with reference to the state of man after death when his soul is free from the Law (cf. *b. Niddah* 61 b; *Yad Mal.* 437), or as a temporary suspension of certain laws (cf. *Sedeh Ḥemed*, Vol. 11; ch. 3. 7), or in a merely homiletical fashion (cf. *Responsa R. Shelomo b. 'Adret* 93). Maimonides (*Comm. Mishnah Sanh.* X, 9; *Yes. Hat.* 9) declares with reference to Deut. 13.1 that the Law will never be modified nor changed for another Law (cf. the line in the *Yigdal Hymn*, 'God will not alter nor change His Law to everlasting for any other'). In *Moreh* III, 34, he makes the same statement. He explains that the Law being perfect (Ps. 19.8), it is not subject to change. Albo (*'Ikkarim* III, 14-20) argues against Maimonides that, on principle, the Law could be altered (with the exception of the Decalogue) if the prophet who announced a new law were superior to Moses; but this possibility, he emphasizes, is precluded by Deut. 34.10. In Jewish mysticism, the Midrashic utterances quoted above are given depth and significance by the theory of World Periods (*Shemitōt*) as explained in the book *Temunah* (about 1250). It teaches that the Torah is to be read in different ways during the various successive periods without, however, being changed in its outward form. In the current period which is that of Stern Judgment, commandments and prohibitions are necessary, in accordance with the present reading of the Torah. But in the coming Aeon the Torah will no longer contain prohibitions since the power of evil will be broken. Cf. Scholem, pp. 175-6; see also pp. 228, 275. The followers of the Jewish Pseudo-Messiah Sabbataï Ṣebi, especially the Frankist movement, made ample use of this bold theory, by which they sought to sanction their antinomian doctrine. Cf. Scholem's article in *Kenesset*, 5697, pp. 370 ff.

[3] *le-'olam.*—Albo (*'Ikkarim*, III, 16) denies that the Hebrew word *'olam* necessarily means eternity; it may also be applied, he says, to limited periods, in the same way as the word *neṣaḥ*. In a passage not included in this Selection (*Amānāt*, 138-9; Hebr. 71), Saadya admits that *'olam* can denote a limited period, but asserts that such a meaning is exceptional and cannot be applied without cogent reasons. On the etymology and meaning of *'olam* cf. the Translator's article 'Olam und Aion' in *Festschrift für Jakob Freimann* (1937), pp. 1-14.

long as heaven and earth exist, it necessarily follows that our laws should continue to exist as long as heaven and earth are in being, and this is what he says, 'Thus saith the Lord, who giveth the sun for a light by day, and the ordinances of the moon and of the stars for a light by night, who stirreth up the sea, that the waves thereof roar, the Lord of Hosts is His name: If these ordinances depart from before Me, saith the Lord, then the seed of Israel also shall cease from being a nation before Me for ever' (Jer. 31.35-36).[1]

I found that in the last period of prophecy God exhorted (his people) that they should keep the Law of Moses until the Day of Judgment, which will be preceded by the advent of Elijah; He says, 'Remember ye the law of Moses, My servant, which I commanded unto him in Horeb for all Israel, even statutes and ordinances. Behold I will send you Elijah the prophet before the coming of the great and terrible day of the Lord' (Mal. 3.22-23).

Some people say that in the same way as the reason for our believing in Moses was his performance of wonders and miracles, so it follows that the reason for believing in some other prophet would be the performance of wonders and miracles by the latter. I was greatly astonished when I heard this remark. For the reason of our belief in Moses lies not in the wonders and miracles only, but the reason for our belief in him and all other prophets lies in the fact that they admonished us in the first place to do what was right,[2] and only after we had heard the prophet's message and found that it was right did we ask him to produce miracles in support of it. If he performed them, we believed in him. But if we hear his call and find it, at the outset, to be wrong, we do not ask him for miracles, for no miracle can prove the (rationally) impossible. The case is similar to that of two people Reuben and Simon appearing before the judge. If Reuben claims from

---

[1] Some of the Church Fathers, notably Justin and Eusebius, sought to prove the abrogation of the Biblical Law by reference to Jer. 31.31-4, where mention is made of the 'new covenant' which God will make with the House of Judah. Saadya quotes here verses 35-6 of that very chapter in order to prove that the Law of the Torah is destined to be valid eternally. A direct answer to the Christian exegesis of Jer. 31.31-4 is given in a subsequent passage, not included in this Selection (*Amānāt*, 135; Hebr. 69), where Saadya points out that the 'new covenant' is nothing but the old Law fulfilled and no longer broken by Israel. He refers to verses 32-3 in support of his interpretation.

[2] Arab. *jā'iz*; lawful, right, i.e. conforming to the innate cognition of Reason.

Simon something within the realm of the possible, saying for instance, 'He owes me a thousand dinar', then the judge will ask him to produce evidence, and if he can establish the claim, the money will be awarded to him. But if he claims something in the nature of the impossible, as by saying, 'He owes me the river Tigris', his claim will be void from the outset since nobody owns the Tigris, and it would not be correct for the judge to ask him for evidence for his claim.

So it is with everyone who claims to be a prophet. If he tells us, 'My Lord commands you to fast to-day', we ask him for a sign of his prophecy, and if we see it, we believe it and shall fast. But if he says, 'My Lord commands you to commit adultery and to steal' or, 'He announces to you that He will flood the world again' or, 'He informs you that He created heaven and earth in one year (without allegory),[1] we shall not ask him for a sign because he brings us a message which neither Reason nor Tradition can sanction. Some people carried the discussion a stage further and said, 'What, if he does not pay regard to us, but shows us wonders and miracles, and willy-nilly we see them, what shall we say to him then?' I replied: 'We shall tell him then the same as we would say in case someone showed us wonders and miracles in support of a doctrine which runs counter to the innate dictates of our Reason, with regard to the approval of truth and the disapproval of falsehood, etc.'[2] He would be driven to assert that the disapproval of falsehood and the approval of truth are not dictated by Reason, but are matters of (legal) commandment and prohibition,[3] and so likewise the condemnation of murder, adultery, theft, etc. But when he comes down to that, he is no longer worthy of my notice, and I see no purpose in further discussion with him.[4]

---

[1] Arab. *bilā tāwīl*; i.e. in a literal sense.
[2] i.e. We shall reply that no miracle can prove the rationally impossible.
[3] The Ash'arite view. Cf. above, p. 96, n. 4.
[4] The authority of Reason is above discussion and cannot be disproved by miracles.

CHAPTER IV

ON OBEDIENCE AND DISOBEDIENCE;
COMPULSION AND JUSTICE

1. MAN — THE CENTRE OF THE UNIVERSE[1]

(ed. Landauer 145.1-148.7;
ed. Slucki 75.1-76.17)

I COMMENCE my discussion of this point with the following prefatory observation. In spite of the great multiplicity of created things, we need have no difficulty in deciding which of them is the most essential part[2] of Creation, because this is a point which the Science of Nature is able to elucidate for us. From the teaching of Science on this point we find that Man is the most essential part of Creation, because it is the rule and habit of Nature to place the most excellent (part of anything) in the centre with things of less excellence surrounding it.[3] To take our first illustration from something very small: The grain is in the middle of the grain-sheaf because it is the most excellent part of the stalk; for the plant grows out, and is fed, from the grain. Likewise the kernel from which the tree grows is in the middle of the fruit, no matter whether the kernel is edible as in the case of an almond tree, or whether it is a stone as in the case of the date. In the latter case the edible part of the fruit is of less importance and left at the outside as a protecting shell for the kernel. Likewise the yolk is in the middle of the egg because the young of birds and the chickens develop from it. Likewise, the heart of man is in the middle of his chest because it is the seat of the soul and of the natural warmth.[4] Likewise the pupil[5] is in the middle of the eye because it is the chief organ of sight. We notice that the same observation applies to a great number of things besides. Then we found

[1] For a discussion of this Chapter, cf. S. Rawidowicz, 'Mishnat ha-'Adam le-Ra<u>b</u> Saadya Gaon', in *Metsudah* (ed. S. Rawidowicz), 1943, pp. 112-25.
[2] Lit. 'the final object' (Arab. *al-maḳṣūd*).
[3] Cf. Aristotle, *De caelo*, II, 13, 293 a, 31-2, in the name of the Pythagoreans.
[4] Cf. below, p. 148.
[5] Lit. 'the seeing spirit', an expression borrowed from the Greek ὀπτικὸν πνεῦμα.

that the earth occupied the centre of the universe,[1] entirely surrounded by the celestial spheres.[2] This made it clear to us that the earth[3] was the most essential part in the created universe.[4] Then we examined everything which the earth contains, and observed that earth and water are both inanimate things; the beast we found to be lacking in Reason; there remained nothing superior but Man. This makes it certain for us that he is undoubtedly the ultimate object of Creation.[5] We searched the Scriptures and found therein the Divine proclamation, 'I, even I, have made the earth, and created man upon it' (Isa. 45.12). Moreover, the opening chapter of the Torah first goes through all categories of creatures and at the end of them says, 'Let us make man' (Gen. 1.26), just like an architect who builds a palace, furnishes it, puts everything in order, and then invites the owner to occupy it.[6]

After these preliminary remarks I come to my subject proper.

Our Lord has informed us through His prophets that He endowed man with superiority over all His creatures. Thus He said, 'And have dominion over the fish of the sea, and over the fowl of the air. . . .' (Gen. 1.38). This is also the theme of Psalm 8 from beginning to end. God further informed us that He gave man the ability to obey Him, placing it as it were in his hands, endowed him with power and free will, and commanded him to choose that which is good, as is said, 'See, I have set before thee this day life and good . . .', and concludes, 'Therefore choose life' (Deut. 30.15, 19). The prophets have established this doctrine by signs and miracles, and we have accepted it. Afterwards we studied well the question wherein man's superiority consisted, and we found that he was raised to superiority by virtue of the wisdom which God bestowed

---

[1] Lit. 'Heavens'.

[2] The Aristotelian view of the cosmos, which was commonly accepted in the Middle Ages. Cf. *Moreh*, I, 72.

[3] On the text, cf. Malter, p. 212, n. 484.

[4] Aristotle, followed by Maimonides (*Moreh*, III, 12-14), holds the opposite view: the outer spheres are more excellent than those nearer to the earth, and the earth itself, being most remote from the Prime Mover, is the least of all in excellence.

[5] This view, for which much support can be found in Haggadic literature, was violently opposed by many Jewish authors in the Middle Ages, notably by Abraham Ibn Ezra, Maimonides, and Jedaiah Bedersi; amongst the Karaites, by Yefet ben 'Ali. For the literature see Malter's note 485.

[6] Cf. *b. Sanhedrin* 38 a; *Gen. R.* 8.5; 15.4.

upon and taught him, as is said, 'Even He that teacheth man knowledge' (Ps. 94.10). By virtue of it man preserves the memory of deeds that happened long ago, and by virtue of it he foresees many of the things that will occur in the future. By virtue of it he is able to subdue the animals so that they may till the earth for him and bring in its produce. By virtue of it he is able to draw the water from the depth of the earth to its surface; he even invents irrigating wheels that draw the water automatically. By virtue of it he is able to build lofty mansions, to make magnificent garments, and to prepare delicate dishes. By virtue of it he is able to organize armies and camps, and to exercise kingship and authority for establishing order and civilization among men. By virtue of it he is able to study the nature of the celestial spheres, the course of the planets, their dimensions, their distances from one another, as well as other matters relating to them.[1]

If one imagines that the highest degree of excellence is given to some being other than Man, let him show us such excellence or a similar one in any other being. He will not find it. It is therefore right and proper that man should have received commandments and prohibitions, and that he should be rewarded and punished, for he is the axis of the world and its foundation, as is said, 'For the pillars of the earth are the Lord's . . .' (1 Sam. 2.8), and furthermore, 'The righteous is the foundation of the world' (Prov. 10.25).

When I reflected on these fundamental facts and what follows from them, I became convinced that our belief in man's superiority is not a mere delusion, nor the result of our inclination to judge in favour of man; nor is it out of vanity and boastfulness that we make such a claim for ourselves, but it is something demonstrably true and perfectly correct. The reason why God in His wisdom endowed man with this excellence can only be to make him the recipient of commandments and prohibitions, as it says, 'Behold, the fear of the Lord, that is wisdom; and to depart from evil is understanding' (Job 28.28).

---

[1] In a way, Saadya's praise of man recalls the famous Hymn of Man's Glory in Sophocles, *Antigone*, 333 sqq.

2. THE FREEDOM OF THE WILL

(ed. Landauer 150.18-153.12;
ed. Slucki 77.23-78.33)

Having explained the way in which we should approach these questions relating to the Justice of God,[1] I say this: It accords with the justice of the Creator and His mercy towards man that He should have granted him the power[2] and ability[3] to do what He commanded him to do, and to refrain from what He forbade him to do. This is established by Reason and by Scripture. By Reason, because the Wise will not insist that a person should do a thing which lies beyond his ability and strength; by Scripture, as it says, 'O My people, what have I done unto thee? and wherein have I wearied thee? Testify against Me' (Micah 6.3). Furthermore, it is said in Scripture, 'They that wait for the Lord shall renew their strength' (Isa. 40.31); moreover, 'Keep silence before Me, O Islands, and let the peoples renew their strength' (Isa. 41.1), and '. . . When the morning is light, they execute it, because it is in the power of their hand' (Micah 2.1).

I also found that the ability to act must necessarily exist before the act, so as to give man the free choice of either acting or abstaining from the act. For if the ability to act came into existence only at the moment of the act and were co-existent with it, the two would be either mutually inter-dependent or neither of them would be the cause of the other. If, on the other hand, the ability to act were to arise only after the act, man would have the power to take back an act which he had already performed. This is absurd, and the other alternative which we mentioned before is likewise absurd. It, therefore, follows that man's power to act must exist before his action so that, by his power, he may be

---

[1] Next to the problem of the Unity of God, that of God's Justice forms the main subject of Mu'tazilite theology.

[2] Arab. *ḳadar*, which denotes, in the first place, God's 'measure', 'decree', but, in the view of the Mu'tazilites, also man's 'power' over his actions. For this reason, the Mu'tazilites were called *Kadarīyya*.

[3] Arab. *'isti'dāt*.

able perfectly to fulfil the commandment of his Lord and God.[1]

I deem it important to make clear that in the same way as a man's action is a positive act, his abstention from a certain action is likewise a positive act, for by abstaining from that action he does, in fact, the opposite of it. This is not the case with the Creator (be He exalted and glorified), whose abstention from creating things is not an act. For if He abstains from creating the substances and their qualities,[2] it is something to which there exists no opposite, whereas man, whenever he abstains from doing one thing, actually chooses the opposite since his action concerns accidents only: if he does not love, he hates; if he is not favourably disposed, he is angry; there is no intermediate position between these.[3] Thus Scripture says, 'Therefore shall ye keep My charge, that ye do not any of these abominable customs, which were done before you' (Lev. 18.30), and furthermore, 'Yea, they do not unrighteousness; they walk in His ways'[4] (Ps. 119.3).

I must further explain that man does not perform any action unless he chooses to do it, since it is impossible for one to act if he has no free will or fails to exercise his free will.[5] The fact that the Law does not prescribe punishment for one who commits an illicit act unintentionally is not because he has no

[1] This line of argument is only intelligible against the background of the Islamic controversy about the freedom of the will. The extreme orthodox view denied the freedom of the will altogether. Some Mu'tazilite schools suggested the compromise view that the ability to act, i.e. the freedom of the will, arises not before the act but simultaneously with it: Man's freedom consists in the mere act of consent and thus accompanies the act without causing it. Saadya rejects this view, as seen above. He postulates the absolute freedom of the will.

[2] Lit. 'The bodies and what is in them'.

[3] Saadya distinguishes between God's and man's actions: God acts by creating the substances, and when He does not create He does not act at all. Man, who is incapable of creative activity, only acts by producing accidental conditions. He, therefore, is acting even if he abstains from an explicit act: if he fails to love, he hates, etc. Saadya introduced this distinction first in connection with the problem of Creation in Chapter I (ed. Landauer 71; ed. Slucki 38). There he points out that before God created the world He did not act at all. In this chapter Saadya wishes to make clear (a) that man's freedom of the will ('his ability to act') is present both in his action and abstention from action, since even his passivity has the positive character of an act; (b) that, on the other hand, God's non-interference with man's freedom must not be understood as an act in analogy with man's abstention from acting, but as absolute passivity. Thus, man's freedom is completely assured.

[4] In both Scriptural passages man's abstention from acting against God's will is described in terms of doing something, i.e. keeping God's charge and walking in His ways.

[5] Saadya means to say that the term action in its full sense implies free choice and responsibility.

free will, but because of his ignorance of the cause and effect of his particular action. Thus, we say of one who killed a person unintentionally that, for instance, the hewing of the wood was done intentionally and with his free will, whereas his failure to prevent the accident was unintentional.[1] Or to quote the case of one who has desecrated the Sabbath,[2] the gathering of the sticks may have been intentional, but the person forgot that that particular day was the Sabbath.

Having dealt with all these points, I maintain further that the Creator (be He exalted) does not allow His power to interfere in the least with the actions of men, nor does He compel them to be either obedient or disobedient. I have proofs for this doctrine founded on sense perception, Reason, Scripture and Tradition.

In regard to sense perception, I have found that a man observes from his own experience that he has the power to speak and to be silent, the power to seize a thing and to abandon it; he does not notice any other force that would hinder him in any way from exercising his will-power. The simple truth is that he directs the impulses of his nature by his Reason, and if he follows the bidding of Reason, he is prudent, if he does not, he is a fool.

As to the proof based on Reason, our previous arguments have already shown how untenable is the idea that one action can be attributed to two agents.[3] Now one who thinks that the Creator (be He exalted and glorified) interferes with the actions of men, does in fact ascribe one single action to God and Man together. Furthermore, if God used compulsion against man, there would be no sense in His giving him commandments and prohibitions. Moreover, if He compelled him to do a certain action, it would be inadmissible to punish him for it. In addition, if men acted under compulsion, it would be necessary to mete out reward to believers and infidels alike, since each of them did only what he was ordered to do. If a wise man employs two workmen, the one that he may build, and the other that he may destroy, it is his duty to pay wages to both. Moreover, it is impossible to assume that man acts under compulsion, for if this were the case, he would

---

[1] Cf. Deut. 19.1-3.   [2] Cf. Num. 15.32-36.
[3] Cf. *Amānāt*, pp. 50-1 (26-7).

have to be excused since one knows that man is unable to prevail against the power of God, and if the infidel offered the excuse that it was not within his power to believe in God, it would be necessary to consider him as justified and to accept his excuse.

As to the proofs based on Scripture, we have already mentioned the verse, 'Therefore choose life' (Deut. 30.19). The sinners are told, 'This has been of your doing; will He accept any of your persons?' (Mal. 1.9). Moreover, the Creator explains clearly that He is innocent with regard to their sins, as He says, 'Woe to the rebellious children, saith the Lord, that take counsel, but not of Me' (Isa. 30.1). He makes it clear that He is innocent with regard to the doings of the false prophets, saying 'I have not sent these prophets, yet they ran; I have not spoken to them, yet they prophesied' (Jer. 23.21), and other similar pronouncements.

As to the proofs based on Tradition, our ancient Teachers have told us, 'Everything lies in the hands of God except the fear of God, as it says, "And now, Israel, what doth the Lord Thy God require of thee, but to fear the Lord Thy God"' (Deut. 10.12).[1]

3. PROVIDENCE AND FREE WILL

> (ed. Landauer 153.19-156.17;
> ed. Slucki 78.40-80.10)

All this explanation brings me to the following question, which will no doubt be asked: 'If what you have said is true, viz. that the will of God has no share in the disobedience of those who disobey Him, how is it possible that there should exist in His world anything which does not find His approval, or to which He does not give His consent?'[2] The answer to this is not far to seek. It is this: *we* regard it as strange that a wise man should tolerate within the realm of his power anything which is undesirable from his point of view, and to which he cannot give his consent. This is intelligible in the case of

---

[1] *b. Ber.* 33 b.

[2] Mu'tazilite theology formulates the above problem as follows: 'whether God has power over the evil deeds and injustices'. Cf. al-Shahrastānī, I, 53, 60; Guttmann, p. 169, n. 2.

a human being since he dreads those things which cause him harm, but our Lord does not dread disobedience on account of Himself, since it is impossible to assume that any sort of accident should affect Him. He abhors disobedience for our own sakes because it has a harmful effect on us. For if we sin against Him and fail to acknowledge His Truth, we act foolishly, and if we sin against each other, we endanger our lives and positions. Since this is quite clear and manifest[1], it is not strange that there should exist in His world things which we consider to be strange. When He explains to us that He abhors certain things, He does so for our own sakes in His way of mercy, as He made it clear in Scripture by saying, 'Do they provoke Me? saith the Lord; do they not provoke themselves, to the confusion of their own faces?' (Jer. 7.19).

Perhaps, someone will ask further: 'If God knows that which is going to be before it comes into being, He knows in advance if a certain person will disobey Him; now that person must by necessity disobey God, for otherwise God's fore-knowledge would not prove to be correct'.[2] The fallacy underlying this question is even more evident than that underlying the previous one. It is this: He who makes this assertion has no proof that the knowledge of the Creator concerning things is the cause of their existence. He merely imagines this to be so, or chooses to believe it. The fallacy of this assumption becomes quite clear when we consider that, if God's knowledge of things were the cause of their existence, they would have existed from eternity, since God's knowledge of them is eternal.[3] We do, however, believe that God knows things as they exist in reality, i.e. of those things which He creates, He knows in advance that He is going to create them, and of those things which are subject to man's free will He

[1] An alternative translation: 'since the Commandment (of God) has been revealed for this purpose'.

[2] Saadya formulates here for the first time in Jewish philosophical thought a problem which has since occupied the minds of both Jewish and non-Jewish scholastic thinkers, i.e. the problem of the reconciliation of man's freedom of will with the foreknowledge of God.

[3] Cf. Yehudah Hallevi, *Kuzari*, V, 20 (ed. Cassel, pp. 415, 418, n. 4), where the above argument is stated in the name of the Mutakallimūn. Yehudah Hallevi adopts Saadya's solution of the problem, whereas Albo ('*Ikkarim*, IV, 1 ff.), after quoting both Saadya and Hallevi, expresses the view that it is no solution at all: if reality, he says, does not depend on God's knowledge, but, on the contrary, God's knowledge depends on reality, God's omniscience is no longer upheld.

knows in advance that man is going to choose them. Should one object, 'If God knows that a certain person will speak, is it possible for that person to be silent?' we answer quite simply that if that person was to keep silent instead of speaking we should have said in our original statement that God knew that this man would be silent, and we were not entitled to state that God knew that this person would speak. For God knows man's ultimate action such as it will be whether sooner or later after all his planning; it is exactly the thing God knows, as is said, 'The Lord knoweth the thoughts of man' (Ps. 94.11), and furthermore, 'For I know their inclination how they do even now' (Deut. 31.21).

I found people who asked on this point: 'How can it be reconciled with God's wisdom that He gives commandments and prohibitions to the righteous knowing as He does that they will always obey Him?[1] I found there are four ways of answering this question. (1) The commandments were given in order to inform man what God desired of him; (2) in order that man's reward should be complete, for if he acted in conformity to God's will without being commanded to do so, he would have no claim to reward[2]; (3) if it were proper for God to bestow reward upon man for something concerning which He did not command him, it would be equally proper to punish him for something concerning which he issued no prohibition. This, however, would be unjust; (4) the commandments were given in order to enjoin, for a second time, through the prophet, the commandments which are already established by Reason so that man, being warned and well prepared, should be particularly careful to perform them, as it says, 'If Thou warn the righteous man, that the righteous sin not, he shall surely live, because he took warning' (Ezek. 3.21).

People ask further: 'How can it be reconciled with God's wisdom that he sends prophets to those who deny Him, knowing as He does in advance that they will refuse to believe?

---

[1] 'Obedience' must be taken here in the sense of conformity on the basis of Reason to the Divine will. Cf. above, pp. 95-7.

[2] Although good and evil can be determined on rational grounds, Saadya holds that reward and punishment pre-suppose a Divine revelation. Cf. above, pp. 93-4. This constitutes an interesting compromise between the Ash'ariya, who held that without Revelation there was neither obligation (*taklīf*) nor reward, and the Mu'tazilites, who believed that both were independent of Revelation.

Does this not seem to be useless?' I found there are six ways of answering this argument. (1) If God did not send a prophetic message to those who deny Him calling on them to believe, they would be able to offer the excuse: if only the prophet had come to us, we would have believed in God.[1] (2) If that which exists in God's foreknowledge has not yet become reality in the form of a human act, God cannot mete out retribution, since otherwise reward and punishment would follow God's foreknowledge, not man's actions.[2] (3) In the same way as He established in the world[3] rational and sensible proofs of His existence for believers and unbelievers alike, so it is necessary that the proofs of prophecy should likewise be universal and embrace believers and unbelievers alike. (4) It is evident to us that if a man bids another person commit a crime which that person refuses to do, he has tried to harm that person and must be called a fool; in the same way, one who bids another person do something good which that other person refuses to do has, nevertheless, tried to benefit that person and must be called a wise man. (5) If the command of one who bids a person do something good is to be regarded as foolish when that person refuses to accept the command, simply because of that person's refusal, then the command of one who bids a person commit a crime would have to be regarded as wisdom in the case of that person accepting it. The essential natures of good and evil would thus be liable to be reversed according as they are accepted or not, which is absurd. (6) In the same way as God put the two classes on the same footing so far as Reason and Free Will are concerned, so it was necessary to put them on the same footing so far as the commandments and the prophetic message are concerned.

In addition to all these arguments I maintain that only that which arises from an action which does not benefit anybody can be called useless, whereas the prophetic message of God to the unbelievers, although they have chosen not to benefit nor to derive improvement from it, is yet one from which the

---

[1] Cf. al-Shahrastānī, I, 67.

[2] The above interpretation of the text (which is corrupt) follows Guttmann (p. 171, n. 3).

[3] Wolff's emendation fi-l-'ilmi ('in the knowledge') for fi-l-'ālami ('in the world') is unnecessary.

believers and the rest of mankind did benefit in that they paid good heed to it, as one can see from the fact that to this day people have recounted, and will do so in the future, the stories of the Flood, of the people of Sodom, of Pharaoh, and so forth.[1]

---

[1] Saadya means to say that although God's commandments were rejected by the unbelievers, a fact which God could foresee, they helped the righteous to appreciate the binding character of the Law: in remembering the stories of the Flood, etc., they were strengthened in their belief in the God of Justice.

CHAPTER V

ON MERITS AND DEMERITS[1]

1. THE IMPRESS OF MAN'S ACTIONS ON HIS SOUL

(ed. Landauer 165.7-167.14;
ed. Slucki 84.1-85.13)

OUR LORD (be He exalted and glorified) has informed us that
acts of obedience to God, if repeatedly performed by men, are
termed merits,[2] and acts of disobedience, if repeatedly performed, are called demerits[3]; moreover, that He preserves the
record of every deed of every one of His servants, as it says,
'Great in counsel, and mighty in work; whose eyes are open
upon all the ways of the sons of men' (Jer. 32.19); and it
further says, 'For His eyes are upon the ways of a man' (Job
34.21). He also informed us that the deeds of men leave an
impress on their souls, either purifying or defiling them, as it
says, with regard to the transgressions, 'He shall bear his
iniquity; he shall bear his sin' (Lev. and Num. *passim*); 'Their
souls bear their iniquity'[4] (Hosea 4.8); 'The iniquity of
that soul shall be upon it' (Num. 15.31). Though this impress
on the soul is hidden from men and is not manifest to them,
it is manifest to God (be He blessed and exalted), as it says,
'I, the Lord, search the heart, I try the reins' (Jer. 17.10). He
produced wonders and miracles in support of this doctrine,
and we accepted it.

This being the accepted doctrine, I began to submit it to the
test of Reason in the same way as the problems of the previous
chapters. I noticed that there are certain arts of which the
mass of men have little knowledge, so that they place the good
and the bad on the same level until an expert distinguishes
between them. Take for example the art of judging coins.

---

[1] This chapter seems to have circulated as a separate treatise under the title, *Sefer
hat-teshubah le-Rabbenu Saadya* at the time of R. Yehudah he-Ḥasid (died 1217),
who made extracts from it. Cf. Malter, pp. 362-3.

[2] Lit. 'Good deeds'.

[3] Lit. 'Evil deeds'.

[4] Saadya's exegesis of this verse is faulty unless he read *we-'eth* instead of *we-'el*.
Some MSS read *nafsham* instead of *nafshō*. Cf. A. B. Ehrlich, *Randglossen*, V, p. 173.
This seems also to have been Saadya's reading.

You will see that the ignorant man who does not understand it treats the valuable *denarius*[1] and the worthless one alike until the coin-tester distinguishes between them. Or take the art of medicine. You will find that the uninitiated[2] examine the pulsation of the veins without knowing from their dilation and contraction which quality is predominant in the body.[3] This only the expert physician knows. So too with the students of physiognomy, who examine the lines of the face and feet, and from them tell the difference between people,[4] which is a mystery to those who are not initiated into this art. The same applies to the art of knowing the difference between jewels such as rubies, pearls, and other sorts of jewellery, which is a matter for the expert only. In short, in all technical matters most of the defects pass unnoticed by the uninitiated and are seen by the expert only.

When I found that this was the case with technical matters, as I have described, I clung even more firmly to my belief that the defects of the soul, i.e. the transgressions and sins, although invisible to men, because they are not subject to sense perception, are yet visible to their Maker since He created the souls and called them into being. For the soul is a rational and pure substance, surpassing in purity the substances of the planets and the spheres, so that we are unable to perceive it with our senses. How then should we obtain evidence of any impress left on the soul and obscuring its light? It is, however, manifest to its Creator Who is also the Creator of the spheres, and for this reason Scripture has compared the planets and the heavens to the soul in this respect, as it says, 'And the stars are not pure in His sight, how much less man...' (Job 25.5); 'Yea, the heavens are not clean in His sight, how much less one that is abominable and impure, man who drinketh iniquity like water' (Job 15.15). God says that the soul is a light unto Him like the light of a lamp by which He searches all secret chambers

[1] A gold coin.
[2] Lit. 'The common people'.
[3] According to Hippocrates and Galen, whose authority in Medicine was undisputed in medieval times, man's state of health depends on the mixture of the four qualities (warm, cold, dry, moist) in the body. The predominance of one particular quality is of decisive importance in this respect.
[4] The art of physiognomy, which included chirology, was held in high esteem by Aristotle. It also plays an important part in Jewish mysticism and Kabbalah. The oldest chiromantic document known to us is a fragment belonging to the pre-Kabbalistic *Hekalōt* mysticism. Cf. Scholem, p. 48.

and dark places, and illumines all that is hidden (in them), as is said, 'The spirit of man is the lamp of the Lord, searching all the inward parts' (Prov. 20.27). He says furthermore that He is unto the soul like the fire that melts the gold and the silver in the furnace and purifies them, as it says, 'The refining pot is for silver, and the furnace for gold, but the Lord trieth the hearts' (Prov. 17.3). I said, is this not a strange thing that a person should partake of two kinds of food, one that is permitted and one that is forbidden, and should find both nourishing; or that he should have sexual intercourse in two cases, one being lawful, the other being unlawful, and should find pleasure in both of them. He may think that the two actions are of one and the same kind. But the Examiner (God) examines the impress they leave in the soul, as we explained, and as it says, 'Every way of man is right in his own eyes, but the Lord weigheth the hearts' (Prov. 21.2). It then became clear to me that if the good deeds are predominant, the soul becomes bright and shining, as is said, 'And his life beholdeth the light' (Job 33.28); furthermore, 'That he may be enlightened with the light of the living' (Job 33.30). If, however, the evil deeds are predominant, the soul becomes dim and clouded, as is said of those who are of such a quality, 'They shall never see the light' (Ps. 49.20).[1]

2. The Ten Degrees of Merit and Demerit

(ed. Landauer 169.3-13; 175.5-176.5; 176.12-177.17; 178.16-179.7;
ed. Slucki 86.1-9; 88.18-34; 88.40-89.18; 89.36-90.4)

I consider that from the point of view of merit and demerit men[2] may be placed in ten classes: (1) the pious; (2) the impious; (3) the obedient; (4) the disobedient; (5) the blameless; (6) the negligent; (7) the offender; (8) the rebellious;

[1] Saadya's thesis that every action of man leaves an impress on his soul, of which he may not be conscious but which is nevertheless existent and patent to the supreme intelligence of God; f rthermore, that this impress has an influence on the substance of the soul in that it either ennobles or debases it, may be regarded as a crude anticipation of the modern *Psychology of the Unconscious*. The idea that man's actions either purify or defile, illumine or obscure the soul, can also be found in the doctrines of the 'Faithful Brethren' (cf. Dieterici, *Logik und Psychologie*, p. 154; Guttmann, p. 176, n. 1), but the stress on the *unconscious* character of these impressions is Saadya's distinctive contribution.

[2] Lit. 'servants' (of God).

(9) the unbeliever; (10) the penitent. There is also the 'half-and-half' person[1], whom we set apart for separate discussion.[2] It is desirable that I should explain each of these categories and their implications.

(1) I say that a person is called pious[3] if the greater part of his actions are good deeds, and (2) he is called impious[4] if the greater part of his actions are evil deeds. This classification is analogous to that made in natural science. Thus, the scholars call a thing warm if the warmth which is contained in it preponderates over the cold; they call it cold if the cold which it contains preponderates over its warmth. They say that a body is healthy if the health is predominant in it, and they say that it is sick if the sickness is predominant in it. Designations in the realm of prophecy are applied in an analogous manner: a man is called pious if the greater part of his actions are of a pious nature.

(3) As to the obedient,[5] he is one who singles out for himself one particular law from which he never deviates throughout his life. Hence, though his attitude towards the rest of the laws may be one of either compliance or non-compliance,[6] this particular law he will not neglect by any means. Thus, a person may fix his mind upon the duty never to miss the times of prayer, or never to miss an opportunity of honouring his parents, or never to embezzle money, or never to tell a lie,[7] etc. Our ancient Teachers said, 'If a person fulfils but one single commandment, he benefits from it; his days will be prolonged, and he will inherit the land' (b.Ḳiddushīn 39 b). They explained that this applies to one who singles out for himself a particular commandment to fulfil, e.g., the honouring of father and mother (loc. cit.). One who never misses an occasion of observing such a commandment is called obedient.

(4) As to the disobedient,[8] he is one who singles out one particular law which he makes it a rule always to transgress.

---

[1] One whose merits and demerits balance each other.
[2] Saadya's view concerning the 'balanced' person is that God's mercy places him in the scale of merit. Cf. Amānāt 181 (92). For a similar division see Maimonides, Hil. Teshuḇah, ch. 3.
[3] Arab. ṣāliḥ; Hebr. ṣaddīḳ.   [4] Arab. ṭāliḥ; Hebr. rasha'.   [5] Arab. muṭī'; Hebr. ōḇed.
[6] Guttmann (p. 184) misunderstood this passage. cf. Margulies, p. 286.
[7] Ibn Tibbon's version varies slightly with regard to the examples enumerated.
[8] Arab. 'āsin; Hebr. mamreh.

Our ancient Teachers call him an apostate (*meshummad*).[1] As an illustration of this type I might imagine one who holds that a certain law is too severe, and therefore turns away from it; and holds that another law is practicable, and therefore resolves to observe it. There is, for instance, a person who deems as too severe the law of usury, or the dietary law, and he does as he thinks fit regarding each one of these. It is, therefore, said that all men have a separate law seeing that their desires are so much at variance. (5) As to the blameless,[2] he is one who holds that the right thing for him to do is to abide by the commandments and prohibitions in their totality without neglecting any of them. He is called the perfectly pious. Although people think that the existence of such a type of person is improbable since no one is likely to remain free from blemish in all his ways, I hold that man is able to rise to this level, for if this were impossible, God in His wisdom would not have given him the Law.[3]

(6) As to the negligent,[4] he is one who makes light of commandments which bid us do certain things. He is termed, 'one that transgresses a positive commandment'; to this group belongs one who makes light of the commandments concerning *Tefilin, Succah, Lulab, Shofar*, and similar precepts of the Law belonging to this class.

(7) As to the offender,[5] he is one who transgresses a prohibition, but not a major one, for the punishment which is meted out to him in this world for transgressing it is not of a severe nature. He is termed, 'one who transgresses a negative commandment'; to this group belongs one who makes light of the prohibitions of *nebelah* and *trefah*, or wears a garment of two kinds of stuff mingled together (*sha'atnez*), or believes in augury and omen, or commits similar transgressions of the same category.

(8) As to the rebellious,[6] he is one who commits a major

---

[1] This statement is incorrect. The proper rabbinic designation of this type is *mumar le-dabar 'ehad* (persistent offender against a particular law).

[2] Arab. *kāmal*; Hebr. *shalem*.

[3] Saadya explains Eccl. 7.20 ('For there is not a righteous man upon earth, that doeth good and sinneth not') to mean that the righteous has, like the sinner, the *choice* of evil, but need not do it.

[4] Arab. *mukassir*; Hebr. *mekasser*.   [5] Arab. *mudhnib*; Hebr. *hōte'*.

[6] Arab. *fāsik*; Hebr. *mezīd*.

transgression, i.e. one which entails the punishment of 'cutting off' (*karet*) or death at the hands of God or capital punishment at the hands of the Court of Justice, which shows that it is a major transgression, such as incest, the desecration of the Sabbath, the partaking of food on the Day of Atonement, or of leavened bread on the Passover, and whatever is in this line and belongs to this category.

(9) As to the unbeliever,[1] he is one who repudiates the root-principle, i.e. the One and All-embracing (be He blessed and exalted).[2] This rejection can take place in three ways. Either he worships beside Him some image or man, or the sun, or the moon, as is said, 'Thou shalt have no other gods before Me. Thou shalt not make unto thee a graven image ...' (Ex. 20.3-4). Or he does not worship anything beside God, but at the same time he does not worship God either. In fact, he is worshipping nothing, be it the true God or a false one. Thus we read in the story of Job, 'They said unto God: "Depart from us; for we desire not the knowledge of Thy ways"' (Job 21.14). Or he may find himself in a state of doubt with regard to his religion, yet he calls himself a religious person and, perhaps, offers his prayers and invokes God's help, whilst his heart is not firmly believing, and thus he lies and is deceitful both in his speech and in belief, as it says of the multitude, 'They beguiled Him with their mouth, and lied unto Him with their tongue, for their heart was not steadfast with Him, neither were they faithful in His covenant' (Ps. 78.35-6). Such a person is called, 'One that profanes the name of God', and he belongs to the category of the unbeliever.

In all these cases, the sin of the sinners is completely forgiven in both worlds, if they repent of their sin, except in case the sin is one regarding which God has written in His law that 'He will not hold (the sinner) guiltless'.[3] In such a case it is indispensable that punishment should be meted out to the sinner in this world,[4] as I shall explain.

---

[1] Arab. *kāfir*; Hebr. *kōfer*.

[2] The unbeliever denies the existence of God and the principle of His unity.

[3] Ex. 20.7; 34.7; Num. 14.18; Deut. 5.11; Joel 4.21; Prov. 6.29, 19.5, 9.

[4] Not 'eternal punishment' as Tibbon's rendering (*ra'ah 'ōlamīt*) suggests, but 'this-worldly punishment'. Cf. Wolff, p. 83. Cf. the same expression *Amānāt* 171.16 (87.1). Saadya explains later on (*Amānāt* 181 (91)) that a man is punished in this world for the crimes of false swearing, bloodshed, adultery, and false witness (cf. the

The 10th degree is that of the penitent who carries out all the requirements of penitence. The requirements of penitence are four in number: the abandonment of sin, the feeling of remorse, the petition for forgiveness, and the giving of an assurance never to repeat the sin.

When all these four conditions are fulfilled, they represent the 'terms of penitence'. I am not afraid lest the majority of my nation should be found wanting in these 'terms of penitence' except for the last one, i.e. the assurance not to repeat the sin. For I am confident that at the time of prayer and supplication people abandon their evil ways, feel remorse, and ask for forgiveness; but it seems to me that they still have the idea of relapsing into their evil ways. I therefore asked: Is there any device whereby to eradicate from their hearts the tendency of falling back into their evil ways? My answer was: By the composition of poems[1] which express the renunciation of this world and remind man of his state of frailty, wretchedness and toil; of his vanity, of his eventual death and the decomposition and decay of his body; of the account which he will have to render and the punishment which he will receive, and all that is bound up with his human condition so that he will renounce this world. When he has renounced the world completely, his sins will be included amongst the things which he has forsaken, and when he has renounced his sins, his faith will grow stronger. For this reason, I believe, we find that our Sages introduced the custom of reciting on the Day of Atonement compositions such as these; 'Thou knowest the secret thoughts of the heart . . .'; 'Do not lead us into judgment . . .'; 'Thou art the master of everything created . . .'[2]

[1] Obviously Saadya refers here to the fact that he himself wrote a number of liturgical poems designated for this purpose. Some of his penitential prayers (*Seliḥōt*) are preserved. Cf. Malter, p. 334.

[2] The first of the above-mentioned *Seliḥōt* (*'attah meḥin sar'afē leḇ*) can be found in Luzzatto's *Betulat bat Yehudah* (ed. Prague, 1840, p. 11). It reflects precisely the ideas set out in the above paragraph. Saadya's *Siddur* contains some 30 *Seliḥōt* of which a few may be his own compositions. There are about 230 anonymous and 740 acrostically named *Seliḥōt*. Solomon ha-Babli (980) is the first known author of *Seliḥōt*. Cf. L. Zunz, *Literaturgeschichte der synagogalen Poesie* (1865), pp. 93 ff.; 219-20; 232.

passages referred to in the preceding note) even if he repents. Having been punished for these sins in this world, man enters into the future life free of guilt. There are, however, certain grave crimes such as idolatry which are liable to eternal punishment in the after-life. Cf. *Amānāt* 276-7 (141). See also below, p. 135, n. 2, and p. 190, n. 1.

3. REWARD AND PUNISHMENT IN THIS WORLD

(ed. Landauer 168.2-21; 169.19-172.2;
ed. Slucki 85.19-33; 86.13-87.6)

God has further told us that during the time we stay in this
World of Action,[1] He observes every single deed of ours and
reserves its reward for the Future World which is the *World
of Reward*. That world He will call into being when the total
number of men which He decided in His wisdom to create will
be complete.[2] There He will reward everyone according to
his actions, as the wise king said, 'The righteous and the wicked
God will judge' (Eccl. 3.17), and furthermore, 'God shall bring
every work into the judgment concerning every hidden thing,
whether it be good or whether it be evil' (Eccl. 12.14). In
Chapter IX of this book we shall deal with the Time of Reward
in the appropriate manner.

Nevertheless, God by no means leaves his servants without
reward for their merits, and punishment for their sins, even in
this world, thus giving us a sign and a hint of all that is reserved
for the time when the harvest of all human actions will be
gathered in. For this reason we find that in the Torah He sets
forth the blessings in the passage, 'If ye walk in My statutes'
(Lev. 26.3-13; Deut. 28.1-14). Of such blessings it is said,
'Work in my behalf a sign for good' (Ps. 86.17). He also sets
forth the curses in the passage, 'But if ye will not hearken unto
Me' (Lev. 26.14-45; Deut. 28.15-68). With regard to them it
is said, 'They shall be upon thee for a sign and for a wonder'

---

[1] The term 'World of Action' (*dār al-'amal*; Tibbon: *ōlam ham-ma'asseh*) used by
Saadia is not to be confounded with the same term in the kabbalistic doctrine of the
Four Worlds, according to which our visible world is called 'World of Action' (*ōlam
ha'assiyah*). On the kabbalistic doctrine see Scholem, art. 'Kabbalah' in *EJ*, Vol. IX,
col. 686 ff.

[2] According to the Midrash (*Gen. R.* 24.4; *Lev. R.* 15.1; *Midr. Kohelet* 1.6), 'The
king Messiah does not come until all the souls which God decided to create are
created'. A different version occurs in the Talmud (*b. Yeḇ.* 62 a, 63 b; *Aḇ. zarah* 5 a;
Niddah 13 b), which runs, 'The son of David will not appear until all the souls (stored
up) in the "Guf" have vanished', i.e. been incorporated. According to the second
version the souls are not created at the time when the body is formed, but are pre-
existent, 'Guf' denoting the heavenly abode of the souls. Saadya, who denies the
pre-existence of the soul (cf. Chapter VI), must have explained 'Guf' as the 'body'
of man: the Messiah does not come until the complete number of souls have been
created and joined to their respective bodies. Abarbanel, too, explains 'Guf' as the
'body of man', although he adopts the view that the souls are pre-existent. Cf.
Theodor-Albeck, p. 233.

(Deut. 28.46). Their evidence and sign is in this world; the total sum of the merits is, however, stored up like a treasure for the righteous, as is said, 'Oh how abundant is Thy goodness, which Thou hast laid up for them that fear Thee' (Ps. 31.20), and the total sum of demerits is stored up and sealed up for the wicked, as is said, 'Is not this laid up in store with Me, sealed up in My treasuries?' (Deut. 32.34).[1]

With reference to this matter we say further that God in His wisdom has decided that He should requite His servants in this world only for that class of deeds (good or evil) which are in the minority in order that there may remain for the Future World the class of deeds which are in the majority. For it cannot be thought that God should shift their souls in the coming world from one rank to another seeing that each of the two classes of retribution is destined to last eternally,[2] as it says, 'Some to everlasting life, and some to reproaches and everlasting abhorrence' (Dan. 12.2). He has arranged the retribution for the class of deeds which are in the minority to be meted out in this world, in the way in which He has explained that the total sum of good deeds of a pious man is stored up for the Future World, whereas the few good deeds of an impious man are rewarded in this world, as it says, 'Know therefore that the Lord thy God, He is God; the faithful God, who keepeth covenant and mercy with them that love Him . . . and repayeth[3] them that hate Him to their face, to destroy them' (Deut. 7.9-10). To illustrate this: The two leaders Moses and Aaron committed only light offences, and they were punished on account of them in this world, as it says, 'Because ye believed

[1] The pious man receives the reward for the sum total of his merits in the Future World, and the impious man receives the punishment for the sum total of his demerits in the Future World. Reward in this world is meted out only to the impious for the few good deeds he has to his credit; similarly, punishment in this world is meted out only to the pious for the few misdeeds which he has committed. Cf. later in the text. In this way reward and punishment in this world are only of minor importance; they merely serve to indicate (as 'signs') the retribution which awaits us in the Future World.

[2] Here Saadya opposes the Ash'arite doctrine, according to which the souls of the pious are first punished in the Future World and, after their expiation, introduced into Paradise. Saadya holds that the sins of the righteous are expiated by suffering in this world, and that theirs is eternal reward in the next world. He also disagrees with the Mu'tazilite view that there are varying degrees of reward and punishment in the Future World, for which view support can be found in Rabbinic literature. On the Islamic controversy with regard to this matter, cf. Guttmann, pp. 178-90.

[3] i.e. the reward for their few good deeds. Saadya follows the traditional Jewish interpretation of this verse.

not in Me, to sanctify Me . . . Therefore ye shall not bring this assembly into the land' (Num. 20.12). Another example: Abijah the son of Jeroboam performed one single good deed, and God rewarded him on account of it in this world, as it says, 'For he only of Jeroboam shall come to the grave, because in him there is found some good thing' (1 Kings 14.13).

On the strength of this principle it often happens that a pious man[1] who has committed a fairly large number of sins incurs punishment throughout the greater part of his life, and a wicked person who has performed a fairly large number of good deeds is privileged to enjoy well-being for the greater part of his life. Our ancient Teachers said on this point, 'One whose sins exceed his merits is granted a good life, and he is on a par with one who has observed the whole Torah, whilst one whose merits exceed his sins is given a sorry life, and he is on a par with one who has burnt the whole Torah' (*b. Kiddushīn* 39 b).[2]

This statement applies, however, only to one who commits his good or evil deeds without change of heart, that is to say who in doing the good deed does not regret his previous misdeeds, and in doing the evil deed does not regret his previous good actions. But if one who has a great number of good deeds to his credit regrets having done them, he loses all of his merits on account of his regret, and of him it is said, 'When the righteous turneth away from his righteousness, and committeth iniquity . . . none of his righteous deeds that he hath done shall be remembered' (Ez. 18.24). And if one who has committed a great number of evil deeds feels remorse for them and carries out all the conditions of repentance,[3] he has thereby removed them from his soul, and of him it is said, 'If the wicked turn from all his sins that he hath committed . . . none of his transgressions that he hath committed shall be remembered against him' (Ez. 18.21-2). Our ancient Teachers state this explicitly with regard to one who regrets his past actions (*b. Kiddushīn* 40 b).

[1] i.e., one whose good deeds are in the majority, but who has, nevertheless, evil deeds to his discredit. Cf. the definition of the 'pious' above, p. 130.

[2] Saadya's theory of the workings of Divine retribution follows the Talmudic pattern, which, incidentally, also solves the problem of Theodicy, as Saadya explains in the following chapter. He exhibits great ingenuity in the application of this doctrine.

[3] Cf. above, p. 133.

On the strength of this principle it may sometimes happen that a pious man whose merits are recorded for reward in the Future World will regret them, whereupon his reward in the Future World is cancelled, and his portion of reward is meted out to him in this world. People may notice that his adoption of an irreligious life coincides with an improvement in his material conditions, and be led astray by this, not understanding that the well-being which he now enjoys is not due to his adoption of an irreligious life, but is the payment to him, in this world, of the happiness that was reserved for him in the Future World, and is now thrown in his face.[1] It is also possible that an impious[2] man whose demerits are recorded for punishment in the Future World may feel regret for them and repent, whereupon his punishment in the Future World is cancelled, and punishment is meted out to him in this world, since punishment he must receive in this world despite his penitence, as I shall explain later.[3] People may observe that immediately upon his turning away from sin he was visited with grief and affliction, and they will be at a loss to understand it, not knowing that the suffering which has befallen him is not the result of his fresh start in life, but is the legacy of the past which he relinquished. When people try to understand these classifications, their doubts will disappear and their hearts will gain new strength in the service of God, as is said, 'The righteous holdeth on his way, and he that hath clean hands waxeth stronger and stronger' (Job 17.9).

4. THE SUFFERING OF THE RIGHTEOUS AND INNOCENT

(ed. Landauer 172.11–173.18;
ed. Slucki 87.15–38)

I find that suffering befalls the pious in this world in one of two ways: either as punishment for the relatively small number of their transgressions, as I have explained before;[4] or, alternatively, as a visitation from God in order to test them, provided

---

[1] An allusion to the verse quoted before, '. . . and repayeth to them that hate him *in the face*'.

[2] The Arabic text reads, 'Pious', which is obviously a mistake. The Hebrew version is correct; it reads, *rasha'*.

[3] Cf. p. 132, n. 4.

[4] Cf. above, pp. 135 ff.

He knows that they will be able to endure it.[1] Later He compensates them for their sufferings, as it says, 'The Lord trieth the righteous; but the wicked and him that loveth violence His soul hateth' (Ps. 11.5). God, however, is not wont to act in this way with one who is unable to bear it, since no useful purpose would be served in such a case, whereas the endurance of the pious serves a useful purpose in that it enables mankind to understand that God has not chosen them gratuitously, as you learn from Job and his endurance.[2]

If the suffering of a man is of the order of punishment and he asks his Lord to let him know the reason, God has enjoined that he should be informed, as it says, 'And it shall come to pass, when he shall say: "Wherefore hath the Lord our God done all these things unto us?" then shalt thou say unto them . . .' (Jer. 5.19). Telling him the reason of his suffering will have the good effect of making him depart from his sins. If, however, the suffering of a man is of the order of a test, and he asks his Lord to let him know the reason, He does not allow him to be told about it, but has enjoined that he should be kept ignorant of it, as our Teacher Moses says, 'Wherefore hast Thou dealt ill with Thy servant? and wherefore have I not found favour in Thy sight . . .?' (Num. 11.11) and God did not reveal it to him. Likewise Job asked, 'Make me know wherefore Thou contendest with me' (Job 10.2), and He did not reveal it to him. This again will have a good effect in that people will not consider the endurance of the pious as something easy, nor will they say: 'He endured it because God had told him of the magnitude of his reward.'

I say furthermore that it is reasonable to suppose that even a blameless man[3] should be tested and later compensated, since I find that suffering is inflicted even on little children.[4] I have

---

[1] Cf. *Gen. R.* 54.1: 'The potter does not test those vessels which easily break, but the vessels which are strong. In the same way God does not test the wicked, but the pious'.

[2] Saadya means to say that the authority of godly men will remain undisputed if they have stood the test of suffering and emerged with their faith unimpaired.

[3] Cf. above, p. 131.

[4] The suffering of little children constitutes a problem of Theodicy which from Plato (*Republic* X, 615 C) down to the Mu'tazilites (cf. al-Shahrastāni I, 60, 86, 144, 146, 152) and Christian theologians, baffled religious thinkers. Saadya classifies this with that of the suffering of the innocent in general, and his answer is that there are, in addition to the sufferings of punishment and test, 'sufferings of love' for which there is a special reward. Saadya is following here a well-known Talmudic doctrine. Cf. *b. Berakōt* 5 a.

no doubt that they will be compensated, and that the suffering which God in His wisdom inflicts on them is like the punishment which they receive at the hands of their father who may strike and confine them in order to protect them from some harm; it also resembles some nasty and bitter medicine which their father bids them drink in order to relieve them from an illness, as it says in the Torah, 'And thou shalt consider in thy heart, that, as a man chasteneth his son, so the Lord thy God chasteneth thee' (Deut. 8.5); in a similar way, it says, 'For whom the Lord loveth, He correcteth, even as a father the son in whom he delighteth' (Prov. 3.12). Should someone object that God has the power to bestow happiness upon the innocent in the measure of His intended compensation even without inflicting suffering previously, our answer is the same as we gave in the first place,[1] namely that God shaped our destiny for a more abundant portion of happiness, since our happiness is greater if it is in the nature of reward than it would be if it were in the nature of grace.

[1] i.e. when this problem was first touched upon in the beginning of Chapter III. Cf. above, pp. 93-4. The Arabic text has here a gloss (cf. Margulies, pp. 285-6) which reads: 'Which concerns the creation, from the outset, of the Future World', a reference to the question posed in the beginning of Chapter IX: why did not God, instead of inflicting so much suffering on man in this world, create him immediately and from the outset in the blissful state of the Future World? As Margulies has rightly pointed out, it is most unlikely that Saadya should have anticipated in the above context a problem which he raises in Chapter IX. The answer which he gives to his question in Chapter IX refers to the solution suggested in Chapter III, as is also the case here.

CHAPTER VI

ON THE ESSENCE OF THE SOUL, DEATH, AND WHAT FOLLOWS IT[1]

1. THEORIES ABOUT THE NATURE OF THE SOUL

(ed. Landauer 188.10-191.11;
ed. Slucki 95.1-96.29)

OUR Lord (be He blessed and exalted) has informed us that the soul of man is created in his heart at the moment when the form of his body is completed, as it says, 'The saying of the Lord, who stretched forth the heavens, and laid the foundations of the earth, and formed the spirit of man *within* him' (Zech. 12.1). Moreover, He told us that He has set a time-limit to the combined existence of body and soul, and that, when it expires, He separates them again until the time when the number of souls which His wisdom has decided to call into being is completed. At that time, He re-unites them with their respective bodies and metes out their reward.[2] Our prophets have established this doctrine by miracles, and we accepted it without hesitation. Thereafter we set our mind on demonstrating these matters by way of speculation in accordance with the pattern we followed in the preceding chapters.

The first thing to be investigated is the actual nature of the soul. For I have found that people disagree on this point to an extraordinary degree and are greatly perplexed about it. I think there is no need to quote all the theories, and shall select only seven.[3]

---

[1] For a treatment of this chapter see Guttmann, pp. 194 ff.; S. Horovitz, *Die Psychologie Saadias*, pp. 12 ff.; Julius Guttmann's (Hebr.) article in the *Magnes Anniversary Book*, Jerusalem (1938), pp. 80-8.

[2] After the completion of the number of souls and the subsequent creation of the Future World (*ōlam habā'*) eternal reward and punishment will be meted out to body and soul together. Cf. below, pp. 154, 155, 181-2.

[3] Similar lists of theories concerning the soul are to be found in Nemesius, Plutarch and Stobaeus. It is likely that Saadya used some such list. Some theories advanced by him in the course of this chapter are also taken from the Greek works on the subject which had probably been translated into Arabic. Cf. Julius Guttmann, *loc. cit.*, p. 82.

(1) I have met people who hold the view that the soul is one of the *accidents*.[1] I fancy they have been led to this opinion by virtue of the fact that the soul is invisible, and that only its activities can be seen. They thought that since it was too subtle to be perceived by the sense organs, it must be an accident, seeing that accidents are of a very subtle nature. There are five theories current amongst them on this subject. Some think that the soul is a 'self-moving number'.[2] Others believe that it is the 'perfection of a natural body'.[3] Again others imagine that it is the composition of the 'four natures'.[4] Still others conceive it as the co-ordination of the senses.[5] Finally some have laid down that it is an accident which originates from the blood.[6] After carefully examining these theories, all of which have in common the view that the soul is an accident — since number, perfection, composition, co-ordination, and production are all accidental — I found them all to be wrong for several reasons. One reason is that an accidental phenomenon cannot be the source of the boundless wisdom and wonderful intelligence displayed in the order of the world and its progress, as I have shown in a preceding chapter.[7] Furthermore, an accident cannot be affected by other accidents[8] — this is unthinkable — and yet we find that

[1] i.e. not a substantial and separate entity, but merely an accident of the bodily substance. This was generally the view of the Mu'tazilites. On the notion of *accident* see above, p. 55, n. 2.

[2] This view is held by Xenocrates, as Plutarch testifies. Cf. Guttmann, p. 195, n. 2; Nemesius, *De natura hominis*, attributes it to Pythagoras. Cf. Julius Guttmann, *loc. cit.*, p. 81. The above reading occurs in a marginal gloss of the Leningrad Version and in the Hebr. Paraphrase. As Horovitz, *loc. cit.*, p. 13, n. 19, has shown, it is to be preferred to the ordinary reading, 'a self-moving accident'.

[3] This is Aristotle's famous definition of the soul as ἐντελέχεια σώματος φυσικοῦ. Cf. *loc. cit.*, II, 1, 412 b5. Saadya, like the Mu'tazilites, does not distinguish between *form* and *accident*.

[4] Cf. *Amānāt*, pp. 55-7 (29-30), where Saadya opposes the view ascribed to Hippocrates that the world was created from the *four natures* (qualities). The theory that the soul is composed of the *four natures* was also attributed to Hippocrates. Cf. Avicenna, *Kanon*, ed. Venice, 1608, p. 12 b.

[5] The context below (Amānāt 195.6 (98.9)), where the same term ('irtabāṭ; Tibbon: hitḳasher) is used, shows that Saadya refers to Aristotle's *sensus communis*. He insists that the sensus communis is only a function of the soul, but not identical with it. Cf. also *Amānāt*, p. 64 (34).

[6] Cf. Aristotle, *loc. cit.*, I, 2, 405 b, 5-8, where Critias is reported to hold the view that the soul is of the nature of the blood. It appears that Saadya took it to mean that it is not identical with the blood, but an 'accident' arising from it.

[7] Cf. above, pp. 116-7.

[8] According to the Mu'tazilite doctrine only a substance can be the carrier of an accident. Saadya thus beats the Mu'tazilites, who declare the soul to be an accident, with their own weapon by pointing out that the soul is affected by accidents.

the soul is affected by many accidents: it is either ignorant or knowing, either righteous or wicked, either loving or hating, either satisfied or displeased, and liable to many other natural dispositions, with which we are all familiar. In view of these conditions of the soul it is not permissible to assume that it is in itself only an accidental phenomenon. It is more appropriate, on account of its liability to contradictory qualities, to recognize it as a substance.[1]

(2) I have met people who imagine that the soul consists of air.[2]

(3) I have met people who imagine that the soul consists of fire.[3] I have found these two theories to be likewise absurd, for if the soul consisted of air, its nature would be warm and moist, and if it consisted of fire, its nature would be warm and dry, whereas our experience does not bear this out.

(4) The fourth theory asserts that the soul consists of two parts, one rational[4] and imperishable, with the heart as its seat, and the other of animal nature, diffused in the other parts of the body, and perishable.[5] I proved that this theory too was mistaken, for if the rational part were separate and distinct from the part which is diffused in the body, it would be impossible for the two to combine, seeing that the one part existed from eternity and the other was newly created, the one being perishable and the other being imperishable. Moreover, the rational part of the soul would not be able to hear or see or perform any other sensual function.[6] One cannot meet this

[1] In addition to the Kalam argument (see the preceding note), Saadya uses the Aristotelian principle that only a substance can be the carrier of two *contradictory* qualities. Cf. Julius Guttmann, *loc. cit.*, pp. 84-5. In opposing the view that the soul is an accident, Saadya seems to be inspired by the platonic and neo-platonic doctrines, which also prevailed in Christian theological circles. See Guttmann, *ibid.*

[2] Cf. Aristotle, *loc. cit.*, I, 2, 405 a, 21-2. The view is ascribed to Diogenes.

[3] Cf. Aristotle, *loc. cit.*, I, 2, 405 a, 8-13, 25-9. The view is reported in the names of Democritos and Heraclitos.

[4] Lit. 'reasonable and logical'.

[5] As Julius Guttmann (*loc. cit.*, p. 83) has shown, the above account combines the platonic view (attested by Plutarch) that the basic division of the soul is a dichotomy into a rational and an irrational part (the latter to be further subdivided into a noble and an ignoble element) with the view held by Democritos and Epicurus (also testified by Plutarch) that the rational part is placed in the heart whilst the irrational part is diffused in the other parts of the body.

[6] The rational soul would be completely separate from the irrational part and therefore unable to benefit from the sense perception of the animal soul. Reason would thus be deprived of all data of sense experience.

argument with the answer which I gave in another context, namely that the experiences of the various senses, although they occur independently of one another, are yet co-ordinated by a rational faculty,[1] as I explained in Chapter I.[2] That answer does not apply here because according to this theory the two parts of the soul are distinct and unrelated to each other.

(5) The fifth theory holds that the soul consists of two kinds of air, one being within the body, and one coming from without. They were led to this view by the observation that the soul cannot exist save through the inhaling of air from without. They thought that the external air had the function of complementing the internal other half of the soul.[3] But, in fact, the purpose of respiration is to cool the natural warmth of the heart in which the soul resides, just as one blows excessive smoke away from a fire.[4]

(6) The sixth theory is held only by 'Anan[5] as he explains it in his book,[6] and this view identifies the soul with the blood.[7] What misled him was the passage in the Torah, 'For the blood maketh atonement by reason of the soul' (Lev. 17.11), but he failed to remember the preceding words, 'For the soul of the flesh is in the blood' (loc. cit.), which testify that the blood is the seat and centre of the soul. The strength of the soul manifests itself in the strength of the blood, and the weakness of the soul becomes apparent in the weakness of the blood. Whenever the soul is glad and reveals its happiness, then the blood shows itself; whenever the soul draws back in dread of something which inspires fear, the blood recedes from the surface of the body. The expression used by the Torah, 'For the blood . . . by reason of the soul' must be understood in accordance with the rules of language. Sometimes a thing is called after

---

[1] i.e. the *sensus communis*.

[2] Cf. *Amānāt* 64 (34). See above, p. 142, n. 5.

[3] This view recalls the Stoic notion of πνεύματα. Ventura (p. 321) traced it to the theory of al-Bāķillānī.

[4] Cf. Aristotle, *De respiratione*, V.

[5] 'Anan ben David, the founder of Ķaraism in the eighth century, against whom Saadya wrote a polemical treatise under the title, 'Refutation of Anan' (*Kitāb al-radd 'alā 'Anān*).

[6] Called *Sefer ham-miṣwōt*. Cf. A. E. Harkavy, *Studien und Mitteilungen*, Vol. 8.

[7] Saadya distinguishes between the view that the soul is an 'accident originating from the blood' (cf. above, p. 142), and that which identifies the soul with the blood. He ascribes the latter to Anan 'only' although it is, in fact, Critias' opinion. Cf. above, p. 142, n. 6; Julius Guttmann, *loc. cit.*, pp. 82-3.

the place which it occupies. Thus wisdom is called 'heart', as, for instance, in the verse, 'A young man void of heart' (Prov. 7.7), because wisdom has its seat in the heart; or language is called 'lip', as, for instance, in the verse, 'And the whole earth was of one lip' (Gen. 11.1), because language flows from the lips.[1]

(7) The seventh theory is the one which we hold to be true, and I shall explain it with the help of God.

2. THE TRUE NATURE OF THE SOUL

(ed. Landauer 193.12-194.13; 195.1-196.8;
ed. Slucki 97.23-39; 98.5-28)

From what I have already explained about the creation of all existing things and the impossibility that anything except the Creator should be eternal, it is evident that the soul must be something created. God says that He 'formed the spirit of man *within him*' (Zech. 12.1), which indicates that He creates the soul at the moment when the bodily form of man is completed, as expressed in the words, 'within him'. Likewise the formula which our fathers still use when they take an oath contains the expression, 'As the Lord liveth, that *made us this soul*' (Jer. 38.16).[2]

The quality of the soul is that of a pure substance similar to the substance of the celestial spheres.[3] When the soul receives the light[4] it becomes more brilliantly illuminated than the sphere when it receives its light[5]; its substance becomes more refined than that of the celestial spheres. It is because of this that it is endowed with intellect. I derived this view from two excellent sources of knowledge: Firstly from the pure Reason.

[1] Saadya means to say that the apparent identification of blood and soul in the second part of the above quoted verse is caused by the habit of language to name a thing after its place. Since the soul has its seat in the blood of the heart, it can be called 'blood'.

[2] Like al-Fārābī, Saadya opposes the Platonic view of the soul as coeternal with God. His view also differs from the Talmudic doctrine that all souls were created in the First Man and are thus pre-existent in relation to the body. He teaches that the souls are created (a) individually, and (b) at the time when the body is created. The same doctrine is advanced by Christian theology. Cf. Julius Guttmann, *loc. cit.*, p. 86.

[3] Saadya follows here the view of Heraclitos, who defines the soul, according to Stobaeus, as 'something shining', and, according to Philoponos, as 'an etherial, i.e. heavenly body'. Cf. Julius Guttmann, *loc. cit.*, p. 87.

[4] Of wisdom and good deeds. Cf. above, pp. 128-9.

[5] From the stars. Cf. below, p. 146.

I observed the traces of the soul's wisdom and forethought when joined with the body, and I saw the body deprived of all that excellence after the soul had departed it. Were the soul of the same nature as the terrestrial bodies, it would not be able to perform any of these great works; and if it were of the same nature as the celestial bodies it would, like them, be lacking in Reason. It thus follows that the soul is a substance even finer, clearer, purer and simpler than that of the celestial spheres.[1] The second source of knowledge to which I referred is Scripture: it testifies that the righteous souls shine like the brilliance of the celestial spheres which are illumined by the stars,[2] as is said, 'The wise shine as the brightness of the firmament' (Dan. 12.3), whereas the wicked souls do not shine, and their light is less than that of the celestial spheres as such,[3] as is said, 'Behold, He putteth no trust in His holy ones; yea, the heavens are not clean in His sight. How much less one that is abominable and impure, man who drinketh iniquity like water' (Job 15.15-16). I maintain that Scripture would not compare the one type of man with celestial spheres which are illumined, and the other type with something less than the celestial bodies as such, if the soul were not something similar to the substance of the spheres. . . .

Then it became clear to me that for various reasons the soul must be intelligent on account of its own nature. One of my reasons is that it cannot possibly acquire knowledge through the body, seeing that it is not the nature of the body to know. Furthermore, it has been established that sometimes a blind person is able to see images in his dreams. Since he does not perceive such images by virtue of his body, he must surely perceive them by virtue of his soul.[4] This point is ignored by

[1] Saadya does not share the view held by Maimonides that the spheres are beings endowed with intellect. Although he holds that the soul resembles the celestial spheres, he regards their substance to be only of a corporeal nature. For Maimonides' view of the spheres, cf. *Moreh*, II, 4.

[2] Noble deeds inspired by wisdom add splendour to the substance of the soul, whereas evil deeds dim its light. Cf. above, pp. 128-9.

[3] i.e. of the celestial bodies with no light reflected on them from the stars.

[4] Saadya concludes from the experience of the blind that the soul possesses a source of knowledge within itself and quite apart from the data of sense perception. Modern psychologists speak of the 'haptic perception' of the blind, which creates 'a synthesis between his tactile perceptions of external reality, and his own subjective experiences'. Cf. V. Löwenfeld, *The Nature of Creative Activity*, London, 1939, pp. 82, 90, quoted by Herbert Read, *Education through Art*, London, 1943.

those who believe the soul to be the co-ordination of the senses as well as their inter-relation and combination.[1] For it is the soul which imparts the faculty of perception to the sense organs; how then could they give the soul its substance? This would, in my opinion, be quite illogical and the opposite of truth.

It then became clear to me that the soul can act only through the instrumentality of the body,[2] for the activity of every created being requires an organ for its performance. Only when body and soul are combined can the three faculties of the soul manifest themselves. These three faculties are the faculty of *discernment*, the faculty of *appetite*, and the faculty of *courage*.[3] For this reason the Hebrew language has three different names for the soul; they are *nefesh*, *ruaḥ*, and *neshamah*. By the name *nefesh* is indicated the soul's faculty of *appetite*; e.g. in the phrases, 'Because thy soul (*nefesh*) desireth' (Deut. 12.20); 'And his soul is made to abhor dainty food' (Job 33.20). By the name *ruaḥ* is indicated the faculty of passion and courage; e.g. in the phrases, 'Be not hasty in thy spirit (*ruaḥ*) to be angry' (Eccl. 7.9); 'A fool spendeth all his spirit' (Prov. 39.11). By the name *neshamah* is expressed the faculty of knowledge; e.g. in the phrases, 'And the breath (*neshamah*) of the Almighty giveth them understanding' (Job 32.8); 'Whose breath came forth from thee?' (Job 26.4).[4]

Concerning these faculties, the opinion of those who believe that the soul consists of two separate parts, one residing in the heart and one residing in the rest of the body, is mistaken. All the three faculties are the functions of one and the same soul.[5]

The Hebrew language employs two more names of the soul in addition to those mentioned above — *ḥayah* and *yeḥidah*. It is called *ḥayah* ('the living one') because of the immortal life which is imparted to it by its Creator. It is called *yeḥidah*

---

[1] Cf. above, p. 142, n. 5.

[2] Aristotle (*De anima*, II, 1, 413 a, 4) describes the body as the instrument of the soul.

[3] This is the well-known Platonic division of the soul into the three parts, λογιστικόν; ἐπιθυμητικόν; θυμοειδές.

[4] The three faculties of the soul are more fully discussed in *Comm. Yeṣ.*, pp. 33-4 (55), where the corresponding Hebrew names of the soul are given exactly as here.

[5] Saadya opposes Plato's view that the three faculties of the soul have to be considered as three separate parts, and not merely separate functions, of the soul. Maimonides opens his 'Eight Chapters' by the same emphatic insistence that the soul is one and indivisible despite its manifold aspects.

('the unique one') because there is nothing resembling it in the whole of the created universe, neither in the celestial world nor upon earth.

Then it became clear to me that the seat of the soul is in the heart of man, since it is evident that the two nerves which impart sensation and movement to the body issue from the heart.[1] Certainly I am well aware that large branches of nerves ramify not from the heart, but from the brain. But I also know that these branches of nerves have no psychic functions. They are the sinews of the body and its ties. For this reason Scripture always mentions heart and soul together, e.g. in the phrase, 'With all thy heart and with all thy soul' (Deut. 6.5; 11.13), and similar expressions.

3. A GNOSTIC ARGUMENT AND ITS REFUTATION

(ed. Landauer 196.9-13; 197.11-200.16;
ed. Slucki 98.29-32; 99.8-100.25)

I found people who argued thus: 'How can we reconcile the wisdom of the Creator (be He exalted and glorified) with the fact that He placed this noble soul, which is purer than the sphere, within this ignoble bodily frame?' They were inclined to believe in their hearts that God had inflicted evil upon the soul.[2] I feel it my duty to dwell on this subject and to explain it in clear terms.

My view is that the soul by itself is, on account of its nature, incapable of action, and that, for this reason, it was necessary

---

[1] Cf. Aristotle, *De animalium historia*, III, 4.5; Galenus, *De usu partium*, I, 16. In translating the Arabic word *sharāyin* by 'nerves' (not 'arteries' as the word normally means) we follow Ventura's example; he considers the Hebrew translation *gidim* (nerves) to be more accurate than the Arabic original. Ventura's view is borne out by a paragraph in R. Josef ben Yehuda's *SeferMussar* (ed. W. Bacher), p. 169. See the Translator's article in *Melilah* (ed. E. Robertson and M. Wallenstein), p. 12, n. 67.

[2] According to Plato, who reflects an earlier tradition (that of Orphic mysticism), the body must be considered as the 'prison' of the soul. The sharp distinction between body and soul was later accentuated by the Gnostic movement, which profoundly influenced the rise of Christianity, and, to some extent, the school of Jewish mysticism. Saadya's attitude is opposed to the Gnostic vilification of the body. He defends God's wisdom of uniting body and soul. He denies that any impurity is attached to the body as such. His spirited apology makes it obvious that he is addressing himself to contemporary Jewish thinkers who were influenced by the Gnostic (notably Manichaean) philosophy. He is, however, not entirely free from an ascetic tendency. Cf. above, p. 133, where he demands the renunciation of the world.

to join it to something through which it became capable of virtuous activities so as to attain by such activities eternal bliss and perfect happiness. As we explained in Chapter V, obedience to God makes the substance of the soul bright and luminous, whereas disobedience causes it to become dim and faint. Scripture bears testimony to this by saying, 'Light is sown for the righteous' (Ps. 97.11), and 'The light of the righteous rejoiceth, but the lamp of the wicked shall be put out' (Prov. 13.9). It is the Lord of the universe who examines the soul and discerns all its actions. Scripture has compared Him to the fire which purges gold and silver from its dross, so that its true nature becomes manifest: the solid gold and silver remain, whereas the admixture of dross[1] is partly consumed and partly dispersed, as is written, 'The refining pot is for silver, and the furnace for gold, and a man is tried by his praise' (Prov. 27.21), and furthermore, 'I will bring the third part through the fire, and will refine them as silver is refined, and will try them as gold is tried' (Zech. 13.9). The righteous and pure souls which are freed from the dross are honoured and exalted, as is said, 'For He knoweth the way that I take; when He hath tried me, I shall come forth as gold' (Job 23.10). But those who resemble the impure dross sink into contempt, as is said, 'In vain doth the founder refine, for the wicked are not separated. Refuse silver shall men call them . . .' (Jer. 6.29-30). Nevertheless, as long as the impure souls are still joined to their bodies, it is possible for them to return to God and to become purified and clean. Thus penitence is accepted as long as a man lives. But once the soul has departed the body, it has lost the possibility of cleansing itself from its admixtures, and there is no longer any hope, as it says, 'When a wicked man dieth, his expectation shall perish' (Prov. 11.7).

Some say that it would have been better for the soul if God had left it by itself, because it would then have remained free from sin, impurity and suffering. My answer in explanation to these people is that God would have done so if it were a better thing for the soul to remain separate. In addition, we have already learned that if the soul had remained separate, it would not have attained bliss, happiness, and the eternal life.

[1] Another reading, *elixir* (Arab. *al-'iksir*).

For all this can only be achieved by obedience to God, and obedience to God is only possible through the instrumentality of the body, for such is the constitution of the soul that it can act only through the body, just as fire cannot become active[1] unless it is attached to combustible material. Similarly many kinds of things cannot complete their actions except by the aid of other things. Had, therefore, the soul remained single, it would not have been capable of action; how much less the body, which would certainly not have been in a condition to act. If, in consequence, both had remained without activity, it would have been purposeless to create them, and if their creation had been without purpose, the same absence of purpose would have applied to the creation of heaven and earth and all that exists between them, seeing that everything was created for the sake of man only, as I explained in the beginning of Chapter IV.[2] The Verse commencing 'who stretched forth the heavens and laid the foundations of the earth' (Zech. 12.1), concludes by saying, 'And formed the spirit of man within him'. We have already explained that the whole work of creation was for the sake of man.

Some people may argue that God could have left the soul by itself aloof from the body whilst at the same time endowing it with the ability to act and thus to achieve the purpose for which it was created. I would point out that such a suggestion resembles the previous one which amounted to asking that the body of man should be like the substance of the stars and angels. Our answer, therefore, is that such a request is tantamount to asking that the soul should not be a soul, seeing that the rational soul is an entity that cannot act without the body. If it could act without the body, it would be either a star or a sphere or an angel. But in such a case its nature as a soul would be obliterated, and one who puts forward the above suggestion is asking that the soul be obliterated without saying this in so many words. It is like asking that the fire should, by its own nature, move downward, and that the water should, by its own nature, rise upwards, which amounts to the obliteration of their essences. Or to use another example, it is

[1] Lit. 'achieve its form'.
[2] Both the Arabic and Hebrew versions read 'Chapter III', which must be corrected as above.

like expressing a desire that the fire be cold and the snow be warm, which again means obliterating their essences. Whosoever desires such a thing does violence to the truth,[1] for the truth is that which corresponds to things as they really are and are known to be. It is no sign of wisdom to suggest that things should be as one desires and wishes them to be. Thus Scripture says, 'Woe unto him that striveth with his Maker' (Isa. 45.9).

As to the soul being exposed to the possibility of sin, which some people make a ground of complaint against God, we must bear in mind that sin is the result of the soul's own evil choice as it acts in opposition to the wishes of the Creator; as it says, 'Behold this only have I found, that God made man upright; but they have sought out many inventions' (Eccl. 7.29). As to the complaint of the soul being subject to impurity and defilement, we declare that there is nothing impure about the human body, on the contrary, it is perfectly pure, for impurity is a thing the existence of which is neither patent to the senses nor discoverable by virtue of Reason.[2] It is known to us only from the Law, which has declared certain human secretions to be impure after their separation from the body. As long as they are still within the body one cannot consider them as impure, unless one presumes to lay down the law for himself. We denounce such a view as monstrous and we will not accept it as law.

With regard to the sufferings of the soul, to which attention has been drawn, they must of necessity belong to one of two categories: either the suffering was incurred by the soul through carelessness, as for instance in the case of a person walking about at the time of darkness or excessive heat or cold. In such a case the fault lies with the soul, and not with God, for He has endowed it with Reason and commanded it to protect itself against such harm, but it disobeyed Him, as it says, 'A prudent man seeth the evil, and hideth himself, but the thoughtless pass on, and are punished' (Prov. 27.12). Where, however, the suffering is inflicted upon the soul by God, it is

---

[1] Lit. 'wisdom'.

[2] In his Refutation of Ḥiwi al-Balkhi Saadya makes the same point: 'Know thou that there is nothing unclean in the innermost parts of man, that all his fluids are not called unclean until they separate (from the body)'. (Davidson, pp. 46-7.) See Niddah, 5.1; b. Niddah 41 b.

because of His justice and mercy, and is meted out to it only in the way of chastisement with the object of bestowing upon it happiness in return, as is said, 'That He might afflict thee, and that He might prove thee, to do thee good at thy latter end' (Deut. 8.16), and furthermore, 'Happy is the man whom Thou chastenest, O Lord . . . That Thou mayest give him rest from the days of evil' (Ps. 94.12).

4. ON DEATH AND THE AFTER-LIFE

> (ed. Landauer 204.14-205.1; 205.15-207.3;
> ed. Slucki 102.15-22; 102.35-103.17)

Having explained all these matters it is desirable that I should now describe the state of the soul at the moment it departs from the body. Our teachers have informed us that the angel sent by God to separate body and soul appears to man in the form of a yellowish flame, full of eyes shining with a bluish fire, holding in his hand a drawn sword pointed at the person to whom death is coming. At this sight the person is greatly terrified, and the breath of life departs from the body.[1] In consulting Scripture, I found that it describes the condition in a way similar to what our teachers have told us. Speaking of a time of pestilence, Scripture says, 'And David lifted up his eyes, and saw the angel of the Lord standing between the earth and the heaven, having a drawn sword in his hand stretched out over Jerusalem' (1 Chron. 21.16). . . .[2]

If one asks for the reason why the soul is not visible at the moment when it departs from the body, our answer is: Because of its fineness and air-like transparency. The same applies to the spheres. They are invisible because of the purity and fineness of their substance. I am accustomed to give the following illustration: If one should take ten lamps of fine glass, put one inside the other, and place a light in the middle, no one looking from a distance would think that the light is surrounded by ten lamps, because owing to the transparency

[1] Cf. b. Aḫ. zarah 20 b. The account given in this Talmudic passage somewhat differs from Saadya's description. As to parallels in Greek, Christian and Islamic folk-lore see Malter, p. 228, n. 509 a, and Ventura, p. 243, n. 85.

[2] Other Scriptural passages quoted by Saadya in support of the above view are 1 Chron. 21.27, 30; Ezek. 1.13; 6.12; Deut. 5.25.

of the glass the vision passes straight through it and strikes the light therein. This is quite obvious.[1]

I will now deal with the question what is the condition of the soul after its departure from the body. My answer is that, as I have already mentioned, the soul is stored up until Judgment Day, as is said, 'He that keepeth thy soul, doth He not know it? And shall not He render to every man according to his work?' (Prov. 24.12). The place where the pure souls are kept is above, the place for the impure is below. I have already quoted, in a previous context, the verse, 'And they that are wise shall shine as the brightness of the firmament' (Dan. 12.3), and 'Who knoweth the spirit of Man whether it goeth upward?' (Eccl. 3.21).[2] Likewise, our ancient teachers have said, 'The souls of the righteous are stored up beneath the Throne of Glory, and the souls of the wicked roam about in the world' (b. Shabbat 152 b). This and other differences are to be found between the righteous and the wicked souls.[3]

In the first period after its separation from the body, the soul is for some while without a permanent abode until the body is consumed, that is to say, its parts are decomposed.[4] During this time the soul is greatly disturbed to see the body in its state of decay, just as one would be overwhelmed by grief to see the house in which one used to live laid in ruins and transformed into a place where thorns and thistles grow. This suffering of the soul varies in degree according to its merits, just as the painfulness of its abode below varies in degree according to its merits. Our ancient teachers likewise said, 'The worm hurts the dead body as the needle hurts the living' (b. Shabbat 152 a). They found support for this view in the words of Scripture, 'But his flesh grieveth for him, and his

[1] 'This illustration is to explain why the celestial lights alone are visible to the human eye, while the spheres in which they are set and which, in ancient astronomy, were supposed to be ten in number, cannot be discerned. Indirectly it serves also as an explanation for the invisibility of the soul, which is of transparent material like the spheres.' (Malter, p. 229.)

[2] Saadya gives to this verse, which obviously questions the immortality of the soul, an affirmative meaning. See also Amānāt 191-4 (96-8). Saadya's interpretation is borne out by the vowel-signs of the Massoretic Text. Cf. S. D. Luzzatto in Geiger's Wissenschaftliche Zeitschrift für jüdische Theologie, V, 1844, p. 124; Malter, p. 224, n. 502; Ventura, p. 233, n. 37.

[3] The view that God rewards the soul not immediately after death but only after its re-union with the body at the time of the resurrection was also current in Islamic theology. Cf. Guttmann, pp. 209-10.

[4] Cf. b. Shabbat 152 b.

soul mourneth over him' (Job 14.22). They call this doctrine by the name of *Din hak-Keber* ('The Judgment of the Grave') or *Hibbut hak-Keber* ('The Beating of the Grave').[1]

I further say that the soul remains in its separation from the body until the time when all souls which God in His wisdom decided to create have been called into being and are gathered together. This will happen in the end of days. When their number is complete and they are gathered together, God will re-unite the souls with their respective bodies, as I shall explain in the next chapter, and bestow upon them their reward according to their merits.

---

[1] Cf. *b. Ta'anit* 11 a. In a somewhat different form, this doctrine found its way into Islamic theology. The term 'Beating of the Grave' (*'adhāb al-kabr*) occurs as the title of a book by Ibn Karrām. Cf. al-Shahrastānī, I, 119. On the Jewish conception of *Hibbūt ha-Keber* see the article in *Oṣar Yisrael*, ed. J. D. Eisenstein, Vol. 4, p. 242.

CHAPTER VII

THE RESURRECTION OF THE DEAD IN THE PRESENT WORLD[1]

1. Refutation of the Allegorist Interpretation

(ed. Landauer 211.8-213.19)

As to the Resurrection of the Dead, regarding which our Lord has informed us that it will take place in the Future World of Reward,[2] this is something on which our whole people is agreed. Their agreement is based on the view already mentioned in the preceding chapters,[3] that Man is the final object of Creation; that the reason of his distinction lies in his obedience (to God); and that the fruit of his obedience is the eternal life in the World of Reward.[4] Prior to this period God deemed it right to separate soul and body only until such time as the (number of) souls was completed and all of them were gathered together as I explained.[5] We know of no Jew who

---

[1] The text of this chapter differs widely in the two extant MSS. (i.e. the Oxford and Leningrad Recensions). The above translation is based on Landauer's text, which follows the Oxford Recension. For our reason see Introduction, pp. 21-2. Tibbon's translation is based on the text which is given in the Leningrad Recension. The anonymous Paraphrase follows partly one and partly the other recension. An abridged version of Chapter VII as it appears in the Paraphrase was published as a separate treatise in Mantua (1556) under the title *Sefer ha-tehiyyah* ('Book on Resur- rection'). Cf. Malter, pp. 362-4. On the subject of Resurrection cf. A. Löwinger, 'Die Auferstehung in der jüd. Tradition' in *Jahrbuch für Jüdische Volskunde*, ed. Max Grunwald (1923), Vol. 25, pp. 23-122. An exposition of Saadya's view is given there on pp. 99-104. See also Israel Lévi, 'Les Morts et l'avènement de l'ère messianique' in *REJ* (1919), Vol. 69.

[2] Arab. *dār al-'āchir* (Hebr. '*ōlam haba*'); in contradistinction to *dār al-dunyā* (Hebr. '*ōlam hazeh*), which occurs in the title of the chapter. Saadya teaches that the messianic period will be initiated by the resurrection of the pious of Israel, who will thus receive a special reward for the suffering they had to endure during the long period of Israel's exile. This resurrection will take place in the present world as part of the scheme of Israel's Redemption, and constitutes an act of justice on God's part. Cf. *Amānāt*, p. 225-6. This resurrection of the pious of Israel will later be followed by the resurrection of the dead of all peoples at the time when the Future World, the World of Reward, will be inaugurated. In this Future World God will mete out justice to every man, pious and impious. In this chapter Saadya deals with the resur- rection in the messianic period.

[3] Cf. above, pp. 115-7.

[4] Saadya deals with the World of Reward in Chapter IX.

[5] Cf. above, p. 154.

opposes this doctrine,[1] or finds it difficult from the point of view of his Reason that God should revive the dead, since it has already become clear to him that God created the world *ex nihilo*. He can find no difficulty therefore in believing that God should, by a second act, create something from something disintegrated and dissolved.[2]

God stated, furthermore, in Scripture that there will take place for us a Resurrection of the Dead at the time of the Redemption of Israel.[3] His prophets have established this doctrine for us by miracles. I found, nevertheless, that in regard to this doctrine of the Resurrection of the Dead in the Present World opinions are divided. The large majority of our people declare that there will be a resurrection at the time of the messianic Redemption, and they interpret all that is found in the Scriptural passages on the Resurrection of the Dead according to its plain meaning,[4] and fixed its time without question for the time of the Redemption. I saw only a small minority of the whole nation interpret figuratively the passages which speak of the Resurrection of the Dead at the time of the Redemption as references to the revival of our Kingdom and the restoration of the people.[5] That which is not fixed for the time of the Redemption they transfer to the Future World.[6] I have reserved this chapter for a treatment of this point.

I declare in regard to this matter that after careful examination I have ascertained beyond doubt for myself what forms the opinion of the majority of the nation, namely, that a resurrection of the dead will take place at the time of the Redemption. I deemed it right to confirm this so that it may

---

[1] Arab. *'amānāt*; i.e. of the Resurrection in the Future World.
[2] The same argument occurs also in the Leningrad Recension. Cf. ed. Bacher, p. 100; ed. Slucki 107.
[3] The term used by Saadya throughout this chapter for the Redemption of Israel is the Hebrew word *yeshu'ah*, salvation, which he invariably cites in Hebrew characters. In Chapter VIII he uses the Arabic *furkān*. Cf. below, p. 167, n. 1.
[4] Arab. *ẓāhir*, manifest, literal (meaning).
[5] Abū Yūsuf Ya'kūb al-Kirkisāni, a contemporary of Saadya's, mentions that some Karaites asserted that the messianic salvation had already taken place during the time of the Second Temple (cf. below, pp. 175 ff), and that others interpreted the Scriptural passages dealing with the Resurrection of the Dead in the sense of allegorical descriptions of Israel's rise from exile. Cf. Bacher, *loc. cit.*, p. 224.
[6] i.e. the references to Resurrection which are unconnected with the Redemption of Israel they understood to apply to the Resurrection in the Future World. With this Saadya agrees.

serve as a guide and give a lead[1] (to our people) like the matters dealt with before. I declare in the first place that one of the things of which we can be certain[2] is that every statement found in the Scriptures must be taken in its plain sense. Only for one of four reasons it is not permitted to take a statement in its plain sense. These four reasons are the following: (1) If sense perception rejects the plain sense of the passage, as in the statement, 'And the man called his wife's name Eve; because she was the mother of all living' (Gen. 3.20), seeing that we witness the fact that ox and lion are not the children of woman so that it is necessary for us to believe that the statement refers only to man[3]; (2) in case Reason repudiates it, as in the statement, 'For the Lord thy God is a devouring fire, a jealous God' (Deut. 4.24), seeing that the fire is something created, required for use and extinguishable; it is, therefore, not permitted, from the point of view of Reason, to assume that God should be like it; it, therefore, follows that we must understand the statement in an elliptical sense, namely, that God's *punishment* is like a devouring fire, in the same way it says, 'For all the earth shall be devoured with the fire of My jealousy' (Zeph. 3.8); (3) in case there exists some clear text which renders the plain meaning of a passage impossible; it then follows that this clear text should be used to interpret the text which is not clear, as in the statement, 'Ye shall not try the Lord your God, as ye tried Him in Massah' (Deut. 6.16), and it is further said, 'And try Me now herewith — if I will not open you the windows of heaven' (Mal. 3.10). Both statements agree in this respect, that one should not try our Lord as to whether or not He is able to do a certain thing, after the manner of those of whom it was said, 'And they tried God in their hearts by asking food for their craving; yea, they spoke against God, they said: "Can God prepare a table in the wilderness?" ' (Ps. 78.18-19). Of these it is said, 'As ye tried Him in Massah'. But man[4] may try the power of his Lord as to whether or not He is able to

---

[1] According to the Leningrad Recension, Saadya's meaning is that the belief in the Resurrection of the pious of Israel in the messianic era is bound to guide and strengthen the people amidst the trials of exile. Cf. ed. Bacher 99; ed. Slucki 106.

[2] Lit. 'according to our knowledge of the true realities of things'. Cf. above, p. 107.

[3] i.e. 'All living' means 'All men'.

[4] Lit. 'Servant' (of God).

produce a sign and miracle for him, in the same way as Gideon asked, 'Let me make trial, I pray thee, but this once with the fleece' (Judges 6.39), or as Hezekiah asked (II Kings 20.8), and others besides them, which is permissible; (4) if to the statement of Scripture is attached some tradition[1] which modifies it, we must interpret the passage in conformity with the reliable tradition, as in the case of the tradition that flogging consists of 39 stripes, although it is written, 'Forty stripes he may give him' (Deut. 25.3). We take this to be a figure of speech[2]; the flogging consists of 39 stripes, and the text of Scripture mentions a round figure,[3] in the same way as it says, 'After the number of the days in which ye spied out the land, even 40 days, for every day a year . . .' (Num. 14.34), although in fact it was only 39 (years) because in the first year they had not yet entered into this punishment.[4]

There are only these four reasons which necessitate the interpretation of the plain meaning of the Scriptural passages in an allegorical sense[5]; there exists no fifth reason which would justify an allegorical interpretation. Now we find that the Resurrection of the Dead is not rejected by sense experience because we do not assert that the dead will be revived by themselves, but we say that their Creator will revive them. Nor is it rejected by Reason because the second creation of a thing which was already in existence and became dissolved, is more acceptable to Reason than the *creatio ex nihilo*. Nor is it precluded by any other text of Scripture; on the contrary, other texts corroborate it by stating in clear terms that the son of the woman of Zarephat (I Kings 17.17-24) and the son of the Shunammite woman (II Kings 4.32-7) were revived in this world. Nor does any tradition make it necessary to interpret it in an allegorical sense; on the contrary, the whole of tradition supports it. Thus it follows that this doctrine must be left in its original meaning in accordance with the clear

---

[1] Arab. *athar*.

[2] Arab. *majāz*.

[3] Arab. *jabara*; lit. 're-unite broken parts'; the word *Algebra* is derived from this Arabic root.

[4] The Leningrad Recension contains the same exegetical canon, but in a slightly less elaborate form than presented here. Cf. ed. Bacher 102-3; ed. Slucki 109. A similar exegetical canon was evolved by Ibn Ḥazm, but with the omission of a possible conflict between Scripture and Reason. Cf. I. Goldziher, *Die Zahiriten*, pp. 122-3; 142-5.

[5] Arab. *tā'wīl*.

sense of the text, namely, that God will revive the dead of His people at the time of the Redemption.[1]

2. EVIDENCE FROM SCRIPTURE[2]

(ed. Landauer 213.21-216.12)

I consider that the Song of Moses (*Shīrat Ha'azīnū*) outlines the whole history of Israel. It commences with the beginnings of our election by God, and says, 'Remember the days of old, consider the years of many generations . . . when the Most High gave to the nations their inheritance . . . for the portion of the Lord is His people' (Deut. 32.7-9). Then, at the second stage, the Song mentions God's favours towards us, and says, 'He found him in a desert land . . . He compassed him about, He cared for him, He kept him as the apple of His eye' (10). Then, at the third stage, it mentions our prosperity[3] and sinfulness, and says, 'But Jeshurun waxed fat, and kicked . . .' (15). Then, at the fourth stage, it mentions our punishment, and says, 'And the Lord saw, and spurned . . . and He said: "I will hide My face from them" . . .' and what follows (19-25). Then, at the fifth stage, it mentions the punishment of our enemies, and says, 'For their vine is of the vine of Sodom . . .' (32-5). Then, at the sixth stage, it speaks of our relief and succour, namely from the verse, 'See now that I, even I, am He, and there is no god with Me' (39) until the end of the Song. And within this historical account occurs the state-

---

[1] In a passage not included in this Selection (ed. Landauer 216-8; ed. Bacher 106-7; ed. Slucki 112-3), Saadya seriously considers whether the Resurrection of the Dead may not, after all, merely express, in symbolic language, the promised rise of the Jewish kingdom 'From its dust'. He quotes Ps. 113.7, II Kings 16.2, Ps. 88.5-6, 31.13, 71.20 as evidence that Scripture is wont to use such and similar expressions for the rise of man from humbleness to glory. His counter-argument is that unless we are prepared to accept the doctrine of Resurrection in its plain literal sense, there is nothing to prevent us from dissolving the whole Torah, its laws and miracles, into a nebulous allegorism. Saadya's anti-allegorism is in striking contrast to Philo's allegorical interpretation of the Torah, including its laws.

[2] According to the Mishnah (*Sanh.* 10.1), 'One who declares that the Resurrection of the Dead is not proclaimed by the Torah, has no share in the Future World'. Saadya endeavours to trace this doctrine both in the Torah and the later Scriptures. In so doing he elaborates some of the arguments produced by the Talmud in order to prove that this doctrine is already found in the Torah.

[3] Lit. "Walking proudly"; also "importance" (Arab. *chatir*).

[4] Lit. 'High rank' (Arab. *chatar*); the Leningrad Recension reads *tarhum*, 'their sprouting'. Cf. ed. Bacher, 108.

[5] Lit. 'Arrangement' (Arab. *nazām*); the same expression is used in the opening sentence of this paragraph.

ment, 'I kill and I make alive; I have wounded, and I heal'
(39), namely, in the days of Redemption. And lest we imagine
that the meaning of the verse is, 'He killeth some people and
maketh other people live',[1] as is the way[2] of the world, He says,
'I have wounded, and I heal', so as to let us know that in the
same way as it is the sick body which is healed, so it is the
dead body which will be revived.[3] And all this will take place
at the time of the Redemption, as is evident from the following
verses[4]: 'For I lift up my hand to heaven and say, "As I live
for ever, if I whet My glittering sword, and My hand take
hold on judgment" ...' (40-42); 'Sing aloud, O ye nations,
of His people', the meaning of which is the same as in the
verse, 'Sing with gladness for Jacob ...' (Jer. 31.7).[5]

I declare furthermore: The Creator knew that whispers
might reach us of the difficulty of believing in the Resurrection
of the Dead of our people.[6] He, therefore, met this point in
advance by the prophecy of Ezekiel. He said unto him, 'Son
of man, those bones are the whole house of Israel; behold,
they say: "Our bones are dried up, and our hope is lost; we
are clean cut off"' (Ezek. 37.11). Then He commanded him
to announce to us that we shall rise from our graves, and that
all of our dead will be revived, in the following words,
'Therefore, prophesy, and say unto them: ... "Behold, I will
open your graves, and cause you to come up out of your
graves, O my people"' (12). And lest we should think that
this promise only relates to the Future World, He added at
the end of this verse, 'And I will bring you into the Land of
Israel' (12), so that we may be sure that it will happen in the
present world. And He further added that every one of us,
when revived by God, will remember that he is the one who
lived and died and was revived. Thus He says, 'And ye shall

---

[1] i.e. not that God revives those who are killed, but He kills people and causes
others to live.
[2] Lit. 'nature'; Arab. *binya*.
[3] Saadya borrows this argument from the Talmud (*b. Sanh.* 91 b).
[4] Since the verses following upon the announcement of the Resurrection speak of
the messianic Redemption, the Resurrection must necessarily form part of this
period.
[5] The same paragraph occurs, in a slightly different form, also in the Leningrad
Recension. Cf. ed. Bacher 108; ed. Slucki 113-4.
[6] Lit. 'The resurrection of the dead amongst us'. The reference is to the special
resurrection of the pious of Israel in the messianic period prior to the general resurrection in the Future World.

know that I am the Lord, when I have opened your graves . . . and ye shall know that I the Lord have spoken, and performed it . . .' (13-14). And He repeats the mention of Palestine in order to corroborate our belief that it will happen in this world, as He says, 'And I will put My spirit in you, and ye shall live, and I will place you in your own land' (14).[1]

I declare furthermore: The prophet (Isaiah) has announced something similar to this promise when he says, 'Thy dead shall live' (Is. 26.19), which in effect corresponds to Ezekiel's statement,[2] 'They say: "Our bones are dried up, and our hope is lost" '.[3] This state (of Resurrection) resembles the condition of one who awakens from his slumber, as it says, 'Awake and sing' (ibid.), which corresponds to Ezekiel's statement, 'And ye shall know that I am the Lord, when I have opened your graves'.[4] The Resurrection is also likened to the 'Dew of light' (ibid.), because man's nature[5] is built up from the four elements: The earth is there already, and the moisture God brings to it from the essence[6] of dew; then He brings to it the spirit[7] from the essence of light, because the soul is luminous like the light as we explained.[8] 'And the earth shall cause the shades to fall' (ibid.)[9] means to say that the unbelievers[10] will

---

[1] The above paragraph on Ezekiel's prophecy appears in a different version also in the Leningrad Recension. Cf. ed. Bacher 104-5; ed. Slucki 111. In the Talmud (b. Sanh. 92 b), opinions are divided as to whether Ezekiel's vision was in the nature of a simile (mashal) or portrayed a real event.

[2] Lit. 'to what is said there', i.e. in Ezekiel, chap. 37.

[3] In the Leningrad Recension this paragraph occurs in a modified form. Cf. ed. Bacher 105; ed. Slucki 111. There Isaiah's words, 'Thy dead shall live', are said to correspond to Ezekiel's words, 'Behold, I open your graves'; and the second part of Isaiah's verse, 'My dead bodies shall arise' is stated to correspond to Ezekiel's words, 'I will cause you to come up out of your graves'. The answer to the despairing words, 'Our bones are dried up', is said to be given by Isaiah's words, 'For Thy dew is a dew of light'.

[4] The Leningrad Recension elaborates this point by adding, 'For one who awakens relates in his waking state what he saw in his dream, and knows that it is he who slept and awoke'.

[5] Arab. binya.

[6] Arab. ma'nā.

[7] Arab. ruḥ; Saadya takes the spirit (breath) to consist of air and fire.

[8] Cf. above, pp. 145-6. — In the Leningrad Recension the plural 'lights' ('orōt) which occurs in Isa. 26.19 is explained with reference to the sixteen faculties of the soul, a conception which strangely contrasts with Saadya's notion of three faculties of the soul as explained in Chapter VI.

[9] This is how Saadya understands the verse. The Authorized Version renders it, 'And the earth shall bring to life the shades'.

[10] Arab. al-kuffār; Saadya holds that the souls of the unbelievers roam about in the universe until the time of their punishment in the Future World arrives. Cf. above, p. 153.

be cast down to earth and humbled, as we explained, and they are those who ignored the commandment and prohibition of God. Thus it is said, 'The man that strayeth out of the way of understanding shall rest in the congregation of the shades' (Prov. 21.16).

I declare furthermore: I found that our Lord informed Daniel as to what will happen in the end of time, in 47 verses.[1] One verse, namely the first one, describes what will happen in the final period of the Persian Kingdom (Dan. 11.2); 13 verses inform us about the Greek Kingdom, namely, from 11.3 to 16; 20 verses inform us about the Roman Empire, namely from 11.16 to 36; 10 verses inform us about the Arab Kingdom, namely from 11.36 to 12.1; and the last 3 verses deal with the Redemption (of Israel), and one of them reads as follows, 'And many of them that sleep in the dust of the earth shall awake, some to everlasting life, and some to reproaches and everlasting abhorrence' (12.2). He only says, 'And *many* of them that sleep'; he does not say, '*All* of them that sleep', because that would include all children of Adam, whereas this promise[2] includes only the children of Israel. Therefore, he says, 'Many'. And he says, 'Some to everlasting life, and some to reproaches', which does not mean that some of those revived will be rewarded and some punished, since at the time of the Redemption God will not revive those who deserve punishment.[3] But the meaning of the distinction made in this verse is that those who will awake will awake to life everlasting, and those who will not awake will be marked for eternal shame, because all the righteous and penitent will be revived, and only the unbelievers and those who died without repentance will be left over. All this applies to the time of the Redemption.[4]

---

[1] Cf. Dan. 11.2-45; 12.1-3.

[2] i.e. of Resurrection in the messianic period as distinct from the life in the Future World.

[3] Only the pious of Israel will be revived in the messianic period.

[4] The above paragraph on Daniel occurs with some variation in the Leningrad Recension as well. Cf. ed. Bacher 105-6; ed. Slucki 111-2.

3. A KNOTTY POINT[1]

(ed. Landauer 220.17-222.6; 223.2-5)

Having explained these statements,[2] I declare: If one by the exercise of his Reason tries to penetrate more deeply into the subject of the Resurrection of the Dead — an event which will take place at the time of the Redemption[3] and, for all mankind, in the Future World — he will, perhaps, be led in the course of his reflections to the following objection: When any human body, as it exists at its first stage,[4] dissolves into its elements after death, all its parts return to their elemental sources,[5] that is to say the bodily warmth joins the fire, the moisture and the humours the air, the coldness the water, and the dryness remains with the earth. Then the Creator forms the bodies of the second stage from the same materials of which the parts of the first stage were composed. Then the human body of the second stage dies, and, again, its parts return to their elemental sources. Then the Creator forms from them a third stage which, again, is composed in the same way as the two preceding stages. And so with the fourth and the fifth. Now how is it possible to assume that the first stage should be perfect, and the second stage also perfect, and the third stage also perfect, seeing that the parts of every stage have already entered into existence at other stages?[6] To remove all misgivings on this matter I say: God would have need to use the

[1] The exposition which follows occurs, with some modifications, also in the Leningrad Recension. Cf. ed. Bacher 100-101; ed. Slucki 107-8. There it is introduced as an answer to a possible objection which natural science might raise against the doctrine of Resurrection.

[2] Saadya refers to the Scriptural passages quoted before and a number of Talmudic utterances on the subject, quoted on pp. 219-20 (ed. Landauer). See also ed. Bacher 108-9; ed. Slucki 114.

[3] i.e. for the pious of Israel.

[4] Arab. ṭabaḳa; layer, stage, grade. The assumption is that the elements into which man dissolves after death are used again in the process of generation on earth so that the very same materials which formed the body of a man at stage 1 may appear again in the body of another man (stage 2), and so forth.

[5] Arab. ma'din. Cf. above, p. 69, n. 7.

[6] The trend of the argument is this: If we assume that there exists only a limited amount of elementary matter in the universe, then the same matter which has been used already will have to form the substance of all subsequent generation. But if this is the case, its quality must necessarily degenerate. If so, how can we imagine that at the time of Resurrection the human body will still be 'perfect'? The idea that, in a biological sense, mankind is in a process of degeneration has been advanced, from a different point of view, by such modern thinkers as L. Klages and Th. Lessing. The notion that the world grows old is already found in IV Ezra 5.53-5; 14.10, 16; syr. Baruch 85.10.

dissolved parts of the bodies of the first stage for His composition of the second bodies only if there remained amongst the
existing things nothing else but those parts. In this case He
would have had to use them over and over again in perpetuity.[1]
I will make this clear by an illustration.[2] Suppose a man
possesses a vessel of silver of a thousand drachms weight, and
possesses nothing else of worth. Whenever this vessel breaks,
he has to renew it by casting it into the mould and handing it
to the silversmith. But a man who has houses full of treasures
is in a different position: If any of his vessels breaks he puts its
fragments aside until he wants to renew this very same vessel.
But everything which he casts into the mould until such time
is fresh, taken from (the gold of) his treasure house, and there
are not mixed with it the fragments of broken pieces; these he
lays aside until such time as he renews the broken vessels, as
he may have promised to do.[3] I searched and found that, in a
similar way, the original elements of air and fire which form
the atmosphere between the air and the first layer[4] of the
heaven are equal to the volume of the entire body of the
earth including its mountains and oceans, multiplied by 1089.[5]
And since the elements[6] are of such a magnitude,[7] there is no
necessity that the Creator should compose the bodies of the
second stage from the dissolved bodies of the first stage. Thus

---

[1] But, in fact, as Saadya explains later, the amount of elementary matter in the
universe is so ample that the decomposed parts of the human body can be left
unused for the process of continued generation, and only appear again in the resur-
rected bodies.

[2] The Leningrad Recension does not contain this simile.

[3] The rich man has no need to cast the fragments of his broken vessels into the
mould since he has plenty of silver and gold in his treasury to have new and fresh
vessels made. He, therefore, reserves the broken pieces until such time as he is inter-
ested in renewing the very same old vessels. In the same way, God has no need to
use the decomposed parts of the bodies for keeping the process of the world going,
but will use them again only at the promised time of Resurrection.

[4] Lit. 'Part'; cf. p. 54, n. 3.

[5] In the Leningrad Recension (ed. Bacher 100; ed. Slucki 107), Saadya explains in
greater detail that according to the knowledge of the learned ('ulamā') the atmosphere
between the earth and the first layer of heaven is 33 times 33 (=1089) times larger
than the volume of the earth. In his Comm. Yes., p. 84 (107), Saadya mentions that
the measures of the earth and the heavenly bodies have been determined by the
ancient scholars with the help of astronomical instruments and geometrical principles.
As S. Gandz has shown, Saadya's main source is al-Farghānī's Elementa Astronomica.
Al-Farghānī flourished under the famous caliph al-Mamūn (813-833), who organized
an expedition of mathematicians and astronomers to measure one degree of the
meridian of the earth. Cf. Saadya Anniversary Volume, New York, pp. 189-93.

[6] Lit. 'Things'.

[7] Lit. 'Width'.

he stores them away until the time comes for him to fulfil what he has promised them.

Perhaps on further reflection one will say: 'If a man has been eaten by a lion, and the lion was drowned and a fish ate it, and then the fish was caught and a man ate it, then the man was burned to ashes, whence can the Creator retrieve the first man? From the lion, or from the fish, or from the second man, or from the fire, or from the ashes?'[1] I have an idea that this is a question which greatly perplexes the faithful. Before I answer it, I think it is right to state this: We have to remember that no body which exists in this world can destroy another body. Thus, the fire which is quick to burn only separates the parts of a thing so that each part rejoins its element, and the earthly part becomes dust; but it does not destroy anything. It is out of the question to assume that anything should be able to destroy anything so as to reduce it to nothing, except the Creator who created the things from nothing. Since this is clear beyond question, any animal which eats any body does not destroy it, but merely dissolves its parts ... And since things can be explained in this way, the parts of those men who were consumed are not destroyed, but all of them are stored away, no matter whether they belong to a pious one or to a criminal, until such time as all of them are made anew.[2] This is nothing to wonder at in the case of Him who created them originally.

---

[1] The Leningrad Recension quotes the same question, but does not give the detailed example as above. Augustine, *De Civitate Dei* XXII, 12, poses the same problem. Cf. Ventura, p. 249.

[2] i.e. in the Future World when the pious and the wicked of all nations will be judged.

CHAPTER VIII

ON THE REDEMPTION OF ISRAEL[1]

1. 'THEY THAT SOW IN TEARS . . .'

(ed. Landauer 229.22–233.16;
ed. Slucki 118.1–119.34)

OUR Lord (be He exalted and glorified) has informed us through His prophets that He will deliver us, the Congregation of the children of Israel, from the state in which we find ourselves now; that he will gather our dispersed from East and West, and bring us unto His Holy Place, and settle us there permanently; moreover, that we shall be His Chosen People[2] and peculiar possession, as is said, 'Thus saith the Lord of hosts: Behold, I will save My people from the east country and from the west country; and I will bring them and they shall dwell in the midst of Jerusalem; and they shall be My people, and I will be their God in truth and in righteousness' (Zech. 8.7–8). His prophets have amply dealt with this matter and written several books about it. Not only did this knowledge come to us from the later prophets, but ever since the time of the first prophet, our Teacher Moses, we have been sustained by the Divine promise which is mentioned in the Torah, 'that the Lord thy God will turn thy captivity . . .' (Deut. 30.3), and what is further written in that chapter from beginning to end. The prophets produced signs and miracles to confirm this belief, and we accepted it. I began to subject this matter to the scrutiny of my reason, but I found that there was nothing in it which required to be discussed, and that

---

[1] The short Arabic title of this chapter reads, 'On the Salvation' (*fī-l-furkān*). The larger part of this chapter appeared in 1556 as a separate treatise under the title, *Sefer hap-pedūt we-hap-purkan* in the translation of the anonymous Paraphrase. It has since been edited several times. R. Jacob Emden published it with a short Introduction in 1769. Cf. Malter, p. 367. For a full treatment of this chapter see A. Marmorstein, 'The Doctrine of Redemption in Saadya's Theological System', in *Saadya Studies* (ed. E. I. J. Rosenthal), 1943, pp. 103–18.

[2] Saadya, like Baḥyah and Yehudah Hallevi, expresses the idea of the 'chosen people' (*'am segullah*) by the Arabic term *ṣafwa* which means originally 'something pure' and, in a derivative sense, 'the best thing'. It does not imply an act of choice, but denotes a peculiar quality which is considered either as inborn, or as acquired by way of self-education. Cf. I. Heinemann, in *Keneset*, Tel Aviv, 5702, p. 270, n. 1.

everything is clear save for one matter which I shall mention in the middle of this chapter.[1]

The fact of Redemption is undeniable for various reasons: (1) Because it is confirmed by the miracles performed by Moses, the first prophet, in announcing the message of Redemption, and because it is confirmed by the miracles which happened to the prophet Isaiah and to the other prophets who announced the Redemption of Israel. God who sent these prophets will undoubtedly fulfil his promise, as is said, 'That confirmeth the word of His servant, and performeth the counsel of His messengers' (Isa. 44.26). (2) Because He is just and will not do wrong. Having inflicted on our people heavy and prolonged sufferings — some, no doubt, as punishment, and some as a test[2] — He must certainly have set a time limit to them. It cannot be thought that they should be unlimited. When the end comes, the punishment meted out on account of sins will necessarily cease, and those who endured sufferings as a trial will be rewarded, as it says, 'Bid Jerusalem take heart and proclaim unto her that her time of service is accomplished, that her guilt is paid off; that she hath received of the Lord's hand double for all her sins' (Isa. 40.2). (3) He is a faithful keeper of His promises, His word endureth and His commandment stands for ever, as it says, 'The grass withereth, the flower fadeth; but the word of our God shall stand for ever' (Isa. 40.8). (4) We judge the promise of final Redemption from the first promise at the time when we were living as exiles in Egypt and God promised us in more precise terms that He would mete out judgment to our oppressors and reward us with great wealth, as it says, 'And also that nation, whom they shall serve, will I judge; and afterwards they shall come out with great substance' (Gen. 15.14). Our eyes have seen the things which He performed for us in dividing the Sea, in feeding us with the manna and the quails, in giving us the Law on Sinai, in causing the sun to

[1] Saadya refers to the computation of the time of the advent of the Messiah. He is conscious of the fact that the subject of the present chapter does not lend itself to a philosophical treatment since it is based entirely on religious tradition. The Leningrad Recension, followed by Tibbon's Version, reads, 'There is nothing in it that requires subtle examination and distinction'.

[2] Cf. pp. 160–62.

[3] With the beginning of the messianic era, the period of retribution will be initiated, although the principal reward and punishment will be left over to the 'Future World' ('ōlam habā').

stand still and similar things. For the future, He promised us wonderful and immeasurable bliss and happiness, and that honour, glory and distinction which He will bestow upon us as a double reward for all the humiliation and misery which He brought upon us, as it says, 'For your shame which was double ... therefore in their land they shall possess double' (Isa. 61.7). Of that which we endured in the past God speaks as of a brief moment, transient like the twinkling of the eye, but of the reward He will give us in the future He speaks in terms of a boundless compassion, as it says, 'For a small moment have I forsaken thee, but with great compassion will I gather thee' (Isa. 54.7). For the trials and ordeals of the past He will give us the double of our double share,[1] which is over and above that which He promised, an amount of bliss not quickly or easily to be measured. Thus it is said, 'And He will do thee good, and multiply thee above thy fathers' (Deut. 30.5). For this reason He mentions to us the Exodus from Egypt so frequently and in so many places. He wants us to remember the things we experienced.[2] If anything which He did for us in the course of the redemption from Egypt is not explicitly included in the promise of the final Redemption, it is implied in the statement 'As in the days of thy coming forth out of the land of Egypt, will I show unto him marvellous things' (Micah 7.15).

For this reason one finds that we patiently endure our sufferings, and wait for Him without casting any doubt on His promise. We do not expire nor does our courage falter, but we grow in strength and in firmness, as it says, 'Be strong and let your heart take courage, all ye that wait for the Lord' (Ps. 31.21). One who sees us in our misfortune is either astounded at us or considers us fools because he has never experienced what we experienced, nor has he the strong faith which we have. He is like one who has never known what it is to sow seed; when he sees, for the first time, the farmer throwing grain into the fissures of the earth to sprout there, he is likely to consider him a fool. But he will realize his

---

[1] Our double share of suffering entails a double measure of the originally promised reward.

[2] The Exodus from Egypt serves as both the model and the assurance of the final Redemption in the messianic era. The Midrash makes ample use of the analogy between the Exodus from Egypt and the future Redemption of Israel.

own ignorance at the time of harvesting when he will see that each measure has yielded 20 or 30 measures. We find an image similar to this in Scripture: 'They that sow in tears shall reap in joy' (Ps. 126.5). He is also like one who has never seen the bringing up of a child, and when he sees, for the first time, a parent willingly bearing all the sacrifices entailed in the rearing of a child, he will mock at him and ask, 'What is this man hoping for?' But after the son has grown up and has become a scholar or a philosopher or a governor or a general, then that person will realize that he has made himself ridiculous. In comparing our hope to the expectation of a child, the prophet says, 'Before she travailed, she brought forth; before her pain came, she was delivered of a man-child' (Isa. 66.7).

I say furthermore: He in Whose sight the measure of the heavens is relatively but a span, how should it be hard for Him to send us a prophetic message from heaven? He in Whose sight the vast spaces of the seas are like the palm of the hand, how should it be difficult for Him to gather our dispersed from them? He Who can take the measure of the dust of the earth, should He not be able to bring us together from the uttermost parts of the earth? He Who can weigh the mountains in the balance, how should it not be easy for Him to build the mountain of His Holy Place? For this reason He opens His message of comfort with these words, 'Who hath measured the waters in the hollow of his hand, and meted out heaven with the span, and comprehended the dust of the earth in a measure and weighed the mountains in scales, and the hills in a balance?' (Isa. 40.12). And He in Whose presence all the peoples are like a drop of water from a bucket, and like the dust of the scales, how should He not be able to humble them for our sake, as is said, 'Behold, the nations are as a drop of a bucket, and are counted as the small dust of the balance' (Isa. 40.15). He shakes them from off the earth as one puts the ends of a cloth together and shakes it, as is said, 'To take hold of the ends of the earth that the wicked be shaken out of it' (Job. 38.13). I might have said simply, 'He Who created the existing things out of nothing', and this alone would have been sufficient for me. But I enlarged upon this topic because Scripture also does so.

It would be wrong on our part to imagine that God does not

know the position in which we find ourselves, or that He is unjust or without compassion. Such a view, if held by us, has already been rebuked by the prophet when he says, 'Why sayest thou, O Jacob ... my way is hid from the Lord?' (Isa. 40.27). Nor must we say that He is unable to help us and to answer our prayers, since it says, 'Behold, the Lord's hand is not shortened, that it cannot save, neither His ear heavy, that it cannot hear' (Isa. 59.1). Nor must we say that He has rejected us and cast us away, 'For the Lord thy God is a merciful God; He will not fail thee, neither destroy thee, nor forget the covenant of thy fathers which He swore unto them' (Deut. 4.31).

2. THE TWO ROADS TO REDEMPTION

> (ed. Landauer 233.16-234.11; 238.13-239.9; 241.2-7; 245.2-246.20;
> ed. Slucki 119.35-120.5; 122.19-34; 123.20-25; 125.12-126.2)

We believe that God has appointed two alternative periods for the duration of our servitude in exile, one extending until such time as we do penitence (*Teshubah*), the other being terminated at a fixed time (*keṣ*). Whichever of these times arrives first, it carries Redemption with it: if our repentance (*teshubah*) is complete, the *fixed time* (*keṣ*) will be disregarded and the words of the Torah will come true, 'It shall come to pass, when all these things are come upon thee ... and thou shalt return unto the Lord thy God ... that then the Lord thy God will turn thy captivity ...' (Deut. 30.1-10). If, however, our repentance is slow, we shall have to wait until the *fixed time* is reached.[1] In this case some of us will have to bear

---

[1] According to the apocalyptic tradition (notably Daniel 12.7), Redemption has to wait until the time fixed for it has arrived. According to the Jewish prophetic tradition, Redemption depends solely on Israel's return to God. The problem formed the subject of a famous dispute between R. Eliezer b. Hyrkanos and R. Joshua b. Ḥananyah. The former held that repentance was the decisive factor, whereas the latter believed that redemption was sure to come at the appointed time (*keṣ*) even without repentance. Their views were harmonized later by R. Joshua b. Levi in the dictum, 'If Israel fail to prove worthy, Redemption has to wait until the appointed time; if they prove worthy, Redemption will be hastened'. A similar compromise can already be found in IV Ezra (4.35). Saadya's theory as set out above follows the Talmudic tradition in combining the two elements of Repentance and *fixed time*. Cf. Marmorstein, *loc. cit.*

suffering as a punishment, others as a test,[1] as we know happens in every general disaster at any time, be it famine, war or pestilence: some people will suffer because they deserve to be punished, others because they are put to a test. Thus, in the Flood there must have perished many young children and infants who were tried so as to be later rewarded; nor can we doubt that amongst our forefathers in Egypt there were many pious people who had to endure their trials until the time arrived which was fixed for their redemption. Let nobody tell us, 'If there were pious men amongst you to-day, your redemption would come to pass', for Moses, Aaron and Miriam (and with them many more pious people like them) had to remain in servitude for over eighty years until the moment of the *fixed time* arrived.

We have learned that in case our repentance is not complete, we must wait until the *fixed time* has arrived. When it is come, and we have not yet repented of our sins, it would not be fitting that salvation should come to us whilst we are still entangled in our sins. God exiled us because of our sins, and should He restore us merely because our stay in exile has been prolonged even though we have not returned to him, and we have not bettered our ways? That would make no sense. Our ancient prophets have, however, handed down to us a tradition, according to which hardships and sufferings will, at the *fixed time*, come upon us in such overwhelming measure that under their impact we shall be forced to choose the way of repentance, and thus become worthy of Redemption. This is what our ancestors said: 'If Israel will do penitence, they will be redeemed; if not, The Holy One (blessed be He) will appoint a king whose harsh decrees will be more terrible than those of Haman, whereupon they will do penitence, and then they will be redeemed'.[2] They say further that this chain of events will be started by the appearance of a man from the descendants of Joseph[3] on the mount of Galilee. Many of the

---

[1] Cf. pp. 137-9.

[2] The well-known view of R. Eliezer, based on Jer. 30.7, 'A time of tribulation will come over Jacob, and thence will come salvation'. See *p. Ta'anit*, I, 1; *b. Sanh.* 97 b.

[3] According to a Midrashic tradition, which can be traced back to a Tannaitic source (*b. Sukkah* 52 b), the real Messiah of the House of David will be preceded by another Messiah of the descendants of Joseph, who will fall in battle. Later Midrashim have elaborated this theme of the suffering Messiah under Gnostic and, to some extent, Christian influences. Cf. G. Dalman, *Der Leidende und Sterbende Messias in der Synagoge*; Israel Lévi in *REJ*, Vol. 74, 77; Siegmund Hurwitz, *Die Gestalt des sterbenden Messias*, 1958.

chief leaders of the nation will gather round him, and he will make his way to the place of the Temple, which will previously have been in the possession of Rome. There he will stay for some while. Later on a man called Armilius[1] will wage war against them. He will fight them, conquer the city, and slay and capture and humiliate the people. That man of the descendants of Joseph will be amongst the multitude of the slain. Terrible hardships will overtake the nation at that time, and the hardest of all will be their degradation amongst the nations, which will lead to their expulsion into the desert and waste places, where they will be left to starvation and misery. Under the pressure of their sufferings, many of them will abandon their faith, but a purified remnant will remain steadfast, and unto them the prophet Elijah will appear to bring them Redemption.

I say furthermore that in either of the two cases, that is to say, in case we fail to do penitence and thus have to go through the experiences which will accompany the advent of the Messiah of the House of Joseph, or, alternatively, we do penitence and shall be spared those sufferings, there will appear unto us the Messiah of the House of David. If he is preceded by the Messiah of the House of Joseph, the latter will act as his messenger, prepare the nation, and pave the way of Redemption, as is said, 'Behold, I send My messenger and he shall clear the way before Me' (Mal. 3.1).

Then the resurrection of the dead will take place as explained in the preceding chapter. First and foremost amongst them will be the Messiah of the House of Joseph, for he is a pious man who suffered trials and merits great reward. Then our Lord (be He exalted and glorified) will renew His Holy Place in the way He described to us, 'When the Lord hath built up Zion, when He hath appeared in His glory' (Ps. 102.17), and its chambers and innermost sanctuary as Ezekiel explained them (Ezek. ch. 40); and in them will be the precious stones and rubies which Isaiah mentioned, 'And I will make thy pinnacles of rubies, and thy gates of carbuncles, and all thy

[1] Probably identical with Romulus, who stands for Rome. According to the Jewish apocalyptic tradition, Rome is the arch-enemy of the Kingdom of God. Although, in Saadya's time, Palestine was in the hands of the Caliphs, Saadya still retains the ancient tradition, which sees in the fall of the Roman Empire a preliminary to the establishment of God's Kingdom on earth. Cf. Marmorstein, *loc. cit.*, pp. 113-4.

border of precious stones' (Isa. 54.12). The whole country will
be inhabited so that there will not remain in it a waste or
empty place, as it says, 'And the parched land shall become a
pool, and the thirsty ground springs of water' (Isa. 35.7).
Then the light of the Divine Presence (*Shekīnāh*) will shine
over the Temple so brilliantly that all the lights around it will
seem dim and faint, for, as I have already explained in Chapter
II, it surpasses in radiance all light,[1] as it says, 'Arise, shine, for
thy light is come, and the glory of the Lord is risen upon thee.
For, behold, darkness shall cover the earth . . . but upon thee
the Lord will arise' (Isa. 60.1-2). Such will be its brilliance that
one who does not know the way to the Temple will only have
to follow the direction of that light, which will extend from
heaven to earth, as is said, 'And nations shall walk at thy
light, and kings at the brightness of thy rising' (Isa. 60.3).
Then the gift of prophecy will abound amongst our nation
so that even our children and servants will prophesy, as it says,
'And it shall come to pass afterward that I will pour out my
spirit upon all flesh; and your sons and your daughters shall
prophesy . . . and also upon the servants and upon the hand-
maids' (Joel 3.1-2). So much so that if one of them goes to
any other country and says there, 'I am an Israelite',[2] people
will ask him, 'Tell us what happened yesterday, and what
will happen to-morrow', if they are desirous to know the
things that are hid from them. If he is able to tell them about
these things, they will be convinced that he is an Israelite, as it
says, 'And their seed shall be known amongst the nations, and
their offspring among the peoples' (Isa. 61.9).

The Israelites will remain in this position for the whole
duration of this world thenceforward, and their condition will
not change, as it says, 'O Israel, that are saved by the Lord with
an everlasting salvation; he shall not be ashamed nor confounded for evermore' (Isa. 45.17). I have an idea that the
expression, 'for evermore' (*'ad 'olmē 'ad*)[3] in this and other
passages is only used in order to emphasize the assurance of
salvation by means of the strongest expression possible and to
repudiate the opinion of those who claim that our salvation

---

[1] Cf. above, pp. 90-1.
[2] Lit. 'One of the Believers'.
[3] Which cannot be taken literally since the present world including the messianic
era will come to an end when the Future World (*'ōlam hābā'*) is created.

will be limited in time and vanish. God furthermore informed us that the people will, in that time, choose obedience towards God, not disobedience, as is explained in Chapter 30 of Deuteronomy, where it is said, 'And the Lord thy God will circumcise thy heart' (6), and in Chapter 36 of Ezekiel, where it is said, 'A new heart also will I give you, and a new spirit will I put within you' (26). They will choose this path for a number of reasons: because of their witnessing the light of the Divine Presence; because of the descent of Divine Inspiration upon them; because of their existence as an independent kingdom in prosperity and freedom from oppression; because of the absence of poverty and distress; because of their complete happiness in every respect. For God has informed us that pestilence, diseases, and calamities will completely vanish, and likewise all grief and sorrow. For them the world will be one of complete joy and gladness so that it will appear to them as if a new heaven and a new earth had been created for them, as is explained in Chapter 65 of Isaiah: 'For, behold, I create new heavens and a new earth; and the former things shall not be remembered nor come into mind. But be ye glad and rejoice for ever in that which I create; for, behold, I create Jerusalem a rejoicing, and her people a joy. And I will rejoice in Jerusalem, and joy in my people; and the voice of weeping shall be no more heard in her, nor the voice of crying' (17-19). How wonderful will such a world be that is full of joy and gladness, full of obedience and service, full of the treasures of reward!

3. AGAINST THOSE WHO BELIEVE THAT THE MESSIANIC PROMISES WERE FULFILLED IN THE PAST

(ed. Landauer 247.2-249.5; 251.5-252.2; 252.12-13;
ed. Slucki 126.5-40; 127.33-128.4; 128.11-13)

After the above explanations I wish to discuss the following point which has been brought to my knowledge: There are so-called Jews[1] who assert that those prophetic promises and

[1] The question as to whom Saadya had in mind in referring to the opinion of 'so-called Jews' who deny the messianic future has exercised the minds of many scholars. For the literature see Malter, p. 239, n. 524. Malter follows Guttmann (p. 214, n. 1) in suggesting that no particular sect was meant. A fresh investigation

messages of Comfort (*neḥamōt*) were all fulfilled at the time
of the Second Temple and have been entirely abrogated so
that nothing remains of their promise. These people base their
opinion on a fundamentally wrong conception. They say that
the emphatic assurances of salvation which we find in the
Scriptures — e.g. 'Thy sun shall no more go down, neither
shall thy moon withdraw itself' (Isa. 60.20); or 'It shall not be
plucked up, nor thrown down any more for ever' (Jer. 31.40) —
were all given *on condition* that the obedience of the people
would be complete. They said that this was similar to the
promise which our Teacher Moses gave to Israel, '. . . that
your days may be multiplied, and the days of your children
upon the land' (Deut. 11.21), and that on account of their sins
their kingdom came to an end and vanished; in the same way,
some of the messianic promises, they say, were fulfilled at the
time of the Second Temple, and then vanished, whereas others
did not come to pass at all on account of the sins of the people.

I fixed my attention on the essential point of the doctrine
proclaimed by these people, viz. the idea of a promise 'on
condition', and subjected it to an examination. I found it to
be unsound from a number of aspects. In the first place, the
promises made by our Teacher Moses were explicitly stated
by him to be conditional, for he said, 'For if ye shall diligently
keep all this commandment . . .' (Deut. 11.22), and furthermore, 'If thou shalt indeed hearken unto His voice and do all
that I speak; then . . .' (Ex. 23.22); moreover, he says, 'And it
shall come to pass, because ye hearken to these ordinances . . .'
(Deut. 7.12), and there are other similar pronouncements.
But so far as these prophetic messages of comfort are concerned, they do not contain a single reference to any condition

by B. M. Lewin (*Ginzē Ḳedem*, Vol. 6, pp. 3 ff.) shows, however, the correctness of
the view held by Rapoport and Poznanski that Saadya is referring to the Ḳaraites.
Cf. also Ventura, p. 265, n. 45. Some Ḳaraites were of opinion (1) that the messianic
promises were 'conditional'; (2) that they were partly fulfilled at the time of the
Second Temple; (3) that the Resurrection of the Dead must be interpreted as a symbol
for the restoration of Israel as a whole. In his *Sefer ha-Galui* (see Malter, pp. 268 ff.,
387 ff.), Saadya mentions that *without an oral tradition* it is easy to believe, as some
so-called Jews do, that the prophetic promises of the messianic future refer to the
period of the Second Temple. The reference to the Ḳaraites is here obvious and
indisputable. Saadya combats the Ḳaraite denial of the messianic future both in the
Sefer ha-Galui and the present book on the same lines. Lewin (*loc. cit.*) discovered
the same line of argument also in one of Saadya's polemical poems found amongst
the Genizah Fragments, which was most probably directed against the Ḳaraite
Solomon b. Yeruḥam.

at all. They are unqualified promises. Moreover, our Teacher Moses felt that it was not sufficient to state the positive case by saying, 'If ye shall keep' or, 'If thou shalt hearken', and then to leave it to the people to put the opposite to themselves, but he pointed out to them that in case they did not fulfil the condition, God would not fulfil those promises. In inverting the terms he made it clear to them that if they did not keep their part, God's promise, too, would be reversed, as is said, 'And it shall be, if thou shalt forget the Lord thy God . . . as the nations that the Lord maketh to perish before you, so shall ye perish' (Deut. 8.19-20); and, furthermore, 'When thou shalt beget children and children's children . . . and shall deal corruptly . . . I call heaven and earth to witness . . . that ye shall soon utterly perish' (Deut. 4.25-6); and, furthermore, 'But if thy heart turn away, and thou wilt not hear . . . I declare unto you this day, that ye shall surely perish' (Deut. 30.17), and similar pronouncements. But so far as the prophetic messages of comfort are concerned, God has attached no condition to them, much less inverted the terms. Moreover, He put those promises in the same category as those which He made with reference to the Flood in the days of Noah. In the same way as He swore that whatever the sins of mankind would be, He would never again bring a Flood upon them, but would punish them in a different way, so He swore unto us that He would not cause our kingdom to vanish for ever, as is said, 'For this is as the waters of Noah unto Me; for as I have sworn that the waters of Noah should no more go over the earth, so have I sworn that I would not be wroth with thee, nor rebuke thee' (Isa. 54.9). If our people were to sin, He would punish them, He said, in some other way, but not by abolishing our kingdom for ever. Moreover, He has already told us that at the appointed time our people will choose the path of obedience and not that of rebellion, as we explained,[1] and knowing as he does all things in advance, as we mentioned before, it is impossible that there should be, at that time, any transgression or sin unforeseen by Him. Now since there will be no sin, there would be no harm even if our Redemption were conditional, much less then, when it is, in fact, unconditional. Moreover, the Torah describes Redemp-

[1] Cf. above, pp. 172-3.

tion as something irrevocably fixed which must necessarily come to pass as we explained,[1] for God has decreed: 'I lift up My hand to heaven, and say, As I live for ever . . . I will render vengeance to mine adversaries, and will recompense them that hate Me . . .' (Deut. 32.40-43). These explanations sufficiently dispose of the baseless and fanciful ideas of these people concerning 'stipulation' and 'condition'.

Having removed the foundation of their structure, I shall now refute their argument by[2] . . . reference to our own experience.

(1) In the messianic age it is expected that all creatures will believe in God and proclaim His unity, as is said, 'And the Lord shall be King over all the earth; in that day shall the Lord be one and His name One' (Zech. 14.9), but do we not see them still clinging to their errors and denial of God? (2) In the messianic age the faithful are supposed to be free and not forced to pay tribute in money and food to other nations, as it says, 'The Lord hath sworn by His right hand . . . Surely I will no more give thy corn to be food for thine enemies; and strangers shall not drink thy wine for which thou hast laboured' (Isa. 62.8). But do we not see that every nation is compelled to pay tribute and obedience to the nation to which it is subject? (3) In the messianic age we expect the abolition of all wars between men and complete disarmament, as it says, 'And they shall beat their swords into ploughshares, and their spears into pruning-hooks; nation shall not lift up sword against nation, neither shall they learn war any more' (Isa. 2.4). But do we not see the nations fighting and contending with each other more violently than ever before? Should one try to explain that Scripture only means to say that there will be no more wars under the banner of religion, is it not the fact that religious wars and quarrels are to-day more intense than ever? (4) In the messianic age the animals are expected to live peacefully one beside the other, the wolf feeding with the lamb, the lion eating straw, and the young child playing with a snake

---

[1] Cf. above, p. 171.

[2] In the original text there follow at this stage ten Scriptural proofs that the messianic promises cannot possibly refer to the time of the Second Temple. Saadya shows that the promises contained in Ez. 34.13, Isaiah 11.11, 60.10, 11, 12, remained unfulfilled at the time of the Second Temple; moreover, that the miracles announced for the messianic age have not yet been fulfilled.

and the basilisk, as is said, 'And the wolf shall dwell with the lamb ... and the cow and the bear shall feed ... They shall not hurt nor destroy. . . .' (Isa. 11.6-9), whereas we see that the evil nature of the wild animals is still the same and they have not changed in any way. Should, again, someone explain that Scripture only means to say that the wicked people will live peacefully alongside with the virtuous,[1] the facts are precisely to the contrary. For nowadays the tyranny and violence of the strong against the weak are more ruthless than ever before.

All these facts prove conclusively that the prophetic messages of comfort have not yet been fulfilled. Our refutation of the opinion held by the people we have referred to applies also to the Christians.

---

[1] This is in fact the symbolic interpretation which Maimonides was later to apply to this messianic prophecy. Cf. *Hil. Melakim* 12.1.

CHAPTER IX

ON REWARD AND PUNISHMENT IN THE FUTURE WORLD[1]

1. A POSTULATE OF REASON

(ed. Landauer 255.2-257.16;
ed. Slucki 130.1-131.16)

OUR Lord (be He blessed and exalted) has informed us that He has fixed a time for the reward of the righteous, and that, at such time, He will distinguish between them and the unbelievers, as it says, 'And they shall be Mine, saith the Lord of Hosts, in the day that I do make ... Then shall ye again discern between the righteous and the wicked ...' (Mal. 3. 17-18). The prophets established this doctrine for us by wonders and miracles, and we accepted it.

It is desirable that I should adduce positive proofs concerning this time called the Future World, from the evidence of Reason, Scripture and Tradition, according to the method, which I laid down in the opening of the book, of finding the prophetic teachings demonstrated by the arguments of Reason. I affirm, in the first place, that it has already become clear from what I stated in Chapters III, IV and VI, that heaven and earth and all that is between them have been created solely for the sake of man, and that, for this reason, he was placed in the centre with all things surrounding him; and for this reason God endowed the soul with distinction and excellence, that is to say, with Reason and Wisdom; and for this reason He imposed on it the duty of obeying commandment and prohibition, and through them He made it fit for life everlasting[2]; and that this life (of the Future World) will supervene when there will be completed (the number of) the human beings which His wisdom has decided to create[3], whereupon He will

---

[1] An analysis of the origin and background of the Rabbinic conception of the Future World ('ōlam habā') is attempted in the Translator's article 'Olam und Aion' in *Festschrift für Dr. Jakob Freimann* (1937), pp. 1-14.

[2] Arab. *al-ḥayāt al-dā'ima*; Tibbon: *ha-ḥayyīm ha-matmīdīm*.

[3] Cf. above, p. 141.

place them in a Second World in which to bestow upon them their reward. We have established this by proofs from Reason, Scripture and Tradition in the chapters mentioned, which can serve us as a sufficient preparation for this chapter. I deemed it proper to add some more points which strengthen and corroborate this belief, and to elucidate it further from the three sources[1] which we mentioned.

I affirm: It is, in addition, a postulate of Reason[2] that, from what we can discern of the wisdom and power of the Creator as well as of His goodness towards His creatures, it is not permissible to assume that the measure of happiness which He intended for the human soul should be limited to what it finds in this world in the shape of earthly pleasure and delight. For every pleasure in this world is associated with evil, every happiness with misery, every delight with pain, and every joy with sadness. I find that either these aspects are equal or that the sorrows outweigh the joys. This being so beyond doubt, it would be absurd to think that the Wise (be He glorified in His glory) should have limited the highest good of the soul to what it can attain under these conditions. No, it is necessary that He should have prepared for it a place where it can find everlasting life and true happiness, to which He may lead it. Moreover, I find that the human beings whom I have known are neither content nor at rest in this world, even if they have attained the summit of power in the kingdom or the highest rank. And this lies in the nature of the soul only because it knows that it has a place more excellent than all the excellencies of this place, and it turns towards it in longing, and its eyes look out for it; but for this, the soul would be satisfied and at rest (in this world). Moreover, God has made loathsome to man's Reason things for which his natural disposition[3] lusts, such as adultery, theft, boasting and revenge by killing and similar things.[4] And when he obeys these commandments, he

---

[1] Arab. *mawād*; Tibbon: *meshakim*. Cf. above, p. 36, n. 1.

[2] Lit. 'Of that which Reason further demands'. — Cf. I. Kant, *Kritik der praktischen Vernunft* I, 2, 2 (4), where the belief in a Future Life is developed as a 'Postulate of Reason'.

[3] Arab. *ṭabʻ*. — Saadya contrasts man's natural disposition (*ṭabʻ*) with his Reason (*ʻaḳl*). The conflict between Nature and Reason is particularly stressed in his *Comm. Prov.* Cf. E. I. J. Rosenthal, 'Saadya Gaon: An Appreciation of his Biblical Exegesis', in *Bulletin of the John Rylands Library*, Vol. 27, 1. See also the Translator's article, 'Saadya's Conception of the Law' in *Bulletin of the John Rylands Library*, Vol. 28, 2.

[4] Cf. above, p. 97.

does so with a sense of grievance and repining, which causes him pain and distress at heart. Surely God would not have treated man thus, unless he intended to give him his recompense. Likewise, God has made attractive to man's Reason the idea of Truth and Justice as well as the commandment of loving-kindness and the prohibition of reprehensible deeds.[1] But if a man seeks to act in this way, he will be pursued by the enmity and hatred of those whom he brought to justice, and of those whom he directed by command and prohibition because he interfered between them and their passions; they may even vilify, beat and kill him. Surely God would not have brought him into such a sorry position by making these ideas attractive to his Reason unless He intended for him, in return, abounding reward.

Moreover, we find that some people treat their fellow men wrongfully, and the wrong-doer as well as the wronged may live either in happiness or in misery. Then both die, and since He (be He glorified in His glory) is the God of Justice, it follows that He must have prepared for both a second place where He will judge between them in equity, and mete out reward to the one according to the pain he suffered at the hands of the wrong-doer, and bring punishment upon the other according to the pleasure which, from his natural disposition,[2] he derived from his wrongdoings and evil acts.

Moreover, we see that unbelievers live in happiness in this world and believers suffer misery in this world. The conclusion can therefore not be avoided that to both classes a second place is allotted where truth and justice decide their fate. Moreover, we find that one who murders one person is killed, and one who murdered ten persons is also killed; similarly, one who committed adultery once and one who committed adultery twenty times. It follows that the justice which remains to be executed for each one of a person's offences will reach him in the Second World. And similarly with everything which belongs to this category.

Someone may ask: Why is it that the Wise (be He glorified in His glory) did not create man from the beginning of things in the Future World so as to save him both the pain and its

---

[1] Arab. *munkar*. Cf. above, p. 99, n. 2.
[2] Cf. above, p. 182, n. 3.

reward? My answer to this question is the same as we have already explained before in Chapter III.[1]

2. WHY THE TORAH MENTIONS CHIEFLY REWARD AND PUNISHMENT IN THIS WORLD

(ed. Landauer 258.7-259.12;
ed. Slucki 131.26-132.4)

Someone may object: In the Torah we do not find an explicit statement on reward except on reward in this world, namely, that which is written in Lev. 26.3-45 and Deut. 28. 1-68. Our answer is that the Wise (God) did not leave the people without the mention of reward and punishment in the Future World, as we shall explain later.[2] But those explicit statements on the happiness and misery in this world are made for two reasons.

(1) Since reward in the Future World is something which Reason can demonstrate as we explained,[3] the Torah omitted a reference to it as superfluous, in the same way as it omitted anything superfluous from the commandment which was given to Adam (Gen. 2.16). It was not said to him, 'I am the Lord thy God, thou shalt not murder, thou shalt not commit adultery, thou shalt not steal', because Reason demonstrates all this. But he was told explicitly, 'Of the tree of the knowledge of good and evil, thou shalt not eat of it' (Gen. 2.17), because Reason does not demonstrate this prohibition. In a similar way the Torah states explicitly the promise of reward in this world because Reason does not demonstrate it, and it omits an explanation of the reward in the Future World because it trusts that Reason will be able to demonstrate it.[4]

(2) It is the habit of prophecy to enlarge upon events which are near at hand and must be urgently provided against; it cuts

[1] i.e. That this world gives man an opportunity of earning reward and thus makes his happiness in the Future World the greater. Cf. above, pp. 93-4.
[2] Cf. below, pp. 85-7. As Saadya explains, the Torah only 'hints' at this doctrine, whereas the other books of Scripture elaborate it.
[3] Cf. above, pp. 181 ff.
[4] Saadya's explanation is not consistent with his general view that Revelation is necessary even in regard to matters which Reason can establish by its own effort. Cf. above, p. 103, n. 1.

short references to events which are far off. Now since at the time when the Torah was written for the people the thing near at hand, and urgently required by them, was the knowledge of matters relating to Palestine, the country they were about to enter, the Torah explained these at length and enlarged upon the fruits which would result from their obedience or rebellion. For this reason it first mentions the rain, as we find in Deut. 11.10 ('For the land whither thou goest in to possess it, is not as the land of Egypt . . .') until the end of the chapter. And it refers to the more distant things only by brief hints without any detailed explanations.

However, the most eloquent proof (from the Torah) is this: We find that our Teacher Moses, the greatest of the God-fearing and righteous ones, did not reap any of the great rewards of this world, such as that contained in the fulfilment of the promise, 'I will give you rains in their seasons . . . And your threshing shall reach unto the vintage . . . And I will make you fruitful, and multiply you . . . And ye shall eat old store long kept . . .' (Lev. 26.4-10), because he did not enter Palestine. Now if the righteous were only to obtain what is mentioned in those chapters, it would be necessary that a specially abundant portion should be given to Moses our Teacher. This fact itself is proof that the greatest reward will be meted out in the Future World.

3. The Testimony of Scripture[1]

(ed. Landauer 260.10-262.22;
ed. Slucki 132.21-133.23)

I consider that there are seven categories[2] (of Scriptural proofs). Each one is indicated by allusions and hints in the Torah, and implicitly and clearly in the other prophetic books. The first section[3] comprises those passages which call what

---

[1] On this subject see J. L. Saalschütz, 'Ideen zu einer Geschichte der Unsterblich-keitslehre bei den Hebräern' in *Zeitschrift für die historische Theologie, Neue Folge*, I.3; J. Wohlgemuth, *Die Unsterblichkeitslehre in der Bibel*, 1899.

[2] Arab. *'ayn*; lit. 'essence'; Tibbon translates, *'inyan*. — Saadya means to say that the Scriptural passages which bear testimony to the doctrine of Reward in the Future World can be classified under seven categories.

[3] Arab. *fasl*; Tibbon translates *shoresh*; root, principle. He probably mistook *fasl* for *'asl* (root).

man acquires through Wisdom and the Law, Life — as it says, 'Which if a man do, he shall live by them' (Ezek. 20.21) — and those which call what results to a fool from his folly, Death — as it says, 'The soul that sinneth, it shall die' (Ezek. 18.20). Furthermore, 'For whoso findeth me, findeth life . . . But he that misseth me, wrongeth his own soul' (Prov. 8.35-6). See also Prov. 15.24; 7.27; Ps. 27.13; 16.10-11; Prov. 11.19. And since this expression cannot possibly allude to the life in this world, seeing that the righteous and the wrong-doers both share in this life, it follows that it must allude to the life in the Future World. Each of the verses quoted could form the basis for a long explanation.

The second section comprises those passages which proclaim that a store of goodness is laid up before God for the righteous, and a store of evil for the wrong-doers. Thus it is said, 'The memory of the righteous shall be for a blessing; but the name of the wicked shall rot '(Prov. 10.7).[1] And it says, 'Remember unto me, O my God, for good, all that I have done' (Neh. 5. 19). And of the wicked it is said, 'Remember, O my God, Tobiah and Sanballat according to these their works' (Neh. 6.14). And this follows upon what the Torah has said, 'And it shall be righteousness unto us, if we observe to do all this commandment' (Deut. 6.25); moreover, 'And it shall be righteousness unto thee before the Lord thy God' (Deut. 24. 13); moreover, 'And thy righteousness shall go before thee, the glory of the Lord shall be thy reward' (Isa. 58.8). Each of these verses could be expounded at length.

The third section comprises those passages which explain that God has, as it were, books and registers in which are recorded the deeds of the righteous and the wicked, as our Teacher Moses said, 'Blot me, I pray Thee, out of Thy book which Thou hast written' (Ex. 32.32); and it is said, 'Let them be blotted out of the book of the living, and not be written with the righteous' (Ps. 69.29). See also Mal. 3.16 and Isa. 65.6. Each of these statements could also be expounded at length.

The fourth section includes those passages which express a warning that God (be He glorified and exalted) has a tribunal[2]

---

[1] It appears that Saadya explains the verse to mean, 'The righteous shall be remembered (by God) for a blessing (in the Future World)'. In his *Comm. Prov.* (p. 56) he offers the usual interpretation of this verse.

[2] Lit. 'stand' (Arab. *mawḳif*).

from which He will mete out retribution to everyone who did good or evil, as it says, 'If thou doest well, shall it not be lifted up? And if thou doest not well . . .' (Gen. 4.7). Moreover, 'The righteous and the wicked God will judge; for there is a time there for every purpose and for every work' (Eccl.3.7). See also Ps. 14.5; 36.13; Job 35.12. Each of these statements could be further elaborated.

The fifth section includes those passages which elaborate the Scriptural statements that God (be He glorified and exalted) is a just Judge who rewards every man according to his work. Thus, it is said, 'The Rock, His work is perfect; for all His ways are justice' (Deut. 32.4); moreover, 'The Lord is righteous in all His ways' (Ps. 145.17). See also Ps. 9.8-9; 119.91; Job 34.21; Prov. 5.21; Jer. 17.10; Eccl. 12.14. Each of these verses could also be expounded at length.

The sixth section comprises those passages which proclaim that there is a Day of the Lord appointed for retribution. Thus, it says, 'The great day of the Lord is near . . . That day is a day of wrath . . . And I will bring distress upon men, that they shall walk like the blind . . . ' (Zeph. 1.14-18; 2.1). Each of these verses requires an explanation which I do not mention in order not to overload the book with exegetical matter.

The seventh section comprises those passages which call the reward the Good, and explain that the wicked shall be excluded from it, as it says, 'That it might be well with them, and with their children for ever' (Deut. 5.26). Moreover, 'Oh how abundant is Thy goodness which Thou hast laid up for them that fear Thee' (Ps. 31.20). Also, 'Though yet I know that it shall be well with them that fear God . . . But it shall not be well with the wicked . . .' (Eccl. 8.12-13).

4. Paradise and Hell

(ed. Landauer 265.18-268.8.; 268.17-269.3; ed. Slucki 135.4-136.12; 136.20-24)

I consider that reward and punishment are two subtle essences[1] which our Lord (be He exalted and glorified) will create at the time of Judgment,[2] and which He will assign to

[1] Arab. *ma'nā*.   [2] Lit. 'Reward'.

every man[1] according to his merit or guilt. They both consist of the same essence,[2] an essence which resembles the particular quality of fire in its capacity both to burn and illumine. It[3] will illumine the righteous, but not the wrong-doers; and it will burn the wrong-doers, but not the righteous. In regard to this, the text of Scripture states, 'For, behold, the day cometh, it burneth as a furnace; and all the proud, and all that work wickedness, shall be stubble; and the day that cometh shall set them ablaze ... But unto you that fear My name shall the sun of righteousness arise with healing in its wings ...' (Mal. 3.19-21). How apt is this comparison with the double activity of the sun in producing both the heat of the day and the bright daylight. The expressions 'The day ... burneth' and 'The sun of righteousness shall arise' both speak of the same thing; for we do find the sun alluded to in the term 'day'. (Cf. Judges 19.11 and 19.9.) The root of this essence which the Creator (be He exalted and glorified) will call into being will resemble the sun, but there is a difference between it and the sun. For in the case of the sun, heat and light are mixed together, and neither of the two can subdue the other, whereas this essence will be at the disposal of the Creator (be He glorified in His glory) to confine its light to the righteous, and gather its heat for the wrong-doers, either by virtue of a particular quality which He will impart to it, or by specially providing[4] that the one group should be guarded from its heat while its light is hidden from the other. The second theory seems the more probable one. For we have seen that God did something similar in Egypt when He gathered the light for the believers and the darkness for the unbelievers by a special provision emanating from His command.[5]

On the basis of these remarks I now affirm that for this reason Scripture calls the reward of the righteous, Light, and

---

[1] Lit. 'Servant' (of God).

[2] Arab. *'ayn*. Cf. above, p. 185, n. 2. Tibbon renders it here by *eṣem*.

[3] i.e. the 'subtle essence' which God will create as a medium of reward and punishment.

[4] Arab. *'araḍ* (accident); i.e. by creative acts which cause the effect desired in each particular case.

[5] Saadya's theory that the Light of the Future World will have opposite effects on the righteous and wicked is obviously based on the Talmudic passage, *b. Ned.* 8 b. On the origin of the Rabbinic conception of the 'Light which is stored up for the righteous' see the Translator's article, 'Gnostic Themes in Rabbinic Cosmology' in *Essays in Honour of the Very Rev. Dr. J. H. Hertz*, pp. 28 ff.

every punishment for the wrong-doers, Fire. As to reward, it is said, 'For with Thee is the fountain of life; in Thy light do we see light' (Ps. 36.10). (See further Ps. 97.11; Prov. 13.9; Job 33.30; and other passages of a similar character.) In regard to punishment, it is said, 'And the strong shall be as tow, and his work as a spark; and they shall both burn together, and none shall quench them' (Isa. 1.31). (See further Isa. 33.11; 26.11; 30.33; Job 15.34; 22.20; 20.26; Ps. 11.6; 140.11, and other passages of a similar character.)

If someone asks us to give him an example as to how body and soul can live everlastingly without food,[1] we quote the example of our Teacher Moses, whom God (be His name blessed) kept alive for 40 days and 40 nights three times without food, as it says, 'And He was there with the Lord 40 days and 40 nights; he did neither eat bread, nor drink water' (Ex. 34. 28). What kept him alive was the light which God created for him and which He caused to radiate from his face, as it says, 'And Moses knew not that the skin of his face sent forth beams' (Ex. 34.29). This can furnish our Reason with an illustration and an analogy of the way in which the life of the righteous can be sustained by Light, without food. In this sense God said to him, 'Before all thy people I will do marvels, such as have not been wrought in all the earth, nor in any nation' (Ex. 34.10). And this is similar to the words of the prophet regarding the righteous, 'And whereof from of old men have not heard, nor perceived by the ear, neither hath the eye seen a god beside Thee, Who worketh for him that waiteth for Him' (Isa. 64.3). But how will God keep alive those who will be undergoing the eternal and everlasting punishment of fire? We do not find amongst the people of the past anyone to whom anything similar occurred so that we could point to him as an example. And since we do not find anything similar to it, Scripture mentions it especially, and says of the unbelievers, 'For their worm shall not die, neither shall their fire be quenched' (Isa. 66.24).

Now, the Reward is called Paradise (*gan 'eden*), because in

---

[1] The above question arises out of Saadya's statement that reward and punishment in the Future World will be in the nature of Light. Since the men who will be revived in the Future World will be 'men with body and soul' (see *Amānāt*, p. 269; ed. Slucki, p. 136), the question naturally arises how they will be able to live. Saadya explains that their life will be of a purely spiritual nature. Cf. *b. Berakot* 17 a.

this world there is found nothing more exalted than this garden in which God placed Adam. And the punishment is called Hell (*Gehinnom*), which is the name of a place in the neighbourhood of the Temple, which Scripture also calls *Tophet*, as it says, 'It shall no more be called Tophet nor the valley (*gey*) of the son of Hinnom' (Jer. 7.32). The *Gehinnom* is also mentioned in the book of Joshua (15.8).

5. LIFE EVERLASTING

(ed. Landauer 272.18-273.19;
ed. Slucki 138.18-139.8)

I will now deal with those Scriptural passages which declare that reward and punishment will be everlasting.[1] There is, in the first place, the statement, 'Some to everlasting life, and some to reproaches and everlasting abhorrence' (Dan. 12.2).[2] There is the further statement, 'In Thy right hand bliss for evermore' (Ps. 16.11); moreover, it is said, 'They shall never ('*ad neṣaḥ*) see the light' (Ps. 49.20). The statement, 'But Thou art the selfsame, and Thy years shall have no end' (Ps. 102.28) is followed by the words, 'The children of Thy servants shall dwell securely, and their seed shall be established before Thee' (29).[3] This implies that in the same way as His existence (be He exalted and glorified) is everlasting[4] without end, so the existence of the righteous (in the Future World) will be everlasting without end. One might make here an objection and say: 'If it is permissible to assume that the created beings will co-exist with God in the "End of Time" *ad infinitum*, it should likewise be permitted to assume that they co-existed with Him in the "Beginning of Time" *ab infinito*'.

[1] Arab. *muʿabbad*; Tibbon: *matmīd*. — The question as to whether reward and punishment in the Future World will be everlasting or of limited duration also exercised the minds of Saadya's Islamic contemporaries. The Muʿtazilites were divided on this question. Cf. Guttmann, pp. 250-55. The views of Jewish theologians on the matter are also divergent. As late as the 17th century, R. Isaac Aboab (1605-1693) of Amsterdam wrote a treatise, 'Nishmat Ḥayyīm', in which he examines the question whether reward and punishment are eternal or not. Unlike Saadya, he decides in favour of the theory that they are of limited duration. Cf. Hebr. MS. Nr. 5, in the John Rylands Library, Manchester.
[2] Cf. above, p. 162.
[3] The emphasis lies on the phrase, 'Before Thee'.
[4] Arab. *baḳāʾ dāʾim*; Tibbon: *kayam laʿad*.

Let me explain the difference between the two things. I maintain that it would be absurd to assume that the created beings co-existed eternally with their Creator *ab infinito*; for the word 'Maker' necessarily implies that the thing made is preceded by its maker. And because the Maker precedes a thing, He has the power to keep it in existence on a certain day we may think of in our Reason; and we may think of Him as being able to keep it in existence also on another day. Now since it is admitted that He may do so, and since He is eternal, this may be true of every day and every time, and there is nothing in this idea which Reason could reject; on the contrary, Reason permits it.[1] If one should ask, what then is the difference between the Creator and the created beings, we say that such a question is not worthy of an answer. How can one compare soul and body, which require time and space, enjoy pleasure, receive commandment and prohibition, and are in need of a preserving force to keep them in existence,[2] unto Him who is exalted above all these and similar things? But man stands before God as one who with his eyes and with his soul waits upon the things God will create for him,[3] as the text says, 'Their seed shall be established before Thee' (Ps. 102.29).

---

[1] Saadya means to say that once created in time, the created beings continue (in the Future World) to exist for ever since their Creator, who is eternal, keeps them in existence. Saadya, who denies the pre-existence of the soul (cf. above, pp. 141, 145), affirms his belief in the everlasting life of man in the Future World. In the above passage he draws a clear distinction between existence without beginning and existence without end. As Malter has shown, this distinction coincides with the scholastic differentiation between eternity and perpetuity as expressed by Isidore of Seville (died 636) in his *Sententiarum Liber* I c. XII. Cf. Malter, p. 225, n. 504.

[2] Cf. above, p. 58, n. 1.

[3] i.e. the reward and punishment in the Future World.

JEHUDA HALEVI: KUZARI

Abridged edition with an introduction and
a commentary by Isaak Heinemann

To my sister Ida Perle and
my brother Max Heinemann

PREFACE

Jehuda Halevi did not write his philosophic works primarily for philosophers. But the fact that the Kuzari is intelligible to the general public in no way signifies that it is shallow. His point of departure is certainly not philosophic argument, with which he is naturally well acquainted, but rather the questioning of a cultured reader on religion and Judaism. But just because he binds neither his reader nor himself to any particular authority or dogmatic notion, he has produced a work in no way inferior in philosophic worth to any produced by expert competitors in the same field.

Our little book does not only present Jehuda Halevi as its subject: it ventures to take the author's generally comprehensible presentation as its model. This study is likewise based on scholarly literature on the subject. But I am well aware that a great number of questions which interest the expert —such as Jehuda Halevi's sources and his relations to certain thinkers of his cultural sphere—are of minor importance to those readers whom Jehuda Halevi himself had in mind. And we certainly believe that he wrote not only for men of his own time. For the thinking Jew of today the main question is: What is Jehuda Halevi's message in the conflict of ideals raging in our own time? What is his contribution and what stimulus can he give us? It is the object of our study to provide an answer to these questions that is scientifically sound and yet intelligible to every honestly thinking reader.

For this purpose an introduction is needed to help the reader to distinguish between the passing and the permanent value of Jehuda Halevi.

We have only quoted from the Kuzari what is of philosophic importance.[1] In particular, we have omitted digressions on

---

[1] Messrs. George Routledge & Sons Ltd. were kind enough to authorize my use of the English translation of Hirschfeld, which they have published. I am also deeply indebted to my friend D. H. Baneth of the Jerusalem

language, calendar, etc., as well as polemics against contemporaries in as far as these do not yield any positive conclusions. We have, on the other hand, added a few poems of philosophic content. The commentary is confined to an exposition of the thought expressed. To more ambitious readers we recommend the English (and German) translations of Hirschfeld, the French selection of Ventura, the commentaries of Cassel (German, 2nd ed. 1869) and Zifrinowitsch (Hebrew), and my exposition of the philosophic poems of Jehuda Halevi in the Hebrew Year Book *Kneset* IX (1945) 261 ff.

Mrs. Hebe R. Mayer-Bentwich is responsible for the revision of my translation of the Arabic text, and for the translation from the German of the preface, introduction and commentary. At my express request she has throughout retained certain technical terms such as 'pick' and 'power', which are explained in the commentary, with the inevitable consequence of a certain inflexibility of style.

Jerusalem, 1946.   ISAAK HEINEMANN

University, who very kindly put at my disposal a manuscript translation into German. It is founded on collations of the Arabic and Hebrew manuscripts and on an excellent command of the languages; in a number of passages (e.g. Book I, § 25) it bears out the fact that Ibn Tibbon's MS. is superior to the Oxford MS. used by Hirschfeld.

INTRODUCTION

THE object of this introduction is to ensure a complete understanding of Jehuda Halevi's teaching, but not to obviate the necessity of studying the original.

It aims at focusing the reader's attention on the pivot of Jehuda Halevi's thought and at presenting his teaching from the modern view-point. Just as Jehuda Halevi (and Hillel before him) strove to conceive Judaism in all its details as evolving from this pivot of religious conception, so should the reader endeavour to conceive Jehuda Halevi himself.

A short review of the experience he derived from life and education will be found necessary.[1]

His early years fell in the period of Christian reaction to the triumphal march of the Moslemin, who had occupied Palestine as early as the seventh century and Spain in the eighth. In both these outposts of Islam, the Christians made important progress in the eleventh century. At the time of Jehuda Halevi's childhood, in 1085, Toledo fell into the hands of the Cid; in his youth, the Crusaders besieged Jerusalem. Whereas in the Holy Land the Moslemin summoned up heart and courage enough to make successful counter-attacks, the pride of Spanish knighthood assumed such proportions that Alfonso VII was able in 1126 to proclaim himself Ruler of the whole of Spain.

Whilst, in the words of Jehuda Halevi, 'Christian and Moslem share the whole world between them' (the 'world' of Medieval Europeans, which scarcely extended beyond the one continent and the Mediterranean countries), the Jew is condemned to nameless suffering. 'They wage their wars and drag us down in their fall,' is his complaint in one of his poems, adding, in a Bible quotation: 'and so it was from the beginning of Israel'. There is nothing to suggest that he envied the knights their bloody laurels; his view of life aims higher

[1] *Cf.* Shirman, *Tarbiz* ix, 35 ff., 219 ff.; Baer, *The Jews in Christian Spain* (Hebrew) i, 49 ff.

than warfare. But the impotence of his people in worldly affairs is not only a burning wound in his side; it becomes a consuming problem, which he attacks with all the weapons that the culture of his time affords him. For notwithstanding the religious conflicts, Jehuda Halevi seems to have found ways and means in his youth of securing a sound introduction to the cultural trends of the time. He is such a master of the Bible that he is able to exploit the whole wealth of its language. The clever use he makes of double meanings in certain verses lends to his poems a peculiar charm: he is as much at home in the poetry of the Aggadah as in his discussions of the Halakah. He was able to write his chief philosophical work in Arabic, and Arabic metre influences most of his poetry. He also knew Castilian; but, both as poet and thinker, he comes mainly under the influence of the great Arab culture. He is specially well acquainted with Arab science (he was a reputed physician) and philosophy, including, of course, its Greek origins. Other details of his life known to us are not important for the understanding of his literary work; but the fact that he really undertook the journey to the land of his dreams which he announces at the end of the Kuzari may be considered the logical outcome of his thinking; he went as far as Egypt and Tyre; it is not sure whether he reached Palestine.

Thus we see that Jehuda Halevi belongs to the class of 'Zweistromland' people (F. Rosenzweig), who seek a synthesis between their Jewish inheritance and general philosophy. But in contrast to most thinkers of whom we know, he was very late in formulating this synthesis in a scholarly way. And when he wrote his 'Kuzari' at the age of about 50, he did not in any way consider himself to be a 'philosopher' in the contemporary sense (Kuzari I, § 1)—i.e. an adherent of definite doctrines, particularly Aristotelian—but rather a man of learning who, as such, did not subscribe to any official 'philosophy'; he aspired, by the use of scholarly methods, to uphold an attitude to the world and Judaism in accordance with the traditions of his religion and no less with his personal conception.

With none of that tendency to penetrating dialectics which Crescas betrayed at a later date, he displays absolute independence in his estimate of the conventional doctrines of philosophy, which were generally accepted uncritically in those times. But with speculative independence he combines the physician's clear apprehension of empiric reality and the urge to check up dull theories through knowledge of life; on the other hand he displays the profound sympathy of the artist for everything that touches the heart of the individual and the soul of his people: 'to wail for thy affliction (O Zion), I am like the jackals, but when I dream of the return of thy captivity I am a harp for thy songs'. His reasoning is therefore never 'sicklied o'er with the pale cast of thought'; he might be termed a 'visual thinker' ('Augendenker'), if we bear in mind that his inward eye, bent on spiritual experience, was no less keen in its vision than the sensual eye.

The title of his book shows with what independence and breadth of view Jehuda Halevi, the visual thinker, conceived the problem of Judaism. The pleasure in rhymes that was so characteristic of his time led him to formulate the title in a little verse: 'the book of argument and proof in defence of a despised religion'. The words for 'proof' and 'despised' rhyme and alliterate in a manner recalling plays on words found in the Bible; thus one word refers to the other: the proof is the answer to the despite and to the spiritual oppression it produces. The task of an apologist of Judaism might seem the same as that of a defender of Christianity and Islam, who also had to fight against attacks of the sister religions. But Jehuda Halevi senses that in the defence of Judaism something else is at stake: the Christian and the Moslem are sure of the esteem of their opponents; the Jew has to defend not only his faith but also his *honour*. The characteristic feature of this book lies in the pointed paradox whereby the most oppressed religious community is proved to be the bearer of the highest, yea, the absolute religious truth. This explains the peculiar form of the book. It is the only genuine dialogue (extending beyond a mere catechism of question and answer) in Jewish philosophy

of the Middle Ages, although one might have expected imitation of the Platonic dialogue to be particularly near to the
Jew, who had examples of philosophic dialogue before his eyes
in the book of Job and in many a text of the Aggadah. It
was probably, in the first place, his artist's sense that prompted
Jehuda Halevi to choose a form where the easy offset of one
theme against another, with frequent surprising turns, lends the
serious subject-matter a real charm and brings the book, which
intentionally only fringes on professional philosophy, well
within the grasp of the serious-minded layman. The artist's
creative instinct betrays itself also in the portrayal of the
young king, somewhat hasty in judgement, but nevertheless
moved by a noble search for truth—the master, imbued with
serene certainty, always ready to admit difficult points in the
various problems and even the faults of his own people, but
deeply convinced, nevertheless, of the fundamental truth of his
doctrine. The dialogue form is also well suited to the contents
of the book. Like the best of Plato's dialogues, its arguments,
setting out from the firm ground of historical event, not only
achieve a change of mind on the part of the king, but a real
spiritual conversion; he is moved from deep contempt of
Judaism, clearly expressed in Book I, § 12, to complete agreement of views, and renders full honour not only to Judaism,
but to the whole Jewish Community.

Jehuda Halevi's answer is as peculiar as his question, not only
in content, but also in method. All other medieval authors, in
presenting Judaism, pass from the general to the particular.
They dwell first on the justification of faith in God, and
consider hereby to have proved the justification of religion
as a contact with God and as a belief in historical revelation.[1]
Starting out from this premise, they justify Judaism by
showing that the revelation of God to Moses has never lost its
force and by dealing with the objections to Christian dogma
and to the personality of Mahomet. Christians and Moslems

---

[1] Maimonides includes his proofs of God only in Book II of his 'Guide'
where he starts to write for scholars, having, in the beginning, intended
his remarks for laymen also.

follow a similar line; it is therefore no wonder if the King of the Khazars holds this to be the only possible line of reasoning (Book I, § 12).

But his 'Master' does not follow it. Judaism is not merely the goal—it is also the *point of departure* of his argument. The fact of the revelation, recognized in ancient times and in their own day, is the proof of the belief in God; whereas the attribution of organic wonders to a cosmic intelligence is, firstly, less convincing and acceptable, and, secondly, only leads to the conception of a God of metaphysics and not to a God of religion, who is concerned for the individual and expects a definite reaction from him. Still less than the *idea* of religion is philosophy able to explain the historical *phenomenon* of religion. Arab philosophy also professes belief in the notion of the prophets and asserts—and *must* assert, if it aspires to be the foundation of our piety—that this highest grade of humanity is attained by the perfection of our spiritual powers, and that therefore philosophical training leads us to it (Book I, § 18; Book V, § 12 middle). But the testimony of history contradicts this claim of philosophy; history shows that prophecy is not found among the philosophers (Book I, § 4; § 99 end); its classical representatives are to be sought pre-eminently among people belonging to a distant group of humanity who have not passed through any school of learning (this is also the case with Christian and Moslem). However, Jehuda Halevi betrays in no way such an absolute negative attitude to philosophy as Luther did; but he does show a marked degree of reserve as regards its claims to the basis of religion. A religious life is to be regarded in the first place as a fact of experience; we cannot reconstruct its terms on bare theory, but we must seek them in experience with the help of such aspects as philosophy of life (biology) has long ago established.

Does, then, religious philosophy have to have a scientific foundation? Certainly. For Jehuda Halevi's visual thinking has two aspects; just as all colourless speculation divorced from experience is foreign to him, so also is any mechanical doctoring which only states the bare essential fact without consideration

of its sources. In this attitude he had great forerunners in
the natural scientists, who were the originators of medieval
culture. The pupils of Hippocrates and Galen were not only
acquainted with the general notions of 'Erbmasse' and
'Milieu'; they already knew of those 'recessive phenomena'
recently exhaustively treated by Gregor Mendel, i.e. they were
aware of the fact that a characteristic which disappears in
the second generation reappears in the third (Book I, § 95
end); they closely investigated influences exerted by conditions of life; a writing produced by the school of Hippocrates
to which Jehuda Halevi alludes (Book I, § 1) deals with the
biological effects of 'winds, waters, and districts'. They distinguished between three grades of life—plant, animal, human
(the two latter grades with the inclusion of spiritual phenomena, Book I, § 31 ff.); the fundamental law by which all life
is influenced by heredity, environment and, in great measure,
by methodic nurture, is applicable in practically the same way
to all three grades. We can draw conclusions from the lower
grades to the higher—just as Mendel's law, to which we
referred, was based on experiments on plants and applied to
the higher grades. On these premises Jehuda Halevi is able to
give biologic explanations of even the loftiest phenomena of
human spiritual life. It is true that according to Jehuda Halevi
(Book I, § 41) the prophet is as far above the ordinary man as
man is above the beast—the beast above the plant—the plant
above the stone—not as an individual, but in his quality as
bearer of special gifts (Book I, § 95 end). But even the highest
life is still life, indeed life in intensified form (*see* p. 140)
and subject to the same laws as all other life, i.e. it is conditioned by blood, earth and nurture; it develops solely within
the chain of mankind that extends from Adam through Shem
to Abraham and Jacob; it attains to full strength only in the
case of men connected with the Holy Land and with those
practices that God has ordained for the fostering of
His 'fire', i.e. of His enlightening influence on the prophetic
spirit of man (Book II, § 26). Thus belief in the reality of
the facts of religion in no way requires of us a 'sacrificium

intellectus'; the miracle that came to light in its lowest form of development in plant life becomes more and more apparent as it passes through the animal to the human and thence to the prophetic life; but the domination in the highest spheres of the same laws as were seen to govern in the lower realms of life is consistent with the claims of analogical schools of thought,[1] and is corroborated by the testimony of history. From this fact we arrive at a solution of the religious and national problem of Judaism. The fact that God is near to man and desires his 'nearness' is shown by the history of the religious 'nucleus' of mankind, particularly since the appearance of Abraham, who is recognized by the devotees of all three religions as the model of faith and trust in God. The status of Judaism now also becomes clear. Its pre-eminence still prevails—even though God's favour at present recedes for lack of the conditions with which it is bound up, namely land and temple-cult. But the seed of heritage will inevitably open out again in full blossom, when the conditions are renewed; not only historical tradition, but also prophetic hope will be fully recognized and justified by scientific knowledge; even at the present day the Jew experiences a flash of the dormant spark in the effect of such laws as were given to cultivate the prophetic spirit, namely the laws governing the Sabbath and prayer, as also through settlement on the Holy soil of Palestine.

This line of thought in the Kuzari finds its complement in the poems, of which we give a few examples. If the Kuzari may be said to show the poet as a thinker, the reverse holds true of the poems; just as reading in the former we realize that Halevi does not disdain to clothe his intuitive feeling in the garment of thought, so in the latter he builds up on the foundation of clear thinking a genuine religious life, comprising the apprehension of God, of Sabbath, and of Zion.

What, then, is Jehuda Halevi's message to mankind today? Naturally he is to a large extent limited by the theories of his time. We know, it is true, that his attitude to the Greek

---

[1] In Arabic 'analogic thought' (qias) often stands for thought in general. The notion often occurs in the Kuzari.

philosophy of nature was that of a very critical outsider. 'Because they furnish proofs concerning logic and mathematics, people accept everything they say concerning physics and metaphysics. Why did you not doubt their theories of the four elements, their search of the fire-world in which they place the etherial fire . . .?' Considering the high authority these doctrines generally commanded in the Middle Ages, we can appreciate the breath of fresh air that was stirred by Jehuda Halevi's criticism.

Nevertheless, as regards his religious views in particular, Jehuda Halevi is unmistakably rooted in medievalism, to a greater extent even than most of the other Jewish philosophers of the time, in one particular point: in his attempt to build up religion on tradition and particularly on the belief in miracles instead of on reasoned considerations. He defends this method of thought by referring to the generally accepted views of his age; even before the advocate of Judaism comes forward, the King declares (Book I, § 8) that miracles alone could convince him of God's sway over world happenings. As late as the nineteenth century, no less a thinker than Dean Mansel takes up the same standpoint in his Bampton Lectures.[1] On the other hand, Maimonides, believing as he did in Biblical miracles, may have doubted whether these Bible accounts were more likely to convince sceptics than the arguments of philosophers; to him—as to most present-day believers—the miracle was perhaps the 'best beloved child' of faith, but not its father!

Although we have here a fundamental difference of opinion between Jehuda Halevi and the majority of his present-day readers, there are two qualifying considerations:

(1) Among the historical miracles to which Jehuda Halevi refers, there are two that he places in the foreground: the miracle of the preservation of Israel and the miracle of

---

[1] Cf. the polemic against him in Bevan's *Symbolism and Belief* (1938), 318 ff. Perhaps Björnson's *Beyond Power* is even better able to enlighten the modern reader on Jehuda Halevi's mode of thought. According to I, § 65, the Biblical theory of creation would have appealed even to Aristotle, had he known it.

prophecy. To the same two facts religious significance has not infrequently been attached in recent times.[1] In particular, a German philosopher, Heinrich Scholz,[2] sees in the revelation of the prophets, which cannot possibly be explained away as an illusion, the most reliable evidence of the truth of religion.

(2) Jehuda Halevi is far from seeking God only in miracles![3] Divine power, it is true, only attains full and convincing penetration on the highest rung of the ladder of organisms (*see* Commentary to Book I, § 31 ff.). But it is always one and the same, in whatever guise it appears, just as light remains the same although it penetrates bodies in varying degrees of strength, displaying its supreme force in the pearl (Book IV, § 15). He who has discovered God in the abnormal will recognize Him also in the 'wonders of every day' (as enumerated in the daily prayers of the Jews, and in Lessing's Nathan 1, 2), in the structure of organisms, which are in no way to be ascribed to an impersonal 'nature' as distinguished from God (Book I, § 69), and in the religious urge of every individual, to which the Kuzari and the poems, such as Song I (on p. 132), bear witness.

This then is the first point in which Jehuda Halevi appears to address us as a contemporary: the recognition of the intrinsic value of religion. Jehuda Halevi makes a much sharper distinction than those who think on similar lines between the philosophic and religious conceptions of God. He who has mustered the proofs of God's existence is, according to him, still far from attaining to true religion; for otherwise prophets would be found mainly among the philosophers (*see* p. 13).

[1] *Cf.*, e.g., Fleming James, *Personalities of the Old Testament* (1943) 1: 'If we can believe in the possibility of any miracles, two facts . . . may well bear that name. One is the Jewish people. . . . The second is Judaism, the religion by virtue of which this people are what they are. Both facts trace their origin to one man.'

[2] *Philosophy of Religion*, 1st edition (the only one available to me here), 1921.

[3] We refer again to Björnson's *Beyond Power*.

The indisputable rightness of the reasoning is apparent to us who are better able to survey the history of philosophy. The classic land of philosophers was Greece; and it is amongst the Greeks (and not, as Jehuda Halevi still believed, Book I, § 63, in the Orient) that the roots of philosophic and metaphysical speculation are to be sought. Yet the classic heroes of religion did not proceed from the Greeks, but from a people who, by its very nature, was even far less susceptible to philosophy than Jehuda Halevi suspected. The experience of history goes to show that intensification of philosophic wisdom has by no means always led to an intensification of religious life and vice versa. Religious life is nurtured by sources quite other than philosophy; and Jehuda Halevi is absolutely right in this fundamental theory, as we can testify today—far righter than he knew.

The same applies to his answer as to what these sources may be. The two answers he gives reappear in modern schools of thought; here indeed, by virtue of the refined method of psychological analysis, they appear much clearer and more convincing in their formulation; indeed, it seems desirable that we should proceed from this conception, which is so much more clearly comprehensible to us, to investigate those of medieval philosophers with all their implications.

The first answer deals with the peculiarity of religious *experience*. It bases itself partly on such works as William James's *Varieties of Religious Experience*, which remains on the high planes of religious emotion, and partly on Rudolf Otto's book *The Idea of the Holy*, which does justice to the character of every kind of religious experience. Although it may be said that both these works are mainly descriptive in character, their arguments serve to establish psychology as the foundation of all religion. 'It (the religious sentiment) may be entirely absent from some, who are insensitive to its peculiar flavour, or only faintly sensitive; a man may be partially or wholly deity-blind as he is stone-deaf . . .; yet most are susceptible to it in their degree as most see colours and not mere grays.'[1]

[1] S. Alexander: *Space, Time and Deity* (1920), II, 378.

He who is capable of such an experience will believe in the reality of the world which affects us [1]; he may admit that the philosopher is his superior as regards clarity of conception [2]; but philosophic knowledge is not an essential pre-requisite of the experience itself or of his conviction of it.

From this idea we can appraise certain thoughts of Jehuda Halevi which are among the most fundamental of the whole book; primarily the distinction between Aristotle's God, to whom 'speculation alone conduces', and the God of Abraham, to whom the soul yearns (Book IV, § 16), [3] and the comparison of the religious genius to the poetic genius, who, though not capable of giving any account of the laws of his art like the metric expert, senses it within himself and has the power of kindling the spark of the artist's exaltation in the hearts of others likewise gifted. [4] This in no way implies any antagonistic attitude to thought—any more than is the case with the more recent thinkers mentioned above. In the last quoted passage [5] Jehuda Halevi attributes to philosophy an apologetic value; and he attaches great importance to the statement that Judaism contains nothing opposed to reason and experience (see Book I, §§ 67, 89). Nevertheless he realizes that thought in itself can as little produce religion as art: religion is more than metaphysics; it has its roots in those depths of the soul that thought can discuss but cannot reach.

Still further removed from rationalism than the psychological justification of all piety, is the second answer to the question on the sources of religion. This answer rests on the analysis of the belief in revelation, an analysis particularly well

[1] 'That which produces effects within another reality, must be termed a reality itself' (a quotation from James by Alexander).

[2] Otto: *The Idea of the Holy*. See beginning.

[3] In the same way Scholz, p. 434, distinguishes between the 'Absolute' in philosophy and the 'Divine' in religion. A near approach to this occurs in one of Pascal's Confessions to the 'Dieu d'Abraham, Dieu d'Isaac, Dieu de Jacob, non des philosophes et des savants' (quoted in Bornhausen, *Offenbarung*, p. 143).

[4] V. § 16; *cf.* our note.

[5] Likewise at the beginning of Book V.

represented in the 'dialectic theology' of the present day.[1]
According to this school neither thought nor mysticism, i.e.
sentiment, can produce the true religious revelation, but only
'the word', i.e. revelation, particularly the completely paradoxical message of the gospels. This harsh attitude to the
'natural' powers of humanity has its root, of course, in
Paulinism, and has found but little support among scholars in
Jewry.[2] Neither does Jehuda Halevi share this opinion. Nevertheless he lays great stress on the fact that religious perception,
in the full sense of the word, according to the Bible, was only
possible from the earliest times on the basis of the word addressed
by God to Man, and that it includes matters (particularly commands) for the complete comprehension of which our natural
faculties do not suffice; thus no road leads to the Father—
but through the Father Himself (Book I, § 98).

The point of the paradox, however, in as far as this is one, is
blunted by Jehuda Halevi's remark that we cannot produce the
conditions of all life *a priori* through deductions of reason; rather
must we humbly learn the secret from experience, however
strange and foreign to us the latter may seem.[3] His irrationalism
appears in truth as a radical empiricism, an acknowledgement
of the fact that the classical representatives of religion, the
prophets, felt themselves addressed, indeed overpowered, by a
power above them[4] and that it was on the ground of their
teachings that full religious experience was evolved.

[1] In the following, reference is made to E. Brunner '*Die Mystik und das
Wort*', a discussion on Schleiermacher, whom Rudolf Otto rightly calls his
forerunner.

[2] In the nineteenth century K. L. Steinheim, whose doctrine has been
revived recently by H. J. Schoeps, comes very near to it.

[3] In occasional remarks (Book II, §§ 23 a. 25) omitted in our selection,
Jehuda Halevi reminds us of the incomprehensibility of the generating
process; and yet we must rely on experience in contrast to the 'alchemists'
who presume to make bees out of beef (we would add: a homunculus out
of a retort).

[4] *Cf.* Heschel's *Prophetie* 1936, p. 42 ff, as a scholarly justification of this
conception; he quotes recent literature, but refers also to the stress on the
connection between prophecy and poetry in medieval Judaism.

The inadequacy of philosophical theology is also manifest in the *form* of the doctrine of God. Of course, Jehuda Halevi agrees, with the philosophers, on the impossibility of ascribing to God any human qualities in the literal sense (Book II, § 2). But he thinks they make a big mistake if they infer from this that it is wrong or even merely superfluous to speak of God in human images (Book IV, § 3). Images such as the prophets envisaged by virtue of their creative power are indispensable for the implanting in our souls of the proper awe of God.[1] Here also Jehuda Halevi is on common ground with the more recent psychological attitude to religious thought, according to which the notion of God can be expressed only through anthropomorphic images; an image such as 'God's hand' or the apostrophizing of God as light has more effect upon us than all abstractions.

This insight into the relative value of anthropomorphism, combined with the insistence on a purely spiritual notion of God, conduces to a deeper understanding of *cult*. For all cult depends on the assumption that the presence of God should become particularly manifest at a certain place,[2] and on the need of 'honouring Him at close hand', as a stoic philosopher of ancient times who despised anthropomorphism expressed it.[3] And cult is a matter affecting the community. Although Jehuda Halevi was a master of individual prayer (Song I (p. 132) suffices to prove this), he nevertheless fully recognizes the advantage of communal prayer in very proper appreciation of the fact that religion, though it is the personal affair of every human being,[4] nevertheless tends much more strongly to communal culture and communal participation than does philosophy, in as far as the latter does not bear a religious

[1] See our commentary on the beginning of Book IV where reference is made to Bevan, *Symbolism and Belief* (1938).

[2] *Cf.* Book I, § 97. He has particularly in mind the worship of the Kaaba.

[3] Dion of Prusa 12, 60, draws his inspiration from him.

[4] Whitehead, *Religion in its Making* (1926) 6, 37, 48; but *cf.* pp. 12, 17, 18 on religion as a 'social phenomenon'.

character.[1] Herewith a definite breach is made in the tendency
of the Middle Ages to put religion on a par with metaphysics,
and a foundation is laid for the true understanding of *all*
religious phenomena. Religion is not merely abstract doctrine,
the highest outcome of which is the meditation of certain
choice spirits; it is union with God, resting on the experience
of our emotions and on the message of history, strengthened
through common service. It finds therefore its justification
not in metaphysical speculation, whose powers of persuasion
were disputed in its own philosophic circles, but in the
religious disposition of man and in the facts of the history
of religion. But as surely as religion is more than metaphysics,
so Judaism is more than religion. As in the question regarding the
essence of religion, so also in the question as to the essence of
Judaism, Jehuda Halevi attacks, in his peculiar way, a problem
that affects our own time not less than the Middle Ages.

In as far as Jehuda Halevi declares Judaism to be the absolute
religion, as opposed to which Christianity and Islam can only
claim to be devitalized imitations (Book III, § 8 ff.) or preparatory stages (Book IV, § 23), he formally adopts the line of
thought of the whole Middle Ages, in which the religious
wars, as he himself stresses (Book I, § 2), were based on the belief
in one absolute religion. But he goes beyond the thinkers of
his time by giving pre-eminence to his own religion, not only,
for example, on the lines of his contemporary and fellow-
countryman Abraham ibn Daûd, who in his book on *Exalted
Religion* stresses the reasonableness of Judaism, but on physiological grounds; the non-Jew who is converted to Judaism is
therefore not quite on a par with the born Jew (in contrast
to Maimonides); and it is only in Palestine that Jewish culture
can open out again in full glory. But this expansion includes
secular culture; that 'pick' of mankind to which Israel also
belongs is at the same time the root-basis of philosophy,
which the Greeks only took over from the East; even the
Hebrew language has its own peculiar advantages (Book II,

[1] This was the case in certain schools of philosophy in Greece, especially
the Pythagorean.

§ 67 ff.). This does not imply any blind satisfaction with the Israel of the present. Quite apart from the fact that Jehuda Halevi admits, as we know, 'recessive phenomena' within the pick of mankind, he remains absolutely loyal to the religious interpretation of the Galuth as the penalty for our sin: it is inflicted upon us in order to train us in the ways of humility (Book I, § 115), and to foster in us an intense yearning for Eretz Israel (Book V, § 27); with deep pain, he admits that the Jewish nation does not realize this significance of its fate; it settles down quite comfortably in the Diaspora instead of responding with a willing spirit to the Divine plan of education. It is, in fact, this most characteristic reproof, together with Jehuda Halevi's determination to draw the consequences of the yearning for Eretz Israel, that illustrates the inseparable connection he makes between the religious values of Israel and its national existence, showing that religious revival of the nation is bound up with the recognition and the abolition of its national calamity; that is to say, it is in no way only bound up with spiritual and ethical enlightenment. Michael Sachs is therefore quite justified in terming Jehuda Halevi 'the most national and the most patriotic of all Jewish poets'.

Jehuda Halevi's nationalism is, as we have seen, nurtured in the soil of Greek biology. The glowing iron of his love for Israel has been welded into steel in the bath of international philosophy. Herein lies the peculiar distinction of his way of thought—the connection between the nation and the faith of Israel being assumed as no longer accidental and arbitrary but as essential—but herein also its mistake. The laws of historical happening cannot be laid down hard and fast like the laws of nature. Eclipses of the sun, both past and future, can be calculated to the second; the cultural development of a nation cannot be foretold nor, as far as we know from history, can it be grasped as the *inevitable* consequence of factors known to us. This applies particularly to Jehuda Halevi's conception of history. Just as surely as the Bible—and it is only as a Bible exponent that Jehuda Halevi claims to count—recognizes special merits of the Israelite group of mankind, just as little does it universally connect prophecy or piety or even the peculiar Divine direction with these factors: we need only refer to the book of Jonah, wherein Jew and Heathen alike are judged according to their behaviour, the heathens appearing no less God-fearing than the prophet. By interpreting the free will of God displayed in the selection of Israel and Palestine as a causal necessity, Jehuda Halevi invests the notion of selection with a crudeness that he himself finds undesirable (Book I, § 28 — 'your words are poor after having been rich') and that, in fact, detracts from the weight of his psychological justification of religion, to which we have just referred; the fact that he does not insist in his story on this exclusiveness of the religious prerogative as formulated by him in Book I, § 115, speaks well for him and for his rootedness in the real Bible heritage: he presents the heathen King of the Khazars as honoured by Divine apparition!

But the clear admission of Jehuda Halevi's over-emphasis inevitably leads us to the recognition of the rightness of his method. For life, as history depicts it, is unquestionably dependent on natural factors; and unaffected by theoretic (or even practical) over-emphasis, the true essential of all nationalism remains the faith in this—that all the cultural characteristics of a people are organically bound up with each other and with the men who have produced them. Even if the belief in revelation is simply taken as the foundation of the religion of Israel, there yet remains that interconnection between faith and people that is stressed in a well-known Midrash, according to which God offered the Torah to all the nations, who refused it each for a reason of its own.

Jehuda Halevi also sees the pre-eminence of his people not in creative force, but in religious aptitude; he held it to be important that this pre-eminence attained its full development in the days of unclouded national freedom, and that it is promised renewal after the return of such freedom; for, like the Hebrew language (Book II, § 68), Jewish culture in its entirety was impoverished by the impoverishment of its bearers (cf. Book I, § 12). Hence, on the one hand, his pride in

Jewish blood and belief in the duty of national preservation for the sake of mankind; on the other hand, his deep consciousness of the unnaturalness of the present-day position of Judaism: we seem to hear Ahad Haam in Jehuda Halevi's statement that the nation is in slavery (Book V, § 25) although individual Jews may fare so well that they do not want to sever themselves from their business and their houses (Book II, § 24); he touches us all to the quick when he hopes that even now, before the final redemption, a healthier and a fuller Jewish life may open up for our people in Palestine.

As an empiricist in the broadest sense of the word, comprising spiritual reality, Jehuda Halevi refuses to interpret his Jewish consciousness in a *purely* religious guise, or to force the religious into the Procrustean bed of a theology subject to philosophic proof. Posterity's opinion of him is based on this peculiarity of his. Whereas in recent times rationalism has focused its main attention on Maimonides, the great representative of philosophic eros, Jehuda Halevi's influence affected above all men of artistic distinction. Michael Sachs[1] evoked his spirit, as we have already mentioned, against 'Israelites of the nineteenth century' whose bartering and trading tendencies induced them to sacrifice the past and future of Judaism to emancipation. A spark of the pure flame of his enthusiasm falls upon the spirit of Heinrich Heine, who represents Jehuda Halevi in the 'Romanzero' as the knight of the sad and beautiful dame Jerusalem and as the poet of the Sabbath, although here, as always, he drowns his own 'Judenleid' in the jingle of the fool's bells.[2] And in the commentary to the translation of Jehuda Halevi's poems[3] which Franz Rosenzweig sets as an 'accompaniment' to the melodies of the poet, the belief in the peculiarity of the Jewish people stands out no less strongly than in the Kuzari; and Rosenzweig protests with even greater emphasis than the Kuzari against all attempts to apprehend Judaism in merely theologic abstractions.

[1] Sachs, *Die Religiöse Poesie der Juden in Spanien*, 2nd ed., p. 300.

[2] *Cf.* Poem No. II, (p. 133), and commentary on p. 139 f.

[3] Jehuda Halevi, *92 Hymnen und Gedichte*, p. 223.

This, then, is the extent of Jehuda Halevi's intentional and actual influence on his descendants. He teaches us to be on our guard against deceptive solutions of the religious and the Jewish problems, and, in the contemplation of our past with critical reference to his own line of thought, to discover the right question and the right answer.

KUZARI
A BOOK OF PROOF AND ARGUMENT:
AN APOLOGY
FOR A DESPISED RELIGION

BOOK I
NON-JEWISH RELIGIONS

1. I was asked to state what arguments I could bring to bear against the attacks of philosophers and followers of other religions which differ from ours and against the sectaries who differ from the majority of Israel. And I remembered the arguments I had heard of a Rabbi who sojourned with the King of the Khazars, who, as we know from historical records, became a convert to Judaism about four hundred years ago: to him there appeared repeatedly a dream, in which it seemed as if an angel addressed him saying: 'Thy (intention) is indeed pleasing to the Creator, but thy way of acting is not pleasing'. Yet he was so zealous in the performance of the Khazar religion, that he devoted himself with a perfect heart to the service of the temple and the sacrifices. Notwithstanding this devotion, the angel came again at night and repeated: 'thy intention is indeed pleasing, but thy way of acting is not pleasing'. This induced him to ponder over the different beliefs and religions, and finally he became a convert to Judaism together with many other Khazars. As I found among the arguments of the Rabbi many which appealed to me and were in harmony with my opinions, I resolved to write them down as they had been spoken. The intelligent will understand me.

It is related: when the King of Khazar dreamt that his intention was pleasing to God, but his way of acting was not pleasing, and was commanded in the same dream to seek the work that would please God, he inquired of a *philosopher* concerning his persuasion. THE PHILOSOPHER replied:

There is no favour or dislike in God, because He is above desire and intention. For an intention intimates a desire in the intending person: by the fulfilment of this desire he becomes complete; as long as it remains unfulfilled, he is incomplete. In a similar way God is, in the opinion of the philosophers, above the knowledge of individuals, because they change with the times and there is no change in God's knowledge. He does not know thee, much less thy intentions and actions, nor does He listen to thy prayers or see thy movements. Even if philosophers say that He created thee, they only speak in metaphor, because He is the cause of causes in the creation of all creatures, but not because this was His intention from the beginning. He never created man, for the world is without beginning, and no man arose other than through one who came into existence before him; in every man we find united physical and intellectual qualities deriving from his parents and other relations not discounting the influence of winds, countries, foods and water, spheres, stars and constellations. Everything is reduced to the Prime Cause—not to a Will proceeding from it, but to an Emanation, from which emanated a second, a third, and a fourth cause. The causes and the things caused are, as thou seest, intimately connected with one another; their connection is as eternal as the Prime Cause and has no beginning. Therefore, every individual on earth has its completing causes; consequently an individual with perfect causes becomes perfect and another with imperfect causes remains imperfect, e.g. the negro is fit to receive nothing more than human shape and speech in its least developed form; the philosopher, however, who is equipped with the highest capacity, derives therefrom moral, intellectual and active advantages, so that he wants nothing to make him perfect. But these perfections exist only in the form of latent powers which require instruction and training to become active, bringing to light this capacity, in all its completeness or with its deficiencies and innumerable grades. To the perfect person there adheres a light of Divine nature, called Active Intellect; his Passive Intellect cleaves so closely to it that it considers itself to be one with the Active Intellect. His organs—I mean the limbs of such a person—only serve the most perfect purposes, at the most appropriate time, and in the best condition, as though they were organs of the Active Intellect, not of the potential and Passive Intellect, which made use of them at an earlier period, sometimes well, but more often improperly. This degree is the ultimate and most longed-for goal for the perfect man, whose soul, purified of doubts, grasps the inward truth of science. The soul becomes the equal of an angel, and finds a place on the nethermost step of seraphic beings. This is what is called, allusively and approximately, God's pleasure. Endeavour to reach it and to reach the true knowledge of things, in order that thy intellect may become active. Keep to the just way, as regards character and action, because this will help thee to effect truth, to gain instruction, and to become like this Active Intellect. The consequence of this will be contentment, humility, meekness and every other praiseworthy inclination, accompanied by the veneration of the Prime Cause, not in order to receive favour from it or to divert its wrath, but solely to become like the Active Intellect. If thou hast reached such disposition of belief, be not concerned about the forms of thy humility, worship and benediction—nor fashion thy religion according to the laws of reason set up by philosophers, but strive after purity of the soul. Then thou wilt reach thy goal, viz. union with the Active Intellect. Maybe he will communicate with thee or teach thee the knowledge of what is hidden through true dreams and positive visions.

2. THE KHAZARI: Thy speech is convincing, yet it does not correspond to what I desire to find. I know already that my soul is pure and that my actions are directed to gain the favour of God. To all this I received the answer that this way of acting does not find favour, though the intention does. There must no doubt be a way of acting, pleasing in itself, and not through the medium of intention. If this be not so, why then do Christian and Moslem, who divided the inhabited world between them, fight with one another, each of them serving his God with pure intention, living either as monks or hermits, fasting and praying? It is, however, impossible to agree with both.

3. THE PHILOSOPHER: The philosopher's creed knows no manslaughter, cultivating only the intellect.

4. THE KHAZARI: And what could be more erroneous, in the opinion of the philosophers, than the belief that the world was created, and that in six days; or that the Prime Cause spoke with mortals—in view of the philosophical doctrine, which declares God to be above knowing details. Moreover, one might expect the gift of prophecy to be quite common among philosophers, considering their deeds, their knowledge, their researches after truth, their exertions and their close connection with all things spiritual; one might also expect that wonders, miracles, and extraordinary things would be reported of them. Yet we find that true visions are granted to persons who do not devote themselves to study or the purification of their souls. This proves that between the Divine power and the soul there are secret relations which are not identical with those thou mentionedst, O Philosopher!

After this the Khazari said to himself: I will ask the Christians and the Moslems, since one of these ways of acting is, no doubt, the God-pleasing one. But as regards the Jews, I am satisfied that they are of low station, few in number, and generally hated. He then invited a Christian scholar and questioned him about his doctrine and his practice.

THE CHRISTIAN SCHOLAR: I believe that all things are created, whilst the Creator is eternal; that He created the whole world in six days; that all mankind sprang from Adam, and after him from Noah; that God takes care of the created beings, and keeps in touch with man; that He is wrathful, takes delight, and is merciful; that He speaks, appears and reveals Himself to His prophets and favoured ones; that He dwells among those who please Him. In short: I believe in all that is written in the Torah and the other books of the Israelites, which are undisputed, because they are generally accepted as everlasting and have been revealed before a vast multitude. Subsequently the Divinity became embodied in the womb of a noble Israelite virgin; she bore Him having the semblance of a human being, which concealed nevertheless a divinity, seemingly a prophet, but in reality a God sent forth. He is the Messiah, whom we call the Son of God, and He is the Father and the Son and the Holy Ghost. We believe in His unity, although the Trinity appears on our tongues. We believe in Him and in His abode among the Israelites; this was granted to them as a distinction, because the Divine influence never ceased to be attached to them—until their masses rebelled against this Messiah, and they crucified Him. Then Divine wrath burdened them everlastingly, whilst the favour was confined to a few who followed the Messiah, and to those nations which followed these few. We belong to their number. Although we are not of Israelitish descent, we are well deserving of being called Israelites, because we follow the Messiah and his twelve Israelite companions, who took the place of the tribes. Our laws and regulations are derived from the apostle Simon (Petrus) and from ordinations taken from the Torah, which we study, for its truth and Divine origin are indisputable. It is also stated in the Gospel by the Messiah: I came not to destroy one of the laws of Moses, but I came to confirm and corroborate them.

5. THE KHAZARI: Here is no logical conclusion; nay, logical thought rejects most of what thou sayest. It is only when both appearance and experience are so palpable that they grip the whole heart, which sees no way of contesting, that it will agree to the difficult, and the remote will become near. This is how naturalists deal with strange powers which come upon them unawares; they would not believe if they only heard of them without seeing them; but when they see them, they discuss them, and ascribe them to the influence of stars or spirits, because they cannot disprove ocular evidence. As for me, I cannot accept these things, because they come upon me suddenly, seeing that I have not grown up in them. My duty is, therefore, to investigate further.

He then invited one of the scholars of Islam and questioned him about his doctrine and his practice.

THE MOSLEM SCHOLAR: We acknowledge the Unity and
Eternity of God and that all men are derived from Adam and
Noah. We absolutely reject embodiment (of God), and if any
element of this appears in the Writ, we explain it as meta-
phoric, serving to make the doctrine acceptable to our
comprehension. At the same time we maintain that our Book
is the Speech of God, being itself a miracle which we are
bound to accept for its own sake, since no one is able to
produce anything comparable to it, or to one of its verses.
Our prophet is the Seal of the prophets, who abrogated every
previous law, and invited all nations to embrace Islam. The
reward of the pious consists in the return of his spirit to his
body in Paradise and bliss, where he never ceases to enjoy
eating, drinking, women's love, and anything he may desire.
The requital of the disobedient consists in being condemned to
fire, and his punishment knows no end.

6. THE KHAZARI: If anyone is to be guided in matters divine,
and to be convinced that God speaks to man, whilst he considers
it improbable, he must be convinced by facts which are generally known and which allow of no refutation. And if your
book is a miracle—a non-Arab, as I am, cannot perceive its
miraculous character, because it is written in Arabic.

7. THE MOSLEM SCHOLAR: Yet miracles are performed by
the Prophet, but they are not used as evidence for the
acceptance of his Law.

8. THE KHAZARI: Yes, the human mind does not incline
to believe that God has intercourse with man, except by a
miracle which changes the nature of things, so that man
may recognize that God alone is able to do so, who created
him from nought. Such a miracle must also have taken place
in the presence of great multitudes, who saw it distinctly.
Then it is possible for the mind to grasp this extraordinary
matter, viz. that the Creator of this world and the next, of
the heavens and lights, should hold intercourse with this
contemptible subject, I mean man, speaking to him, and
fulfilling his wishes and desires.

9. THE MOSLEM SCHOLAR: Is not our Book full of stories of Moses and the Israelites? No one denies what He did to Pharaoh, how He divided the sea, saved those who enjoyed His favour, but drowned those who aroused His wrath, that he granted them manna and the quails during forty years, that He spoke to Moses on the mount (Sinai), that He made the sun stand still for Joshua, and assisted him against the giants; nor do they deny what happened previously, viz. the Flood and the destruction of the fellow-citizens of Lot. Is this not so well known that no suspicion of deceit and imagination is possible?

10. THE KHAZARI: Indeed I see myself compelled to ask the Jews, because they are the descendants of the Israelites. For I see that they constitute in themselves the evidence for a divine law on earth.

He then invited a Rabbi and asked him about his belief.

THE BASIS OF JEWISH FAITH

11. THE RABBI: I believe in the God of Abraham, Isaac and Israel, who led the Israelites out of Egypt with signs and miracles; who fed them in the desert and gave them the (Holy) Land, after having made them traverse the sea and the Jordan in a miraculous way; who sent Moses with His Law, and subsequently thousands of prophets, who confirmed His law by promises to those who observed, and threats to the disobedient. We believe in what is contained in the Torah—a very large domain.

12. THE KHAZARI: I had intended from the very beginning not to ask any Jew, because I am aware of the destruction of their books and of their narrow-minded views, their misfortunes having deprived them of all commendable qualities. Shouldst thou, O Jew, not have said that thou believest in the Creator of the world, its Governor and Guide, who created and keeps thee, and such attributes which serve as evidence for every believer, and for the sake of which he

pursues justice in order to resemble the Creator in His wisdom and justice?

13. THE RABBI: That which thou dost express is speculative and political religion, to which inquiry leads; but this is open to many doubts. Now ask the philosophers, and thou wilt find that they do not agree on one action or on one principle, since they rely on theories; some of these can be established by arguments, some of them are only plausible, some even less capable of being proved.

14. THE KHAZARI: That which thou sayest now, O Jew, seems to me better than the beginning, and I should like to hear more.

15. THE RABBI: But the beginning of my speech was the very proof, yea, the evidence, which makes every argument superfluous.

16. THE KHAZARI: How so?

17. THE RABBI: Allow me to make a few preliminary remarks; for I see thee disregarding and depreciating my words.

18. THE KHAZARI: Let me hear thy remarks.

19. THE RABBI: If thou wert told that the King of India was an excellent man, commanding admiration, and deserving reputation, only because his actions were reflected in the justice which rules his country and the virtuous ways of his subjects, would this compel you to revere him?

20. THE KHAZARI: How could this compel me, whilst I am not sure if the justice of the Indian people is natural and not dependent on their king, or due to the king, or both?

21. THE RABBI: But if his messenger came to thee bringing presents which thou knowest to be only procurable in India, and in the royal palace, accompanied by a letter in which it is distinctly stated from whom it comes, and to which are added drugs to cure thy diseases, to preserve thy health, poisons for thine enemies, and other means to fight and kill them without battle, would this make thee beholden to him?

22. THE KHAZARI: Certainly. For this would remove my former doubt that the Indians have a king. I should also acknowledge that his dominion and his word had touched me.

23. THE RABBI: How wouldst thou then, if asked, describe him?

24. THE KHAZARI: In such terms as were quite clear to me; and I would add such as were at first rather doubtful, but which were later affirmed by the former.

25. THE RABBI: In this way I answered thy question. In the same strain Moses spoke to Pharaoh, when he told him 'The God of the Hebrews sent me to thee'—viz. the God of Abraham, Isaac and Jacob. For the story of their life was well known to the nations, who also knew that the Divine power was in contact with the Patriarchs, caring for them and performing miracles for them. He did not say: 'The God of heaven and earth' nor 'my Creator and thine sent me'. In the same way God commenced His speech to the assembled people of Israel: 'I am the God whom you worship, who hath led you out of the land of Egypt'; He did not say 'I am the Creator of the world and your Creator'. In the same style I spoke to thee, O Prince of the Khazars, when thou didst ask me about my creed. I made mention to thee of what is convincing for me and for the whole of Israel, who knew these things, first through personal experience, and afterward through an uninterrupted tradition, which is equal to experience.

26. THE KHAZARI: Then your belief is confined to yourselves?

27. THE RABBI: Yes. Any Gentile who joins us sincerely shares our good fortune, but he is not equal to us. If the Torah were binding on us because God created us, the white and the black man would be equal since He created them all. But the Torah (is binding) because He led us out of Egypt and remained attached to us. For we are the pick of mankind.

28. THE KHAZARI: I see thee quite altered, O Jew, and thy words are poor after having been so rich.

29. THE RABBI: The poorest ones will become the richest, if thou givest me thy attention, until I have expressed myself more fully.

30. THE KHAZARI: Say what thou wilt.

31. THE RABBI: The (realm of) the organic power comprises nurture, growth, and propagation with their powers and all conditions attached thereto. To this belong plants and animals, to the exclusion of earth, stones, metals, and elements.

32. THE KHAZARI: This is a maxim which requires explanation, but it is true.

33. THE RABBI: Likewise, the realm of the soul's power, expressed in movement, willed action, external and internal senses and such like, is limited to all animated beings.

34. THE KHAZARI: This, too, cannot be contradicted.

35. THE RABBI: Likewise, the intellectual power distinguishes man above all living beings, it leads to the ennobling of his character, to the administration of his home and his country, to government and legislation.

36. THE KHAZARI: This is also true.

37. THE RABBI: And which would be the degree higher than this?

38. THE KHAZARI: The degree of great scholars.

39. THE RABBI: I only mean a degree which distinguishes those who occupy it essentially, as the plant is distinguished from inorganic things, a man from animals. The differences in quantity, however, are innumerable, but are purely accidental, and do not constitute a degree in the true sense.

40. THE KHAZARI: If this be so, then there is no degree above man among tangible things.

41. THE RABBI: And if we find a man who walks into the fire without hurt, or abstains from food for some time without starving, on whose face a light shines which the eye cannot bear,

who is never ill, nor ages—and when he reaches his life's end, dies spontaneously just as a man retires to his couch to sleep on an appointed day and hour, equipped with the knowledge of what is hidden as to past and future: is such a degree not essentially distinguished from the human degree?

42. The Khazari: This degree would be divine and seraphic, if it existed. It would belong to the province of Divine power, not to that of the intellectual, spiritual (soulful) or natural one.

43. The Rabbi: These are some of the characteristics of the undoubted prophet. Through him God made manifest to the people that He is in connection with them, that there is a Lord who guides them as He wishes, according to their obedience or disobedience. He revealed that which was hidden and taught how the world was created, how the generations prior to the Flood followed each other and how man descended from Adam. He described the Flood and the origin of the Seventy nations from Shem, Ham and Japhet, the sons of Noah; how the languages were split up, and where men sought their habitations; how arts arose and how cities were built—and the chronology from Adam up to this day.

ETERNITY OF THE WORLD? NATURE AND GOD

62. The Khazari: What is thy opinion of the philosophers, who, after careful investigation, agree that the world is without beginning?

63. The Rabbi: We cannot reproach the philosophers, because they inherited neither science nor religion. Being Grecians, they belong to the descendants of Japhet, who inhabited the north; whereas (that) knowledge coming from Adam, and sustained by Divine power, is only to be found among the progeny of Shem, who were the 'pick' of Noah's descendants; this knowledge has always been connected with this 'pick' of mankind and will always remain so. The Greeks

only received it, when they became powerful, from the Persians, who had it from the Chaldeans. It was only then that famous philosophers arose in their midst; but from the moment that Rome assumed political leadership, the Greeks produced no famous philosopher.

64. THE KHAZARI: Does this mean that Aristotle's investigations are not deserving of credence?

65. THE RABBI: Yes. He exerted his mind, because he had no reliable tradition at his disposal. He meditated on the beginning and end of the world, but found difficulty in accepting a theory of the beginning as well as of eternity. Finally, he preferred those abstract speculations which pointed to eternity, and he found no reason to inquire into chronology. Had he lived among a people with well-authenticated and generally acknowledged traditions, he would have applied his deductions and arguments to the establishment of a theory of creation, however difficult, rather than to one of eternity, which is even more difficult to accept.

66. THE KHAZARI: Is there any decisive proof?

67. THE RABBI: Where could proof of such a problem be found? Heaven forbid that there should be anything in the Torah to contradict that which is manifest or proved! On the other hand it tells of miracles and the transformations of the normal cause of things, either through new creations or by changing one thing into another, to testify to the power of the Creator, who accomplishes whatever He wills, and whenever He wills it. The question of eternity and creation is obscure, and the arguments are evenly balanced. The theory of creation is outbalanced by the prophetic tradition of Adam, Noah, and Moses, which is more deserving of credence than speculation founded on analogies. But if, after all, a believer in the Torah finds himself compelled to admit an eternal substance and the existence of many worlds prior to this one, this would not affect his belief in that *this* world was created at a certain epoch, and that Adam and Noah were the first human beings.

68. THE KHAZARI: Thus far I find these arguments satisfactory. Now take up the thread of thy earlier exposition. How came about the great conviction that the Creator of bodies, spirits, souls, intellects and angels—He who is too high, holy and exalted for the mind still less for the senses to grasp — that He holds intercourse with creatures, wonderful as their form may appear? For in the smallest worm there are revealed the wonders of His wisdom in a manner unfathomable to our mind.

69. THE RABBI: Thou hast forestalled by thy (last) words much of my intended answer. Dost thou ascribe the wisdom apparent in the creation of an ant, for example, to a sphere or star or to any other object, to the exclusion of the Almighty creator, who weighs and gives everything its due, giving neither too much, nor too little?

70. THE KHAZARI: That is ascribed to the action of Nature.

71. THE RABBI: And what is Nature?

72. THE KHAZARI: It is a certain power, as we have learnt through the sciences. What it really is, we do not know; but no doubt scholars know.

73. THE RABBI: They know as much as we do. Aristotle defined it as the beginning and primary cause through which a thing either moves or rests, not by accident, but by virtue of its inherent essence.

74. THE KHAZARI: This would mean that the thing which moves or rests on its own account, implies a cause by which it moves or rests, and this cause is Nature.

75. THE RABBI: This is his meaning; yet he adds many subtleties and discriminations between accidental and natural occurrences and he makes statements astonishing to those who hear them; but the essence of their doctrine of Nature is just this.

76. THE KHAZARI: Then we are misled by these names, and we are persuaded to add an associate to God, if we say that Nature is wise and active, that perhaps Nature even creates, if we concluded rightly from them.

77. THE RABBI: Certainly. It is true, that the elements, moon, sun and stars have effect, such as warming, cooling, moistening, drying, etc.; yet we should ascribe to them not wisdom but mere functioning labour. Shaping (of the animal being), determining of its size and conception of it, however, and everything that betrays intention, can only be ascribed to Him, who is wise, victorious and who is possessed of the power to decree things. There is no harm in denoting the force which affects matter through heating and cooling as 'Nature'; but all intelligence must be denied it. Thus we deny human beings the faculty of creating the embryo by their intercourse, because they only assist matter to receive human form from the wise Creator. Do not therefore deem it improbable for exalted traces of the Divine to be rendered visible in the low world, when the (low) matter is prepared to receive them. Herein is to be found the root of belief and unbelief.

78. THE KHAZARI: How may the root of belief be also the root of unbelief?

79. THE RABBI: The things which are capable of receiving Divine influence are not under man's control. It is impossible for him to gauge their quantity or quality; and even if their essence were known, yet neither their time, place, constitution, nor preparation are revealed. For this an instruction is required, inspired by God, detailed through sublime evidence. He who has been thus inspired, and who obeys the order with all its determinations and conditions with a pure mind, is the true believer. But an unbeliever is he who strives by speculation and deduction to influence conditions for the reception of this (Divine) power, as revealed in the writings of astrologers, who try to call down supernatural beings, or who manufacture talismans. He brings offerings and burns incense in accordance with his own analogic deductions and conjectures, being in reality ignorant of that which we should do, how much, in which way, by what means, in which place, by whom, in which manner, and many other details, the enumeration of which would lead us too far. He is like an ignorant man who enters

the surgery of a physician famous for the curative power of his medicines. The physician is not at home, but people come for medicines. The ignorant man dispenses them out of the jars, knowing nothing of the contents, nor how much should be given to each person. Thus he kills with the very medicine which should have cured them. Should he by chance have effected a cure with one of the drugs, the people will turn to him and say that it helped them—till they discover that he deceived them; or they note the accidental success of another drug and turn to it. They do not notice that the real cure was effected by the skill of the learned physician who prepared the medicines and explained the proper manner in which they were to be administered, and also taught the patients what food and drink, exercise and rest, sleep, ventilation and kind of bed, etc., was necessary. Men before the time of Moses, with few exceptions, were like these patients. They were deceived by astrological and physical doctrines; they turned from doctrine to doctrine, from god to god, or adopted a plurality (of doctrines and gods) at the same time; they forgot the guide and master of those powers and regarded the latter as helpful factors, whereas they are in reality mostly harmful factors, by reason of their construction and arrangement. Profitable on its own account is the Divine influence, and harmful on its own account, the absence thereof.

THE ORIGIN OF OUR RELIGION

80. THE KHAZARI: Let us return to our subject. Explain to me how thy belief grew, how it spread and became celebrated, how differing opinions became united, and how long it took to lay the foundations of the faith and to build up a strong complete structure. For all religions start, no doubt, from single individuals who support one another in upholding the faith which it pleased God should be promulgated. Their number increases continually, they grow more powerful, either by their own virtue, or through the assistance of a king who compels the multitudes to adopt that particular creed.

81. THE RABBI: It is only rational religion of human origin that spreads in this way. When (such a religion) becomes celebrated and succeeds, it is said to be sustained by God, etc. But the religion of Divine origin arises suddenly. It is bidden to arise, and it is there, similar to the creation of the world.

82. THE KHAZARI: Thou startlest me, O Rabbi!

83. THE RABBI: But the facts are yet more startling. The Israelites lived in Egypt as slaves, 600,000 men above the age of twenty, the descendants of the Twelve Tribes. Not one of them had separated or emigrated into another country, nor was there a stranger among them. They looked forward to the promise given to their ancestors, Abraham, Isaac and Jacob, that the land of Palestine should be their inheritance. At that time it was in the power of seven mighty and prosperous nations, whilst the Israelites groaned in the depths of misery under the bondage of Pharaoh, who caused their children to be put to death, lest they should increase in number. But (God) sent Moses and Aaron, two weak men, and they advanced before the mighty Pharaoh with signs, miracles and change of the course of nature. And Pharaoh could not get away from them, nor harm them, neither could he protect himself from the ten plagues which befell the Egyptians, affecting their streams, land, air, plants, animals, bodies, even their souls; for in one moment, at midnight, died the most precious and most beloved members of their houses, viz. every firstborn male; there was no dwelling without dead, except the houses of the Israelites. All these plagues were preceded by warnings and menaces, and their cessation was signalled in the same way, proving that they were ordained by God, who does what He wills and when He wills, and that they were not ordinary natural phenomena, nor were they wrought by constellations or accident. The Israelites left the country of Pharaoh's bondage, by the command of God, the same night and at the same moment as the firstborn died, and travelled in the direction of the Red Sea, guided by pillars of cloud and fire; their leaders and governors and religious chiefs were Moses and

Aaron, inspired, venerated old men, more than eighty years of age at that time. Up till then the Israelites had had only a few laws, handed down from their chosen ancestors back to Adam and Noah; Moses did not abrogate these laws, but rather added to them. When Pharaoh pursued the Israelites they did not have recourse to arms, being unskilled in their use, but (God) divided the sea and they traversed it; Pharaoh and his host were drowned, and the waves washed their corpses towards the Israelites, so that they could see them with their own eyes. It is a long and well-known story.

84. THE KHAZARI: Here the Divine power is manifest, and the commandment connected with (these facts) must be accepted. No one could imagine for a moment that this was the product of witchcraft, trickery, or imagination. For had it been possible to stimulate belief in any imaginary dividing of the waters and the crossing of them, it would also have been possible to gain credence for a similar trickery as regards their delivery from bondage, the death of their tormenters, and the capture of their goods and chattels. And this would be an atheistic distortion.

85. THE RABBI: And later on, when they came to the sterile desert, He sent them food, which, except on the Sabbath, was produced daily for them and they ate it for forty years.

86. THE KHAZARI: This is also irrefutable, viz. a thing which occurred to six hundred thousand people for forty years. Six days in the week the manna came down, but on the Sabbath it stopped. This makes the observance of the Sabbath obligatory, since Divine power is connected with it.

87. THE RABBI: The Sabbath is confirmed by this fact as well as by the creation of the world in six days and also by another matter to which I shall now refer. Although the people believed in the message of Moses after the performance of these miracles, they retained some doubt as to whether God really communed with mortals, and whether or not the Law was of human origin, only later supported by Divine inspiration. They could not associate speech with a Divine being,

since speech is a corporeal function. God, however, desired to remove this doubt. He commanded them to prepare themselves morally as well as physically, enjoining them to keep aloof from their wives and to be ready to hear the words of God. The people prepared and fitted themselves to receive prophetic inspiration and even actually to hear (in person) the words of God. This came to pass three days later, and was preceded by overwhelming phenomena, lightning, thunder, earthquake and fire, which surrounded Mount Sinai. The fire remained visible to the people forty days; they also saw Moses enter it and emerge from it; they distinctly heard the Ten Commandments, the source and foundation of the Law. One of these is the ordination of the Sabbath. . . . He wrote these Ten Words on two tablets of precious stone, and handed them to Moses.

88. THE KHAZARI: If any one were to hear you relate that God spoke to your assembled multitude, and wrote tablets for you, etc., he could not be blamed for accusing you of believing in the corporeality of God. But you also are free from blame, because these grand and lofty spectacles, seen by thousands, cannot be denied; therefore, you are justified in rejecting analogical conclusions and speculation.

89. THE RABBI: Heaven forbid that we should assume what is impossible or that which reason rejects as being impossible. The first of the Ten Commandments enjoins the belief in Divine providence; and immediately there follows the second command which forbids the worship of other gods, the association of any human beings with Him, His representation in statues, forms, and images, in general, i.e. the belief in His corporeality. We must not, however, reject the tradition concerning that apparition. We say, then, that we do not know how the idea took bodily form, nor how the speech was evolved which struck our ear, nor what new thing God created from naught, nor what existing thing he employed; for nothing is beyond His power. Just so we have to admit that He created the two tablets, and engraved a text on them, in the same way as He created the heaven and the stars by His will alone.

90. THE KHAZARI: This representation is satisfactory.

91. THE RABBI: I do not maintain that this is exactly how these things occurred. Maybe they happened in another way, which is too deep for me to fathom. But the result was that every one who viewed those apparitions became convinced that the matter proceeded from God direct. Thus, the belief in the law connected with those scenes was firmly established in the mind.

92. THE KHAZARI: Take care, O Rabbi, lest too great indulgence for thy people induce thee to overestimate and to overlook what is known of their disobedience despite the revelation. I know that at that time they made a calf and worshipped it instead of God.

93. THE RABBI: A sin which was reckoned all the heavier on account of their greatness. Great is he whose sins are counted.

94. THE KHAZARI: Here is shown again thy obstinacy and thy partiality for thy people. What sin could be greater than this? And must not all right of precedence yield to this?

95. THE RABBI: Bear with me a little and I will prove the pre-eminence of the people. For me it is sufficient that God chose them as His community and people from all the nations of the world; that the Divine power descended on the whole people, so that they all became worthy to be addressed by Him. The power even swayed their women, among whom were prophetesses. Up to that time the power had descended from Adam on isolated individuals only. For Adam was perfection itself, because no flaw could be found in the work of a wise and almighty Creator, wrought from a substance chosen by Him, and fashioned according to His own design—and there was no contaminating influence from the sperm of the father and the blood of the mother, from nourishing and nursing in the years of childhood and growth, from air, water and soil. For He created him in the form of an adolescent, perfect in body and mind. He was endowed, therefore, with the most perfect soul and with the loftiest intellect which it is possible

for a human being to possess, and, surpassing intellect, with
the Divine faculty, viz. an eminence enabling him to enter into
communication with God and spiritual beings and to comprehend the great truths without instruction after slight
reflection. We call him God's son, and we call those of his
descendants who are like him, sons of God. He begot many
children; but the only one capable of taking his place was Abel,
because he alone was like him. After he had been slain by Cain
through jealousy of this peculiar eminence, he was replaced
by Seth, who also was like Adam; he was the pick of Adam's
progeny and his 'heart', while the others were 'husks' and
rotten fruit. The pick of Seth's progeny was Enoch, and in
this way was the Divine power connected with isolated
individuals down to Noah; they were the 'heart', they
resembled Adam, and were styled sons of God. They were
perfect outwardly and inwardly, as regards length of life,
knowledge and power; their lives fix the chronology from
Adam to Noah, as well as from Noah to Abraham. There were
some, however, among them who had no communication
with the Divine power, such as Terah; but his son Abraham
was the disciple of his grandfather Eber, and for this reason
he was called 'Hebrew'; Eber was the pick of Shem's progeny,
Shem the pick of Noah's; accordingly he inherited the tem-
perate zone, the centre and jewel of which is Palestine, the
land of prophecy, whilst Japhet turned toward the north, and
Ham towards the south. The pick of Abraham's sons was
Isaac. Abraham, therefore, removed all his children from the
privileged land, in order to give it over to Isaac alone. The
pick of Isaac's sons was Jacob; his brother Esau was removed,
because the land belonged to Jacob. The sons of Jacob were
all 'picked' and worthy of the (influence of the) Divine power;
they all, therefore, received the country, distinguished through
the Divine power. This is the first instance of the Divine power
descending on a number of people, whereas it was previously
found in single individuals only. Then God tended them in
Egypt, multiplied and fostered them, as we foster a tree with
a sound root until it produces perfect fruit, resembling the

first fruit from which it was planted, viz. Abraham, Isaac, Jacob, Joseph and his brethren. And the fruit ripened in Moses, Aaron and Miriam, Bezaleel, Oholiab and the chiefs of the tribes, the seventy Elders, who were all endowed with the spirit of continual prophecy; then Joshua, Kaleb, Hur, and many others. Then (the Israelites) became worthy of the Divine light and (special) Divine providence. If disobedient men existed among them, they were hated, but remained, without doubt, within the picked; they were part of the picked on account of their descent and nature, and begot children who belonged to the picked. A disobedient man, therefore, received (Divine) consideration by reason of the admixture of picked blood, which appeared in his children and grandchildren, according to the purity of their lineage—as we decided that Terah and others with whom the Divine power was not connected were enabled to beget descendants belonging to the picked, according to their natural disposition, which was not the case with all the posterity of Ham and Japhet. We perceive a similar phenomenon in nature: many people do not resemble their father at all, but resemble their grandfathers; there cannot, consequently, be any doubt that this nature and resemblance was latent in the father, although it did not become visible outwardly, like the nature of Eber in his children, until it reappeared in Abraham.

96. THE KHAZARI: This is the true nobility, which descended directly from Adam, the noblest creature on earth; yours by right, therefore, is the title of nobility among all the inhabitants of the earth. But how to reconcile this nobility with that sin?

97. THE RABBI: All nations were given to idolatry at that time. Even the philosophers, who proclaimed the unity and the government of God, were unable to dispense with an image, and taught the masses that the Divine power was connected with the image, which was distinguished by some miraculous power; no people, therefore, were reconciled to any law without a visible image on which they could depend. The Israelites had been promised that something visible would

descend on them from God on which they could depend, as
they followed the pillars of cloud and fire when they departed
from Egypt; this they pointed out and fell to praising it, and
worshipping God in its presence. Thus they also turned
towards the cloud which hovered over Moses, while God
spoke with him; they rose and worshipped God in its presence.
Now the people had heard the proclamation of the Ten
Commandments, and Moses had ascended the mount in order
to receive the tables which he was to bring down to them
inscribed, and then to make an ark towards which they should
direct their gaze during their devotions. In this was the Divine
covenant and God's latest creation, the tablets. To it belonged
the cloud, the (Divine) Light, and all miracles wrought through
its instrumentality. The people waited for (Moses') return,
clad in the same apparel in which they had witnessed the drama
on Sinai, without removing their jewels or changing their
clothes, remaining just as he left them, expecting every
moment to see him return. He, however, tarried forty days,
although he had not provided himself with food, having only
left them with the intention of returning the same day. Then
distrust overpowered a section of this great people, and they
began to divide into parties and factions. Many views and
opinions were expressed, till at last some of them had recourse
to demanding an object of worship, towards which they could
turn, like the other nations, without, however, prejudicing
the supremacy of Him who had brought them out of Egypt;
they wished only to have something towards which they could
direct their gaze when relating the wonders of God, as the
believers did with the ark, exclaiming 'there is the Lord', as
we do with the sky and every other object which we know to
be set in motion by the Divine will exclusively, and not by any
accident or desire of man or nature. Their sin consisted in the
manufacture of an image, which was forbidden to them, and
in attributing Divine power to a thing made and chosen by
themselves without the order of God. Some excuse may be
found for them in the above mentioned dissension; actually
out of six hundred thousand souls the number of those who

worshipped the calf was below three thousand. For those of higher station who assisted in making it, an excuse might be found in the fact that they wished to separate clearly the disobedient from the pious, in order to slay those who would worship the calf. On the other hand, they sinned in causing what was only a sin of intention to be a sin in deed. This sin was not on a par with an entire lapse from obedience to Him who had led them out of Egypt, as only one of His commands was violated by them: God had forbidden images, and in spite of this they made one. They should have waited and not have created for themselves an object of worship, arranging an altar and sacrifices. This had been done by the advice of the astrologers and magicians among them, who imagined that their actions based on analogical conclusions could approach the true ones. They resembled the fool of whom we spoke, who entered the surgery of a physician and dealt out death to those who had formerly profited from the remedies. The whole affair appears to us so repulsive, because nowadays the majority of nations have abandoned the worship of images; it was less objectionable at that time, because all nations were then idolators. Had their sin consisted in constructing a house of worship of their own, and creating a place of prayer, offering and veneration, the matter would not have appeared so grave; because nowadays we also build our houses of worship, hold them in great respect, and seek blessing through their means. If this were not essential for the cohesion of our community, it would be as unknown as it was in the time of the kings, when the people were forbidden to erect places of worship, called heights; the pious kings destroyed them, lest (any place of worship) be venerated beside the house chosen by God, in which He was to be worshipped according to His own ordinances.

98. THE KHAZARI: Thou confirmest the opinion I formed through meditation and through what I saw in my vision: that man can only attain to Divine 'order' through Divine 'ordinance', viz. through actions ordained by God.

COMMENTARY TO BOOK I

§ 1. Jehuda Halevi is in line with historical tradition. True comprehension of the Kuzari is concerned not with historical facts, but with the question: What did J. H. find set down and how did he bend tradition to accord with his aims?

The tradition is as follows: Bulan, King of the Khazars (who inhabited the area known today as Southern Russia), was a God-fearing man who distinguished himself by fighting against what remained of heathendom. To him appeared an angel in his dream, who said unto him: 'Bulan, I am sent by the Everlasting God to give thee this message: "I (God) have heard thy prayer; I bless thee and will cause thee to be exceedingly fruitful; thy kingdom shall stand for a thousand generations and I shall deliver thine enemies into thy hands."' The following morning the king arose, thanked the Lord and excelled still more in pious actions. Then the angel appeared a second time and said to him: 'My son, I have seen thy ways, and thy deeds please me; I know that thou followest me with all thy soul and all thy might; I will give thee justice and law if thou wilt observe my commandments and keep my laws'. Then the king answered the angel: 'Oh my Lord, Thou knowest my heart's thoughts; Thou hast searched my inmost parts and knowest that my whole trust is in Thee. But the people over whom I reign are unbelieving; I do not know if they will believe me; if Thou hast pity upon me, Thou wilt also appear to their great vizier so that he may help me.' God granted his wish and appeared to the vizier in his dream; the latter informed the King early on the following morning. Now the King sent for his ministers, his servants and all his people and set the matter before them; they were converted to the (true) faith and took refuge under the wings of the Shekinah. In another dream, God demanded the erection of a temple. But then 'the King of Edom and the King of Ishmael' heard about the King and sent their ambassadors laden with costly presents in order to convert the King to their faiths. The King, who was a clever man, sent for a Jewish scholar; the three men held discussions and could not come to an agreement. The King then secretly asked first the Christian, and afterwards the Moslem, which was the better of the two remaining faiths. Both chose Judaism as being founded on truth and because God had performed miracles for the Jews until their sins had brought down His anger upon them. Thereupon the King declared, in a public assembly, that he accepted Judaism; he had himself and his people circumcised and they had learned Jews to instruct them in the particulars of their faith.

J. H. could not make more use of these facts than Goethe did of the descriptions of the life of the alchemist Doctor Faustus. There was the dream—the discussions (in which Christians and Moslems admit the wonders of Jewish history)—the conversion: that is all. On the other hand: the inward process of conversion as known to this tradition was useless to J. H. According to this description, the King was against heathendom from the beginning, hesitating only as to which of the three monotheistic religions to adopt; it is a dream that makes him decide in favour of Judaism. The discussions are not instigated by the King: he only listens to the Christian and the Moslem in order not to offend powerful neighbours. He has no difficulty in accepting Judaism seeing that the two younger faiths are at one in recognizing it (and because there were many respected Jews in his kingdom). In J. H.'s version, on the other hand, the King only learns from the dream that there exists a course of action which is pleasing to God, i.e. an absolute religion; it is only after listening to the representatives of all religions that he attains to the belief that the least popular religion is the true one; thereby he succeeds not only in arousing the human sympathy of the reader but also in shifting the general centre of the interest of the whole story: everything now depends on the content and argument of the ex-positions given by the representatives of the three religions.

Although the presentation of the non-Jewish views is strictly objective, it is, nevertheless, part of the general plan. It is intended to supply an *indirect proof* of the truth of Jewish teaching. Each of the three opposing conceptions contains both points of agreement and of disagreement with Judaism. J. H. attempts to prove that the points of agreement are evident and that the points of disagreement are controversial.

The question that the King sets before the four debaters is briefly this: which are the ways known to you of approach to God, by which we may attain nearness to God in this world and immortality in the world to come?

§ 2. He first questions a philosopher—not about his conception of life (this is critically reviewed in the 5th Book of the Kuzari), but as to whether there is contact with God through the medium of philosophy. The answer is yes and no. No, in so far as God Himself, the Unalterable, the Highest Cause, has no direct contact with the world under the moon—the realm of growth and decay. Yes, in so far as we are influenced by the mediums emanating from God. In the contemplation of this 'world of spirits' (a notion derived from neo-Platonism) we are reminded of the first scene of *Faust*. In particular, the 'Erdgeist' bears a resemblance to the 'active intellect' here mentioned, which is also instrumental in regulating the fluctuations of earthly happenings by giving form to matter. But 'active intellect' has the additional task of passing knowledge of these forms on to man. Hence human intellect is described as 'passive', i.e. 'receptive' in relation to 'active intellect'. But this receptive power is only exerted when man is redeemed from his lower instincts (thus philosophic religion also insists on moral purity) and is able to concentrate on thought. The more he succeeds in doing this, the nearer he approaches to the 'active intellect' until he finally becomes one with it. Through this unification we secure a share in the immortality of the 'active intellect'. Hence devotion to philosophic perception is not merely a scholar's ideal: it is also a means to the attainment of truth, of morality and of immortality. There is no need of any additional dogma or ritual.

The King's verdict on the philosopher's discourse must not be regarded as that of J. H. The praise with which the King begins only applies, according to J. H., to the theory of heritage and environment (*see* our Introduction) and not to the actual philosophical doctrines (Book I, § 13), amongst which the strange theory of emanation is in particular rejected (Book IV, § 25) as being completely unfounded. The King, however, is only concerned with the *religious* content of the discourse. That which appeals to him is best illustrated by the remark he makes later on (Book I, § 8) that reason is opposed to the conception of God being in relation with 'this world' (in Arabic a rather derogatory term is used for this notion) and with humanity. But he cannot lightly make up his mind to declare that the belief of the Churches in absolute religion and in the creation is an illusion; and he cannot see at all why philosophy has failed to produce prophets when its own premises lead us to accept their presence. He therefore turns to the prophetic religions with the object of learning their content and, more especially, the foundation of their doctrines.

§ 4, middle. In the discourses of the Christian and Moslem, the sympathetic and antipathetic is present in inverse proportion to that of the philosopher's discourse. They justify the struggle for supremacy among the religions; in addition, their teaching is of a personal God taking part in our affairs; but they do not satisfy reason; for that which cannot be explained by analogies can only be made plausible by reference to miracles which are unquestionable because they were performed in public. The Moslem refers to such miracles only in connection with the Old Testament foundation of his religion, a foundation he shares with the Christian. Of course, the particular characteristics of Christianity and Islam cannot be established on the basis of these miracles. The King therefore desires to learn about Judaism, which prescribes faith only in such doctrines as are proved by those miracles. 'Empiricism', i.e. the desire to understand historical fact, had prompted him to refrain, at first, from questioning the Jew (§ 4, middle), whose precarious position was apparent evidence against the truth of his religion. But the arguments of the representatives of the other religions (including the philosopher's faith) induce him to hope that he may here find the true religion producing satisfactory evidence of that which is 'beyond reason'.

Though both discourses betray the weak points of the more recent religions, they nevertheless seek to give psychological justification for their propagation. This is found in § 2 (both religions are propagated by means of the sword) and particularly in the remark in the middle of § 5 that one is easily induced to remain true to a faith in which one has been reared. He who favours a simple faith like J. H. (Book V, § 1) is bound to consider such argument very comprehensible. But, of course, it does not prove anything as regards the truth-content of the religions.

§§ 12–17. Note the dramatic trend of the dialogue. The obviously inadequate definition of the Jew not only stimulates logical doubts, but further strengthens the King in his contempt for Judaism. In § 12 he still speaks very condescendingly. The Rabbi answers most politely that the King's criticism rests on an under-estimation of our mode of thought, i.e. generally speaking, we Jews are despised just because what actually constitutes the best part of our teaching is not understood.

§ 15 means: the definition of God is the proof. I believe in God *who* has led us out of Egypt—*because* He has led us out of Egypt.

§ 17 ff. J. H. is not to be interpreted as rejecting evidence of God through Nature and, in particular, through the structure of organisms. But he does not hold this evidence to be as convincing as the evidence of revelation and miracles. Therefore (§ 24) God is primarily to be denoted as the God of revelation and only in the second place as God of the creation.

§ 26 ff. A second surprise! At first the King had cast doubts on the foundations of Judaism—wrongly as he realizes. Now he attempts to refute Judaism by saying that because of its purely historical foundation, it appeals only to Jews and is therefore a separatist religion. The Rabbi attempts to show that the full truth could be revealed only to the chosen few. Hence separatism is an *advantage* of Judaism.

§ 27. J. H.'s doctrine of Israel being the 'pick' of mankind (*see* note to § 95) should not be understood as an extension of the Biblical doctrine of the election of Israel (the Hebrew translation סְגֻלָּה is deceptive). Nowhere does J. H. quote the Biblical passages which deal with the election such as Ex. xix, 5, though the opportunity frequently presents itself, e.g. Book I, § 109. The expression 'pick' rather denotes the religious choice of mankind. In Book I, § 95, the synonym 'heart' is used for a group in contrast to 'shell'. Bahya in his 'Duties of the Heart' often uses the same term with reference to particularly pious men of all nations. But J. H.'s conception is more distinctly racial; this is shown by the line he draws between the white and black races in the immediately preceding context (§ 27), which corresponds exactly to the conception of the philosopher (§ 1). He is of opinion that the gift for religion (unaffected by recessive phenomena) is bestowed on one particular group of mankind (*see* Introduction); in particular it cannot—as the Christian teaches (§ 4)—be transferred by the adoption of a faith (by 'a word': Book IV, § 23).

§ 31 ff. The following remarks of J. H. are fundamental for his conception of nature and religion. In all Nature's 'realms' he sees the working of powers striving towards a definite goal. He denotes these powers by a term that is a literal translation of the comprehensive Greek notion 'Logos', which cannot be absolutely reproduced in any language. In our translation 'force', the characteristic striving towards a goal is insufficiently expressed. The highest of these forces, the 'Divine', is the medium of the highest prophetic grace; as such it is very frequently referred to in the following; the lower forces are sometimes termed 'Divine' only in the broader sense as all issuing from God.

§ 63. J. H.'s instinctive attitude towards the philosophy of Aristotle, and Greek culture in general, is a distinct departure from the rule of nearly all Jewish philosophers. Maimonides, for instance, and the readers for whom he writes, are definitely constrained by the contradictions between Jewish tradition and Aristotle's doctrine, and consider it their duty to give an exact justification of the points of dissension. Jehuda Halevi, however, is not at all disconcerted by such contradictions; how can the Greeks be expected to be in full possession of the truth! His critical attitude, however, is not based on the conviction (natural to us) that no philosophy can be based on authority, but rather on the medieval notion that philosophy, like every other science, is partly based on the fruit of individual intellect and partly on tradition. The opinion that the Greeks inherited their knowledge from the Orientals was common to Jew and Christian alike; it was even borne out—with certain limitations—by individual Greeks themselves; for certain branches of natural science—especially that of astronomy, which was so highly considered in the Middle Ages—it is not lightly to be discarded. It is very characteristic of J. H.'s conception of the 'pick of mankind' that he includes among the chosen in the broader sense the Chaldean astronomers and star worshippers, whom he represents as teachers of the Greeks; he accounts for their superiority by stressing the superiority of their place of residence (as in § 95), i.e. climatically.

§ 67. J. H. does not consider belief in the Creation out of nothing to be fundamental, whereas Saadya bases his whole conception of God on it. What J. H. regards as the essential is God's ministration in this world and especially His power over human fate. Maimonides admits the connection between the belief in creation and the belief in ministration, but does not include the former in his thirteen creeds.

§ 69. The question about the 'creation of the ant' exemplifies the general question: how can we explain the phenomenon of the useful in nature?

The King settles the question in the main by attributing these phenomena to Divine wisdom (§ 68–end). Aristotle, on the other hand, assigns to Nature a force that strives towards a definite goal—not in the passage to which J. H. refers, i.e. Physics II, § 3, end, but in phrases such as 'God and Nature do nothing in vain' (Of Heavens I, 4–end). Arab philosophers, under pantheistic influence, went a step further. J. H. opposes to this recognition of Nature's supremacy two arguments:

(1) that, however learned the distinction between nature and chance may sound, the description of organic processes as 'natural' scarcely explains the wisdom behind the life of organisms . . .

(2) that the recognition of a creative principle besides God (as expressed in the above quoted passage) means religious Dualism; the Arabic has a strong denunciatory term for this; for Islam also is firm in its assertion of the Unity and Peerlessness of God (Book I, § 5, middle).

§ 77, end–§ 79. J. H. submits the following idea. The theoretic recognition that God is active in this lower sphere induces the wish to give practical stimulus to such demonstrations of Divine power. This is at the root of all religions—the true as well as the false. Whereas the devotee of the true religion knows that the way *to* God is only *through* God (i.e. through His revelation), the devotees of the false religion rely on reason. At best they make use of revealed remedies such as sacrifices, days of rest or fasts, but contrary to prescription and, therefore, for the most part without effect (the analogy is to the doctor's assistant!). Still worse is the use of amulets (revealed religion knows nothing of these), or the attempt to evoke the power of the stars in place of God's power through faith in their Divinity. In reality this faith runs counter to the common root of the true and false religions stressed at the end of § 77, i.e. the belief that God alone exerts power over the world. But Jehuda Halevi cannot forgo the rejection of astrological piety (*see* § 97), since it exerted a great influence on all medieval religions; for according to him it is typical of the faith in man's power to approach God through the medium of his own effort.

§§ 80–87. The theme, which is not, of course, accurately formulated by the King, is as follows: Does history establish the pre-eminence of Judaism over other religions which also profess to be based on revelation and miracles?

Affirmation of this question is claimed partly on the assumption that the miracles of Judaism are performed in fuller publicity (*cf.* § 8) and cannot therefore be reckoned as deceit or deception. More significant is the stress on the fact (§ 81) that, according to the evidence of its history, Judaism has developed in a completely different way from Christianity, Islam (and Buddhism), where the sphere of influence was extended from a small inner circle. Recent schools of criticism have pointed out that Jewry is the only community that boasts of a revelation of God to *the whole body of the people;* from this premise, they explain the fact that Judaism, notwithstanding the universalism of its conception of God, knows itself to be bound to the heirs of those who received the revelation. Jehuda Halevi might have accepted this conclusion (*cf.* Book I, § 95); but here he attempts to show that Christianity and Islam originated in the same way as philosophic schools (e.g. the Socratic) and that Judaism, on the other hand, originated suddenly, like the world, being, like the latter, a Divine creation.

§ 85 ff. Here Jehuda Halevi justifies the theory that the Jewish weekly day of rest is the true one because it is distinguished by God Himself. He voices the same thought in Song III (p. 134 f.).

§ 89 beginning. *Cf.* § 67 beginning. The reproach in § 88 has all the more weight from the fact that, according to the philosophic teaching of the time, belief in the corporeality of God is in contradiction to the belief in His Unity, which is the fundament of Jewish-Islamic teaching (everything corporeal being divisible!). Jehuda Halevi therefore stresses the fact that the doctrine of 'Unity', i.e. of the incompatibility of God to all earthly things, is found in the second commandment.

§ 92 ff. Jehuda Halevi in no way feels himself absolutely called upon to appear as an apologist for his people. Quite in line with tradition, he attributes the bad position of the Jewish people to the sins they have committed—conceived by him, indeed, in a very original manner (*see* Book II, § 24). If he seeks to extenuate even the sin of the golden calf, it is because this is the very sin which is often stressed by the Fathers of the Church and by Islam, and to which the loss of the preferential position of Judaism is attributed (Book I, § 4). For this same reason, it is often treated apologetically in the Aggadah. But apparently here again Jehuda Halevi strikes out on his own line. In the first place, he stresses the fact that there is a great difference between the worship of idols and the satisfaction in a forbidden way of the justifiable (Book IV, § 5) need for a perceptible symbol of God's presence; there is a similar difference between Jeroboam and

Ahab (Book IV, § 13 ff.). He then proceeds to explain the sin historically. We no longer admit any cult images, but are easily inclined to
over-estimate the seriousness of the sin committed in a time when the
worship of images was general. Such a historical conception is rare
in medieval Judaism (Maimonides makes use of this method in his
explanation of some of the commandments): but it is exceptionally
well suited to Jehuda Halevi's explanation of religions through
heredity and milieu! In this way Jehuda Halevi is able to show that
the sin of the golden calf rests on that fundamental error which he is
constantly challenging (§ 77, end): the belief that man can find the
way to God by the strength of his own reasoning, not needing
revelation; in the case of the golden calf this belief is said to have
been represented by 'astrologers and soothsayers', i.e. probably by
non-Jews (according to the Midrash Lev. R. 27, 8). Jehuda Halevi's
treatment of the question has therefore not only the apologetic force
that comes out clearly in § 97, end, but also a definite systematic
significance; the latter is clearly emphasized in the King's summary
(§ 98).

A very remarkable interpretation of history is here introduced
(§ 95). It proceeds from primitive man in the same way as the
Christian historical conception. But whereas the latter in general
lays exclusive emphasis on the sin of Adam, Jehuda Halevi lays an
equally exclusive emphasis on the pre-eminence of man created in
the likeness of God, calling Adam the son of God with reference to
Gen. vi, 2, where, according to a widespread theory, the 'sons of
God' who came to the 'daughters of man' are held to be the genuine
heirs of Adam's pre-eminence (cf. Hosea ii, 1, 'Sons of the living
God'). Thus Adam already belongs to the religious supermen mentioned in § 41. Yet his religious competence was not transferred to
all his descendants, but was inherited only by one man in each
generation like the 'true ring' in Lessing's fable (which is perhaps
based on a Jewish model). In particular the inheritor in the line of
Abraham is not Ishmael, as Islam naturally asserts, but only Isaac.
That is why Ishmael is driven out—that he may not inherit together
with Isaac (Gen. xxi, 10), i.e. the land of prophecy, Palestine!
This is also why Abraham sent away the sons of Ketura from his
son Isaac (Gen. xxv, 6) and why Esau leaves Palestine with
God's approval (Josh. xxiv, 4). On the other hand, Jacob's
sons, many relapses notwithstanding, were worthy of Palestine;
in this sense they constitute the pick of mankind (cf. § 27

commentary). Arguing thus, the present state of Israel and its future hope become clear. Our present remoteness from the Holy Land hinders us from displaying our prophetic gift in its full glory; if once this hindrance is removed, the ancient times will live again; thus the essence of history and the goal of religion is not the redemption from original sin, but the reattainment of original perfection.

§ 98 is the expression in a pun of a fundamental thought of the book: One can only attain to the effect of Divine power, to which reference is often made in §§ 95 and 97, and, accordingly, to the preeminence of the 'picked' (§§ 27 and 41) through the commandments. In Arabic the same word stands for 'order' and 'ordinance'.

Let us cast a retrospective glance at the first book, the important passages of which are included almost intact in our selection. It obviously falls into two unequal sections: the opening dialogue brings indirect proof of the truth of Judaism, both through the indication of flaws in the other three religions and through the establishment of the fact that the other Biblical religions are able to bring evidence of unequivocal miracles only from the history of Israel. The second part is a direct justification of the doctrines of Judaism. But this part seems, at first sight, to be lacking in plan. The course of the conversation seems not to be set by the Rabbi, who represents the author, but by the King and on the inspiration of the moment. This accounts for the natural, unforced character of the dialogue; as in Plato's dialogue there is nothing pedantic, which would have offended the artistic nature of the author. And yet these questions and their sequence are actually governed, of course, by the author's plan. This is shown by the fact that he puts the conversion of the King not at the end of the conversation or at least at the end of the theologic discussion, i.e. after Book IV (Book V is almost purely philosophical in character), but at the beginning of Book II. That is to say that Book I is intended to present *a general description of Judaism as a whole;* Books II–IV serve as a completion of the argument and Book V as a defence: In other words, Jehuda Halevi's presentation of Judaism is not purely systematic as is Saadya's or H. Cohen's, but is in *concentric circles,* and risks a certain amount of repetition. He may have been influenced in this by consideration for such readers as are not prepared or not able to read the whole book (the plan of Maimonides' 'More Nebukhim' was affected by a like consideration). But even the argument of the Rabbi in Book I is in concentric form. First the main thought is presented: religion, in the full sense of the word, can only be traced from the history of revelation to the pick of mankind (§§ 11–43). This thought is elucidated by the clear exposition of the relation to Greek philosophy and to the sister religions. In this way the outcome of the preliminary dialogue (§ 1 ff.) attains a definite profundity. It now appears that philosophy in no way deserves the confidence the layman (§ 2) places in it; on the contrary, its doctrine of the everlastingness of the world rests on a weak foundation, and its conception of nature is a mere bluff (§§ 62–77); indeed, these flaws are not surprising, seeing that the Greeks were not bearers of the true tradition and this could not be made good for all their perspicuity. On the other hand, it appears that Judaism remains fundamentally separated from the sister religions by virtue of the history of its origin (§ 81) and that, as the King had already noted, the common good of the three Biblical religions—the belief in the revelation to Moses and in the Torah (*cf.* § 4, middle–§ 5, middle)— is true and can be defended against the attacks of the philosophers (§ 88 ff.); but that the statement that Israel, possibly through the sin of the golden calf, had forfeited its right of pre-eminence cannot be maintained (§ 92 ff.); in a passage not included here, Jehuda Halevi adds, incidentally, that our sufferings are not evidence against us, seeing that other religions even boast of their sufferings (§ 113).

This presentation is interrupted here and there by digressions such as occur also in Plato; for in ancient and medieval times a text used to include points that we would nowadays add in notes or in 'learned appendices'. But one cannot mistake Jehuda Halevi's intention of creating a foundation on which the elucidation of important notions can be superimposed in the following books.

BOOK II

THE UNITY OF GOD

1. AFTER this the Khazari and his Vizier travelled to the deserted mountains on the seashore, and arrived one night at the cave in which some Jews used to celebrate the Sabbath. They disclosed their identity to them, embraced their religion, were circumcised in the cave and then returned to their country. The king, studying the Torah and the books of the prophets, employed the Rabbi as his teacher, and put many questions to him concerning Hebrew expressions. The first of these questions referred to the names and attributes ascribed to God and their seeming anthropomorphism, which is opposed to reason and to the unmistakable doctrine of the Law.

2. THE RABBI: All the names of God, save the Tetragrammaton, are predicates and relative attributes, derived from the way His creatures are affected by His decrees and measures. He is called merciful, for the improvement in the condition of any man whom people pity for his sorry plight; hence, they attribute to Him mercy and compassion, although these attributes, in us, testify in truth to a weakness of the soul and irritability of nature. This cannot be applied to God. He is a just judge; He ordains the poverty of one individual and the wealth of another; without any change in His nature, without feelings of sympathy with one or anger against another. We see similar impartiality in human judges; they decide the questions put to them according to the law, making some people happy, and others miserable. He (God) appears to us according to His doings, sometimes a 'merciful and compassionate God' (Ex. xxxiv, 6), sometimes 'a jealous and revengeful God' (Nahum i, 2), whereas He never changes from one attribute to the other.

All attributes—except the Tetragrammaton—are divided into three classes, viz. active, relative and negative. The active attributes are derived from acts emanating from Him through natural intermediaries, e.g. 'making poor or rich, exalting or

casting down, merciful and compassionate, jealous and revengeful, strong, almighty (Shaddai)' and the like. Relative attributes
are, for example, 'blessed, praised, glorified, holy, exalted, and
extolled'; they are taken from the reverence paid to Him by
mankind; however numerous these may be, they produce no
plurality in God, and do not affect his unity. Negative attributes are, for example, 'living, only, first and last'. They are
given to Him in order to negate their contrasts, but not to
establish them in the sense familiar to us. For we cannot understand life unaccompanied by sensibility and movement; God,
however, is above these; we describe Him as living in order to
negate the attributes of rigidity (minerals) and deadness (bodies),
in accordance with the prejudice that all which does not live is
dead—a prejudice rejected by reason. One cannot, for example,
speak of time as being endowed with life; yet it does not follow
that time is dead, since its nature has nothing to do with either
life or death. Life and death are, therefore, only applicable to
material bodies, whereas the Divine essence is transcendent. On
the other hand: if one says 'life, but not like ours', it coincides
with our opinion. In the same way we take the term 'One',
viz. to controvert plurality, not to establish unity as we understand it; for we call a thing 'one', when the component parts
are coherent and of the same materials, e.g. one bone, one
sinew, one water, one air; in a similar way we speak of time, in
comparison with a compact body (saying) 'one day, one year';
the Divine essence is not subject to complexity or divisibility,
and 'one' only stands as the negation of plurality. In the same
way (we style Him) 'First' in order to exclude the notion of
later origin, but not to assert that He has a beginning; thus also
'Last' stands to negate the idea of finality, but not to fix a term
for Him. None of these attributes touch on the Divine essence,
nor do they imply multiplicity in connection with it.

   The attributes connected with the Tetragrammaton describe
creations of God, produced without any natural intermediaries,
as e.g. Creator, Producer, Maker, 'who *alone* doeth great
wonders' (Ps. cxxxvi, 4), i.e. by His bare intention and will, to
the exclusion of any assisting cause. This is perhaps meant in the

passage (Ex. vi, 3) 'I appeared to Abraham . . . as El Shaddai (באל שדי)' viz. in the way of power and victory, as is said 'He suffered no man to do them wrong, and He reproved kings for their sake' (Ps. cv, 14); but He performed no miracles for them as He did for Moses, saying (Ex. l.c.) 'but by my name (ושמי) YHVH was I not known to them', meaning ובשמי (instead of ושמי), since the ב in באל שדי refers to the following (also). But for Moses and the Israelites he performed wonders, which left no manner of doubt in their souls that the Creator of the world created them according to His purpose, as the plagues of Egypt, the dividing of the Red Sea, the Manna, the pillar of cloud and the like. The reason of this difference was not because they were higher than Abraham, Isaac, and Jacob, but because they were a multitude, and had nourished doubt in their souls, whereas the Patriarchs had the utmost faith and innocence of mind, so that their faith in God would not have suffered, had they been pursued by misfortune all their lives. Therefore, they wanted no signs.

We also call (God) 'wise of heart' (Job ix, 4), because He is the essence of intelligence and intelligence itself; but (intelligence) is no attribute. As to 'almighty' (l.c.), it belongs to the active attributes.

3. THE KHAZARI: But how do you explain those attributes which are of a yet more corporeal nature, viz. seeing, hearing, speaking, writing the tablets, descending on Mount Sinai, rejoicing in His works, grieving in His heart?

4. THE RABBI: Did I not compare Him with a just judge in whose qualities no change exists? If by His decrees people attain prosperity and good fortune, they say that He loves them and takes pleasure in them; if He decrees against others destruction of their houses or extirpation, they say on the contrary that He is filled with hate and wrath. Because nothing that is done or spoken escapes Him, He is called seeing and hearing; because the air and all bodies are under the order of His will and assume shape by His command, as did heaven and earth, He is described as 'speaking and writing'. Likewise from the fine and spiritual

substance, which is called 'holy spirit', arose the spiritual forms called 'glory of God' (כבוד ה'); metaphorically, it is called YHVH, who 'descended' (Ex. xix, 20) on Mount Sinai.

7. THE KHAZARI: The secret of the attributes is now clear, and I understand the meaning of 'The glory of God, Angels of God and Shekinah'. These names are supplied to visionary objects seen by the prophets, for example 'Pillar of Cloud, Consuming Fire, Cloud, Mist, Fire, Splendour'. In a similar way we say of light in the morning, in the evening, and on cloudy days that the rays of light go forth from the sun, although the latter is not visible, and we say that the rays of light belong to the sun itself, although in reality this is not so: it is the terrestrial bodies which, being opposite to it, are affected by it, and reflect its light.

8. THE RABBI: Also the glory (כבוד) of God is only a ray of Divine light, which has a salutary effect on His people and on His country.

THE PRE-EMINENCE OF THE COUNTRY

9. THE KHAZARI: What thou meanest by 'His people' is now intelligible to me, but thy word 'His country' is difficult for me to appreciate.

10. THE RABBI: But no difficulty is attached to (the assumption) that one country may have higher qualities than others. Obviously there are places in which particular plants, metals, or animals thrive well, or where the inhabitants are distinguished by their form and character—through the mingling of humours resulting in the perfection or imperfection of the soul.

11. THE KHAZARI: Yet I have not heard that the inhabitants of Palestine are better than other people.

12. THE RABBI: It is the same case as with your hill on which you say the vines thrive so well. If they had not planted vine branches on it and cultivated them well, it would never have

produced grapes. So precedence belongs to those particular people who, as stated before, represent the 'pick' and the 'heart' (of mankind); the land has also its part in this and so have the religious acts connected with it, which I would compare to the cultivation of the vineyard. But no other place could share with this pre-eminent people the influence of the Divine power, whereas other hills are also able to produce good wine.

13. THE KHAZARI: How can this be? Were there not prophets in other places, between Adam and Moses, as Abraham in Ur-Kasdim, and Ezekiel and Daniel in Babylon, and Jeremiah in Egypt?

14. THE RABBI: Whosoever prophesied, did so either in Palestine or for its sake, viz. Abraham to reach it, Ezekiel and Daniel on account of it, to prepare the return. The two latter, moreover, lived during the time of the first temple and under the influence of the apparition of the Shekinah, through which any member of the 'picked' people who was duly prepared became able to prophesy. But Adam had there his native place, and died there, according to tradition: 'in the cave of Makpelah were buried the four pairs: Adam and Eve, Abraham and Sarah, Isaac and Rebeccah, Jacob and Leah' (Gen. Rabba lviii, 4). This is the land which bore the name 'before the Lord' and of which it is said 'the eyes of the Lord thy God are always upon it' (Deut. xi, 12). It was also the first object of jealousy and envy between Cain and Abel: they desired to know which of them would be Adam's successor, his 'picked one' and his 'heart' to inherit the Land, and to stand in communion with the Divine power, whilst the other would be merely the 'shell'. Then Abel was killed by Cain, and the realm was without an heir. Cain 'went out of the presence of the Lord' (Gen. iv, 16), which means that he left the land; (for) he says: 'Thou hast driven me out this day from the land, and from thy face shall I be hid (iv, 14); in the same way it is said: 'Jonah rose up to flee unto Tarshish from the presence of the Lord' (Jonah i, 3); he only fled, indeed, from the place of prophecy; God, however, brought him back there out of

the belly of the fish and there He appointed him prophet. When Seth was born, who was like Adam—for 'be begat in his own likeness, after his image' (Gen. v, 3)—he took Abel's place; for Adam says 'God has appointed me another seed, instead of Abel, whom Cain slew' (iv, 25). He merited to be called 'son of God', like Adam, and to live in that land, which is the next step to paradise. The land was then the object of jealousy between Isaac and Ishmael, till the latter was rejected as the 'shell'; the words 'I have blessed him and I will multiply him exceedingly' (Gen. xvii, 20) refer to worldly prosperity; but the following words 'my covenant will I establish with Isaac' refer to the emanation of the Divine power and happiness in the world to come; with Ishmael and Esau there was no covenant, in spite of their prosperity. About this land there arose also the jealousy between Jacob and Esau for the birthright and the blessing, till Esau was rejected, despite his strength, in favour of Jacob, despite his weakness. Jeremiah's prophecy in Egypt was inspired by Palestine and was made for its sake. This was also the case with Moses, Aaron and Miriam. Sinai and Paran are reckoned as belonging to Palestine as they are on this side of the Red Sea, as it is said: 'I will set your bounds from the Red Sea, even unto the sea of the Philistines, and from the desert unto the River' (Ex. xxiii, 31). There were the altars of the Patriarchs, who were answered by fire from heaven and the Divine light. The 'binding' of Isaac took place on a desolate mountain, viz. Moriah; in the days of David, when it was inhabited, the secret was revealed that it was the place specially fit and suitable for the Shekinah; Arauna the Jebusite tilled it at that time. Thus it is said: 'And Abraham called the name of the place the Lord sees—about which will one day be said: 'In the mount the Lord shall be seen' (Gen. xxii, 14). In the book of Chronicles (2, iii, 1) it is stated clearly that the Temple was built on Mount Moriah. There (in Palestine) are, without doubt, the places worthy of being called the gates of heaven. Dost thou not see that Jacob ascribed the vision which he saw, not to the purity of his soul, nor to his belief, nor to his integrity, but to the place, as it is said: 'He was afraid and said: How awful is this place' (Gen. xxviii, 17): prior to this it is said: 'He lighted upon the place' (xxviii, 11), viz. the distinguished place. Abraham, the 'heart' of the 'picked' people, when he came to maturity and was ready to accept the influence of the Divine power—was he not removed from his country to a place where his perfection could mature, as the agriculturist who finds the root of a good tree in a desert place transplants it into properly tilled ground, in order that the wild root may be transformed into a cultivated one, producing much in the place of little? Having been found in an accidental moment at an accidental place, it produces a luxuriant crop. It was the same with the gift of prophecy among Abraham's descendants in Palestine: it was an asset of many as long as they remained in the land and observed the necessary conditions, viz. purity, worship, and sacrifices, and, above all, the influence of the Shekinah. For the Divine power, one might say, is attendant on the man who appears worthy of the favour, waiting to be attached to him and to be his God, as in the case of the prophets and the pious man; thus Reason is attendant on those whose natural gifts are perfect and whose soul and character are so harmonious that it can find its perfect dwelling among them, viz. philosophers; thus, likewise, the Soul is attendant on a being whose natural powers are perfected to such a degree that a higher power is able to dwell within it, viz. animals; so also Nature (organic power) is attendant on a harmonious mingling of qualities in order to dwell therein, and to form the plant.

15. THE KHAZARI: These are the general rules of a complete science which must be specified. Continue thy discourse about the advantages of Eretz Israel.

16. THE RABBI: The land was appointed for the instruction of mankind and apportioned to the tribes of Israel from the time of the confusion of tongues, as it is said: 'When the Most High divided among the nations their inheritance, when He separated the sons of Man, He set up the frontiers of the

nations according to the number of the sons of Israel' (Deut. xxxii, 8). Abraham, also, was not fit to be associated with the Divine power and to enter into a covenant with Him—the covenant 'of the pieces of sacrifice' (Gen. xv)—until he had reached that land. And what is now thy opinion of a 'picked community' which has merited the appellation 'people of God', in a land, called 'the inheritance of God' (1 Sam. xxvi, 19; Ps. lxxix, 1), and of seasons fixed by Him, not agreed upon or settled by astronomical calculations, and therefore styled: 'feasts of the Lord', of the observance of rules regarding purity and worship, prayers and performances fixed by God and therefore called 'work of the Lord' and 'services of the Lord'?

17. THE KHAZARI: In such a way we may expect the glory of God to be manifest.

20. THE RABBI: Thus the knowledge of the 'sabbath of the Lord' and the 'festivals of the Lord' (Lev. xxiii, 38 and 2) depends upon the country which is called 'the inheritance of the Lord', and, as thou didst read, 'His holy mountain', 'His footstool', 'gate of Heaven' (Gen. xxviii, 7); it is also said 'for the Torah goes out from Zion' (Micah iv, 2). How greatly did the Patriarchs strive to live in the country, whilst it was in the hands of pagans, how they yearned for it and ordered their bones to be carried thither as, for example, Jacob and Joseph (Gen. xlvii, 30; l, 25). Moses prayed to see it; he considered it a misfortune when this was denied him, and as an act of grace, when the land was shown to him from the summit of Pisgah. Persians, Indians, Greeks, and other nations begged to have sacrifices offered and prayers to be said for them in that Holy House, and they spent their wealth on it, though they believed in other religions, since the true religion did not admit them. Today, also, the country is honoured, although the Shekinah no longer appears in it; all nations make pilgrimages to it, long for it—excepting we ourselves, being oppressed and homeless.

23. THE KHAZARI: If this be so, thou fallest short of thy religious duty, by not endeavouring to reach that place, and

making it thy abode in life and death, although thou sayest: 'Have mercy on Zion, for it is the house of our life', and thou believest that the Shekinah will return thither. And had it no other distinction than that the Shekinah dwelt there nine hundred years, this would be sufficient reason for the souls to trust in it and to purify themselves there, as it has been done near the abodes of the pious and the prophets; moreover, it is the gate of Heaven; all nations agree on this point: Christians believe that the souls are gathered there and then lifted up to heaven; Islam teaches that it is the place of Mahomet's Ascension and that prophets are made to ascend from there to heaven, and further, that it is the place of gathering on the day of Resurrection. Everybody turns to it in prayer and visits it in pilgrimage. Thus, thy bowing and kneeling in the direction of it is either hypocrisy or thoughtless practice. Yet thy earliest forefathers chose it as an abode in preference to their birthplaces, and lived there as strangers rather than as citizens in their own country.

24. THE RABBI: That is a justified reproach, O King of the Khazars! It was that sin which kept the Divine promise with regard to the second Temple from being fulfilled: 'Sing and rejoice, O daughter of Zion; for I come to dwell in the midst of thee' (Zechariah ii, 14). For the Divine power was ready to prevail in Zion as it had in the first place, if they had all willingly consented to return. But only a part of the people were prepared to do so; the majority and the men of rank remained in Babylon, preferring dependence and slavery, because they were unwilling to leave their houses and their easy circumstances. The power of the promises was weakened in accordance with their weakness. For the Divine power inspires human power only in such measure as the latter is prepared to receive it: if the readiness is little, little will be obtained, and much will be obtained, if it be great. Were we prepared to meet the God of our forefathers with a pure mind, we should find the same salvation as our fathers did in Egypt. But when we only say: 'Bow to His holy hill, bow to His

footstool' (Ps. xcix, 9, 5), 'He who restoreth His glory to
Zion', and similar words, this is but as the chattering of the
starling and the nightingale. We do not realize what we are
saying through these and other words, as thou observest, O
Prince of the Khazars!

SACRIFICES AND TEMPLE

25. THE KHAZARI: Enough on this subject! Now I should
like thee to make plausible to me what I have read about the
sacrifices; for reason cannot accept such expressions as 'My
offering, My bread for My sacrifices made by My fire, a
sweet savour unto Me' (Num. xxviii, 2); here is said that
the sacrifices are God's offering, His bread, and His savour!

26. THE RABBI: The expression 'My fires' removes all
difficulty. It states that offering, bread and sweet savour,
ascribed to 'Me', only belong to 'My fires', i.e. to the fire
which was influenced by His power and fed by the offerings,
the remaining pieces of which were used as food for the
priests. The purpose of these commandments was to create
a workable system, in order that the King could 'sit enthroned'
there, in the sense of distinction of the place, not in a local
sense. Compare the Divine power with the reasoning soul,
which enters the body governed by organic and animal
powers. If its organic faculties are harmonized and the relation
between higher and lower powers is regulated for the reception
of a higher condition than the animal, then it is ripe for the
entrance of King Reason, who will guide and direct it and
remain with it, as long as harmony is undisturbed, but departs
from it, as soon as this harmony is impaired by disease. A fool
may imagine, therefore, that Reason requires food, drink
and scents, because he sees it subsisting as long as these things
subsist, and removed when they are removed; but this is not
the case; and similarly with the Divine power. It is beneficent,
desirous of doing good to all. Wheresoever a being is found
well prepared to receive its guidance, it does not refuse it nor
hesitate to shed over him light, wisdom and inspiration. If,

however, the order is disturbed, this light cannot be perceived and is then lost, although the Divine power itself is exempt from all exhaustion or damage. Hence: if the whole order of sacrificial service, its proceedings, offerings, burning of incense, singing, eating, drinking, is to be performed in the utmost purity and holiness, and if, therefore, terms such as 'service of God, bread of God' are applied to it, all this expresses only His pleasure in the beautiful harmony prevailing among the people and its priests, and His readiness to accept—so to say—their hospitality and to dwell among them in order to distinguish them; He, however, is too holy and too exalted to find pleasure in their meat and drink. . . . The fire was created by the will of God, when the people found favour in His sight, being a sign that He accepted their hospitality and their offerings. For fire is the finest and noblest element beneath the sphere of the moon. Its seat is the fat and vapour of the sacrifices, the smoke of the incense and oil, since it is in the nature of fire to cling to fat and oil, as natural heat clings to the finest fatty globules of the blood. God commanded therefore the (construction of the) altar of burnt offerings, the altar of incense, and the candlestick, with their holocausts, incense, and the lamp oil. The altar of burnt offerings was destined to bear the visible fire, the golden altar (to bear) the invisible and finer fire, the candlestick to bear the light of wisdom and inspiration, the table to bear the gift of abundance and material provisions. All these implements stood in the service of the Holy Ark and the Cherubim, who protect it, as the lungs protect the heart. For all of them, auxiliary implements were necessary, as the wash-basin and its foot, tongs, firepans, etc. To guard the implements a house was required, viz. the Tabernacle, tent and cover—and to guard the whole, the court of the Tabernacle with its appurtenances. All this is graduated and arranged by the wisdom of God. I do not—God forbid—assert that the intention of that service was exactly as here expounded; indeed it is more obscure and loftier. It is commanded by God; and he who accepts it with all his heart, without scrutiny or scruple, is superior to the man who scrutinizes and investigates. He, however, who descends from this highest grade to scrutinizing, does well to seek a wise reason for these commandments, instead of casting misconstructions and doubts upon them, leading to corruption.

27. THE KHAZARI: Rabbi, thy comparison is excellent; but I have not heard thy comparison for the head and the senses, nor for the consecrated oil.

28. THE RABBI: Quite so. The root of all knowledge was deposited in the Ark, which took the place of the heart, viz. the Ten Commandments; their 'branches', viz. the Torah, at its side, as it is said: 'Put (the book of the Torah) at the side of the Ark of the covenant' (Deut. xxxi, 26). From here there branched out a twofold knowledge: first, scriptural knowledge, whose bearers were the priests; secondly, prophetic knowledge, whose bearers were the prophets. Both were, so to speak, the people's councillors, seers and admonishers, its secretaries and chroniclers; they, therefore, were the head of the people.

ISRAEL AMONG THE NATIONS

29. THE KHAZARI: So you are today a body without either head or heart?

30. THE RABBI: So it is. Or rather: we are not even a body, only scattered limbs, like the dry bones Ezekiel (ch. xxxvii) saw. However, O King of the Khazars, these bones, which have retained a trace of vital power and have once been the seat of a heart, head, spirit, soul, and intellect, are better than bodies formed of marble and plaster, endowed with heads, eyes, ears, and all limbs, in which there never dwelt the spirit of life, nor can it dwell therein, since they are but imitations of men, not men in reality.

31. THE KHAZARI: It is as thou sayest.

32. THE RABBI: The dead religious communities, which desired to be equal to the living one, achieved nothing more

than an external resemblance. They built houses to God, but no trace of His (presence) was visible therein. They lived as hermits and ascetics in order to derive inspiration, but they did not derive it. They deteriorated, became disobedient, and wicked; yet no fire fell down from heaven upon them, nor swift pestilence, to be distinguished as God's punishment for their disobedience. If their heart—I mean their temple—was destroyed, their status has not changed; it changed only in proportion to their greatness or smallness, strength or weakness, disunion or unity, according to natural or accidental causes. We, however, since our heart, the Holy House, was destroyed, were also lost; if it be restored, we, too, will be restored, be we few or many, and whatever be our status. For our leader is the living God; He is our King, who keeps us in our present status of dispersion and exile.

33. THE KHAZARI: Certainly. Such a dispersion of a people is inconceivable without the same people being absorbed by another, especially after so long a period. How many nations which lived after your (ruin) have perished without leaving a trace, as Edom, Moab, Ammon, Aram, the Philistines, Chaldeans, Medians, Persians, Greeks, Brahmans, Sabaeans and many others!

34. THE RABBI: Do not believe that I, though agreeing with thy (former) words, admit that we are like the dead. We still hold connection with that Divine power through the laws He has placed as a link between us and Him, e.g. circumcision, of which is said 'My covenant shall be in your flesh for an everlasting covenant' (Gen. xvii, 13), and the Sabbath, which is called 'a sign between Me and you throughout your generations' (Ex. xxxi, 13). Besides this there is the covenant with the fathers and the covenant of the Torah, first granted on Horeb and then in the plains of Moab, in connection with promises and warnings (Deut. iv, 25 ff.) and His words: 'If any of thine be driven out into the utmost parts of heaven, thence will God gather and fetch thy people' (xxx, 4); and 'thou shalt return unto the Lord thy God' (xxx, 2)

and the song 'Give ear, O heavens' (xxxii), and other places. We resemble, therefore, not the dead, but rather a person sick unto death, who has been given up by the physicians, and yet hopes for recovery through miracles or extraordinary events, as it is said: 'Will these bones live' (Ezek. xxxvii, 3), and in the parable (Jes. lii, 13 ff.): 'He is ugly and homely, like one from whom men hide their faces' (liii, 2, 3), which means that, on account of his deformity and repulsive visage, he resembles an unclean thing, which man only beholds with disgust, and rejects; 'despised and rejected of men, a man of pain, acquainted with disease' (liii, 3).

35. THE KHAZARI: How can this serve as a comparison for Israel, as it is said (liii, 4): 'Surely he has borne our diseases'? That which has befallen Israel, befell it on account of its sins only!

36. THE RABBI: Israel amidst the nations is like the heart amidst the organs: it is the most sick and the most healthy of them all.

37. THE KHAZARI: Make this clearer.

38. THE RABBI: The heart is visited without interruption by all sorts of diseases, as sadness, anxiety, envy, wrath, enmity, love, hate, and fear. Its constitution changes continually according to the vigour and weakness of respiration, inappropriate meat and drink, movement, exertion, sleep or wakefulness. These all affect the heart, whilst the limbs rest uninjured.

39. THE KHAZARI: I understand how far it is the sickest of all organs. But in which sense is it the healthiest of them all?

40. THE RABBI: Is it possible that in the heart there should settle a humour producing an inflammation, a cancer, a wart, etc., as is possible in other organs?

41. THE KHAZARI: Impossible. For the smallest trace of these would bring on death. On account of its extreme sensibility, caused by the purity of its blood and its abundance of animal spirit, it feels the slightest symptom and expels it as long as it is able to do so. The other organs lack this fine

sensibility, and it is, therefore, possible for humours to settle in them which produce diseases.

42. THE RABBI: Thus its sensibility and feeling expose it to many diseases, but they are also the cause of the expulsion of the same at the very beginning, before they have taken root.

43. THE KHAZARI: Quite so.

44. THE RABBI: The relation of the Divine power to us is the same as that of the soul to the heart. For this reason it is said: 'You only have I known among all the families of the earth, therefore I will punish you for all your iniquities' (Amos iii, 2). He does not allow our sins to accumulate—and to destroy us completely by their multitude, as He did in the case of the Amorites, of whom it is said: 'The iniquity of the Amorites is not yet full' (Gen. xv, 16); God left them alone, till the ailment of their sins became rooted and deadly. And just as the heart is pure in substance and matter, and of even temperament, in order to be accessible to the intellectual soul, so is Israel in its substance and matter; but in the same way as the heart may be affected by diseases from the other organs, viz. the lusts of the liver, stomach and genitals, by reason of their bad temperament, thus also diseases befell Israel in consequence of its assimilation to the Gentiles, as it is said: 'They were mingled among the heathens and learned their works' (Ps. cvi, 35). It cannot seem strange, therefore, that it is said: 'Surely, he has borne our disease and carried our griefs' (Jes. liii, 4). Now we are oppressed, whilst the whole world enjoys rest and prosperity. But the trials which meet us serve to purify our piety, to cleanse us and to remove all taint from us.

RELIGIOUS DUTIES

45. THE KHAZARI: But I should expect to see more hermits and ascetics among you than among other people.

46. THE RABBI: I regret that thou hast forgotten those fundamental principles which I explained to thee and to which thou didst agree. Did we not concur that men cannot

approach God except by means of deeds commanded by Him? Dost thou think that this 'approaching' is meekness, humility, and nothing else?

47. THE KHAZARI: Certainly, and rightly so. I think so, and I read in your books: 'What doth the Lord thy God require from thee, but to fear the Lord thy God' (Deut. x, 12), 'What doth the Lord thy God require of thee (but to do justice, to love charity and to wander in meekness before thy God') (Micah vi, 8) and many similar passages.

48. THE RABBI: These are the rational laws, being the basis and preamble of the Divine law, preceding it in character and time. They are indispensable in the administration of every human society: even a gang of robbers must have a kind of justice among them; otherwise their confederacy cannot last. When the disloyalty of the Israelites had come to such a pass that they disregarded the rational and social principles— which are as absolutely necessary for society as are the natural functions of eating, drinking, etc., for the individual—but held fast to sacrificial worship and other Divine ritual laws, God was satisfied with even less, and it was told to them: 'Would you had observed those laws which are appreciated by the smallest and meanest community, laws which refer to justice, virtue and recognition of God's bounty'. For the Divine law cannot become complete till the social and rational laws are perfected; and rational law demands justice and recognition of God's bounty; and what has he who fails in this respect to do with offerings, Sabbath, circumcision, etc., which reason neither demands nor forbids, ordinations especially given to Israel as a corollary to the rational laws, through which it received the privilege of the Divine power, without knowing why they are necessary; in the same way they did not know how it came to pass that the 'Glory of God' descended upon them, and that the 'fire of God' consumed their offerings, how they could hear the voice of the Lord and how events came to pass which reason would refuse to believe if they were not guaranteed by irrefutable evidence.

Therefore it was said to them: 'What doth the Lord require of thee?' (Micah vi, 8), 'Add your burnt offerings to your peace-offerings' (Jer. vii, 21), and similar verses. Can it be conceived that an Israelite should observe 'the doing of justice and the love of charity' only and neglect circumcision, the Sabbath and the other laws—and yet turn out well?

49. THE KHAZARI: No—after all that thou hast argued. In the opinion of the philosophers, he only becomes a pious man who does not mind in which way he approaches God, whether through Judaism or Christianity, etc., or in a way he himself contrives. Thus we return to reasoning, analogies, speculating and dialectics, where every one may endeavour to invent a religion according to his own speculation—which would be absurd.

50. THE RABBI: The Divine law imposes no asceticism on us. It rather desires that we should keep the balance and grant every mental and physical faculty its due, without over-burdening one faculty at the expense of another: if a person gives preponderance to desires, he blunts his mental faculty, and vice-versa; and he who gives preponderance to violence, blunts other faculties. Long fasting, therefore, is no form of worship for a person whose desires are checked and whose body is weak; for him feasting is a religious duty and victory over self. Neither is a diminution in income an act of worship, if the earning is lawful and easy, and does not interfere with study and good works, especially for the man who has a household and children, and endeavours to spend part of his earnings in aims agreeable to God; then it is even more suitable to increase earnings. Our law, as a whole, is divided between fear, love and joy; through each of them thou mayst approach thy God. Thy contrition on a fast day does no more to bring thee nearer to God than thy joy on the Sabbath and holy days, if the latter is the outcome of devotion. For just as penitential prayers demand attention and devotion, so also pleasure in God's command and law demands attention and devotion; thou shalt delight in the law itself

through love towards the Law-giver and consciousness of how He has distinguished thee; feel as if thou hadst been His guest, invited to His festive board, and thank Him in mind and word, and if thy joy induces thee to sing and dance, thy song and thy dance become worship and a bond of union between thee and the Divine power. Our law did not leave all these things to chance, but laid down decisive injunctions concerning them; since it is not in the power of man to apportion to each faculty of the soul and body its right measure, nor to decide what amount of rest and exertion is good, or to determine how much crop the soil must produce, in order that it may rest unploughed in the years of release and jubilee, and that the tithe, etc., may be taken from it; He ordained, therefore, the repose of Sabbath and holidays, and the repose of the soil. All this is also 'remembrance of the exodus from Egypt' and 'remembrance of the work of creation'; these two (events) belong together, because they are the outcome of the absolute Divine will, not of accident and natural phenomena, as it is said: 'Ask of the days past, since the day that God created man upon the earth, whether there hath been any such thing as this great thing is, or hath been heard like it? Did ever a people hear the voice of God speaking out of the midst of the fire, as thou hast heard, and live? Or hath God assayed to go and take Him a nation from the midst of another nation, according to all that the Lord your God did for you in Egypt before your eyes?' (Deut. iv, 32 ff.). The observance of the Sabbath is, therefore, an acknowledgement of His omnipotence, an acknowledgement, however, through the medium of deeds; for he who observes the Sabbath because the work of creation was finished on it, acknowledges, no doubt, the creation itself; and he who acknowledges the creation, acknowledges the Creator and Originator; he, however, who does not believe in it, tends to the belief in the eternity of the world, and his conviction concerning the Creator is not undisturbed. The observance of the Sabbath brings us, therefore, nearer to God than worshipping, asceticism and retirement.

Behold now, how the Divine power—which attached itself to Abraham and afterwards to his whole 'picked' progeny and the Holy Land—followed the people step by step and guarded its prosperity, preventing all decrease of it; placed them in the most sheltered and fertile place (Goshen) and caused them to multiply in a miraculous manner, till it transposed them and planted them in a soil suited to the picked people. He is, therefore, called God of Abraham and of the land (Gen. xxviii, 13) as He is called 'dwelling between the Cherubim' (1 Sam. iv, 4), 'dwelling in Zion' (Ps. ix, 12), 'abiding in Jerusalem' (cxxxv, 21), these places being compared to heaven, as it is said 'dwelling in heaven' (cxxiii, 1), since His light shines in these places as in heaven, although through the medium of a people fit to receive this light, and on whom He shed it. This shedding is called 'God's love'; it has been taught us, and we have been enjoined to believe in it as well as to praise and thank Him (for it) in the prayer 'with eternal love Thou lovest us', bearing in mind that it originally came from Him, but not from us, as we say, for instance, that an animal did not create itself, but that God formed and fashioned it, having found matter fit for that form. In the same way it was He who initiated our delivery from Egypt in order that we should become His legion and He our King, as He said: 'I am the Lord your God, who brought you out from the land of Egypt, to be your God' (*cf.* Num. xv, 41).

56. The influence of the Divine power is recognized, therefore, not in well-chosen phrases, raising the eyebrows, twisting the eyeballs, in weeping and praying, movements and words behind which there are no deeds, but in a pure intention, manifested in actions which by their nature are difficult to perform, and yet are performed with the utmost zeal and love.

COMMENTARY TO BOOK II

§ 1 ff. We already know (Book I, § 88) that Jehuda Halevi conceives the 'Unity' of God in the strict sense adopted by Arab philosophers. He now returns to this important point, seeing that the King understands sufficient Hebrew (§ 1) to follow the argument on such expressions as כבוד, שכינה.

Knowledge of the fact that the Torah preaches the unity of God (Book I, § 89) is here assumed (§ 1, end). But Christianity also professes this doctrine; and yet (according to the general Arab-Jewish opinion) it does not bear it out consistently, seeing that it attributes emotions to God (Book I, § 4) and expressly names three persons in the one God concept. With definite reference to Christianity, Jehuda Halevi declares:

1. Judaism recognizes no name for God in the strict sense of the word—that is: no Divine person; 'names' such as 'Shaddai' are attributes; for the Tetragram, see below.

2. It admits of no positive attributes for God, since these always contain a hint of anthropomorphism, but only negative attributes and evidence of God's relation and attitude to his creatures; in particular it attributes to God neither affects nor changes.

3. Physical phenomena, such as glory, are not to be referred to God, but to God's creations which were seen by the prophets (see Book IV, § 3, for the necessity of these).

These views are supplemented in passages such as Book II, § 50, end (we believe in God's love, but not in the literal sense). They correspond to the views of more recent theologists, namely that the anthropomorphic expressions applied to God are only to be interpreted in the sense of 'Ideograms'. They are also in line with medieval philosophy. Even the apparent exception to the doctrine of the negative attributes (§ 2, end), namely, the opinion 'that God can be termed wise', was shared by certain Aristotelians—our reason passing as something Divine which has only entered us 'from without'.

Thus, criticism of philosophy in no way hinders Jehuda Halevi from agreeing whole-heartedly with it wherever it appears to formulate nothing more than the old Jewish doctrine of the incomparableness of God.

On the other hand, Jehuda Halevi is original in the manner in which he distinguishes between the Tetragram and other names (*cf.* Book IV, § 15).

§ 14. Jehuda Halevi attempts to give scientific proof of Palestine's pre-eminence. This is shown particularly at the end of the paragraph, where reference is made to the same ascending order of the four realms of organic life (plant, animal, human, superhuman) as discussed in Book I, § 31 ff. On the other hand, he attempts to give historical proof for the fact of pre-eminence. In this he supports his argument partly on unquestionable Biblical tradition, and partly on a peculiar interpretation of verses such as Gen. xxii, 14, 'the place of which it is said to this day. . . .', where Jehuda Halevi interprets the Hebrew יאמר היום as 'of which it will be said one day'; he may have interpreted the following words as translated above (similar to the Greek Bible version), or 'He will appear on the mount of the Lord'. As regards the quarrel between Isaac and Ishmael, he possibly has in mind Gen. xxi, 10 ('for the son of this bondwoman shall not be heir with my son'). What he says regarding the burial of the first man in Palestine, the quarrel between Cain and Abel, and Jonah's flight, is in accordance with Rabbinic tradition. At the end of § 20 he seems to take passages such as Psalms ii, 6; xcix, 5; 9, as references to Palestine.

Before § 20 we omit an argument about the appointment of the festivals and before § 23 a list of sayings by the Rabbis on the sacredness of Palestine.

§ 24. Note here again the dramatic turn of the conversation. The Rabbi admits the King's reproof to be justified, and even uses it to demonstrate the difference between his conception of the superiority of Palestine (based on natural science) and the general conception! *Cf.* the Zion poem on pp. 135 ff. below.

§ 25. As already mentioned in Book II, § 2, Jehuda Halevi rejects all anthropomorphism. He obtains an acceptable rendering of the expressions in § 25 by deriving the word 'לְאִשֵּׁי' not from 'אִשֶּׁה' (fire offering), but from 'אֵשׁ' (fire) and by interpreting these 'fires' not as intended for God, but as the fiery apparitions emanating from God as on Sinai and in the Burning Bush. Thus the sacrificial rites—and in general all ritual performances—are not services rendered by us to God in His own interest, but rather arrangements which God has instituted for the religious perfection of man. In illustration of this idea, Jehuda Halevi conceives the Temple, as in

Book III, § 19, the State, as 'men in big', in line with the well-known designation of man as a microcosm (world in small); and he interprets the laws dealing with sacrifice and Temple ritual on the basis of the analogy of the organic, spiritual, intellectual and prophetic realms of life (Book I, § 31). If higher forces (e.g. intellectual) are to be displayed, the lower ones on which they are founded (i.e. the physical) must be fully developed; he who protects the latter from illness, etc., indirectly serves the former; this theory is followed up by Jehuda Halevi, in a passage omitted by us, down to the smallest detail. In the same way certain physical conditions are essential, particularly the kindling of prescribed fire, for the drawing down of Divine fire; according to Book III, § 23, the connection between prescribed action and supernatural effect is puzzling, but not more puzzling and not less essential than the connection between the bond of man and wife and the origin of new life.

§ 28. Jehuda Halevi only answers the questions on the parallel to the human head. He approaches the question of the senses only in so far as he refers fairly clearly, in his presentation of the functions of priest and prophet, to the doctrine (of Galen) of the three 'inner senses' (powers of imagination, of thought and of memory). He could safely assume the fact of anointing oil being used for the priests to be well known.

§ 30 ff. Jehuda Halevi sounds the peculiar character of Jewish history. The dispersion, the preservation and the hope of Israel's future rest on peculiar foundations. While the history of other peoples is affected by nature's laws, Israel's national life is bound up with the existence of its Temple, i.e. of its heart (§§ 29, 32). But the enigma of Israel's preservation testifies to the effect of a life-giving power within, lacking in other nations. This is the 'Divine Power', conceived here not only as a power leading to God, but even more as a power emanating from God. True, its effect is diminished by 'assimilation'. Here again, Jehuda Halevi makes use of a physiological simile. His readers are already acquainted with the term 'heart' denoting the religious aristocracy of mankind (Note to Book I, § 27), but 'heart' is here used only in the usual sense: the 'core'; hence its contrary is the 'outer skin'. Jehuda Halevi uses the simile quite seriously: the heart is affected by diseases of the body; hence the natural consequence: Book IV, § 23 — the recovery of the heart brings health to the whole body!

In comparing Israel to the seemingly dead, Jehuda Halevi comes near to comparisons such as those used by the Rabbis Taanith 20a: Israel is *like* a widow (Lamentations i, 1), i.e. the resemblance is only external; Israel is not a widow, but a wife whose husband is on a distant journey, but will return to her.

§ 48. All those who have philosophized on Judaism down to the present day had to tackle those passages in the Bible that appear to lay more stress on the laws governing sacrifice, and other ritual precepts, than on the moral laws. The 'rationalists', particularly Jehuda Halevi's contemporaries Ibn Daûd and Maimonides, held that, in point of fact, the observance of the moral laws was more important—not by way of criticizing the ritual law, but in as much as they considered the training of character more important than the training of the mind, without contesting the value of the latter in any way. Jehuda Halevi, on the other hand, bases his argument on Plato's theory (The State, 351 C) that not even robbers and thieves can dispense with justice in their relations towards each other, without damage to themselves. It is therefore no wonder that the prophets reproach such people as do not even observe this minimum of moral duty, thus placing themselves below the standard of intelligent criminals. But on the other hand, the fact that the ritual laws were made solely for the aristocracy of mankind renders it all the more essential that we should attach a special value to them.

The justification of the ritual laws in the following criticism of the Ascetics (§ 50) goes much deeper. Jehuda Halevi rejects the 'mortification of the flesh' as definitely as the 'sacrifice of the intellect' (Book I, § 88; Book II, § 1). The ritual laws prescribe neither the one nor the other; they are irrational as is religion in general; but like the latter they are not anti-rational; reason cannot explain them—but it does not reject them; the pious Jew does not consider the great number of the precepts to be a burden (§ 56; *cf.* Book III, § 14); on the contrary: the love and delight with which he observes them are the test of his piety. Yet while Judaism recognizes the deep seriousness of the fast-days, it considers the joyous commands no less important. It is not joy of life *as such* that is held to be religious as in the religion of Dionysos. For we regard as religious only that which is in direct connection with the God of creation and of history (Book IV, § 15); but this is the God who is proclaimed by the Sabbath; and hence our joy, when it is governed by the thought of creation and redemption, bears as religious a character as the practice of atonement. This day of remembrance of our redemption reminds us of the 'love' of our God (*see* Book II, § 1, for the figurative conception of this notion); hence this very day can be described as the gift of Divine love (e.g. in the Kiddush); and to this love there corresponds the 'joy' of man, as a natural reaction.

BOOK III

RELIGIOUS LIFE

1. The servant of God does not withdraw himself from secular contact lest he be a burden to the world and the world to him; he does not hate life, which is one of God's bounties granted to him, as it is said: 'The number of thy days I will fulfil' (Ex. xxiii, 26); 'thou mayest prolong thy days' (Deut. xxii, 7). On the contrary, he loves this world and a long life, because they afford him opportunities of deserving the world to come: the more good he does, the greater is his claim on the world to come. He would like, in fact, to attain to the level of Enoch, who 'walked with God' (Gen. v, 24), or of Eliah, in order to be freed (from worldly matters) and to remain in the society of angels; then he would not feel lonely in seclusion and solitude but would experience pleasure; lonely would he feel himself in a crowd, since he is deprived there of the view of the Divine realm, which frees him from the need of eating and drinking. To such persons complete solitude is suited, they might even welcome death, since they have attained to a height which nobody may hope to surpass. Philosophic scholars also live in solitude to purify their thoughts; nevertheless they desire the society of disciples who stimulate their research and retentiveness; such was the stage attained by Socrates and those who were like him. But these are outstanding men, and there is no hope today of attaining their level. When the Shekinah dwelt in the Holy Land among the people capable of prophecy, there were persons who lived an ascetic life in deserts, associated with people of the same frame of mind; they did not seclude themselves completely, but they supported each other in the knowledge of Law and in the practice of its commandments which brought them near to that stage 'in holiness and purity': these were the 'disciples of prophets'. But in our time and place, among this people 'whilst no open vision exists' (1 Sam. iii, 1), acquired knowledge being diminished and natural knowledge wanting,

he who desires to retire into ascetic solitude, can only count on pain of soul and body. The misery of sickness is visible in him, and one might regard it as the consequence of humility and contrition, but he lives as a prisoner and disdains life out of disgust for his prison and pain, not because he enjoys his seclusion. And how could it be otherwise? He has not achieved connection or association with any Divine light as the prophets did; nor has he acquired knowledge to absorb him and to enjoy as did the philosophers. Suppose he is God-fearing, excellent, desiring to meet his God in solitude, waking, humbling himself and reciting as many prayers and supplications as he can remember, (his) satisfaction of these self-prompted actions lasts only a few days as long as they are new; when his tongue repeats them frequently, they do not affect his soul and do not make for humility or submission. Thus he remains night and day, whilst his soul urges him to exert its inherent powers of seeing, hearing, speaking, moving, eating, cohabitation, gain, house-managing, helping the poor, upholding religion with money in case of need. Must he not regret this life to which he has tied his soul, and must not such a regret remove him further from the Divine power which he desired to approach?

2. The Khazari: Describe the conduct of one of your pious men today.

3. The Rabbi: Pious is he who takes care of his country, who gives to its inhabitants provisions and all they need in just proportions, who treats them righteously, without wronging or preferring anyone—who finds them, when he requires them, obedient to his call and obsequious to his order and prohibition.

4. The Khazari: I asked thee concerning a pious man, not a prince!

5. The Rabbi: The pious man is no other than a prince obeyed by his senses and by his mental as well as his physical faculties, which he governs like a city, as it is said: 'He who rules his spirit (is better) than he who occupies a city' (Prov.

xvi, 32). He is fit to rule; for if he were the prince of a country, he would be as just as he is to his body and soul. He subdues his passions and restrains them from excesses, but he gives them their share, satisfying them as regards moderate food, moderate drink, moderate bathing, etc. He subdues further the urge towards superiority, but allows it as much freedom as is required for the discussion of scientific or practical views as well as for the reprimand of the evil-minded. He concedes to the senses their fair share according as he requires them, using hands, feet, and tongue for necessary or useful actions, likewise hearing, seeing, and the general perception which unites them, as well as imagination, instinctive judgement, thought, and memory; finally will-power which commands all these, but is in its turn subservient to the decision of the intellect. He does not allow any of the limbs or faculties to perform their various tasks without restriction, nor does he allow them to encroach on each other. Thus, when he has satisfied each of them, giving to the organic limbs the necessary amount of rest and sleep, to the animal ones waking and movement in worldly occupation, he calls up his troop as a respected prince calls up his disciplined army, to assist him in reaching the higher or Divine degree, which is to be found above the degree of the intellect. He arranges his troop in the same manner as Moses arranged his people round Mount Sinai. He orders his will-power to receive every command issued by him obediently and to carry it out forthwith, leasing the faculties and limbs to do his bidding without contradiction. He admonishes the will, bidding it not to obey and trust the two tempters, instinct and imagination, without taking counsel with the intellect—to obey them if intellect accords with them, otherwise to resist. The will obeys his admonition and resolves to execute it. It (the will) directs first the organs of thought and frees them from all worldly ideas which filled them before; it charges the imagination to produce, with the assistance of memory, the most splendid pictures possible, in order to approach the Divine power which it seeks, e.g. the scene of Sinai, Abraham and Isaac on Moriah, the Tabernacle of Moses, the Temple service, the presence of (God's) glory in the Holy House, and the like. The pious man then orders his memory to retain all these, and not to forget them; he warns his instinctive judgement and its 'tempters' not to confuse the truth or to trouble it by doubts; he warns his irascibility and greed not to influence the will to lead it astray nor to subdue it to wrath and lust. After this preparation, the will-power stimulates all his organs to work with alertness, pleasure and joy. They stand without fatigue when occasion demands; they bow down when he bids them to bow; they sit at the proper moment. The eyes look as a servant looks at his master; the hands do not play nor join together; the feet stand straight; all limbs are frightened and anxious to obey their master, paying no heed to pain or fatigue. The tongue agrees with the mind and does not talk idly nor speak in prayer in an automatic way like the starling and the parrot, but every word is uttered thoughtfully and attentively. This hour of Divine service constitutes the maturity and essence of time, whilst the other hours represent the road which leads to his goal; for in the one hour he becomes like the spiritual beings (angels) and is removed from the animal ones. And as these times of prayer are the 'fruit' of his day and night, so is the Sabbath the 'fruit' of the week, because it is appointed to establish the connection with the Divine power that he may serve Him in joy, not in contrition, as has been explained before (Book II, § 50). All this stands in the same relation to the soul as food to the body; he prays for the sake of his soul, as he takes nourishment for the sake of his body; and the blessing of one prayer lasts until it is time for the next, just as the strength derived from lunch lasts till supper. But the further the soul of the pious man is removed from the time of prayer, the more it is darkened by his coming in contact with worldly matters—still more when necessity brings him into the company of children, women, or wicked people, and he (the pious man) hears dissolute words or seductive songs, which he is unable to master—so that his soul is oppressed by them. Prayer, to be sure, purges his soul from all that has passed over it and prepares it for the future; but in spite of this arrangement no week elapses in which both—his soul and body—are not satiated with weariness, oppressive elements having multiplied in the course of the week; and these cannot be cleansed away except by consecrating one day to service with corporeal rest. On the Sabbath, therefore, the body makes good what it lacked during the six days, and prepares itself for the work to come, and the soul remembers what it lacked as long as it looked after the body; it cures itself of past illness and provides against future sickness, as Job did with his children every week, saying: 'it may be that my sons have sinned' (and he sacrificed for them: Job i, 5). He then provides himself with a monthly remedy on the 'season of atonement for all that may happen during this period' (prayer for Rosh Hodesh). He further observes the Three Festivals and the very holy Fast Day, on which he casts off his former sins and makes up what he may have missed on the weekly and monthly days (of atonement). Then the soul frees itself from the whisperings of instinct, wrath, and lust, and turns away from any inclination to second these in thought or deed; and even if it cannot escape from thoughts, by reason of the weight of the conceptions, stirred by the remembrance of songs, tales, etc., heard in youth, it turns away, at least, from the deeds and begs pardon for the thoughts, but resolves never to allow them to escape his tongue, much less to put them into practice, as it is written: 'I think, but my thought does not proceed from my mouth' (Ps. xvii, 3). The fast of this day is such as to bring him near the angels, because it is spent in humility and contrition, standing, bowing, praising and singing. All his corporeal faculties are denied their natural requirements, being devoted entirely to religious service, as if there were in him no animal element at all. And so does the pious man always behave when he fasts: he curbs eye, ear, and tongue completely to the service of such things only as bring him nearer to God; it is likewise with the innermost faculties, such as imagination and mind. To this add wholesome practice.

6. THE KHAZARI: The Practice is known to all.

7. THE RABBI: Generally known are only social institutions and rational laws. Divine practice, however, added in order that it might be observed by the people guided by the 'Living God', was not known until it was exhibited and explained in detail by Him. Even the social and rational practices are known only by their main feature, not by their measure. We know that charity and chastening of the spirit by means of fasting and meekness are incumbent on us; that deceit, immoderate intercourse with women, and cohabitation with relatives are abominable; that honouring parents is a duty, etc.; but the limitation and moderation of these duties in accordance with common welfare is God's. And the 'Divine actions' are entirely beyond the sphere of our intellect; it does not reject them, but it must obey the order of God, just as a sick person must obey the physician in applying his medicines and diet. Circumcision has nothing to do with analogic thought or with the constitution of social life; yet Abraham, although this commandment is against nature and although he was a hundred years old, subjected his person and his son to it, and it became the sign of the covenant, that the Divine power might be connected with him and his descendants, as it is written: 'I will establish My covenant between Me and thee and thy seed after thee throughout their generations for an everlasting covenant, to be a God unto thee' (and thy seed after thee) (Gen. xvii, 7).

8. THE KHAZARI: With good reason you duly accepted this command and you perform it with the greatest zeal, with public solemnity and ceremonies, praising (God) and mentioning the root and origin of the practice in the formula of blessing. Other peoples desired to imitate you, but they only had the pain, without the joy which can only be felt by him who remembers the cause for which he bears the pain.

9. THE RABBI: Just so it is with other imitations: no people succeeded in equalling us. Look at those who appointed a day of rest in the place of the Sabbath. Could they reach a higher

plane of resemblance than that which exists between statues and living human bodies?

10. THE KHAZARI: Having reflected about you, I understood that God employs means in preserving you and that He appointed the Sabbath and the Festivals as the strongest means of preserving your life and vigour. For the other peoples would have dispersed you and employed you as servants on account of your intelligence and acumen, and made you warriors, were it not for these festive seasons observed by you so conscientiously, because they originate with God and are based on great causes, such as resemblance of the creation, of the exodus from Egypt and of the giving of the Torah—Divine (ideas), inciting you to observance. Had these (festivals) not been, none of you would put on a clean garment, nor would you hold congregations to remember the law—in view of your deep depression as a result of your everlasting degradation. Had they not been, you would not enjoy a single day in your life; by them, you spend the sixth part of your life in rest of body and soul. Such is not granted even to kings; for their souls have no respite on their days of rest; if the smallest business calls them on that day to trouble and stir them, they stir and trouble themselves, complete rest being denied to them. Had these holidays not been, your toil would be for the benefit of others, since it would be exposed to plundering. Whatever you spend on these days is your profit for this life, and also for the next, because it is spent for the sake of God.

11. THE RABBI: The excellent man among us fulfils the Divine laws, which justifies him in saying: 'I have not transgressed any of Thy commandments, neither have I forgotten them' (Deut. xxvi, 13), without counting vows, free gifts, voluntary offerings and the free adoption of the Nazirite vow. These are the religious laws, most of which are performed through priestly service. Social laws are as follows: 'Thou shalt not murder, commit adultery, steal, nor bear false witness against thy neighbour' (Ex. xx, 13), honouring the parents, 'Thou shalt love thy fellow creatures' (Lev. xix, 18),

'love ye the stranger' (Deut. x, 19), 'thou shalt not deal
falsely nor lie' (Lev. xix, 11), the avoidance of usury, the
giving of correct weights and measures, the leaving of the
gleanings, such as the unpicked grapes, the corners, etc. Laws of
the mind are: 'I am the Lord thy God; thou shalt have no
(other gods before Me); thou shalt not take the name of the
(Lord thy God in vain)' (Ex. xx, 2 f.), with the doctrine, proved
by our religion, that God observes not only the actions and
words of man but also his secret thoughts, and requites good
and evil, that 'God's eyes wander over the whole earth'
(Zechariah iv, 10). So the excellent person never acts, speaks or
thinks without believing that he is observed by eyes which see
and take note, reward and punish, and call to account for every
thing objectionable in word and deed. He is, therefore, in
walking or sitting, like one afraid and timid, who is ashamed of
his doings; but at times he is glad and rejoices; he is full of self-
confidence, whenever he has done a good action, as if he had
paid, as it were, a tribute to his Lord in enduring hardships in
order to obey Him. Altogether he bears in mind and takes as
rule of conduct the words: 'Consider three things, and you will
not commit any sin: understand what is above you, a seeing
eye and a hearing ear, and all your actions written in a book'
(Abot ii, 1); and he finds convincing proof (of them) in David's
word: 'He that planted the ear, shall He not hear? He that
formed the eye, shall He not see?' (Ps. xciv, 9) and in the whole
Psalm cxxxix, beginning: 'O Lord, Thou hast searched me
and knowest (me)'. (According to this Psalm) he considers
that all his limbs are placed with consummate wisdom, in
proper order and proportion. He sees how they obey his will,
though he know not which part of them should be moved. If,
for example, he wishes to rise, he finds that certain limbs he
does not even know of raise his body like obedient servants;
and it is the same when he wishes to sit, walk or assume any
other position; this is what is meant by the words: 'Thou
knowest my downsitting and my uprising; Thou searchest out
my path and my lying down, and art acquainted with all my
ways' (v. 2, 3). For one must not consider the work of creation

to be similar to an artisan's craft. When the latter, for example, has built a mill, he departs and the mill does the work for which it was constructed. The Creator, however, creates limbs, endows them with their faculties and grants them continually what they need; let us imagine His providence and guidance removed only for one instant, and the whole world would perish. If the pious man remembers this with every movement that he makes, it is as if the Shekinah (Divine Presence) were with him continually, and the angels accompanied him virtually; yet if his piety is eminent and he abides in places worthy of the Shekinah, they are with him in reality, and he sees them with his own eyes, occupying a degree just below that of prophecy. Thus the most prominent of the Sages, during the time of the Second Temple, saw a certain apparition and heard a Bat Kol (Divine voice). This is the degree attained by the holy men, and higher still is that attained by the prophets. The pious man attunes his mind to the Divine power through various means, some of which are prescribed in the written Law, others by tradition. He wears the phylacteries on that part of the head which is the seat of mind and memory—a strap falling down on his hand, that he may see it hourly—and the hand-phylacteries above the heart, the mainspring of the faculties. He wears the fringes, lest the senses entrap him in wordly thoughts, as it is written: 'that ye go not about after your heart and your eyes' (Num. xv, 39). By such means love and fear (of God) enter the soul, no doubt; but they are limited through the limitations of the Law, lest joy on Sabbaths and holy days degenerate into extravagance, debauchery, idleness, and neglect of the appointed hours of prayer, and lest fear deepen into despair of forgiveness, so that he spends all his life in defection and transgresses the command to feel pleasure in the gifts of God: 'And thou shalt rejoice in all the good which the Lord thy God hath given unto thee and unto thy house' (Deut. xxvi, 11); his gratitude for God's bounties would also be imperfect; for gratitude attends joy. Then there applies to him the word: 'Because thou didst not serve the Lord thy God with joyfulness (and with gladness of the heart), therefore thou shalt serve thine enemy' (xxviii, 47). Zeal in 'rebuking the neighbour' (Lev. xix, 17) and in scientific discussions should also not go too far and pass into wrath and hatred, disturbing the purity of the soul during prayer. The pious man is so deeply convinced of the 'justice of God's judgement', that he finds in this belief protection and help from the miseries and troubles of this world. For he is convinced of the justice of Him who created the living creatures, sustains and guides them with a wisdom our intellect cannot grasp in detail, but only in a general way, when it beholds perfection in the most wonderful structure of animals; these reveal the intention of an all-wise God and the will of an omniscient all-powerful Being, who endowed small and great with all the necessary internal and external senses, the limbs, and the organs corresponding to their instincts. He gave to the hare and the stag the means of flight and their timid nature, to the lion its ferocity and the instruments for delaceration. He who considers the formation and use of the limbs, and their relation to the animal instinct, sees in them so just a proportion and so perfect an arrangement, that no doubt or uncertainty can remain in his soul concerning the justice of the Creator. And if the tempter, instinctive judgement, upbraids the injustice to the hare or to the fly that falls prey to the lion and the wolf or to the spider, reason refutes and reprimands it as follows: How can I charge a wise being with injustice, since his justice is beyond question for me and he has no need of injustice? If the lion's pursuit of the hare, and the spider's of the fly were mere accidents, I should charge the accident; I see, however, that this wise, just, and purposeful Being equipped the lion with the means of hunting: ferocity and strength, teeth and claws, and the spider with cunning, with the art of weaving webs without having learnt to do so, and with the instruments required; He has consequently appointed the fly as its prey just as many fishes serve other fishes for food. Can I then say aught but that there is a wisdom which I am unable to grasp, and that I must submit to 'the Rock whose doing is perfect' (Deut. xxxii, 4)? Whoever has gained this solid conviction, will become like Nahum of Gimzo, of whom it is related that he said in every accident of misfortune: 'This, too, is for the best'; he will, then, spend his life in happiness, and lightly bear the tribulations; he will even welcome them if he is conscious of a sin that weighed on him and of which he is cleansed by them, as one who has paid his debt, and is glad to be discharged from it. He enjoys looking forward to the reward and retribution which await him, instructing mankind in patience and submission to God, and thereby gaining a good reputation. So he overcomes his own troubles—and also those of the community. If his instinctive judgement calls to mind the length of the exile and the diaspora, the decrease and the degradation of his people, he finds comfort first in 'acknowledging the justice of (God's) decree', as was said before, then in the hope of being cleansed from his sins, then in the reward and recompense awaiting him in the world to come, and in the connection with the Divine power in this world. And if his tempter makes him despair of it, saying: 'Can these bones live?' (Ezek. xxxvii, 3) our traces being thoroughly destroyed and our memory wiped out, as it is written: 'they say: our bones are dried' (v. 11), he thinks of the circumstances of the delivery from Egypt and 'for how many favours we owe gratitude to God' (Pesah-Haggada); then he will find no difficulty in picturing our restitution, though only one of us may have remained, as it is written 'Thou worm Jacob' (Jes. xli, 14; that is to say): what remains of a man when he has become a worm in his grave!

12. The Khazari: Such a man will live a happy life even in exile and gather the fruit of his faith in this world and the next. He, however, who bears the exile unwillingly, almost loses his rewards in both worlds.

13. The Rabbi: And that which strengthens and enhances his joy is the duty of saying blessings for all he enjoys or suffers in this world.

14. The Khazari: How can that be? Are not the blessings an additional burden?

15. The Rabbi: Is it not true that a cultured man finds a completer pleasure in eating and drinking than a child or an

animal, even as an animal enjoys food and drink more than a plant, though the plant is continually taking nourishment?

16. THE KHAZARI: Certainly, because he is favoured with the observation and the consciousness of enjoyment. For if a drunken person were given all he desires, whilst being completely intoxicated, and if he were to eat and drink, hear songs, meet his friends and be embraced by his beloved, when told of it, he would regret it and regard it as a loss, not a gain, since he did not enjoy these things in a state of consciousness and clearness of the senses.

17. THE RABBI: Expectation of a pleasure, the experiencing of it and thinking of its lack in former times doubles the feeling of enjoyment. Such advantages result from the blessings for him who is used to saying them with attention and comprehension. For they make us feel pleasure and gratitude towards the Giver of that (pleasure) which we were prepared to do without; and this enhances the joy. You say ' (Blessed art Thou who) hast kept us alive and preserved us', having been prepared for death: now you feel gratitude for life and regard it as gain; should sickness and death be near you, you despise them; for having made an account, you see that you have obtained profit from your Lord, since you ought on account of your nature to abjure all enjoyment, being dust; yet God presented you with life and joy. You thank him therefore, and if He takes away these benefits you praise him and say: 'The Lord has given, the Lord has taken — (the Lord's name be praised)' (Job i, 21). So you will remain cheerful for your whole life. Whoever is unable to pursue such a course, must count his pleasure not human, but brutish, since he lacks consciousness like the drunkard alluded to above.

In such a way the pious man realizes the meaning of each blessing, its purpose and what is connected with it. When he says 'He who created the lights', he realizes the order in the celestial world, the greatness of the heavenly bodies and their usefulness, but also that in the eyes of their Creator they are no greater than worms, though they appear to us immense on account of the profit we derive from them. The proof of this estimation by their Creator may be found in this, that His wisdom and guidance appear in the creation of the ant and bee not less than in that of the sun and its sphere; the traces of providence and wisdom are even finer and more adorable in the ant and bee, since such faculties and organs are found in them notwithstanding their minuteness. This he bears in mind, lest he overrate the celestial lights and be seduced by the tempter to the views held by the worshippers of (celestial) spirits, and believe that these help or injure by their innate (power), whereas (they have effect) by their qualities only, like wind and fire.—At the blessing 'with eternal love' he realizes, in a similar way, the connection of the Divine power with the community fit to receive it, as a smooth mirror receives the light, and that the Torah is the outcome of His will to reveal His sway on earth, as in heaven.—(Following on from this blessing) he takes upon himself the Divine Law, reciting the 'Shema Israel' (Deut. vi, 4 ff.) and after it the passage 'True and certain', containing the confirmation of the acknowledgement of the Torah: after having clearly and unmistakably imbibed all that preceded (the Shema), he binds his soul and asserts that he regards all this as obligatory as his forefathers did, and that his children too shall regard it as obligatory up to the last generation, saying: 'Upon our fathers, and upon us, and our children, and our generations (it is) a good word, firmly established, that never passes away'. To this he attaches the articles of faith which complete the Jewish belief, viz. the recognition of God's sovereignty, His eternity, the providential care bestowed on our forefathers, the Divine origin of the Torah, finally the proof for all that: the exodus from Egypt, saying: 'It is true that Thou art the Lord our God; truly from everlasting is Thy name; the help of our fathers (hast Thou been); from Egypt didst Thou redeem us'. Whoever pronounces all this context with pure attention is a true Israelite, and may hope to obtain that contact with the Divine power which is exclusively connected with the Israelite among all nations; he is worthy to stay before the Shekinah and to receive an answer as often as he asks. We are obliged, therefore, to follow the blessing for the redemption with the chief-prayer, standing upright and reciting the blessings relating to all Israel—prayers of individual character having their place in the paragraph ending 'He who hears the prayer'. In the first benediction, called 'fathers', (the worshipper) remembers the excellence of the patriarchs and the firm covenant God made with them, unshakable for all days, saying 'He brings the Redeemer to their children's children'. In the second, called 'mighty deeds', (he remembers) that the (course of the) world is ruled by God eternally and not, as asserted by the Naturalists, by the known elements; he realizes that He 'revives the dead' whenever He desires, however far removed this may be from the analogic thought of the Naturalists, and likewise 'He causes the wind to blow and the rain to descend', etc., and 'delivers prisoners' according to His desire. All this has been established in the history of Israel. After having expressed his consent to the passages 'fathers' and 'mighty deeds', which might cause us to imagine that God is entangled in this corporeal world, he extols and sanctifies God and raises Him above all participation with or entanglement in corporeal qualities by the benediction 'holiness' (beginning:) 'Thou art holy', realizing in reciting it all that the philosophers have preached regarding His sublimity and holiness, but only after having acknowledged His omnipotence and sovereignty in the passages 'fathers' and 'mighty deeds', convincing us that we have a King and Law-giver; without them we should live in doubt in view of the Aristotelian and materialistic theories; the passages 'fathers' and 'mighty deeds' must therefore precede 'holiness'.—After having acknowledged God's sublimity, he begins to pray for his wants, included in those of the world of Israel, exceptions being admitted in supplements only. For a prayer, in order to be heard, must be recited by a multitude or in a multitude or by an individual who outweighs a multitude; but such men are no longer found.

18. THE KHAZARI: Why is this? Is not retirement preferable for man, better for the purity of his soul and the undisturbed attention of his mind?

19. THE RABBI: No, community is preferable for many reasons. Firstly, the community does not pray for what is hurtful to an individual, whilst the individual sometimes prays for something to the hurt of other individuals, and these pray for something that hurts him; a prayer, however, can be heard only if its object is profitable to the world and noways hurtful. Moreover: an individual rarely accomplishes his prayer without digression of mind and negligence; we are therefore commanded that the individual recite the prayers of a community, and if possible in a community of not less than ten persons, so that one makes up for the digression or negligence of the other, in order that a perfect prayer, recited with unalloyed devotion, may be made, and its blessing bestowed on the community, each individual receiving his portion. For the Divine power resembles the rain which waters an area, if the inhabitants deserve it (Deut. xi, 14), although perhaps some of them do not deserve it: but they profit from the consideration of the majority; on the other hand, rain is withheld from an area whose inhabitants do not deserve it, although some of them perhaps might deserve it; but they suffer with the majority. This is how God governs this world; He rewards these individuals in the world to come, and even in this world He gives them the best recompense and bestows blessing upon them which distinguishes them from their neighbours (Gen. xix, 29); but rarely are they completely exempted from general affliction. A person who prays but for himself is therefore like one who wishes to keep in repair his domicile only, refusing to associate with his fellow-citizens in the repair of the walls; in spite of his great expenditure he remains in danger; he, however, who joins the majority spends little, but remains in safety; for one replaces the defects of the other; thus the community attains the best possible condition, all its inhabitants enjoying its prosperity with but little expenditure, in justice and concord. Plato (cf. Rep. 369 C) calls therefore that which is expended on behalf of the law 'the portion of the whole'. If, however, an individual neglects the ' portion of the whole' which belongs to the welfare of the commonwealth of which he forms a part,

thinking to keep it for himself, he sins against the commonwealth, and more against himself; for the relation of the individual to the commonwealth is as the relation of the single
limb to the body: should the arm, in a case where bleeding is
required, refuse its blood, the whole body, the arm included,
would perish; it is, therefore, the duty of the individual to bear
hardships, or even death, for the sake of the welfare of the
commonwealth. So particularly must the individual be careful
to contribute the 'portion of the whole' without fail. Since it
cannot be fixed by analogic conclusions, God prescribed it:
tithes, holy gifts, offerings, etc., are the portion of our property;
Sabbath, Holidays, years of release and jubilee, etc., are the
portion of our actions; prayers, blessings, thanksgivings are the
portion of our words; love, fear and joy are the portion of our
mind.—Among the requesting prayers the first place is due to
the prayer for intelligence and enlightenment to serve the Lord;
for in this way man approaches God. Therefore (the prayer)
'Thou graciously givest reason to man' precedes the following, 'He who taketh delight in repentance', in order that
this 'wisdom, knowledge, and intelligence' be directed to the
way of the Torah and Divine service as the prayer continues:
'Restore us, O our Father, to Thy Law and bring us near to
Thy service'. But since a mortal cannot help sinning, a prayer is
required for forgiveness of transgressions in thought and deed;
this is done in the passage 'the Merciful who forgiveth much'.
Connected thereto is the outcome and token of forgiveness,
viz. the redemption from our present condition: this passage
begins 'behold our misery', and ends 'redeemer of Israel'.
After this the pious man prays for the health of body and soul
and in connection with it for the bestowal of food to keep up
his strength, in the 'blessing of the years'. Then he prays for the
reunion of the whole people in the passage: 'He who gathereth
together the scattered of His people, the house of Israel'; in
connection with it he prays for the reappearance of justice and
restoration of our former condition in the words 'rule over us
Thou alone'; then he prays for the removing of cinders and
destruction of thorns in the 'blessing against heretics' and in

connection with it for the preservation of the picked in 'pious and just', then for the return to Jerusalem and its restoration as seat of the Divine power, and in connection with it for the Messiah, the son of David. This concludes all worldly wants. There follows the prayer for the 'acceptance of prayers' and in connection with it for the revelation of the Shekinah before our eyes, just as it appeared to the prophets, the pious and the generation delivered from Egypt, in the passage beginning 'may our eyes see' and ending 'He who restoreth His Shekinah to Zion'. He imagines the Shekinah standing opposite to him and bows down in the 'blessing of thanks and acknowledgement', which contains the acknowledgement and gratitude for God's grace. He attaches the blessing 'who maketh peace', in order to take leave from the presence of the Shekinah in peace.

RABBINIC JUDAISM AND ITS BRANCH SECTS

64. THE KHAZARI: Please illustrate for me the manner of tradition, because this (manner) must prove its trustworthiness.

65. THE RABBI: Prophecy was prevalent about forty years in the period of the second Temple among those elders who had the support of the Shekinah from the first Temple; the people after its return still had Haggai, Zechariah, Ezra and others. Forty years later there arose that assembly of Sages called 'the Men of the Great Synod'. They were too numerous to be counted. They had returned with Zerubbabel and relied in their teachings upon the prophets, as it is said: 'the prophets handed (the Law) down to the Men of the Great Synod' (Abot i, 1). Then came the generation of the High Priest Simon the Just and his disciples and colleagues, then the celebrated Antigonos of Soko; among his disciples were Sadok and Boëthos, the originators of sectarianism; Sadducees and Boëthosians are called after them. Then Joseph ben Joëzer, 'the most pious among the priests', and Joseph ben Johanan and their colleagues. Then Joshua ben Perahja, whose history is

known; among his disciples was Jesus the Nazarene, and
Nittai of Arbela was his contemporary. Then Jehuda ben
Tabbai and Simon ben Shetah and their colleagues. At this
period there arose the sect of the Karaites, in consequence of an
incident between the Sages and (King) Jannai. He was a priest,
and his mother was under suspicion of being violated (and
therefore forbidden to be married to a priest). One of the sages
alluded to this, saying to him: 'Be satisfied, O King Jannai,
with the royal crown, but leave the priestly crown to the
seed of Aaron'. His friends excited him to vex, expel, scatter
and execute the Sages. He replied: 'If I destroy the Sages, what
will become of our Law?' 'The written Law is in our hands,'
they answered, 'whoever wishes to study it, may do so; the
oral Law one should not mind.' He followed them and expelled
the Sages, among them Simon ben Shetah, his son-in-law.
Rabbinism was laid low for some time; people tried to maintain the Torah by means of analogic conclusions, but they
failed; finally Simon ben Shetah and his disciples returned
from Alexandria and tradition was restored. Karaism had,
however, taken root among people who rejected the oral law
and combated it by fallacies, as you see them doing today.
Sadducees and Boëthosians are unbelievers who deny the
world to come; they and the 'sectarians' are alluded to in our
prayers; the followers of Jesus are called meshumadim
(Baptists), having joined the mamudiyya who were baptized
in the Jordan. The Karaites interpret the roots with their intellect; but in the case of the branches (particulars) they make
mistakes; the damage sometimes extends to the roots, but
through ignorance, not through intention.

R. Akiba reached a degree so near prophecy that he had
intercourse with the spiritual world, as it is said: 'Four persons
entered paradise; one of them peeped in and died; the other
peeped in and was hurt; the third peeped in and cut down the
plants, and only one entered in health and left in health: R.
Akiba' (Hagiga 14b). The one who died belonged to those
who cannot bear the sight of the celestial world without the
destruction of the body. The second became a demoniac,

seized by Divine frenzy, and men did not benefit from him.
The third repudiated practice, having perceived theory; he
said: 'these actions are but means and instruments to attain
spiritual rank; I have attained it and I do not need to bother
about religious actions'. So he was corrupt and corrupted
others, erred and caused others to err. R. Akiba, however, conversed with both worlds without harm; it was said of him: 'he
was as worthy of connection with the Shekinah as Moses,
but the period was not worthy'. He was one of the 'ten
martyrs' executed by the Roman government; during his
torture he asked his pupils whether the time of reciting the
Shema had arrived. They answered: 'O our master, even
now—?' And he replied 'All my days I was afflicted by
reason of the commandment: Thou shalt love the Lord thy
God with all thy heart and all thy soul (Deut. vi, 5), viz: even
if He takes away thy soul; now, the opportunity being given,
shall I not fulfil it?' And he protracted the word 'ehad' (the
One) till his soul fled.

66. THE KHAZARI: Such a man must spend a happy life, and
die a happy death, and then enjoy the eternal life in never-
ceasing bliss.

67. THE RABBI: These are a few of the many tales and traditions about our Sages. They treated the Mishnah with the
same care as the Torah, guarding the traditions in such a
manner that no suspicion of arbitrary invention could arise.
Besides this, the Mishnah has preserved a large amount of pure
Hebrew expressions which are not borrowed from the Bible.
The terseness of its language, the beauty of its arrangement,
the excellence of composition, the complete consideration of
all aspects of the objects in a lucid diction, leaving neither
doubt nor obscurity, are so striking that every one who
scrutinizes it genuinely must become aware that no mortal is
capable of composing such a work without Divine assistance.
It is opposed by those only who do not know it and never
endeavoured to read and study it; having heard through the

traditions of the Sages only popular sayings and homiletic interpretations, they judge them senseless and foolish, just as one
who judges a person to be foolish after meeting him by accident,
without having examined him or conversed with him for any
length of time. As regards the traditions and traditionalists of
the Talmud, however, their methods, their sayings and parables,
it would lead us too far to investigate them. If there is in them
many a thing which appears less attractive to us, we should remember that they were usual and caused pleasure in those days.

68. THE KHAZARI: Indeed, several details in their sayings
seem to contradict thy general description of their qualities,
e.g. they interpret verses of the Torah in a manner opposed to
analogic thought and contradicting the literal sense, as testified
by our feeling, for legal deductions and for homiletic purposes;
and many of their tales and stories are also contrary to reason.

69. THE RABBI: Hast thou noticed how strictly and minutely
they comment the Mishnah and Baraita, what accuracy and
care they employ without any negligence as regards expressions
or even things?

70. THE KHAZARI: I have assured myself that they attained
the climax of evidence; even their arguments cannot be subject
to any objection.

71. THE RABBI: Can we assume that he who penetrates the
Mishnah with such thoroughness should not understand a
Bible verse as well as we?

72. THE KHAZARI: This is impossible. Two cases only are
imaginable: either we do not know their methods of interpreting the Torah, or the interpreters of the Mishnah are
different from those of the Torah.

73. THE RABBI: Let us rather assume another alternative:
either they had inherited secret methods, unknown to us, of
interpretation of the Torah according to the 'thirteen (traditional) rules', or they use some Biblical verses as a kind
of fulcrum—they call it 'asmakta'—and make them a sort
of reminder of their traditions. The verse 'God the Lord

commanded the man, saying: of every tree of the garden thou mayest freely eat' (Gen. ii, 16), e.g. is interpreted as an allusion to the seven laws given to the descendants of Noah: 'commanded' refers to jurisdiction, 'the Lord' to forbidding blasphemy, 'God' to prohibition of idolatry, 'the man' to murder, 'saying' to incest, 'of every tree of the garden' to robbery, 'thou mayest freely eat' to prohibition of flesh from a living animal. How wide is the difference between all that and the verse! But these seven laws were generally known by tradition and were connected with the verse as an aid of memory. Perhaps both reasons mentioned above were effectual or others which are lost to us. In every case, however, it is our duty to acknowledge the authority of the Sages, considering their celebrated wisdom, piety, zeal and their great number, which excludes arbitrary invention; we must not object to their words, but must put the blame on our own intelligence, as we do in the Torah, in cases where the contents are not evident to our intellect: there, too, no objection is taken, but we charge only our own insufficiency. As to the haggadot (homiletic interpretations), many of them serve as basis and introduction for explanations and injunctions. For instance: 'The Sages said: when the Lord of the worlds descended to Egypt'—this passage is designed to confirm the belief that the exodus from Egypt was a deliberate act of God, and not an accident, nor achieved by mediation of human plotting, stars' spirits, angels, jinn or other beings occurring to our mind, but by God's commandment alone. In such cases they used (the word) 'kivejakol' ('so to say', literally: 'if it were possible'), meaning: 'if it could be so, it would be so'. For the rest, this anthropomorphistic passage is not to be found in the Talmud, but only in certain prayerbooks for Pesah. If thou findest similar passages, explain them in this way. Some haggadot are tales on visions of spirits. In the case of such excellent men it is not strange at all that they saw visions, either in imagination, in consequence of their lofty thoughts and pure minds, or even in reality, as did the prophets. Similar is the nature of Bat Kol (literally: daughter of voice), often heard in the time of the second Temple, which ranks after prophecy and Divine voice; do not consider strange what R. Ishmael said: 'I heard a (Divine) voice cooing like a dove' (Berak. 3a), or similar passages; for the visions of Moses and Eliah prove that such a thing is possible; when there is a trustworthy tradition, it must be accepted. And the words attributed to God in this passage: 'Woe unto me that I have destroyed my house' are to be explained in the same figurative way as 'It repented the Lord and it grieved Him in His heart' (Gen. vi, 6). Other (haggadot) are parables employed to express mysterious teachings which are not to be made public, because they are of no use for the masses, and only handed over to selected individuals for research and investigation, in order that a person who is mature for them— one in an age or even in several ages—may be aware of them. Other haggadot seem absurd in their literal sense, but their meaning appears after a little reflection; e.g. 'Seven things were created before the world: Paradise, the Torah, the pious, Israel, the throne of Glory, Jerusalem, and the Messiah, the son of David' (cf. Pes. 54a). This is similar to the saying of some scholars: 'the first in thought is the last in execution' (Aristotle). For the aim of (Divine) wisdom in creating the world was the Torah, which is the essence of wisdom; its bearers are the pious; among them stands 'the Throne of Glory'; the origin of the truly pious can be only in the 'pick' (of mankind), in Israel; conforming to them is alone the most distinguished of all regions, Jerusalem; only the best of men, the Messiah, son of David, is able to guide them; and the place they attain to is Paradise. They all must therefore be said to have virtually existed before the world. Another passage whose literal sense is absurd: 'Ten things were created in the twilight (of the sixth day of creation): the mouth of the earth (which swallowed Korah), the mouth of the spring, the mouth of the ass, etc.' (Abot v, 9). The aim of this passage is to bring into unison natural science and Torah, the former showing conformity to the law of nature, the latter preaching deviation from it: unison is brought about by doctrine, that uniformity is also founded in nature, since their origin was fixed by the primordial will in the days of creation on certain conditions.

However, I will not deny, O King of the Khazars, that there are matters in the Talmud which I am unable to explain satisfactorily or to bring into line with the whole. They are incorporated in the Talmud by the zeal of disciples who followed the principle that 'even commonplace talk of the Sages requires study' (Avoda zara 19b). They took care to reproduce only that which they had heard from their teachers, but they strove at the same time to hand down everything they had heard from them, and they endeavoured to render it with the same words; it may happen that they did not grasp the meaning and said: 'thus have we been taught and have heard'; the teachers, however, probably had certain purposes concealed from the pupils. The matter having come to us in this form, we think little of it, because we do not know its purpose. But all this does not relate to permissions and prohibitions; it is therefore unimportant to us from the practical point of view and does not reduce the value of the Talmud, even apart from the points of view mentioned above.

74. THE KHAZARI: Thou hast reassured me greatly, and strengthened my belief in tradition. But now give me further illustrations of the names of God.

COMMENTARY TO BOOK III

§ 1 ff. The discussion of the Jewish doctrine of duty begun in Book II, § 50, is continued in Book III in a more graphic form. Jehuda Halevi describes the life of a pious man in our times (§ 2), i.e. in times when there are no longer such exceptional people as the prophets (§ 1, 17, end); he does not adhere too strictly, however, to this time limit, and refers also to the sacrificial laws (§ 11), which can no longer be observed at the present day. His description forms an intentional parallel to Plato's picture of man as a miniature of a well-ordered state; but Jehuda Halevi (§ 5) compares the pious man not to the state, but to the one who directs the state. There are also clear references to Aristotle's doctrine of the 'middle way' and to the Pythagorean esteem of harmony. The division of the soul into three sections (thought, courageous desire, base lust) is also Platonic; added to this is the Arab doctrine of what we may call an 'instinctive judgement' (in approximate rendering of the Arabic), i.e. such judgements or prejudices as we find expressed by young children, uncontrolled by reason and often in flagrant opposition to it. Then there is the doctrine (of Galen), strongly developed in Islam, of the 'inward senses' and the 'general perception', i.e. the spontaneous combination of various sensual impressions (the sight of the whip arouses in the animal the thought of the pain of which it is the cause). But the foreign matter Jehuda Halevi works upon is merely the raw material with which he builds up his characteristic Jewish conception of life. In contrast to Plato, his ideal of life is based entirely on a religious foundation (*see* below); but his religious sense is quite opposed to that disparagement of this world and that condemnation of a natural joy of life of which distinct traces are found in the doctrines of the Church and Islam, but which also penetrated into certain Jewish circles; true, he uses the very expression that the Arabic has coined for 'secularity'—but he uses it generally in a much milder sense. The pious optimism shown in his conception of life is in no way the outcome of any under-estimation of the suffering of the world (as demonstrated in natural phenomena, in the fate of the individual, and, not least, in the fate of the Jewish nation). It proceeds from the realization that the pious man conceives this suffering in the religious sense; in particular, in his religious conception of duties he discovers sources of joy that were not open to other religions; circumcision, which is no symbol of covenant for the Arab, cannot have for him the religious significance that it bears for us (§ 81); nor can the Sabbath mean for the Arab or the Christian what it signifies for the Jew, who is reminded by it of the exodus from Egypt. Compare, in this connection, Songs II and III, pp. 133-4.

§ 11, 2nd half. Jehuda Halevi approaches in a noteworthy manner the problem of the paradox of faith. Many a phenomenon inexplicable to us in nature (the suffering of animals), in the fate of the individual and, above all, in the fate of Israel, must induce us either to consider all that happens as the sport of chance or to believe in a Divine wisdom superior to ours. According to Jehuda Halevi, the latter belief can be justified logically on the ground of certain signs of Divine working, particularly in the structure of organisms and in the history of our nation; there is therefore no 'credo quia absurdum!' But psychologically we can maintain this belief in all situations that life presents only if it has not only taken root in our minds, but if we also keep up the feeling of submission to God by remembering constantly those signs of His wisdom that are emphasized by religious symbols (e.g. tefillin, reciting of the blessings).

§ 12 ff. It may appear somewhat strange to us that here, and in § 10 where he deals with the Sabbath, Jehuda Halevi assigns to religion the task of enhancing our earthly happiness. It would appear that he contradicts not only our mode of thought (influenced by Kant), but also that of the Talmud, where the phrase: 'מצוות לאו ליהנות ניתנו' (the laws are not given for our pleasure) apparently rests on a distinction between duty and pleasure. It is not sufficient to remember that 'הצלחה' (=luck) and the exactly corresponding Arabic word embrace both the notion of external well-being and a deeper happiness independent of any influence of fate. The real reason is to be found in the realization that, according to Jehuda Halevi, the highest human force—i.e. the religious, can only come to maturity when the lower animal forces have been given full play (see § 5 beginning); the Jewish people, in particular, could not have maintained their religious susceptibility, if the festivals had not preserved them from the convulsion of their vital strength. The idea (§ 10) that the Sabbath raises the Jew temporarily to the high sphere of kings, which gains double force from being presented as the utterance of a king, anticipates Heine's 'Prinzessin Sabbat'; this idea stands out still more prominently in the Sabbath poems.

§ 17. Here Jehuda Halevi refers not to prayer in general, but only to the compulsory prayer that Islam designates by a special expression, considering it to be a most important religious act. But in accordance with his fundamental conception that the way to God is not to be found without the direction of the divinely inspired man, he holds it to be unquestionable that prayer prescribed by the wise men of Israel is higher than the prayer of one's own invention, although he himself was one of the inspired authors of prayer! True to this assessment, prayer is for him, as for S. R. Hirsch, less an expression of our feeling than a recitation intended to serve as an elucidation of our philosophy of life.

The public morning service begins according to him, as also according to Maimonides, with ברכו. His commentary on the first blessing (the heavenly lights) appears to be based on the fact that this blessing includes the seemingly unconnected verse from the Psalms: 'How great are Thy works, O Everlasting God! Thou hast created them all in wisdom—the earth is full of Thy possessions!' Jehuda Halevi seems to detect here a polemic against the religion of the stars, a polemic resting on the doctrine that God's wisdom is revealed still more clearly in the structure of organisms than in the splendour of the heavenly bodies. The second saying praises God as 'He who has chosen His people Israel in love'. The human affect, love, cannot in its literal sense be attributed to God (Book II, § 2); rather does the expression denote the act by which God distinguishes the 'aristocracy' of mankind (s. Book I, § 95). Jehuda Halevi rightly holds it superfluous to emphasize the instructive character of the following extract from the Torah (שמע, etc.). He has no difficulty in demonstrating that the following passage beginning with the words: אמת אתה הוא מעולם contains and emphasizes the fundamental doctrines of the Jewish religion. He explains the instruction to follow this passage (ending with the words: גאל ישראל) immediately with the main prayer (the so-called שמונה עשרה) by saying that only he who has strengthened himself in the fundamental truths of his faith can hope to be heard. He points out that this prayer also begins as a prayer of confession; true, in history (the Patriarchs) as in nature (and in the miracle of the resurrection) God rules; but He Himself is 'holy', i.e. He is raised above all the merely natural.

§ 17, end–§ 19. Jehuda Halevi proves the superiority of public prayer to individual prayer, in line with the ancient theory that the state is a living organism and that the individuals only represent its limbs (Livy II, ii). This theory seems, at first, out of place, though in fact it is absolutely in place preceding as it does a discussion on the prayer for the salvation of the community.

§ 66 ff. Jehuda Halevi defends Rabbinic tradition against the Karaites and the Christians. He presents the whole chain of tradition (we have omitted details) and gives an account of certain approved traits which tend to prove the reliability of the carriers of the tradition; he refers in § 67 (middle) to the beauty of the Mishnah to prove the collaboration of Divine forces, just as the Moslem does in Book I, § 5, with reference to the Koran. (This clarity of the Mishnah is also praised by Maimonides in his preface to 'Mishne Torah', and stands out clearly enough, especially in contrast with the intentionally unsystematic arrangement of the Talmud.) On the other hand, he points out that the anti-Rabbinic heresies have their origin in very human motives. This is clearly specified in references to the Sadducees, the forerunners of the Karaites; as regards the Christians, Jehuda Halevi is forced to content himself with two insinuations: his remark about the Karaites, who spare the roots though they prune the branches, contains a reproach aimed at the Christians, who do not even admit the authority of the Torah; moreover he hints that Jesus was, according to Rabbinical tradition, the pupil of R. Joshua, and he probably assumes the reader to know the sequel of this account (Sanh. 107 b and elsewhere), according to which Jesus forsook Judaism as the result of an over-emphatic, but not undeserved, reproof of his teacher. But with this presentation of the historical course of events, Jehuda Halevi in no way considers himself exempt from discussion of the main arguments of those opposed to tradition. The Karaites, whose services to exegesis are not disputed even by the Jews (Kuzari iii, 22), object particularly to those Bible interpretations of the Rabbis that undoubtedly fail to correspond with the literal sense and have been characterized by later opponents of tradition as the products of a very muddled exegetic faculty. Jehuda Halevi opposes this argument by stressing with absolute justice (§ 69) the fact that the peculiar methods used in the Rabbinical interpretation of the Bible do not appear in the Talmudists' interpretation of the Mishnah, and therefore cannot be attributed to methodic incapability but rather to intentional purpose; even in cases where this purpose remains hidden from us, it is our duty to react as we do to the obscure passages of the Torah (§ 73, beginning) and, let us add, to the enigmas of nature and of history (*see* note to Book III, § 11 above), i.e. to seek the fault in ourselves! Hereby Jehuda Halevi clears the way to the understanding of the 'creative exegesis' of the Midrash (*cf.* my study on 'Altjüdische Allegoristik', 1936, p. 77), which does not claim to be the interpretation of Divinely revealed records in the scientific sense, but does claim to be their organic continuation and therefore follows special laws. In particular, such interpretations as that quoted in § 73 (beginning) are explained by the fact that, according to Rabbinical opinion, in many cases words used in the Bible cannot quite free themselves within the context from the meaning attached to them outside of the context.

Moreover, he admits, with admirable frankness, that certain passages in the Aggadah probably do not appeal to the taste of a later period (§ 67, end). Even in Talmudic times one finds traces of similar criticism; but he stresses the fact that this does not, of course, in any way affect the distinguishing characteristic of Rabbinical Judaism—the belief in the reliability of the lawful tradition (§ 73, end).

BOOK IV

THE NAMES OF GOD

1. THE RABBI: Elohim is a term signifying Him who reigns over or disposes of all things. It is employed in connection with the universe, if we mean the Sovereign of the world, and in connection with certain sections, if we mean the power of the spheres or of nature or of a human judge. The plural form of the name (signifying God) is to be explained from its usage by the Gentiles; they made idols and believed each of them to be invested with astral and other powers; each of them was considered as 'Eloah' (God); their forces altogether were called 'Elohim'; they swore by them, and (regarded) them as judges over themselves. An exact expression and characterization (of God) is found only in the sublime name written Yod, He, Waw, He (=the Lord). This is a proper name, the bearer of which can only be indicated by attributes, not by location like corporeal beings, He being unknown or only named by the common noun Elohim; whereas the Tetragrammaton (=the LORD[1]) signifies Him alone.

2. THE KHAZARI: How can I indicate a being I am not able to characterize, but can only infer from his actions?

3. THE RABBI: No, God can be designated by prophetic visions and through the spirit. For the way of inference is misleading and may produce heresy and error. What else was it that led the Dualists to assume two eternal causes? And what led the Materialists to teach that the sphere was not only eternal, but its own primary cause as well as that of other matter? Inference also was the source of error of the worshippers of fire and of the sun. True, there are differences in the ways of demonstration; some of them are exact, others insufficient; but the most exact of all are the ways of the philosophers, and even they are led by their inferences to say that God neither benefits nor injures, nor knows

[1] Where we have put block letters, Jehuda Halevi uses the Hebrew terms אלהים (= GOD) and ה (= the LORD).

anything of our prayers or offerings, our obedience or disobedience, and that the world is as eternal as He Himself! None of them has therefore a definite proper name for God; but only such as hear His address, commands and prohibitions, His approval of obedience and reproof of disobedience, bestow on Him a name to designate the One who spoke with them and convinced them that He is the Creator of the world from naught. The first of these was Adam. He would never have known God, if He had not addressed, rewarded and punished him and created Eve from one of his ribs. By this he was convinced that He was the Creator of the world, and he characterized Him by words and attributes and called Him 'the LORD'. Had it not been for this experience he would have been satisfied with the name GOD; he would not have perceived what God was, whether He is one or many, whether He knows individuals or not. Cain and Abel also perceived God, after having been taught by their father, through prophetic vision. Then Noah, Abraham, Isaac, and Jacob, down to Moses and the later prophets called Him 'the LORD' by reason of their visions; and so did the people, having been taught on their authority, and through their authority, in as far as God's influence and guidance is with man and in as far as the pick of mankind enters into connection with Him, viewing Him through intermediaries called 'Glory, Shekinah, Dominion, fire, cloud, likeness, form, appearance of the rainbow', etc., all proving to them that He had spoken to them.

9. He who is capable of seeing these lights is the real prophet; the place where they are visible is the true direction of worship; for it is a Divine place; and the religion coming forth from it is the true religion.

10. The Khazari: Later religions, too, if they admit the truth and do not dispute it, all respect the place; they admit the existence of prophecy in Israel and the distinction of Israel's forefathers. They also perform pilgrimages to this hallowed place.

11. THE RABBI: I would compare them to those proselytes who may not have accepted the whole law with all its branches, but only the fundamental principles—if their actions should not belie their words. They praise the place of prophecy in words, but they turn in praying to places of idolatry, if by accident the greatest number of their people happen to live there, although no sign of Divine presence be visible in them. They retain the relics of ancient idolatry and feast days, changing nothing but this, that they have demolished the idols, without doing away with the rites connected with them. I might almost say that the verse oft repeated 'you will serve there other gods, wood and stone' (Deut. xxviii, 64, 36; iv, 28) alludes to those who worship the wood (cross) and the stone (Kaaba), towards which we incline daily more and more through our sins. But it is true that they believe in God, like the people of Abimelek and Nineveh, and like the philosophers who meditated on God's ways. The leaders of religions are said to have perceived the Divine light at its source, viz. in the Holy Land; it is said that there they ascended to Heaven and were commanded to lead all the inhabitants of the globe in the right path. They turned in prayer towards the Land; but after a short time a change took place and people turned towards the place where the greatest number lived. Isn't it as if a person wished to guide all men to the place of the sun, because they are blind and do not know its course—he, however, leads them to the south or to the north pole and tells them: 'here is the sun, turn towards it, and you will see it', but they would see nothing of it? The first leader, Moses, however, caused the people to stand before Mount Sinai, that they might see the light which he himself had seen, so far as they should be able to see it in the same way; he, then, invited the Seventy elders, and they saw it, as it is written: 'They saw the God of Israel' (Ex. xxiv, 10); afterwards he assembled the second Seventy, and so much of the prophetic light was passed on to them that they equalled him, as it is written: '(God) took the spirit that was upon (Moses), and gave it unto the seventy elders' (Num. xi, 25).

12. The Khazari: But the other religions approach nearer to you than the philosophers.

13. The Rabbi: There is a broad difference, indeed, between the believer in a religion and the philosopher. The believer seeks God for the sake of various benefits, apart from the benefit of knowing Him; the philosopher seeks Him only that he may be able to describe Him accurately, as he would describe the earth, (saying) that it is in the centre of the great sphere, but not in that of the zodiac, etc.; ignorance of God would therefore be no more injurious than ignorance concerning the earth by those who consider it flat; the real benefit is to be found only in the cognizance of the true nature of things, through which man becomes akin to the Active intellect. . . . But they had no other approach to theology but analogic thought. The fairest among them speak therefore to the believers in religions like Socrates who says: 'Citizens, I do not contest your doctrine of God; I say only that I do not penetrate so far; I only understand the doctrine of man!' But those religions, although they are nearer to us, withdrew from us. Otherwise Jeroboam and his party would have approached nearer to us; but they passed for idolators, although they were Israelites, practised circumcision, observed the Sabbath and other commandments, with the exception of a few which administrative emergency forced them to neglect; they acknowledged the God of Israel, who delivered them from Egypt, as we pointed out (Book I, § 97) with regard to the worshippers of the golden calf in the desert. The later religions are superior to them inasmuch as they did away with idols. But since they altered the direction of prayer and seek the Divine power where it is not to be found, altering at the same time most of the ritual laws, there is a broad difference between us and them.

15. But let us return to the discussion of attributes, from which we digressed. I should like to explain the matter by a simile of the sun. The sun is uniform; but the bodies receiving its (light) react in different ways. Those most fitted to receive its lustre are the ruby, the crystal, pure air and water; such

light as these receive is therefore called transparent. On glittering stones and polished surfaces it is called glittering, on wood, earth, etc., feeble light, and on all other things it is simply designated as light without any specific qualification. The general light corresponds to what we call Elohim (GOD), according to our explication (§ 1); transparent light corresponds to 'the LORD' (Tetragram), that name expressing only the relation between Him and His most perfect creatures on earth, viz. the prophets, whose souls are transparent and susceptible to His light, which penetrates them as the sunlight penetrates crystal and ruby. These souls take their origin from Adam, as has been explained before (Book I, § 95); his 'pick' (Book I, § 27) and 'heart' (Book II, § 36) are transmitted from generation to generation, from age to age; besides it the large mass of mankind is like husks, leaves, resin, etc. As god of this 'heart' He is called 'the LORD'; and because He entered into connection with Adam, the name God (Gen. i, 1–ii, 3) was replaced after the creation by 'the LORD GOD' (2, 4 ff.)— 'a full name over a full universe' (Gen. Rabba xiii, 3); for the world was only completed in Adam, who was the 'heart' of all that was created before him. No intelligent person can contest the idea conveyed by 'GOD'; but there can be some discussion as to 'the LORD', because the gift of prophecy is strange and rare even in individuals, and much more so in a multitude. For this reason, Pharaoh disbelieved and said 'I know not the LORD' (Ex. v, 2); he conceived this name as meaning a penetrating light and understood it as a god whose light is connected with and penetrates man; Moses added therefore 'the God of the Hebrews', alluding to the patriarchs, whose prophecy and distinction through marvels were acknowledged. The name 'GOD', however, was widespread in Egypt; the first Pharaoh said to Joseph 'forasmuch as GOD hath shown thee all this' (Gen. xli, 39) and 'a man in whom the spirit of GOD is' (ibid. 38). The meaning of 'GOD' can be grasped by way of speculation, a Guide and Manager of the world being inferred by Reason; opinions about Him differ among men according to their faculty of thought; the

most evident of them is that of the philosophers. The meaning
of 'the LORD', however, cannot be grasped by analogic
thought, but only by that prophetic intuition by which man
ascends, so to say, from his kind and joins the angels, 'another
spirit' (Num. xiv, 24) entering in him, as it is written 'Thou
shalt be turned into another man', 'God gave him another
heart' (I Sam. x, 6, 9), 'a spirit enwrapped Amasai' (I Chr.
xii, 19); 'the hand of the LORD was upon me' (Ezek. xxxvii,
I) 'munificent spirit may uphold me' (Ps. li, 14). All these are
symbols of the Holy Spirit which enwraps the prophet in
the hour of prophecy, the Nazirite and him who is anointed
for priesthood or prophecy, when a prophet anoints him or
when God guides him in any matter; or the priest, when he
makes prophetic utterances through secret science after having
consulted the Urim and Tummim. Then there vanish all
previous doubts of man concerning GOD, and he despises
all these analogic proofs by means of which men endeavour
to attain to knowledge of His dominion and unity. Then he
becomes a servant who loves his master, and is ready to
perish for the sake of his love, finding the greatest sweetness
in his connection with Him, the greatest sorrow in separation
from Him. Otherwise the philosophers: they consider Divine
worship only as refinement of conduct and confession of
truth, so that they extol Him above all other beings, just as the
sun is to be extolled above all other visible things—and the
denial of God only as a mark of a low standard of the soul
which acquiesces in untruth.

16. THE KHAZARI: Now I understand the difference between
GOD and the LORD and I see how great is the difference
between the God of Abraham and the God of Aristotle. To
the LORD we yearn, tasting and viewing Him, to GOD we
draw near through speculation. And this feeling invites its
votaries to give their life for the love of Him and to suffer
death for Him. Speculation, however, tends to veneration
only as long as it entails no harm, nor causes pain for its own
sake. We must not take it amiss that Aristotle thinks lightly

of the observation of religious laws, since he doubts whether God has any cognizance of them.

17. THE RABBI: Abraham, on the other hand, bore his burden honestly, in Ur Kasdim, in emigration, circumcision, removal of Ishmael, in the painful resolution to sacrifice Isaac; for he conceived the Divine power by tasting, not by speculating; he had observed that no detail of his life escaped God, that He rewarded him instantly for his piety and guided him along the best path, so that he moved forwards or backwards only according to God's will. How should he not despise his former speculations? The Sages (Sabb. 156a) explain the verse: 'He brought (Abraham) forth abroad' (Gen. xv, 5) as meaning 'give up thy astrology'. That is to say: He commanded him to leave off his speculative researches into the stars and other matters, and to devote himself to the service of Him whom he had tasted, as it is written: 'Taste and see that the LORD is good' (Ps. xxxiv, 9). The Lord is therefore rightly called 'God of Israel', because this seeing is not found elsewhere, and 'God of the land', because the peculiarity of its air, soil, and heaven aids this vision, together with (actions) such as the cultivating and tilling of the soil for the higher prosperity of the species. All followers of the Divine law follow these 'seeing' men; they find satisfaction in the authority of their tradition, in spite of the simplicity of their speech and the clumsiness of their similes, not in the authority of philosophers, with their graphic elegance, their excellent dispositions, and their brilliant demonstrations. For all that, the masses do not follow them, as if the soul had a presentiment for truth, as it is said 'the words of truth are recognizable' (Sota 9b).

20. THE KHAZARI: The light thou hast described is so completely extinguished that we can hardly believe in its reappearance; it is lost, and there can be no thought of its return.

21. THE RABBI: It seems only extinguished for him who does not see us with a clear eye, who infers the extinction of our light from our degradation, poverty, and dispersion, and

concludes from the greatness of others, their dominion on earth and their power over us, that they have a share in the (Divine) light.

22. THE KHAZARI: I should not like to conclude in that manner. For I see two conflicting religions prevailing, and the truth cannot be in both contrary affirmations, but in one of them or in neither! Thou hast shown me also (Book II, § 34) that, according to the chapter 'my servant shall prosper' (Jes. lii, 13 ff.), humility and meekness conform more to the Divine power than greatness and pride. This is acknowledged also by the two religions themselves. Christians do not glory in their kings, heroes, and rich people, but in those who followed Jesus all the time, before his faith had taken firm root, who were expelled or who hid themselves or were killed wherever one of them was found, suffering dreadful humiliations and slaughter for the victory of their belief: these men they regard as worthy of conferring blessing; they revere the places where they lived and died, and they build churches in their names. In the same way, the supporters of the founder of Islam bore many humiliations, until they succeeded; but in these their humiliations and martyrdom they glory—not in the princes who excelled by wealth and power; no, in those who were clad in rags and fed scantily on barley. Yet, O Rabbi, they lived so in utmost solitude and devotion to God. Should I see the Jews acting in a like manner for God's sake, I would place them above the kings of David's house, for I am well aware of what thou didst teach me concerning the words '(I am) with the contrite and humble spirit' (Jes. lvii, 15), viz. that the light of God enters only into the souls of the humble.

23. THE RABBI: Thou art right to blame us: our degradation has not yielded any result! But think of thoughtful men amongst us who could escape this degradation by a word spoken lightly —and even surpass their oppressors! But they do not do so out of allegiance to their faith. Is not such a religious deed worthy of intercession before God and of obtaining remission

of many sins? But if we should fulfil thy demand, we should not remain in our present condition! God, it is true, has a secret and wise design concerning us. It should be compared to the wisdom hidden in the seed which falls into the ground and apparently is transformed into earth, water and dung without leaving a trace—so it seems to the contemplator. But really this seed transforms earth and water into its own substance, carrying them from one degree to another, until it refines the elements and makes them like unto itself, casting off husks, leaves, etc., in order that the 'heart' (of the plant) may appear in purity and become fit to receive this power and the form of the first seed: then the tree bears fruit resembling that from which it had been produced. So it is concerning the religion of Moses: all later religions are transformed into it, though externally they may reject it. They merely serve to introduce and pave the way for the expected Messiah: he is the fruit; all will be his fruit, if they acknowledge him, and will become one tree. Then they will revere the root they formerly despised as we have said in explaining the (chapter) 'my servant shall prosper' (Jes. lii, 13 ff.: cf. Book II, 34).

COMMENTARY TO BOOK IV

§ 1 ff. The following argument on 'God' and 'Lord' (the rendering of the four letters that stand for God's name) is very significant. Through his comparison with the sun and the various forms in which it appears (§ 15) Jehuda Halevi forestalls any mistaken notion of a plurality of gods. To conceive 'the Lord' as solely a national God of Israel is likewise far from his intention; the distinction made by the Rabbis between 'God' as the judge of retribution and 'the Lord' as the dispenser of mercy does not suffice him. Rather do both names serve to set off the religious faith against the philosophic faith in a supreme being. Jehuda Halevi fully admits the justice of the question as to 'who may name Him' (Goethe, 'Faust') (§ 2); in fact we are only justified in using the word Elohim, which is not a 'name' but may be said also to indicate the mortal judge (§ 1), if we know no better approach to the recognition of God than that of the philosophers. But this is not the case; we can therefore name God actually only in as far as we recognize Him through the peculiar channel of revelation, which is the only basis of the *religious* connection between Man and God. True, Jehuda Halevi expressly admits in a passage omitted by us (§ 19 middle) that the philosophers also set up the claim of resemblance to God—this was often done from Plato on (Theaetet 176 B); he also admits that such an approach demands, as Plato puts it, a certain 'escape from life' and upright dealing. But, according to Jehuda Halevi, philosophy certainly cannot constitute the basis of the love of God; we may say even more precisely that the Greek language has no term to designate this religious 'love' other than the words 'friendship' or 'eros'; the former is considered by Aristotle to be absolutely inapplicable to our relation to the Divinity (M. Mor. 1208 b 27). Neither are 'Divine commands' recognized in Greek philosophy. True, the Greeks, and certainly the Romans, were no less conscientious than the Jews in the observance of their ritual customs; the philosophers also had their part in the official cult; but what moved them was the law of the state and not the will of the gods (Seneca), and although Aristotle does not mock at the practice of religious observance as Jehuda Halevi suggests (Book I, § 16), but rather recommends to the king the conscientious practice of the rites for practical reasons (Pol. 1315 a 1), this motivation does in fact amount to a certain contempt of ritual life. The contrast between the philosopher's attitude to religion and the self-sacrificing love of Abraham, who is the model of a pious man for all three religions, is therefore most fittingly drawn. Hence in § 23 Christianity and Islam, having inherited this vigorous piety from Judaism, can be considered as the stepping-stones to the Messianic age. But not even Abraham was possessed by this religious sense from the beginning, but attempted at first to recognize God in Nature; Jehuda Halevi probably deduces this from the prevalent assumption that Abraham was the author of the mystic book of Jesirah (§ 25 ff.). Here Jehuda Halevi seems to hint at his own development—seeing that he too first sought to base religion on nature after the manner of the philosophers and only later arrived at the recognition of the true nature of religious experience.

In this connection Jehuda Halevi devotes a whole series of arguments to the *corporeal anthropomorphic presentation of God* in the prophets and in the mystical books, which can scarcely hold the present-day reader's attention to the same extent but which contain a very noteworthy basic conception. When, for example, the prophets say that God 'thrones' in Heaven or in Zion, such representations are not true with reference to the incorporeal God to which Reason aspires, but apply rather to a conception appealing to the imagination and the senses; they are the outcome of a peculiar 'inward vision' vouchsafed to the prophets (§ 3, second part). And if the philosophers believe that the abstract presentations of God's being and qualities can stimulate awe and love (§ 4), they overlook the fact that it is only tangible description that works upon our feelings, embracing as it does in a single vivid picture all that is spread over a whole series of abstract phrases. Bevan has recently made a similar observation (*Symbolism and Belief*, 1938), declaring that no theistic conception that is not content with mere negations (p. 254) can escape making use of anthropomorphic images (p. 26), and that an image such as 'God's hand' (p. 259) is an impressive presentation of the belief in God's direction of worldly affairs. Bevan devotes a special chapter to the representation (p. 125 ff.) of God as light, which Jehuda Halevi considers to be a particularly apt one. Jehuda Halevi is of the same opinion although he attributes a more lofty reality to the prophetic vision, and he is probably right in assuming that the use of anthropomorphic images betrays neither primitive instinct nor a wide concession to the ignorant masses, but is to be explained and justified through the channels of our own experience.

§ 23. The comparison of Israel in exile with the grain of corn is found in the Talmud Pes. 87 b. Israel is distributed among the nations in order that the Gentile may join it; for it is said: 'I will sow her (Israel compared to a wife) unto me in the earth' (Hosea ii, 25); 'a small quantity is sown that a great quantity may be reaped'. But Jehuda Halevi pursues the comparison in quite a different direction; just as the seed at first appears to be lost, then casts forth at first the less useful parts, and only in the end the most valuable parts, those that guarantee the perpetuation of the plant—so at first has Israel produced the two semi-true daughter religions and only in the end—in the Messianic times—will the latter develop into the true religion. This shows that Jehuda Halevi is far from expressing any 'resentment' against the religions that have oppressed Israel so heavily; he regards them as necessary preliminary stages in the religious development of humanity.

BOOK V

THE PHILOSOPHICAL AND THE RELIGIOUS APPROACH TO GOD

15. THE KHAZARI: Please give me a brief abstract of the views of the fundaments of faith of those whom the Karaites style 'the Masters of the Kalam'.

16. THE RABBI: This would be of no use, except as an exercise in debating, contributing to the fulfilment of the dictum 'Be careful to learn what to answer an Epicurean' (Abot ii, 14). A plain wise man like the prophets can only impart little to another person in the way of instruction; nor can he solve a problem by dialectic methods. The lustre of erudition, however, shines upon the master of Kalam (= dialectics) and his hearers prefer him to this pious and noble man whose learning consists in unshakable principles. But the highest pitch to which the dialectic may attain through all his learning and teaching is that in his soul and that of his disciples there may enter those principles which are found in the soul of this naturally pious man; in some cases dialectic even destroys many true principles, in consequence of the doubts and the change of opinions it produces. Dialecticians resemble metric experts, who measure the length of syllables; here we have much empty noise and erudite words on an art which offers no difficulties to the naturally gifted, who sense the metres and no fault can be found in them; the highest pitch which those scholars can attain is to be like the latter, who appear to be ignorant in metres, since they cannot teach it, whereas the former are able to do so; but the naturally gifted can teach another naturally gifted with the slightest hint. In the same manner sparks are kindled in the souls of people naturally gifted for religious life and approach to God by the words of the pious—sparks which become luminaries in their hearts; whilst those who are not naturally gifted must have recourse to dialectics, which often produces no benefit at all but even harm.

21. Set alone the argument of the Karaites taken from David's last will to his son: 'Solomon, my son, know the God of thy father and serve Him' (1 Chr. xxviii, 9): they conclude from this verse that we must first conceive God in truth, and only afterwards are we obliged to serve Him. As a matter of fact, David urged his son to obey the authority of his father and his ancestors in their belief in the God of Abraham, Isaac, and Jacob, whose solicitude was with them, and who fulfilled His promises that their descendants should be numerous, that they would obtain Palestine, and that His Shekinah would dwell among them. The verse 'gods you did not know' (e.g. Deut. xi, 28) does not mean 'conceiving in truth', but 'beings from whom you saw issuing neither good nor evil' and therefore deserving neither confidence nor fear.

JOURNEY TO ERETZ ISRAEL

22. After this the Rabbi resolved to leave the land of the Khazars and to betake himself to Jerusalem. The King regretted the parting, and he began a conversation with him. 'What can be sought in Palestine nowadays, since the Shekinah is absent from it? Through pure intention and strong desire we may approach to God in every place! Why dost thou expose thyself to the dangers of land and sea and to risks incurred by contact with other peoples?'

23. THE RABBI: To be sure, the visible Shekinah has disappeared, revealing itself only to a prophet or to a community pleasant to God in the distinguished place; we look for that, as it is said 'they shall see, eye to eye, the Lord returning to Zion' (Jes. lii, 8) and as we say in our prayer, 'Let our eyes behold when Thou returnest to Zion, Thy residence'. But the invisible and spiritual Shekinah is with every born Israelite of pure life, pure heart and sincere devotion to the Lord of Israel. And Palestine has a special relation to the Lord of Israel. Pure life can be perfect only there; many of the Israelite

laws lose their force for him who does not live in Palestine. Sincere devotion and purity of life reach perfection only in a place which is believed to have a special relation to God, even though this belief be founded on an imaginary or comparative conception; how much more so if it is right, as we have shown (Book II, § 14)! Then the yearning is bound to be strengthened, and the desire for God must be sincere, especially in him who travels to the Land from a great distance; still more in one who wishes to atone for past transgressions! It is true: the way of offerings is ordained by God for intentional and unintentional sins; but he relies on the saying of the Sages: 'emigration atones for sins' (Maccot 2b), especially since he emigrates to the place of God's choice. Through the risk he runs on land and sea he does not transgress the prohibition: 'you shall not tempt the Lord' (Deut. vi, 16), which refers to risks which one takes e.g. when travelling with merchandise in the hope of gain. Even if he incurs greater risks on account of his ardent desire of God and in order to obtain forgiveness, he is free from reproach for the sake of the dangers; it is as if he had closed the account of his life, expressed his gratitude for his past life and his contentment with it, and devoted to his Lord the rest of his days. Running into danger, he praises God if he escapes; and should he perish through his sins, he forbears and acquiesces in his fate, being confident that he has obtained atonement for most of his sins through his death. He acts more wisely than those who risk their lives in war, in order to obtain the reputation of bravery and distinction or to gain high reward; and this kind of risk is even inferior to the risk of those who march spontaneously in a (religious) war for the sake of heavenly reward.

24. THE KHAZARI: I thought that thou didst love freedom; but now I see thou strengthenest thy bondage by imposing duties which are obligatory only if thou residest in Palestine and bidest not here.

25. THE RABBI: I seek freedom—from the service of those numerous people only whose favour I shall never obtain even

if I work for it all my life and which would not profit me, even
if I could obtain it: I mean the service of men and the courting
of their favour. But I seek the service of One whose favour
is obtained with the smallest effort and profits in this world
and the next: this is the favour of God; His service is freedom,
and humility before Him is true honour.

26. THE KHAZARI: If thou meanest all thou sayest, God
certainly knows thy pious intention; and intention is sufficient
before God, who knows the intentions and discloses what is
hidden.

27. THE RABBI: This is true—only when action is impossible.
But man is able to endeavour and also to work! He deserves
blame when he does not apply for visible reward through
visible action. For this reason it is written: 'Thou shalt sound
an alarm with the trumpets . . . and thou shalt be remembered
before the Lord thy God' (Num. x, 9), 'they shall be to you for
a memorial (before your God)' (x, 10), 'a memorial of blowing
of trumpets' (Lev. xxiii, 24). God need not be reminded or
directed; but actions must be perfected to claim reward.
Prayerful thoughts also are to be pronounced in the most
imploring and submissive manner. Only when intention and
action are brought to perfection are they rewarded. This
execution of thoughts is like reminding in the human sphere;
and 'the Torah speaks in a human manner' (cf. Nedarim 3a).
Actions without intention and intentions without action are
vain, except in that which is impossible; in such cases it is
useful to bring to the fore the good intention and to exculpate
before God the omission of action, as we do saying 'on
account of our sins have we been driven out of our land' and
in similar prayers. If we provoke and instil love of this sacred
place among men, we may be sure of obtaining reward
and of hastening the (Messianic) aim; for it is written: 'Thou
shalt arise and have mercy upon Zion; for it is time to favour
her, the moment is come. For Thy servants love her stones and
pity her dust' (Ps. cii, 14, 15). This means: Jerusalem can only

be rebuilt when Israel yearns for it to such an extent that we sympathize even with its stones and its dust.

28. THE KHAZARI: If this be so, it would be a sin to hinder thee; it is, on the contrary, a merit to assist thee. May God help thee: may He be thy protector and friend, and favour thee in His mercy! Peace be with thee!

COMMENTARY TO BOOK V

§ 15 ff. Jehuda Halevi at first holds out prospects of discussing the theological school of the Mutakallimun (literally the talkers or dialecticians), who exerted a strong influence not only on the Karaites, but also, for instance, on Saadya. Actually he appends to his mention of the name of this school a fundamental exposition of the relation of religion to religious philosophy, compared by him to the relation between poetry and the science of metre; today we should carry the simile further and say: between art and æsthetics (in the Middle Ages the latter was in its initial stage). Just as the genuine artist is not produced by knowledge of the laws of art and certainly not by intellectual superiority, but by a special gift—a 'feeling'—so it is with religion: the religious man is not he who knows how to talk about religion, but he who experiences it; his task is not to convince by dialectics, but to stimulate by his example those who believe as he does.

The Arab thinker Ghazzali had already pointed out that 'to explain' and 'to have' were two different things; the drunken man cannot explain his intoxication, but he 'has' it (Obermann, 'Der Subjektivismus Ghazzalis,' 36 ff.). Jehuda Halevi probably knew of this simile; he adapts it and gives it a new turn. For intoxication, which even the Arab looked upon as contemptible, he substitutes art, thus placing religion in the realm of those values that reason comprehends and can analyse, but cannot produce by virtue of its own power.

§ 21, middle. On the limitations of the perception of God, see the commentary on Song I. The verse: 'Know the God of Thy father' is taken as a reference to philosophic perception, not only by the Karaites, but also, for example, by Bahya (*Duties of the Heart*, i, 3) and Maimonides (*More* iii, 51), together with other verses on the perception of God. This contrast again demonstrates clearly the difference between the speculative formulation of religion as given by most philosophers and the more historical foundation of Jehuda Halevi.

§ 22. It is known that Jehuda Halevi started out on a journey to Palestine notwithstanding the serious remonstrances of his friends; he did so not only because, according to the convictions of all three religions, pilgrimages were laudable and effected the forgiveness of sin, but also because he hoped the soil of Palestine would exert a favourable influence on religious life (Book II, § 12) and because a shortening of the exile was to be expected from the immigration of Israel into Palestine (Book II, § 24; *cf.* Dinaburg's Study in Yellin Jubilee vol. [Hebrew], p. 157 ff.).

The first of the King's criticisms (§ 24) is based on the observation that Jehuda Halevi apparently feels the slavery of Israel in exile more intensely than most of his co-religionists (Book I, § 115; Book II, § 24; Book IV, § 23); the answer is that he only rejects service of mankind in order that he may serve God. The second criticism (§ 26) has been cleverly circumlocuted in the Hebrew translation through the Talmudic saying 'God only demands the heart'. The rejection of this gives Jehuda Halevi an opportunity of stressing once more one of the main ideas of the book—the belief in the value of Divine service notwithstanding the importance of the religious inner life. He interprets the Talmudic saying 'The Torah speaks the language of man' in the sense in which it was understood by most philosophers, namely, that in its form of expression the Torah assigns human attributes to God.

SONGS

I

Lord, where shall I find Thee?
High and hidden is Thy place!
And where shall I not find Thee?
The world is full of Thy glory!

5 Found in the innermost being,
He set up the ends of the earth:
The refuge of the near,
The trust for those far off.
Thou dwellest amid the Cherubim.
10 Thou abidest in the clouds,
Yet art raised above their praise.
The (celestial) sphere cannot contain Thee;
How then the chambers of a temple?

And though Thou be uplifted over them
15 Upon a throne high and exalted,
Yet art Thou near to them,
Of their very spirit and their flesh.
Their own mouth testifieth for them,
That thou alone art their creator.
20 Who shall not fear Thee,
Since the yoke of Thy kingdom is their yoke?
Or who shall not call to Thee
Since Thou givest them their food?

I have sought Thy nearness;
25 With all my heart have I called Thee;
And going out to meet Thee
I found Thee coming toward me.
Even as in the wonder of Thy might
In the sanctuary I have beheld Thee.
30 Who shall say he hath not seen Thee?—

Lo, the heavens and their hosts
Declare the fear of Thee
Though their voice be not heard.

Doth then, in very truth,
35 God dwell with man?
What can he think—every one that thinketh,
Whose foundation is in the dust?
Since Thou art holy, dwelling
Amid their praises and their glory,
40 Angels adore Thy wonder,
Standing in the everlasting height;
Over their heads is Thy throne,
And Thou upholdest them all!

II

To love of thee I drink my cup:
Peace to thee, peace, O Seventh Day!

Six days of work are like thy slaves.
While toiling through them, full of restlessness,
5 All of them seem to me but as a few days,
For the love I have to thee, O day of my delight!

I go forth on the first day to do my work,
To set in order the next Sabbath day's array;
For God hath placed the blessing there:
10 Thou alone art my portion for all my toil.

The lamp for my holy day is from the light of mine Holy
One.
The sun and stars are jealous of my sun.
What care I for the second day or third:
Let the fourth day hide his lights.

15 I hear a herald of good tidings from the fifth day forth:
Tomorrow cometh fresh life for my soul!
The morning for my labour, the evening for my
freedom:

I shall be summoned to the table of my King, my
    Shepherd.

I find upon the sixth day my soul rejoicing,
20 For there draweth nigh to me the time of rest.
    Albeit I go about, a wanderer, to find relief,
    At even I forget all my weariness and wandering.

How sweet to me the time between the lights
    To see the face of Sabbath with mien renewed!
25 O come with apples, bring ye many raisin cakes—
    This is the day of my rest, this my love, my friend.

I will sing to thee, O Sabbath, songs of love:
    So it befitteth thee, for thou art a day of enjoyments,
    A day of pleasures, yea, of banquets three,
30 Pleasure at my table, pleasure of my couch.

III

Thou hast bestowed great splendour on the Sabbath
    Through the bond of peace and life.
    And thou hast sanctified it, that it may distinguish
    Between Israel and the other nations.

 5 Who utter mere empty words
    When they would compare their days with my holy day—
    Edom later on the first day—and Arabia earlier on
       the sixth—
    Can the deceit of Ishmael and Edom mislead the men
       of truth?
    They compare dross with jewels,
10 The dead with the living.

And can there ever be for our neighbours, who think
    To ascend the king's throne,
    God's day of rest and man's,
    Upon which God has set His blessing—
15 The first, the holy day of festival,
    Which has endured since the beginning?
    The tree of life springs forth from its sanctification.

In its shadow we live among the nations.
The host who rules as priest in Thy name
20 And who leans upon Thy name,
Behold—he mourns upon Thy bosom;
And rejoices at Thy table
He has refreshed himself with Manna (doubled on the
    Sabbath)
With yet a little flask-full left over.
25 This is known to the islands,
Celebrated among the nations.

Stretch forth Thy hand a second time
To renew Thine erstwhile kingdom
To Thy people wandering in the dark.
30 Dispersed to the left and to the right—
Then shame will befall Arabia and the Greeks.
Renew the priesthood of Aaron
That there may be sanctified in the camp of the Levites
Thy name, which is desecrated among the nations!

IV

Thy words are compounded of sweet-smelling myrrh
And gathered from the rock of mountains of spice,
And unto thee and the house of thy fathers belong
    precious virtues
Whereunto praises fail to attain.
5 Thou comest to meet me with sweet speeches,
But within them lie men in wait bearing swords—
Words wherein stinging bees lurk,
A honeycomb prickly with thorns.
If the peace of Jerusalem is not to be sought,
10 While yet with the blind and the halt she is filled,
For the sake of the House of our God let us seek
Her peace, or for the sake of friends and of brothers;
And if it be according to your words, see, there is sin
Upon all those who bend towards her and bow down.

15 And sin upon those sires who dwelt in her as strangers
And purchased their vaults for their dead,
And vain would be the deed of the fathers who were
    embalmed
And their bodies sent to her earth—
And they sighing for her sake
20 Though the land was full of reprobates;
And for naught would the fathers' altars have been built,
And in vain their oblation offered there.
Is it well that the deed should be remembered,
And the Ark and the Tablets forgotten?
25 That we should seek out the place of the pit and the
    worm,
And forsake the fount of life eternal?
Have we any heritage save the sanctuaries of God?
Then how should we forget His Holy Mount?
Have we either in the east or in the west
30 A place of hope wherein we may trust,
Except the land that is full of gates,
Toward which the gates of Heaven are open—
Like Mount Sinai and Carmel and Bethel,
And the houses of the prophets, the envoys
35 And the thrones of the priests of the Lord's throne,
And the thrones of the kings, the anointed?
Unto us, yea, and unto our children hath He assigned her;
And though wild beasts abide in her, and doleful creatures,
Was it not so she was given of old to the fathers—
40 All of her the heritage of thorns and thistles?
But they walked through the length and the breadth of her
As one walketh in an orchard among the green boughs,
Though they came as strangers and sojourners, seeking
But burial place and a lodging there, like wayfarers.
45 And there they walked before the Lord
And learnt the straight paths—
And they said that here arise the shades
And those who lie under the bars of earth come forth,
And that here the bodies rejoice,

50 And the souls return to their rest—
  See now, yea see, my friend, and understand
  And turn aside from the lure of thorns and snares,
  And let not the wisdom of the Greeks beguile thee,
  Which hath no fruit, but only flowers—
55 Or her fruit is: that the earth was never outstretched
  Nor the tents of the sky spread out.
  Nor was any beginning to all the work of creation
  Nor will any end be to the renewal of the months.
  Hark how the words of her wise are confused,
60 Built and plastered up on a vain unstable base;
  And thou wilt come back with a heart stripped empty
  And a mouth full of dross and weeds.
  Wherefore, then, should I seek me out crooked ways
  And forsake the mother of paths?

Notes to the Songs:

Song I

17—*Nearer than* their own spirit and their flesh
18—Their own mouth testifieth *with regard to them*
26f. *And when I went out to meet Thee*
    I found Thee coming towards me.
28—'Even as'—not in the original text—
38—*But* Thou art holy . . .
40—Angels *proclaim* Thy wonder.

Song II

 4—*While toiling through them*, I am full of restlessness
11—'*The light* of my holy day is from the light of my holy
    One.'
24—'To see the face of the Sabbath *as a new visitor*'
    (A reference to the custom by which every day of the
    wedding week brings new visitors.)

Song IV

47—And they *say* . . .

COMMENTARY TO THE SONGS

Songs I, II and IV are reprinted from 'Selected Poems of Jehuda Halevi', translated into English by Nina Salaman, with permission of the copyright owners, The Jewish Publication Society of America. In passages where I disagree with the translator's rendering, I have added my version in the notes. Song No. III has been rendered into English by Hebe Mayer-Bentwich with reference to my German version.

Jehuda Halevi's religious lyrics obviously aim not only at satisfying æsthetic requirements like his secular poems, but, consciously or unconsciously, they serve a religious inspiration. In so far they support the arguments of the Kuzari. The relation between the two is illustrated in the Kuzari, Book V, § 16, where a comparison is drawn between the 'metric expert' and the poet, and between the inspirations emanating from either. Like the metric expert, the philosopher can appeal to any man of intellectual grasp; the poet, on the other hand, can only inspire the æsthetically gifted, for whom a slight hint is sufficient. The same applies to religious inspiration, which certainly does not emanate from the words alone, but also from the life of the devout man and, not least, from the direct expression of his experience in the religious lyric. In truth the same applies to the national sentiment, when it is expressed in the lyric; here also the words of the poet kindle sparks that inflame the heart of the reader.

Not all of Jehuda Halevi's poems can be taken as voicing his personal feeling. Very often there is an admixture of conventional expression of sentiment. But in some of his poems expression is given to thoughts of the Kuzari. They are a still purer and more impressive revelation of experience than the philosophic discourse. We have therefore appended a few of these and here add some short commentaries:

Song I

This poem, which is inserted in the passage of the morning prayers where the praise of God is proclaimed by the angels 'from His place', has as its theme an antinomy of religious consciousness. On the one hand, a religious man seeks God's traces 'in every place'; he considers it blasphemy when men attribute the wonders of organisms to nature instead of to God (Kuz., Book I, § 76). But, on the other hand, is it not a degrading of God to 'find' Him, i.e. to claim perception of Him in any 'place' (Kuz., Book V, § 21), or to place Him in relation to this lowly mortal world (Book I, § 8, *cf.* line 18 ff. of our poem)?

Jehuda Halevi is not the first to stress this antinomy. His predecessor Bahya solves the problem by admitting that it is only God's traces that we perceive and not His being. Jehuda Halevi would not exactly have opposed this conception; for according to Kuzari, Book II, § 2, we come much nearer perceiving God's working than His qualities. In our poem the poet is not seeking a way out. He allows the tension to stand and overcomes it only by the idea, expressed in line 26 ff., that in searching for God we find God. Pascal's idea: 'tu ne me chercherais pas si tu ne m'avais pas trouvé'.

Among the numerous parallels to this poem in European literature, the best known is the 'Confession' of the young Goethe in 'Faust': 'Wer darf ihn nennen und wer bekennen: ich glaub' ihn? Wer empfinden und sich unterwinden zu sagen: ich glaub' ihn nicht?' But Goethe calls God 'unsichtbar-sichtbar' in a sense different from Jehuda Halevi. He knows that the pantheistic feeling for nature, which penetrates him, is akin to the religious and yet remains a thing apart; it is no mere accident that the confession scene ends with the fall of the hero and the mocking laugh of the devil. Jehuda Halevi, on the other hand, 'possesses' God; and his doubt, as to whether he, an unworthy human being, may perceive God, emanates—from religion!

Song II

Jehuda Halevi is the first poet to sing of the Sabbath. Many before him had produced prayers for the Sabbath: he is the first to give expression in song to the *experience* of the Sabbath. The first words reveal the experience of that love and joy the religious significance of which is expressed in Kuzari, Book II, § 48. It is true that the Rabbis had preceded him in religious experience when they greeted the Sabbath with the exclamation: 'Come, O bride!' (Sabb. 119a), and as this exclamation inspired the best-known of all Sabbath lyrics, Heinrich Heine was not so wrong when he said that Jehuda Halevi had learnt from the Aggadah, and even when he confused him with Solomon Halevi, the author of the לכה דודי! But what in ancient times found its sole expression in symbolic acts finds poetic expression in the Middle Ages and in the Kabbalah through Bible reminiscence. As the years he served for Rachel seemed unto the Patriarch Jacob but 'as so many days' for 'the love he bore her'—so for Jehuda Halevi (line 5) the weekdays are but swiftly passing forerunners of the 'beloved' day of cherishing (cf. Jer. xxxi, 19); the apparently worldly joys are only symptoms of this love: line 25 is reminiscent of the Song of Songs ii, 5, 'stay me with flagons, comfort me with apples: for I am sick of love'. But as God is the initiator of the fascination of the Sabbath (line 9, cf. Ex. xx, 11), the glory of this day is the irradiation of heavenly light—line 11. Heine is certainly wrong in assuming that Jehuda Halevi rejected the Halakah, i.e. the legal discussion. For the highly poetic conception of the Sabbath as the ruler of the weekdays —its slaves (line 3)—is taken from the legal provision that the week-day should be a preparation for the Sabbath (line 8), not the other way round; this appears even in the Talmudic discussion 'about the fatal egg which a hen had laid on the festival'. It was Jehuda Halevi's special merit that he gave voice to the inarticulate poetry of the Jewish law, thus converting it for us into a living experience.

Song III

In this poem, the belief in the peculiarity of the *Jewish* day of rest is still more strongly emphasized. The charm of this poem lies partly in the contrast—stressed by the rhyme—between חיים (= life or life's blessing) and בויים (nations, especially non-Jewish). The explanation of this contrast is found in Kuzari, Book II, § 32, where Israel, i.e. Israel's faith, is represented as 'living', the other faiths being but imitators of this life, just as the statue is but an imitation of the living organism. This, according to Kuzari, Book III, § 9, is particularly true of the Sabbath; the imitation of the other nations resembles the original only in the sense in which the statue resembles the human body. Hence our poem opens with the words: 'Thou hast honoured the Sabbath by the bond of peace and life and hast hallowed it that it may distinguish between Israel and the nations'. And if they quibblingly proclaim their 'days' the equal of my holy day—Edom advancing it to the first, and Arabia setting it back to the sixth—how can their hoax deceive the bearers of the truth? In the same way one might set rags on a par with jewels (עֲדִים לַעֲדָיִים) and the living on a par with the dead. Do our neighbours indeed find that 'rest of God and man'—that absolute rest which, in the words of the King of the Khazars (Book III, § 10), raises the simple Jew above princes (*cf.* Heine), and saves the people from enslavement? Are their holy days days of remembrance of the rest-day of the creation (line 9) and, as such, the expression of our belief in the Creator? Do they call to mind the miracle of the manna, in which the non-Jews also believe (line 14 = Kuzari, Book I, §§ 4 and 9), as the basis of our trust in God's provision for the lower world? The comparison of man-made beliefs with the Divine appointment of the Sabbath must appear a blasphemy to Jehuda Halevi, debasing as it does the peculiar character of the Sabbath, which cannot be postponed or replaced at will.

Song IV

The belief in the pre-eminence of Palestine which Jehuda Halevi seeks to establish in Kuzari, Book II (§§ 13–24) finds expression in a number of his poems, of which the best known is the Zion Ode (translated by Nina Salaman, pp. 3 and 151). Although the poet speaks there in the name of the community (as 'the harp of its song'), his glorification of the land often bears his own stamp; the words 'how can other countries compare their vanities with your Urim and Tummim (which the High Priest wore)' are reminiscent of Song III with its message of the incomparableness of our religion; still closer in spirit is the thought 'that at that time it was not the sun nor the moon which gave light, but God's glory'. The phrase 'the air of Thy Land is the breath of life' is a reference to a Talmudic remark, but bears a special significance in the mouth of Jehuda Halevi, who believes in the superiority of Eretz Israel to all other countries; and the words 'I would take delight in thy stones and be tender to thy dust' attain their full significance through Jehuda Halevi's belief that only through such tenderness and love of the land can redemption be brought about (Kuzari, Book V, § 27).

The poem here quoted has a much more personal stamp. It contains the answer to the poem of a friend dissuading him from the journey to Palestine, seeing that only 'the blind and the lame', i.e. misbelievers, live there now, and that the land therefore has as little present significance as Greece, which also was once the cradle of culture.

After a few respectful words on the form of the poem, Jehuda Halevi's indignation at its contents bursts forth: 'for God's sake and for the sake of our brothers' (line 11 ff.), for religious and national reasons, Eretz Israel has a unique value. At first he contents himself with indirect proof. Were it a country like any other, why did the patriarchs want to live, sacrifice and be buried only here (17 ff., *cf.* Gen. lvii, 29; l, 25), although even at that time unbelievers dwelt there (line 20 = Kuzari, Book II, § 23, end)? And they were right! For still higher than the veneration for the graves to which we pilgrimage must we reckon the reverence for the source of life (line 26) in which God has revealed Himself (Kuzari, l.c. 2nd phrase)! In addition to these religious considerations, we have national reasons: it has been promised to us and our children (lines 37 ff.) and, according to Gen. xiii, 14 ff., Abraham wandered around the Land (line 41) only because he considered it to be the inheritance of his descendants. And is it not the Land of marvellous hopes, even in the eyes of younger religions (lines 47 ff. = Kuzari, Book II, § 23, middle)?

On the other hand, Greece, like all other religions apart from the Jewish (Kuzari, Book IV, § 23), produced no 'fruit' or, what amounts to the same, only poisonous fruit (lines 54 ff.) such as the doctrine that the creation (מעשה בראשית) had no 'beginning' (ראשית) and no 'end' (אחרית), i.e. purpose (lines 57 ff.)! The worth of Greek profane science, which was appreciated by Jehuda Halevi as a disciple of Aristotle and the physicians, is not belittled by the statement that it cannot compare with the absolute worth of Palestine from both the religious and national aspects.

INDEX

I. NAMES AND SUBJECTS

(ASTERISKS REFER TO FOOTNOTES)

Aaron, 42, 43, 47, 66
Abel, 46, 65, 66, 81, 114
Abimelek, 115
Abraham, 14, 15, 19, 33, 35, 42, 46,
    47, 58, 63, 65, 66, 67, 68, 79, 87,
    90, 114, 118, 119, 123, 142
Abraham ibn Daûd, 22, 83
Adam, 14, 30, 32, 37, 38, 43, 45,
    46, 47, 58, 65, 66, 81, 114, 117
Aggadah, 12, 57, 81, 105, 106, 111,
    112, 139
Ahab, 58
Ahad Haam, 25
Akiba, R., 102, 103
Alexander, S., 18*
Amasai, 118
Anthropomorphism, 21, 63, 80, 81,
    105, 123
    see also: Attributes
Antigonos of Soko, 101
Arab philosophy, 13, 56, 80, 108
Arauna, 66
Aristotle (Aristotelians), 10, 16*, 19,
    38, 39, 55, 56, 80, 98, 106, 108,
    118, 122, 142
    see also: Greek philosophy
Art, 19, 125, 130, 138
Astrology, 40, 41, 49, 56, 58, 97,
    110, 119
Attributes and names of God, 61, 62,
    63, 64, 80, 81, 113–123, 131
    see also: Anthropomorphism

Babylon, 69
Baer, 9*
Bahya, 54, 130, 139
Baraita, 104
Bevan, 16*, 21*, 123
Bezaleel, 47

Biology, 13, 14, 20, 23
Björnson, 16*, 17*
Boëthos, Boëthosians, 101, 102
Brunner, E., 20*
Buddhism, 57
Bulan, 50

Cain, 46, 65, 66, 81, 114
Calf, Golden, 45, 47, 48, 49, 57, 58,
    60
Chaldeans, 38, 55
Christianity (Christians), 22, 29, 30,
    31, 53, 57, 58, 60, 69, 80, 90, 102,
    108, 109, 111, 115, 120, 121, 123,
    124, 140
Circumcision, 73, 76, 77, 90, 109,
    119
Cohen, Hermann, 59
Crescas, 11

Daniel, 65
David, 66, 92, 126
Dialectic theology (modern), 19, 20
Diaspora, *see:* Galuth
Dinaburg, 131
Dion of Prusa, 21*
Dionysos, 83

Eber, 46, 47
Eliah, 85, 106
Enoch, 46, 85
Esau, 46, 58, 66
Eve, 65, 114
Ezekiel, 65, 72
Ezra, 101

Festivals, 68, 77, 78, 89, 91, 93,
    100
    see also: Sabbath

2. BIBLE PASSAGES

THE EDITORS

HANS LEWY was born in Berlin in 1901 and died in Jeru-salem in 1945. Educated at the University of Berlin and the Hochschule für Wissenschaft des Judentums, he ac-quired mastery both of classic Hebrew thought and Greek and Hellenistic philosophy. He made Philo his particular specialty, although he concentrated as well on the view of Judaism reflected in the work of such classic writers as Tacitus, Cicero, and particularly Josephus. The last twelve years of his life were spent in the Department of Classics at the Hebrew University in Jerusalem.

ALEXANDER ALTMANN was born in Germany in 1906. He was rabbi and lecturer in the Berlin Rabbinical Seminary until 1938, when he was appointed the community rabbi in Manchester, England. In England he published exten-sively on Jewish philosophy and theology and in 1953 founded the Manchester Institute of Jewish Studies. He is presently at Brandeis University. Among his works are *Isaac Israeli* (with S. Stern) and *Between East and West,* which he edited.

ISAAK HEINEMANN was born in Germany in 1876 and died in Israel in 1957. From 1919 he lectured at the Bres-lau Rabbinical Seminary and from 1920 he served as edi-tor of the *Monatschrift für Geschichte und Wissenschaft des Judentums.* Having settled in Palestine in 1939, he continued to pursue his studies of Jewish philosophy in the classical and medieval world.